1970

GERMANY'S THREE REICHS

GERMANY'S
THREE REICHS

Their History and Culture

BY

EDMOND VERMEIL

Translated by
E. W. DICKES

NEW YORK

Howard Fertig

1969

First published in English in 1944
by Andrew Dakers Limited

HOWARD FERTIG, INC. EDITION 1969
Published by arrangement with the Estate of Edmond Vermeil

Library of Congress Catalog Card Number: 68-9638

PRINTED IN THE UNITED STATES OF AMERICA
BY NOBLE OFFSET PRINTERS, INC.

PREFACE TO THE ENGLISH EDITION

THIS book had just been written and published, and a few copies had reached their owners, even on English soil, when France's defeat came. The occupation authorities naturally suppressed the book, and no doubt they destroyed the copies at the publishers' and the booksellers'. The author is happy to see this work appear in London in an English translation. In it he has attempted a synthesis that sums up about forty years' labours on Germany. In bringing it up to date he has contented himself with adding a paragraph to Chapter IX on the present war, and with modifying the concluding chapter on certain essential points. Such as it is, he offers the work to the British public, hoping·that it will meet with a favourable reception, which, on top of the kind and generous hospitality extended to him here, would be one more reason for the boundless gratitude he feels.

I wish to thank Mr E. W. Dickes for the excellent translation he has made of this book: owing to its subject, the text presented quite special difficulties.

E. V.

LONDON,
Spring 1944.

PREFACE

THE simple title of this book reveals in full the venture it undertakes. This attempt at a complete interpretation, without being a formal history of German civilization, follows the evolution of our neighbour people from its origins to our own days—no doubt the first attempt of its kind published in France. Good judges will say that the venture is not a little ambitious. But the momentous nature of our epoch demands an attempt at synthesis. It is no longer sufficient to accumulate article after article, book after book, on Germany. She is more than ever the Enemy, since her plan of European domination, now being carried out under our eyes, requires our destruction. It is necessary, therefore, to know her, and, to that end, to have a full view of her. The author will surely be forgiven for the endeavour.

The average Frenchman, a reasonable creature, instinctively turns to look at a Germany to whose claims there is no end, and does his best to understand her. Since the armistice of 1918 he has done so with an earnestness which the Germans themselves, sensitive as they are on this point, could not ignore with a good grace.

But can he succeed? The question is bound up with the crisis of our time, the last act of an age-long drama on which this essay proposes to throw a little light.

History teaches us that, from the middle of the ninth century, Germany and France, formerly united under the Carolingians, obeyed their natural tendencies by following divergent paths. The modern epoch has seen the dissimilarity in their destinies so tragically accentuated as to provoke in the course of a single century three sanguinary struggles—in 1814, 1870, and 1914.

At the end of the revolutionary and Napoleonic era France was vanquished by an Eastern coalition led by Prussia; later she was again defeated by a Germany whose States Bismarck had just regrouped. In the First World War she assured her victory with the aid of a Western coalition. In the first conflict and in the third Great Britain played a decisive part.

6

Some then conceived the legitimate idea, on the morrow of a disaster that seemed to be leading Europe to a fresh balance of forces, that a sort of compensatory system might be established, under Britain's benevolent supervision, between the development of Germany and that of France. In March 1918 I wrote, when still in uniform:

"Logically, the grouping of the Anglo-Saxons and the French should devote all its energies to its further organization. This is the most immediate task, the most indispensable effort. Do not let us organize ourselves like the Germans; let us organize ourselves quite simply for ourselves and against them. The danger . . . for nations of the Germanic type is excess of organization, meticulous, pedantic, mechanical regulation. The danger for us is rather that we may abandon ourselves to a pleasant, easy-going anarchism, refusing to make the effort that any attempt at organization demands of the individual." [1]

It was a lamentably vain aspiration. Less than twenty years later these two dangers, exactly complementary of each other, once more became cruelly evident. Have we ever seen Germany more tense, more ready for the permanent and total mobilization of her industrial and military energies? Have we ever seen the West more divided, more undecided, less single-minded?

The Allies could have returned to the tradition of Richelieu and once more dismembered Germany, destroying her Bismarckian structure and her central power, based on Prussian hegemony. That would have been a policy of bold realism, but of cynical brutality, and above all an idle policy, because it would have been out of date and contrary to the natural evolution of modern nations.

On the other hand, they could have resuscitated the Carolingian past, closely uniting the two great Continental peoples in a vast and entirely renovated social edifice, in which the use of both languages would have been introduced everywhere and the opportunity created of beneficent marriages. But that was a Utopian idea, impossible to carry out in a period dominated by bitterness and cruel memories, and in countries in which the sense of psychological differences had been impregnably established by the work of centuries.

Overcome as they were, after a long struggle, by a very natural lassitude, and baffled by the mass of problems to be considered, the Allies found themselves driven to a compromise. They themselves assured the maintenance of German unity, but

[1] *Revue de Métaphysique et de Morale*, September–December 1918, pp. 920–921.

without preparing the decisive and fruitful *rapprochement* that was expected. At the same time they destroyed the old Dual Monarchy and Balkanized the whole of Central Europe south of Germany.

The essential defect of the treaties signed in 1919 lay in their counting on Germany's lasting weakness. On the morrow of the armistice Ernest Lavisse declared that Germany had "her back broken." For all time? How could the extraordinary recovery of 1933 have been foreseen, a reversal of the situation that enabled the Reich to blow down the League of Nations and the treaties of 1919 like card castles?

From this point of view the event which the Germans call the "revolution" of January to March 1933 might seem to partake of the miraculous. Some people were almost tempted to compare Hitler with Joan of Arc, at the very time when the Führer, in the midst of apparently unbroken peace, had seized the power offered to him by the weakness or the complicity of the ruling classes.

It is too little known that this supposed miracle had been long in preparation with German care and thoroughness, and carefully concealed meanwhile from indiscreet investigation, under a plan cleverly drawn up, with nothing left to chance—just such a plan as Paul Valéry described in his prophetic vision of 1897.[1]

When, in September 1918, General Ludendorff drafted his instructions for the military commission charged with the negotiation of the armistice, he considered it his duty, after he had led his country to disaster, to formulate a paradoxical programme, a truly insane programme, but one which the even more frantic insanity of the world was later to justify with disconcerting precision.

True to his own ideas and to the old military traditions, Ludendorff conceived the armistice as no more than a momentary suspension of hostilities. This conception in no way prevented him from contemplating immediate peace, which had become a necessity, and the grave consequences it would entail. Accordingly he advised his people to go shrewdly to work, playing off against France the candid idealism of the Americans and the obstinate belief of the British in the virtues of the Balance of Power. By setting Wilson's Fourteen Points, thought Ludendorff, against the French demands, it would be possible to

[1] "La Conquête allemande, essai sur l'expansion germanique," *New Review*, January 1897.

embroil the Anglo-Saxons with their Ally of yesterday. When the Allies had withdrawn their troops and abandoned her, the German army, with its strength renewed, would settle its account with France, left to her solitary defence against it.

It was an absurd plan in 1918, but only because the Allies had not then attained the degree of disunion and weakness that would have made them the victims of the clumsy German Machiavelli. Ludendorff's scheme was premature. Its very cynicism condemned it. But when, from 1918 to 1932, disunion and weakness, with the slow but sure growth promoted by the deceptive mirage of victory, had poisoned Western minds, the Prussian general's plan automatically materialized, step by step.

Who will contradict me if I suggest that Ludendorff's prevision was strikingly confirmed by events? The German defeat of 1918 gradually changed, under our startled eyes, into a Ludendorffian armistice. France, with her three threatened Continental frontiers, saw rising against her, with the possibility of Italian support, a German army of which it might be said that it was far from being equal to that of 1914, but which had had plenty of time in fifteen years to profit from the lessons of the war, to strengthen itself with new military conceptions, and to assemble the most perfected material resources. This army had the support of a dictatorial régime capable of placing in its service, through the agency of permanent total mobilization, the resources that the nation possessed in soldiers, workers, finance, and resolute patriotism.

This was what the German nationalists called "winning the revolution." [1] Having won it, Germany could feel in a position to win the universal war which was bound to come as the continuation of the preceding one. Already she saw herself attaining the European hegemony which for so many centuries had been her most persistent dream. She was able to live in that faith and to entertain that insane hope so long as France, lacking confidence in her destiny, failed to consolidate her forces, so long as Britain gave her only lukewarm support, so long as the United States contented themselves with threats from afar or vain promises, so long as the democracies failed to unite their forces and their resources against the common enemy.

There can no longer be any doubt about this. We have nursed too many illusions not to find in them the explanation of the recent surrenders, and have lost too many to be able to

[1] In the phrase of Möller van den Bruck.

invent for ourselves the fiction of a security that exists no longer. In the sixteenth century the sudden offensive which the Germany of Luther and of the territorial States declared against Rome threw all Europe into religious and political insecurity. The same surprise has been suffered to-day. Germany and Italy, with their rear temporarily covered by the immense Russia, have been destroying, by the disciplinarian régime which they have adopted, the very foundations of international order, forcibly throwing us back into complete uncertainty in the gravest crisis we have known, according to our best historians, since the Hundred Years War.

We had imagined Germany beaten and poor, and ourselves victorious and wealthy for a long time to come.

Victorious in 1918 we certainly were, thanks to the unity of command and the constant renewal of our forces, which four years of heroic struggle had constantly threatened to exhaust. Those who, like the author of this work, had followed from General Headquarters the military collapse of Germany between August and October 1918, and who knew her true strategic situation at the beginning of November, had good reason for our certainty.

We were equally convinced that Germany had been the first to attack, for reasons which she had invented for herself at the time, and that she bore the principal responsibility for the catastrophe. Nobody, however, was unaware that Germany, even the Germany of Weimar, while violently repudiating that responsibility, had no intention at all of enabling the world to feel confident that she would never again take up arms against the periphery of Europe. There was nothing to prevent her from furnishing that guarantee to her former enemies. By so doing she would have induced the Allies to free themselves from the necessity of assuring their military superiority at all costs for at least half a century. In face of such disturbing obstinacy, how could this liberation be conceivable?

The tragedy is that there suddenly came a momentary military inferiority, without that liberation having been secured. The defection of the United States, the ambiguous British tactics, favouring vanquished Germany rather than victorious France, the hostility of Mussolinian Italy, the growing isolation of France, herself weakened by internal struggles, in face of Germany, the changes imposed on military strategy and tactics by the progress of aviation, the formidable example of permanent mobilization

given by Fascism, and the entirely novel problems of material
and of fortifications, were serious enough without the sudden
rise on German soil, after two years of the Hitler régime, of the
new army, which was virtually ready about 1932, and its linking
up with the Italian army. The German army had become a
terrifying menace to us, in spite of certain weaknesses of which
our experts were well aware.

The fateful character of this sudden shifting of relative strength
was due no less to the financial and economic means employed
to secure that double military recovery, stretching a sort of iron
bar across Central Europe. These methods, in spite of the
inconveniences incidental to autarky, ended by giving the nations
reputed to be poor the aspect of rich nations, and to the States
that still believed in the mirage of their secular wealth an air of
poor relations. For the Third Reich, to consider that alone,
had the advantage over us not only of an economic apparatus
and a production potential unrivalled in Europe. In contrast
with the countries that have remained faithful to the principle
of the dispersed ownership of private property, to the method
that consists in the distribution of the national income between
innumerable individual shares, the German system, which had
liquidated internal and external debt by measures of unexampled
brutality, had had every opportunity of devoting to a basic plan,
that of rearmament, a concentration of resources and of effort
such as was impossible, at all events for some time, for the
countries paralysed by the class struggle.

We misinterpreted the great crises of 1918–33. I am thinking
particularly in this connexion of the inflation of 1922–23 and the
catastrophe of 1929–32. We imagined that they sufficiently
accounted for German patriotic excesses and for the launching
of neo-Pan-Germanism. The reverse is the truth. German
nationalism, both the proud and aristocratic nationalism of the
old ruling classes and the dynamic popular type of National
Socialism and its paramilitary formations, had been in full swing
and in full activity since 1919. Its history is outlined behind
that of the Weimar régime. It drew its strength from the
republican disintegration at which it worked with desperate
energy. It was this nationalism that deliberately provoked the
crises, from which it drew profit with diabolical cleverness,
imposing on the masses terrible sacrifices of which the democratic
peoples have no idea.

It is easy to demonstrate this in the case of the inflation. I have always considered the inflation as not only the greatest affliction endured by the German people since 1918, and one of which we know too little, but also as *the symbolic commencement of the systematic rupture which was to take place between Germany and the Western system.* It has been well said that German capitalism, by ruining the middle classes as it had done, sawed off the branch on which it was sitting. The inflation destroyed within Germany the normal juridical relation between debtor and creditor and, indirectly, the fundamental relation between conquered Germany, with her debt for Reparations, and the victor States, her creditors.

Not that we have any intention of justifying the way the Allies proposed and tried to solve this problem. The inflation does nevertheless represent the first attempt ventured on by Germany to suppress the treaties of 1919 and to offer wild resistance to them. It was a very naïve view that supposed that if Germany could not meet her obligations it must be because of the inflation. On the contrary, in her refusal to meet them she herself brought about that collapse, that absolutely complete cataclysm. At the same time she made the occupation of the Ruhr inevitable. That occupation we were unable either to avoid or, after its success, to turn to account. Germany produced that catastrophe knowingly and deliberately. It was a policy that seemed to be one of pure madness, carried on by such magnates as Cuno and Stinnes and the rest, but it was a far-reaching policy that shook all Europe and, by the sudden ruining of the German masses, created within the population of the Reich the despair and rancour and injured pride and the rest of the conditions necessary for the birth very soon of National Socialism. The immediate result of this diabolical manœuvre, in which capitalists of Germany and of other countries were associated, was *the boosting of nationalism among the German masses and the first wave of Hitlerism.*

The years 1929–32 bear similar witness. The essential aim of the Young plan was to efface the past at least in some degree, and to reduce the volume of Reparations. Yet did we not see at that very moment the opening in Germany of the great campaign, astutely orchestrated by Schacht, against the enslavement to which it was pretended that the Allies were condemning her? Were not steps taken, in the struggle against Stresemann and against his whole policy of meeting Germany's obligations and of *rapprochement,* to produce a great economic crisis, in order once more to exasperate the nationalism of the masses, which had been quiescent during 1924–28, those years of pseudo-recovery? A terrible chronological table is that of the years 1929–32! After 1914, after 1923, Germany rocked Europe a third time by sapping the foundations of her own structure. Now she was out to destroy world trade in order to defend herself against the consequences of the new blockade which she would have to suffer in the next war. She turned to autarky and to the reconstruction of her armed might. To this end she sacrificed in four years a much larger part of her national income than would have been represented by the successive annuities envisaged by the Young plan.

From these astutely calculated shocks, from these convulsions which were spontaneous only in appearance, issued Hitler's National Socialism, fully armed. Germany's rulers had played a dangerous game, at the expense of their own people. The Reich declared the recommencement of the eternal offensive against all Europe and the world, clear proof of the rooted aggressiveness, the iconoclastic tendencies, of which the attentive observer should never lose sight when considering Germany and her policy.

On this already volcanic soil, cleverly "volcanized," if the term may be permitted, by Germany, the doctrinal pacifism of the democracies, with its effort to lull the indispensable vigilance of the West, cut a sorry figure.

It was this element that made the parliamentary régimes slack and sleepy. It was this element that prevented them from emerging from their confusion. There was argument about social and political justice, but life went on by routine, societies were built up in which plutocrats and unemployed faced each other in mortal combat, and in Europe, to crown all, badly drawn frontiers were maintained. At the very time when the Germans were attacking the treaties of 1919—and with what vigour!—and energetically rebuilding their military strength, they were left a free hand. The democratic game was played in face of the fiercest and the most systematic anti-democratic policy the world has ever seen. Above all, the fatal path was entered on of indulgences that weakened the givers without in the least contenting the recipient. Compulsory military service, the remilitarization of the Rhineland, the war in Spain, the annexation of Austria, the destruction of Czechoslovak democracy, were all rigorously logical links in this tragic chain.

That is the true enigma—the temporary apathy of the two great Western democracies, but lately surrounded with all the prestige of victory. For too long they remained inert, undecided, paralysed by a sort of hidden malady that consumed them, and by no less secret connivances and betrayals that rendered them indulgent toward the totalitarian régimes. Let us not dwell only on the collapse of German democracy, due to the absurd pact which, at the time of the armistice, the Social Democrats and the Centre Party had concluded with the Counter-revolution, as though they had no knowledge of its appalling appetite for power, still so keen even after defeat. Apart from international reasons, there were certainly intrinsically German motives that explained the Weimar collapse in 1932. It is true that neither France nor Britain had any manifest desire for Fascism. But did they want democracy as the Americans seemed to do? The Americans knew how to redouble their energy without adopting to that end a dictatorship that was death to all liberties, without renouncing their traditions of political independence. How can we explain this incredible propensity to play for time and to allay public vigilance in face of countries whose rhythm of existence was entirely different from ours, countries in which the mobilization of energies was more and more perfected every day?

We are too ready, in the European democracies, to imagine that disarmament is economically all gain. It is true that armaments claim an undue share of certain productive capacity and a considerable quantity of human energies of high quality. But they assure work for the nations and to that extent diminish unemployment. Disarm? It has still to be established that disarmament is an absolute obstacle to war, or that rigorous equality of armaments would be a reinforcement of the spirit of peace. What we actually did, for all sorts of fallacious reasons, was to favour and facilitate German rearmament, instead of being absolutely adamant on a point of such capital importance. Only so could the military superiority so hardly won have been preserved.

Instead of the firm and effective establishment of such superiority, a League of Nations was set up with no authority over the States Members of it, a sort of international extension of the "social contract," absolutely incompatible with the tragic and implacable laws that govern the formation and the duration of States. Mussolini and Hitler brought down in a moment that fragile instrument, which had afforded them temporary shelter. Deliberately they substituted for the era of pacts of conservation that of struggle between opposing forces.

Thus, through the force of circumstances of which we had lost the mastery, we were faced with a German-Italian offensive which, thanks to frenetic rearmament, to the annexation of Austria, to the destruction of Czechoslovakia, and finally to its successes in Spain, had just attained the last stage of its development. If we had continued to show weakness, its programme would have attained complete realization. Give way? Capitulate? What could be more utterly contrary to the interests of our country? What should we have done in face of that Central Europe, totally armed to the teeth, totally militarized? Ought we to have accepted in advance the end, not only of those small States whose every right to existence the leaders of the Third Reich denied with supreme disdain, but also of the two Western empires which those same leaders considered incapable of assuring to the white race its traditional primacy and its existing "*Lebensraum*"?

Had we done so, had we made that renunciation of our own destiny, the sinister prophecy of Oswald Spengler would have found fulfilment. Upon our dislocated empires and our passive populations there would have swooped the most implacable Cæsarism, because the most systematic and the best armed, that Europe has ever known. Prussia would then have proclaimed herself the one and only Protector of the white races in the world. Over the enslaved Continent would have reigned the Pax Teutonica.

At Neumünster, in Schleswig-Holstein, on June 16, 1939, Deichgräber, Nazi gauleiter of the island of Alsen, declared to his audience that the Germans of northern Schleswig would never abandon their mission as intermediaries between north and south. *He added that the National Socialist doctrine would soon have conquered all civilized peoples, and that, just as Prussia had been the primitive cell, the nucleus, of Greater Germany, so Germany in turn would be the cell and nucleus of the whole white race: the new Germany would thus become the Prussia of Europe.*

These were not empty phrases. The programme had begun to be carried into execution, and it was time for our leaders to cope with the danger that was not only investing us on all sides but attacking us from within.

September 1939.

CONTENTS

BOOK III: THE HITLER REICH

INTRODUCTION[1]

GERMANY'S OFFENSIVE AGAINST HUMANISM

ANYONE who turns to the problem of the relations between Germany and the Western nations needs to know the precise reasons for which in the course of her history, and especially in modern times, Germany has set up, with increasing energy, her ideal of national community in opposition to the declarations and the hopes of Western humanism.

By tradition and almost despite ourselves we have been the supporters of an *abstract universalism* which, without ignoring racial differences, is mainly concerned with the man of all ages and of all countries. The Germans, on the contrary, defended a *centralized universalism* that would assure them, by the simple irradiation of their power, domination over the whole European periphery.

What, then, is Western humanism? Why has Germany an irresistible tendency to break with it? This rupture she rightly calls her "Revolution." This act of violence, according to her most authoritative publicists, is *revolutionary* in that it breaks with foreign influences and foreign importations, which are charged with having corrupted the Germanic spirit and institutions; and *conservative* in the sense that it would lead the straying Germany back to her true traditions and to a mode of government more in conformity with her natural genius. Since the World War, and since the Revolution of November 1918 which is in such ill odour beyond the Rhine, German nationalism, whether aristocratic or popular, has constantly given this definition in advance of the Revolution to come.

I

To-day we are able to reconstruct the genesis and the history of Western humanism. We may be sure that there has always been, and is to this day behind the Hitlerite façade, a humanist Germany. There is thus nothing to prevent us from giving to

[1] Written in March 1939.

19

this term "Western," for the moment at all events, the most comprehensive definition, and taking "Western Europe" to mean the whole of the countries west of the Russian world.

Within the frame thus defined, it seems to me that the total heritage of Western humanism may be reduced to four essential elements, which entered successively and in the most rigorous chronological order into the fabric of our Continental history. These are the spirit of Græco-Roman civilization, which comes to us from the ancient culture with its *static* quality; the spirit of Christianity, split up since the Reformation between three great confessions of faith or institutional churches, but characterized by its *missionary* energy; the spirit of liberal rationalism, summed up on the economic and political plane by the belief in *dynamic progress*; and, finally, the spirit of Socialism, made manifest by the hope of *universal social justice*. Such seem to be the main aspects of eternal humanism.

Let us note at once that in German literature before and during the First World War, and thus before the appearance of National Socialism, there were already many publicists who were announcing the inevitable end of the era in which these diverse forms of humanism developed. In their eyes these three or four thousand years of civilization all belonged to the past. A new period was opening in the history of mankind. It was opening under the sign of *racialism*. And it was precisely every essential manifestation of humanism that the Hitlerites attacked.

The two earliest cultures, ancient and Christian, were so intimately associated in the distant past that it is scarcely possible to separate them. They were not inspired, however, by the same ideal, since the former envisaged a purely earthly order and the latter an order transcending earthly existence.

In spite of certain forms taken by its thought, and in spite of the crises it underwent and its final decay, Græco-Roman humanism had this special feature: it almost always regarded the universe *in its relation to man*. Its thought naturally followed the system of Ptolemy, who regarded our world as the centre of the universe. Christianity preserved and deepened this heritage. It proclaimed that in the person, both human and divine, of Christ an absolute value entered this life and suffered on earth, in the very midst of mankind, to whom, for man's salvation and regeneration, God sent His only Son.

There is no doubt that Christianity drew its power of growth from this fundamental belief, which further established a radical distinction between West and East. But these two first forms of humanism, which historic evolution has so closely intermingled, these two first conceptions of human society, whether in the Platonic "Republic" or the "City" of Augustine, had a certain static quality, a certain fixity of thought and action, which were inevitably bound to be fatal to mediæval Christianity when new aspirations began to be formulated all over Europe.

It required a Luther and a Copernicus to inflict on Christianity the tragic loss of its security, which had seemed to be won for all time. A religious Reformation, a scientific Renaissance! How deep a gash in the web of eternal humanism! Human thought, emerging from a system which it had supposed to be established for all time, was at first bewildered by the universe of which it seemed suddenly to have divined the unity and the infinity. For the moment it found in it nothing but perplexities and perils. How could new points of refuge be established in it? All that men saw were the claims of a new spirit of heroism, which was obligatory upon all without exception.

It is true that this modern vision of the world did not destroy the vital principles either of antiquity or of Christianity. Did not the Renaissance recommend the return to the Greek and Roman writers; did not the Reformation encourage a nostalgic memory of the earliest days of the Church? But this prodigious intellectual change was to result in the replacement of mediæval fixity by a new dynamism.

This indispensable transition was assured by Western Protestantism. Through Calvinism it created the active personal religion which, inculcating labour and thrift, underlay modern capitalism and the remarkable work done in the world by the Western middle class. To this class Christianity still lent, at all events for a time, the solid support of its theocratic system. This in turn collapsed, and in the seventeenth and eighteenth centuries man once more stood alone, lost in the infinite immensity of the universe, face to face with a nature that he knew to be hostile to his plans and his works and ready at any time to destroy the beings it engendered.

Did man lose courage and confidence in his destiny? Not at all. Descartes and, later, the French Revolution came in due time to establish a fundamental agreement between human and universal law, and to introduce harmony and justice even into Nature with her disturbing mysteries. There was, indeed, a partial destruction of the idea of an unchanging, eternal order prescribed to men by divine revelation: that notion subsisted only in the three churches between which Christian energies were shared. The new value that tended to take its place was the idea of *progress*, the idea of an unending march forward, step by step, pursued simultaneously by all mankind. This faith in the Light, one of the great principles of the European West, conquered in the eighteenth century not only the principal elements of German culture but Russia, which Peter the Great had westernized.

This was above all a *middle-class* conception. To speak of enlightenment is to speak also of technical advance and its marvels. The reader of Jaurès' *Armée Nouvelle* will see the lyrical enthusiasm with which that great Socialist praised the achievements of the Western middle class in building vast empires such as the British and French, empires that did not crush mankind beneath their weight because they were inspired, on the whole, by the ideas of liberty and justice.

Nevertheless, these unprecedented successes gave birth, with industrialism and plutocracy, to the tragedy of the growth of the proletariat, a tragedy that has spread to all nations and over every continent as industrialization became universal and entailed universal rivalry. It was from that tragedy, so close to us, that the fourth and last form of humanism proceeded, the vision of a social order, common to all States, imposed on all peoples by a truly universal Revolution, establishing a fruitful alliance in the world between material prosperity and social justice—the real and lasting refuge of mankind in face of the formidable determinism of nature and of the economic process. It is a hope no less imperishable than those that preceded it; a sense of *justice* as firmly anchored in the human spirit as the Greek notion of *beauty*, the Roman belief in *social order*, the faith of the Christian in an *invisible Church of souls*, or the fidelity of Liberals to the *Parliamentary Democracy* of free discussion, free competition, and free exchange.

These four historic aspects of humanism have this in common, that they are based on the belief in the eternal human, in what the Germans themselves, at the time when their classicism was flourishing, called *das Allgemeinmenschliche*. It seems, moreover, that these four forms of thought and action are rigorously bound up with one another. The last link is no less essential than the first. I will go so far as to say that it is because of the neglect of it, because of the failure to solve the social problem on a truly universal plane, that the whole system is at present in danger of collapse. Frightened by the spectre of Communism, emasculated by that bogy, which is virtually an accusing conscience, the Western middle classes have permitted the creation and the world-wide extension of the present crisis, a crisis not only political and social but, above all, *spiritual.*

I will add—and this is an absolutely capital point—that these four forms of thought and action are in no sense "ideologies." Let us admit our debt to Count Keyserling for having so soundly demonstrated that the Western spirit is characterized by faith in man. Not that it does not change or revise traditional forms. But, in one way or another, it firmly proclaims the fundamental agreement between universal law and human law, of which we have just been speaking. It matters little whether this agreement is conceived as existing through all eternity under a precise form, or as achieved either progressively or through a sudden revolution. The Greek ideal conquered the whole world. The affirmations of Christian love have won acceptance, at least in some degree, from all the peoples of the world. The idea of universal progress and of unlimited liberation of political, economic, and intellectual energies has not disappeared, in spite of the German predictions of the end of Liberalism. As for the hope of social justice, it lives in the masses even now when nationalism has, for the time,'reduced the world proletariat to a collection of fragments which cannot at present be reassembled.

Beauty, love, liberty, justice—are these ideologies? But the enemies of humanism are wonderfully skilled in making use of the term "ideology," of *the suspicion of ideology,* to submerge beneath a fatal relativism, cause of so much apathy and indifference and of so many facile abandonments, the principles which, being bound up with eternal realities, are through that very fact common to all men. These principles imply the renunciation of all *racial privilege,* such as could justify any element of mankind in making claim to absolute superiority, to the right of conquest and domination, or to the exercise of a hegemony assured by violence.

This brief historical account of the forms which humanism has successively assumed is mainly concerned with the differentiations occurring in European civilization from the sixteenth century onward. More than four centuries have passed since 1517, in an increasing anarchy which has resulted from men's rejection of the values acclaimed by hu manism.

It is true that through all these disorders the humanities, with their never-ceasing devotion to the magnificent remains of Græco-Latin literature, art, and culture, have kept afloat. But they have been split up over the most heterogeneous environments, here supporting the narrowest of religious education, Catholic or Protestant, there supporting a secular education usually hostile to Christianity. The humanities have also become a class privilege, taking on an aristocratic tinge that shuts them off from the life of the people and prevents them from exercising real influence over the nations.

Since the Reformation, and especially in the seventeenth century, Western Christianity has undergone an unending process of fragmentation. It does not only comprise three great institutional churches; it is well known how far the splitting up of the churches into sects or denominations of every sort has proceeded in the Anglo-Saxon countries. The chief result of Protestantism has been to multiply special manifestations of Christianity. It has enriched it with an unending variety of nuances, but has bound it up, in the West as in Germany, with a thousand territorial or local interests which visibly weaken its unifying action.

Although in part an outcome of Calvinism, intellectual, economic, and political Liberalism has almost always been an enemy of Christianity, especially where it has come into opposition to the great conservative and reactionary churches. Parliamentary or presidential democracy, centralizing or federalist, which is the most authentic creation of Liberalism alongside the great colonial empires of to-day, has also taken on very varied forms. What is there in common to-day between British, French, and American democracy? In its evolution down to the nineteenth and twentieth centuries, has not democratism in turn been menaced by a mortal anarchy?

The workers' or proletarian International has suffered an analogous fate. Everybody knows that to-day, passing on beyond the Muscovite Third International, it is undergoing its fourth transformation. A veritable abyss has opened between Socialism and Communism. The decay of the Popular Front in every country is due precisely to the causes that separate not only Liberalism from Socialism in general, but moderate or revisionist Socialism from intransigent Communism. That is the whole story of the fatal division of the Left.

Like the Romanticists of the dawn of the nineteenth century, the Europeans of the twentieth are faced with the most tragic dilemma. How to avoid anarchy without depriving Europe of incomparable wealth on the pretext of restoring unity? How, on the other hand, can anarchy be permitted to continue its ravages, just in order to maintain the diversity of European culture?

The suspicion of ideology throws a vivid light on the present crisis. This crisis of humanism and its values dates back to the First World War as its most immediate cause. It has to be admitted that the values on which all human civilization rests can be vanquished, at all events for a time, by the opposing forces, the forces of nationalism and racialism. The First World War, by the very fact that it was possible and that it lasted four years, was a sad demonstration that these values, at the point they had attained in 1914, were powerless to maintain order, to establish a stable equilibrium between the interests and the passions of the Europeans.

There is not the slightest question that the existence of the humanities, that is to say, of a culture with a Græco-Latin basis common to the *élite* of all Europe, counted for little in the struggle to prevent war and to limit its duration. It is no less evident that Rome and the Papacy, the centre of universal Catholicism, proved impotent in face of the terrible cataclysm that shook Europe. Since the end of the Middle Ages there had no longer existed, of course, a European Christendom. Any romantic dream of re-creating it, entertained in Germany or in France at the time of the Holy Alliance, came to nothing. Did not the First World War complete a process of decomposition that had long been sapping the international activities of Catholicism?

Protestantism was bound up with the conflict between the nations by virtue of its origins. Its divisions, particularly the irreconcilable opposition between Lutheranism and Calvinism, condemned it to represent precisely the elements at feud. The general result was that Christianity apparently no longer had the authority necessary for preventing the Continental rupture.

Considered under its most diverse aspects, Liberalism showed itself to be equally impotent. In the economic domain it had presided over the successes of the European middle class, over the magnificent conquest of the globe that had brought such prosperity to Europe. But it was directly responsible not only for the bitter competition let loose within each State but also for the rivalry between nations for the conquest of world markets. By its extension throughout the world, by its encouragement of every inhabited country to industrialize itself, did it not burden the world, and especially over-populated Europe, with the terrible, implacable mechanization in which we are bound to see, with Rathenau, the essential cause of war? The diplomatic history of Europe between 1900 and 1914, one of the most tragic of periods, close to the irremediable catastrophe, throws full light on the economic rivalries that determined the course of events and brought the conflagration of 1914.

Political and intellectual Liberalism had failed in Germany, where its bankruptcy after the defeat in 1918 was virtually final. But in the Western nations it still enjoyed its wonted prestige. It was Liberalism that they had had to defend against Germany's anti-democratic offensive. If the propaganda of the Entente showed real power, if America joined Western Europe, if the idea of law and of civilization won through in the end, thanks to an unprecedented coalition of forces, the Allies owed this to the French Revolution, and to the Western revolutions in general.

On this point did not intellectual and political Liberalism correct, to some extent, the errors and the fatal consequences of economic Liberalism? Britain, France, and the United States shared, of course, all their material resources. But their united effort would not have attained the coherence it did attain in 1918 if their union had not been cemented by the Liberal spirit, furnishing their actions with motives that went far beyond those of mere conservation. We did not fight simply to save our existence and our country. We were concerned, in full unity, to secure the triumph of certain principles. The democracies won through *as democracies*. In their countries the peoples willingly submitted to their leaders, and the leaders of the Allied nations voluntarily subordinated themselves to the unified command. Victory was secured by mutual sacrifices freely agreed to.

Socialism, with the workers' Third International, showed itself far weaker than the democratic international. The illusion harboured by Jaurès, and by official French Socialism, in regard to the attitude which the German Social Democracy would take up in the event of war, is well known. The controversy that arose, shortly before the war, between Jean Jaurès and Charles Andler, when the latter had charged the younger Social Democrats with being as pan-German as the Conservatives, throws a strange light on the disastrous dreams that some then almost consciously entertained. Nobody had the slightest doubt that French Socialism was mainly pacifist. But it is well known for what reasons the revisionist Social Democracy, thoroughly disciplined and faithful to the monarchy of William II and to the great industrial employers who were its source of livelihood, and under the influence of the pan-Germanism that had always inspired its doctrines and its activities, abandoned the cause of the International. The workers' International showed itself as impotent as the others in face of war.

On the morrow of the armistice the fate of Western humanism was intimately bound up with that of the League of Nations, and with all the pacts that preceded or followed its foundation. The present collapse of the Genevan edifice is the clearest and cruellest sign of the crisis through which the traditional forms of humanism are passing, at the moment of collision with their most implacable enemies.

From its creation and throughout its development until the Hitlerite break with it, the League was inspired by the Liberal idea, which had carried the day in the war. Certainly nothing could have been more legitimate or more natural. But while humanist culture and the Christian confessions showed the liveliest interest in the League they never, so far as I am aware, played a leading part in it. On the other hand, the Covenant and the international legislation connected with it are manifestly inspired by the idea on which it may be said that the whole edifice of Western rationalism rests, the idea that the peoples of Europe will never experience stability and a fruitful peace until they submit to common standards and to the principles of a moral system recognized as universal and eternal, until they themselves subordinate their sovereignties to an authority superior to States, an authority whose foundations are laid on the rock of Law. This is a conviction which J. Benda has magnificently developed in his *Discours à la Nation Européenne*. It is also a point of view shared by France's best jurists, including Georges Scelle.

Why did the League fail in its task? There seem to me to be four reasons. To begin with, the League never possessed the authority necessary for the accomplishment of its mission. It never had any sort of coercive power.

Then, it is certain that the Treaty of Versailles, especially because it was badly applied and badly defended, did considerable harm to the maintenance and the efficacy of the principles on which the League of Nations was founded. There is nothing to be gained from an enumeration here of the mistakes made by the great middle classes of the West between 1919 and 1932.

Thirdly, the League never, in its structure, its organization, or its activity, got beyond the stage that had been reached during the war. It was unable to restore Socialist activity. It remained aloof from the masses, formed as it was as an assembly of governmental representatives and professional diplomats. It was a sort of great sovereign, a little distant and aristocratic, even in its great annual sessions. The peoples recognized the existence and the value of the International Labour Organization, but they never really believed in the League and did not animate it with their living breath.

Finally, Germany was admitted at Geneva too late. From 1926 on it was evident that if Germany ever recovered strength, and broke with the League of Nations, the League would never survive so radical an amputation. Six years sufficed to justify the anxiety we shared with many contemporaries.

II

But why did Hitlerite Germany break with the League as early as 1933? And why, by its earlier doctrine or by its later acts, did it deny the validity not only of the Geneva organism but of every International founded by the West, and of Western humanism *in toto*? This rupture gave the German action, and the *aggressiveness on principle* that was characteristic of the Third Reich, its forceful and brutal originality as well as its violence of accent. This unlimited dynamism represented in its consequences and in its own acts the greatest danger that France and Europe had ever known.

The explanation of that aggressiveness on principle is the purpose of this study. To explain it is not in the least, as the Germans believe and say of every Frenchman who takes up a definite position in regard to them, to embark on an act of hostility against Germany. The first thing needed is to understand this aggressiveness, not to minimize the danger that proceeds from it. To do so is also to remove the gravest failure of understanding that can weigh on the normal relations between France and Germany.

The great misfortune is that France does not know, or does not want to know, the profound reasons for this secular aggressiveness. It is true that the French people, which has passed through terrible trials in the course of its history, did not experience after the armistice the same disasters as the Germans; for it formed part of the victorious coalition, and it also possessed the dangerous privilege of the legendary stability due to its own virtues and its political education.

Have the French, indeed, any idea of what it means to suffer a defeat that passes like a relentless wave over the vastest ambitions and the most deceptive illusions ever entertained by the ignorance, almost organized, of an entire people? Have they any idea of the unheard-of ravages of inflation throughout all social classes? Do they realize the crushing nature of the German depression of 1930 to 1933, with unprecedented unemployment and destitution, following so suddenly on four years of illusory recovery, 1924 to 1928, in the course of which foreign capital had been pouring into Germany?

The French people were afraid of Communism because they feared for the things they believe themselves to possess for all time. The upper and lower middle class alike felt this vague alarm. But how many people were aware of the real Bolshevization, the incredible political and social decomposition Germany underwent at the beginning of 1933—as we were able to observe with our own eyes during a six months' tour of Germany? This succession of failures to grasp what had happened, for which the facile explanation is offered that it all went beyond human imagination, explains in turn not only the inability of the two nations to understand each other but the fatal difference, steadily growing between 1933 and 1939, between their respective rhythms of life.

Germany's present attitude [1] is nothing new: on the contrary, it is the result of a long historic process. At all times Germany has been in revolt against the West and the South. At all times she has protested against our humanism, against the universalism that is its ineffaceable stamp and its very essence. But no one will deny that the two most tragic episodes of this struggle are the two last—the war of 1914–18 and, since 1933, the offensive declared by the Nazi iconoclasts with increasing shrillness against the European order consecrated by centuries of civilization.

It was certainly not without grave reason that in 1917 Thomas Mann, in his *Betrachtungen eines Unpolitischen*, defined Germany as

[1] See note p. 19.

the *protesting* country *par excellence*. But to whom was the
protest addressed? To the whole of the West—by which
Thomas Mann, writing in the midst of the war, meant Britain
and the Anglo-Saxon countries, France, and Italy. We know
the elements he attributed to this German protest, and the hidden
motives he ascribed to it. The famous novelist analysed, with
incontestable talent, all the varied nuances of what we call
German dynamism. A problematic psychology, faith in the
middle class, both professional and artistic, a strongly emotional
music, an apologia for the war based on the supposed ascent
of the Reich that began with Bismarck—every possible argument, every form of natural aggressiveness was to be found
here, the whole assembled and linked together with the most
implacable logic by a philosophic writer who, facing the enemy
of 1916 at the moment of Verdun, forged this brilliant but
burdensome and unjust chain.

This fundamental opposition may be traced through the
thread of the centuries.

Everybody knows, to begin with, that the conversion of the
Teutons to Christianity was a long, painful, tragic process,
scarcely completed before the end of the tenth century. After
the vast migration of peoples and races the Græco-Latin tradition
and Roman Catholicism, coming from south, south-west, and
north-west, had brought to the Germanic tribes the elements
of a culture which underwent a magnificent expansion in the
twelfth and thirteenth centuries. But what mythological super-
stitions, what ancient popular beliefs, what irrational violence
and untamable passions still lurked beneath the ashes of these
terrible struggles! Heinrich Heine refers to them in his celebrated essay on religion and philosophy in Germany.[1] He
shows in his witty style that under cover of œcumenical Christianity there was always to be found in Germany, even before
the Reformation, a *purely national religion*.

The Teutons clung to their gods, however "diabolized"
through the good offices of Christianity. The great heroic sagas,
so sombre and tragic, the legends all men knew, the elemental
spirits everybody had at call, the old story of Faust—all these
bear witness to a past never really buried, in face of which it
may well be asked whether Christianity ever really conquered
the old German paganism. The Christian Church, said Heine,
though without mentioning the ancient world or the humanities,

[1] *Zur Geschichte der Religion und Philosophie in Deutschland.*

represents that universal Christianity which strikes no roots in national-ism. There will always rise up against it the popular faith that can feed only on the sap that rises from the soil.

Thus, as regards the most ancient forms of humanism, there is no proof that in the course of history they had entirely conquered the Germanic countries even on the eve of the Reformation. But now we come to the sixteenth century. It was then that there began the great and decisive duel between the German spirit and what we will call the Roman idea.

In this Roman idea German thought detected several elements.

To begin with, the notion of a universal civilization, a culture that would be "culture itself," "human culture *par excellence.*" There is only one culture in the world, said Charles Andler,[1] there are no purely national cultures. A magnificent affirma-tion, in no way ignoring all the vigorous originality, the particular nuances, or the varied linguistic expressions, brought to culture by the most diverse nations.

Conversely, that notion is radically opposed to any idea of a superior racial culture, destined to primacy and hegemony. Clearly we have here a crucial issue.

The Roman idea further embraces three historic realities that have changed the face of Europe. Italian humanism, to begin with, the Renaissance as Italy and France understood it. Then, œcumenical Christianity, represented by Papal Catholicism. Finally a political concept of the highest importance, the re-publican idea, from which has come the modern State.

Does not the very fact that this was a struggle over principles, proceeding in increasingly dramatic phases through the four centuries that separate us from the Reformation, go to prove that Germany showed herself incapable of *accomplishing her true mission, that of welding together Germanism and the Latin world?* Was it not for her to attempt this synthesis, seeing that she was the central country? She had almost succeeded between 1650 and 1750, after the Thirty Years War, with the philosophy of Leibnitz and the music of Bach.

Unhappily she arrogated to herself another mission, that of ruling all Europe by the simple virtue of her intelligence and her methods, to the destruction, if necessary, of the whole of the civilization proceeding from West and South. A terrible claim, which the Germans express almost symbolically when

[1] Celebrated French Germanist, formerly professor at the Sorbonne and at the Collège de France.

they set *Kultur* against *Zivilisation*, on the pretext that the former alone is living and natural and close to the true realities, while the latter is merely artificial, an intellectual abstraction, and consequently a cause of decadence.

We have, then, to see how this struggle grew in modern times and gave birth to the contemporary tragedy.

Let us direct our attention to the German dualism, a dualism over which Germany has never yet triumphed. The contrast is often drawn between North and South Germany, and also between Germany east of the Elbe and the western provinces. It would be more useful, I think, to consider north-eastern Germany as against south-western, since the Elbe, running from south-east to north-west, makes a highly significant cleavage in the country.

It separates the old Western Germany, formerly Carolingian, from the Germany that experienced colonization and Slav influence. This geographical antithesis does not correspond in the slightest to that between "culture" and "civilization." In it I see another opposition and one that is pregnant with consequences for Germany's future, that between *policy* and *civilization*. From the sixteenth century onward, the political direction of the Germanic countries passed by successive steps from the south-west to the north-east, from the most Westernized elements to the Prussian element. The South-west became and has remained the country of civilization.

What does this mean, if not that policy and culture were never again to coincide in Germany? Absorbing the practices and the institutions to which the Germans have given the term "Kultur," policy implacably exiled civilization from the country, and civilization policy. In view of the territorial fragmentation that for centuries paralysed the countries beyond the Rhine, German policy aimed above all at securing greater cohesion and slowly bringing about national unity; but civilization flourished there when Germany was most divided, in the twelfth and thirteenth centuries and at the end of the eighteenth, and was doomed to decline in proportion to German unification.

It was a formidable dilemma for Germany and for all Europe. Either Germany remained divided when, giving herself up to culture, she effected a marvellously rich synthesis between the many introductions from the European periphery; or she gained unity while renouncing them and impoverishing herself psychologically and artistically. This opposition between expanded civilization and territorial contraction has falsified the relations between Germany, the central country, and the European periphery. *It appears that a coherent and strong Germany, centrea upon herself, can possess herself only through a will to absolute domination.* After having broken the bonds and the obligations that attach her to the periphery, she claims to impose upon it her spirit of mystical primitiveness and of stifling discipline. It might be said that the old Roman "limes" left a tragic cleavage in the country for ever.

From the beginning of the fifteenth century German humanism showed hostility to Rome and favoured the cause of Germanism. The reign of Maximilian I witnessed a growth of this new force. The Empire was then no longer the Christian magistracy and the universal power of which the Middle Ages had dreamed. It was becoming more and more a German State, composed of territorial sovereignties. Its writers still used Latin, but used it to celebrate the memory of the old Germania or to extol her genius, her virtues, and her glory. The figure of Arminius rose from the limbo of this forgotten past. The aim was to reconstitute upon the mosaic of the territorial States the moral and spiritual unity of the German people.

It was thus that the humanists with whom Luther associated at Erfurt, Johann Hess, Hermann de Buch, Crotus Rubianus, and Ulrich von Hutten, conceived their mission. Did not Mutianus say that before Christ the Hebrews, the Greeks, *and the Teutons* had received the divine revelation on an equal footing?

Thus this early nationalism was not a simple return to antiquity. It was not in this field that the broad international spirit of Erasmus could flourish. The true scope of the polemic between Luther and him lay precisely in the opposition between a national religion and universal Christianity. But this conflict must not prevent us from realizing the marvellous European effort which Germany had successfully made after the Thirty Years War, at a time when she was entirely destitute of political power. Not only did she re-establish in their rights the Græco-Latin humanities, that cult of Greece which, after passing through the stage of poetic erudition and Anacreontism, was to become the Hellenism of the classics; she also, especially in Leibnitz and Bach, a philosopher and a musician, admirably united the profoundest Germanism with the purest Latinity. It was in the nineteenth century, beginning with Hölderlin, that the cult of Græco-Latin antiquity followed in Germany more and more nationalist tendencies. The political image of the Greece of the past began then to be confused with that of the Germany of the future. Germany was conceived as the direct heir of Greece and Rome, and as destined in their place to exercise the same hegemony. Historians were later to return to this conception, until in our day the Nordic man was declared to be the creator of Greek culture and the memory of Greece served only to exalt National Socialist arrogance. On the other hand, the historical fluctuations we have just summarily recalled show us that the truly humanist Germany is not dead but still lives, at least potentially, alongside the fiercely nationalist Germany.

The same alternation may be noted in the destinies of German Catholicism. In the sixteenth century Rome was the object of a radical animosity of which the causes are well known, and which lay at the root of the Reformation. For that reason the Lutheran confession bears unmistakable marks of Germanism. It has all its elements of ferment. It bears witness to its powerful originality. It is well known that the theology and the religious spirit of Lutheranism are the original sources of German thought and German philosophy. The opposition between faith and works, the notion of material corruption and of a fundamental insecurity as the lot of mankind, the conception of a Christian heroism practising its virtues in daily life, the idea of the communion of souls as the foundation of the invisible Church whose visible structure is intimately bound up with the territorial State, all these were affirmations and principles' which, modernized, were subsequently to dominate German culture, in spite of the universal character which Lutheranism claimed still to possess after the schism.

After that schism, however, Catholicism and Lutheranism followed different paths in Germany.

The partial victory of the Counter-reformation consolidated the positions of German Catholicism in the West and the South. Thenceforward a silent struggle was carried on between Catholicism and Germanism. A time came when Germanism tried to capture German Catholicism, and another when German Catholicism, in its bitter defence of the independence and the liberty of the Church, separated its cause from that of the Reich and fought energetically under the wing of Rome. In the eighteenth century Catholicism was the victim of a narrow and tyrannical territorialism. German thought, rationalist or pietist, attacked the dogmatic and disciplinary rigour of Catholicism.

The attacks of Febronius on the papal power were the prelude to attempts to set up a national Church. This movement was extended and renewed in the nineteenth century with incredible ardour, thanks to romanticism. But from the condemnation of G. Hermes, a Catholic theologian inspired by Kant, in 1835, to the Vatican decrees at the very moment when Bismarck was preparing and achieving the great territorial concentration based on Prussian and Protestant hegemony, the German Catholics, who recognized the decrees of 1870, sided with Rome. This was the direct origin of the *Kulturkampf*, which ended in a partial reconciliation under Bismarck and was followed by an era of greater toleration under William II and by the enthusiastic participation of Catholics in the First World War.

After the war German Catholicism, with its powerful Centre Party, deliberately adhered to the Weimar Republic, took part in the elaboration of its constitution, and profited greatly by the advantages accruing from access to public affairs. But then came, with National Socialism, a pitiless reaction, and, this time, a Nazi attempt on a vast scale to bring about the total destruction of Catholicism in Germany. The full-blooded Teutonism of the Hitlerites had no further use for an auxiliary that at the outset of the last century had been dreaming of a new catholicity under German leadership that might have rebuilt European unity to its own profit. The problem of union between the Germanic body and the Roman Catholic Church was insoluble.

From the first spread of the Reformation to the "German Christians" of to-day—a group more or less docilely accepting Hitler's injunctions—Lutheran œcumenicalism, too, has passed through many vicissitudes. So long as it was confined within the narrow matrix of the territorial States, it played its normal part of a disciplinary Church closely united with the State. Later, in the seventeenth and eighteenth centuries, rationalism and pietism freed it from its shackles. How could the territorial churches, muffled in the most pedantic of orthodoxy, have satisfied all those new aspirations? In the end, for that reason, Lutheranism became secularized. It grew into that diffused piety, philosophical, literary, and musical at once, that constituted the original environment, so difficult to define, within which German classicism spread.

Then it was taken possession of by romanticism, which attempted, on the one hand, to restore orthodox Lutheran pietism, and on the other to bring Lutheranism over to pan-

Germanism, making Luther the revealer of religion for Germany alone, Christ's successor, and the prophet of the future Reich. Finally the day came when, on the eve of world war, the imperialists, more realist in their outlook, reproached it with having compromised the political and economic development of Germany and with having been the cause of her being two centuries behind the Western nations. Pushed into the background, after Germany's defeat, by Weimar Catholicism, incapable of democratizing itself, and thrown in the direction of the old nationalism or of Hitlerism, Lutheranism found itself persecuted in its turn by the Nazis when it tried to maintain its bonds with Christian œcumenicalism, or captured by them thanks to the "German Christian" movement.

Thus German nationalism did not cease to fight against Christian universalism, Catholic or Protestant. Yet there is no possible doubt that this universalism has retained in Germany a multitude of convinced and fervent supporters. But it seems that, as a centralized body dominated by Prussia, Germany cannot reconcile this universalism with her excessively rigid divisions. Such is the paradox that explains the religious drama of the Third Reich! Universal Christianity, the religion above all others of the Divine City transcending the terrestrial world, has been split up in Germany into various confessions closely united to the territories by their churches, and favouring the fragmentation of Germany and the triumph of particularism. *So much so that all free and exalted religious feeling has ended in that strange nation by confusing its own cause with that of pan-Germanism.*

The history of the new forms which humanism has taken on since the sixteenth century is entirely different. The rationalism of the men of the Enlightenment, with its intellectual, political, and economic consequences, so penetrated German minds in the eighteenth century that it ended by driving Germanic thought into a sort of systematic revolt against the European West. On the other hand, German Socialism, especially after the last war, opposed Communist Russia and its ideas of a universal revolution.

The struggle against the West is thus a chapter of capital importance in the history of Germany. It was directed against both France and Britain. France, in Germany's eyes, was either the Catholic and monarchist France of the seventeenth century and before the Revolution, which, following the tradition of Richelieu, succeeded in maintaining the territorial division of Germany, or, especially, the revolutionary and Bonapartist

France that defeated and humiliated her, while introducing on her soil, under Napoleon, an extraordinary territorial simplification, or the modern France with which the Reich had the three sanguinary struggles of the nineteenth and twentieth centuries. Britain, for the Germans, is in essence the Calvinist Protestantism, so different from the Lutheran, that was the true origin of the political and economic might of the British Empire.

But French Catholicism, Anglo-French Free Thought, and Anglo-Saxon Calvinism, in spite of the differences that separate them, are all derivatives of the Roman idea. There is no need to demonstrate this for the first of the three. As for the rationalism of the eighteenth and nineteenth centuries, its appearance in the West explains in itself why Germany turned from Italy to direct the blows of her criticism against the West.

France had, indeed, been the first to separate herself, in virtue of her advanced national centralization, from Christian Europe. She had also succeeded, at the time of the Renaissance, in unifying Germanism and Latinity in her rich and supple culture, a thing Germany had not succeeded in doing. She constituted an intellectual menace through the philosophy of the Enlightenment, and a political menace through the monarchy, the Revolution of 1789, and the Napoleonic empire. Was it not also in France that Calvinism had made its appearance, the Calvinism, inspired by Roman law, that was perhaps a more dangerous adversary of Catholicism and the Papacy than Lutheranism? The Reformation had failed, of course, in France. But rationalist France, lay France, had succeeded, where in the sixteenth century German Lutheranism had failed, in introducing egalitarian democracy.

In adopting Calvinism, with all its consequences for the institutional churches and the sects, the Anglo-Saxon countries had founded, on the basis of democracy, political and economic Liberalism. It was from these prodigious accomplishments that the Western capitalist plutocracy had arisen to create the British and French empires. It is enough to recall this past to explain the great and unconquerable German jealousy. Here were privileged nations on whose soil there flourished three great traditions associated with humanism—that of Greek and Latin studies, that of Christianity, and finally that of Liberal democracy. Endowed with their two empires, differing in size but both considerable, these two nations faced a Germany that had long been divided and powerless. Re-read the history of

European diplomacy, particularly that of 1900–14, and it will be understood why Germany was unable at that time to forgive the Entente Cordiale for having sided with Slavism against pan-Germanism. This antagonism between Germany and the West is now [1] diminishing. Maddened by fear of Communism, many westerners are seeking the support of Germany herself. But are they aware that Germany's hostility to the Anglo-French world has not diminished in the least?

Let us not forget that the Socialist idea also was born in the West. The Germans were the first to contend that the proletariat could be nothing in this connexion but the complementary phenomenon of plutocratic capitalism. It is fair to say that the most solid and durable elements of Marxism came from Western Socialism. Germany, before the First World War, had been able to withstand in her own country the pressure of the Socialist masses. The Bismarckian system had astutely satisfied them. But after Germany's defeat in the World War her Social Democracy had entered into power, and Communism had become a huge party. While, however, the Social Democracy had leanings to the West, Communism kept its gaze obstinately fixed on Moscow. So it was that there was born in Germany, in the middle class, with National Socialism, the great *furor teutonicus*, ultimately directed against Marxism and capitalism as well, a fury cleverly excited by a series of crises, and one from which Hitler drew great profit. A strange story in truth, bringing Germany into opposition to all the forms of humanism at once.

What extraordinary significance, from this point of view, has Nietzsche's ultimate philosophy, with its criticism of European and German nihilism! Greek Socratism, with the notion of the moral conscience, Christianity under the most varied forms, political democracy and intellectual or economic Liberalism, and Socialism, are all, says Nietzsche, *maladies that enfeeble and devour* the soul of Europe. A total offensive, and one of genius, since this philosophy of heroic negation made its appearance under Bismarck, between 1880 and 1888. It was a radical condemnation of all Western humanism, which it considered to be decadent and decrepit, like all the things Germany had introduced from the West. From Nietzsche's time there rose a Germany more and more hostile to the influences coming from West or East.

As remedy for this nihilism whose special strength he found

[1] In the spring of 1939.

in his own country, Nietzsche preached an ideal of super-humanity that had no chance of realization. His doctrine also contains potentially the idea of a chosen *élite* that should lead the masses to the well-being they justly claim. But, at the very moment when Nietzsche disappeared, the real substitute for the values lost was found by pan-Germanism, with Houston Stewart Chamberlain, in racialism, the anti-Semitic racialism of which Hitler, a direct disciple of Chamberlain, formed by his tuition, made the centre of his doctrine and action.

Thus Nazism took up in its turn, with a more powerful and more massive because vulgar and popular argument, the total criticism of Western humanism. This time it discovered the Israelite in every form that humanism had assumed in the course of the ages. This time it found the best of all scapegoats for centring the gaze and collecting the scattered aims of the despairing crowd. This time it invented Race, the biological "ersatz" for the national Community, religious in essence, of which Germany had never ceased to dream throughout her history, and above all since the eighteenth century.

Starting from territorial multiplicity and from the Holy Roman Empire, long since defunct, Germany has carried on both traditions since the sixteenth century. Thanks to the slow elaboration and the solid framework of her State, and thanks also to her accomplishments in unification, Prussia put an end to the splitting up of Germany, and Nazism crowned this relative unification by its familiar *Gleichschaltung*, forcing every element in the great country into step. On the other hand, the Germans have not ceased to cherish the imperial dream; it reappears to-day in the form of the Racial Myth.

It may be asked whether this myth is truly an object of national conviction. It is certainly a practical rallying sign and symbol. *In the past, it was the Reich for the Reich or the State for the State. To-day it is the Race for the Race. But at all times it is a question of the maximum mobilization of German energies.* The German Revolution is an organized romanticism. Or, rather, it romanticizes the organization it gives the nation and it organizes the latent romanticism that fills all German heads, in order to console them for the grey and hard existence beyond the Rhine.

The German revolution is the revolution of nihilism, the revolution of a people in which a pseudo-militarized *élite*, denying all the values on which the civilization of the old Continent has rested, has thrown itself into pseudo-biological authoritarianism.

That is why it is dynamic, and, indeed, destructive. It does not operate by means of social displacements within the country, but, profiting by the forces that formerly worked for humanism, it regroups the elements of the German collectivity in accordance with a new plan, impressing on them a rhythm of life totally different from our own. Will Germany simply take a new and more ample place among the European nations? Or will she acquire, by a crushing victory, a total hegemony? That is to-morrow's secret.

Meanwhile, the effort must be made to understand, and to that end we suggest to the reader the interpretation that follows.

March 1939.

BOOK I

THE HOLY ROMAN EMPIRE AND THE
TERRITORIAL STATES

CHAPTER I

ORIGINS (TO 1500)

IN considering the social and political history of the Germans, and then the development of their civilization, it may be said that they have not at any stage in their evolution had a general will. They talked much of their national unity. In point of fact, they *broke* it, leaving free play to their inveterate particularism; or they *dreamed* of it under the form of an absolutely unrealizable Continental hegemony. They seem to have been condemned to oscillate between a cramped realism and a grandiose idealism, both of which deformed their vision of things. Few of them escaped from this law, which appears to have governed their collective psychology and the course of their activities at all times and in all places.

1. *Preliminaries*

It is true that geography assigned a hard destiny to Germany. What can be more singular than the structure of her soil, or more complex than her general configuration? The most marked contrasts abound. Nowhere are climatic differences more pronounced; nowhere are the roads more divergent. Such immense diversity favours a fatal splitting up of the country. This poor and rough soil, open to contrary winds from west and east, offers no outlet to its population except in the direction of the two isthmuses which, east and west of Germany, separate by about six hundred miles the North Sea and the Baltic from the southern waters.

Vegetable and animal life are alike devoid of all originality. The elements of fauna and flora come more or less from all parts. In addition to this, the racial composition of the German people

presents every imaginable variety and every imaginable contrast.
Not to speak of the original racial groups—Nordic, Dinaric,
Mediterranean, Baltic, and Oriental.   How tenacious we find
the maintenance of the regional temperaments west of the Elbe,
how remarkable the difference between that particularist Germany
and the colonized lands of the east.   Who could ever say which
is the more important contrast, that between north and south
or that between east and west?   It needed the simplifying action
of Prussia, the frenzied industrialism of the nineteenth century,
and, later, the ruthless Nazi dictatorship, to lead the country to
a certain sense of homogeneity and a measure of common will.
And still, what do we know of the unsatisfied diversities that
may lie behind the Hitlerite façade?

Since the end of the Carolingian Empire, and particularly
since the Treaty of Verdun, which in 843 separated from each
other what were to become the future France and Germany,
national sentiment has formed in the Germanic lands according
to a law of its own.   One essential trait marks the tragic
originality of this formation.   Germany has never been, has
never been able to be, and, owing to her circumstances, no
doubt never will be, a *true national State*.   That is the enigma of
her history, an enigma whose nature it is important to learn
and to comprehend if we are to treat Germany *with the equitable
firmness* that will always be indispensable for her immediate
neighbours.

While in France the royal power, true symbol of the nation in
process of formation, worked from the centre to the periphery
in its progressive aggrandizement, giving the country the desired
solidity, in the German countries that power worked from the
periphery toward the centre.   It began by embracing the whole
of the national territory, which it then allowed to proceed to
the most complete fragmentation experienced by any European
people.   *Thus Germany became for all time on the one hand a conglomerate of territorial fragments, which the most important among
them, Prussia, ultimately unified by a long and painful effort, and on
the other hand an empire, a " Reich," virtually all-embracing, and for
that very reason always shifting and indeterminate ; a realm that took
the historic form of the Holy Roman Empire, then subsisted in the
form of a vast dream, and finally sought incarnation in the Hitlerite
Third Reich.*

This curious dualism enables us to understand why the
German can confine himself at will within his little Fatherland

and within the limited horizon of his occupational activities, both ruled by the omnipresent despotism of the territorial powers; or, to ward off the danger of atrophy, will readily launch out into the wide spaces of dreams and imagination, ready to take the risk of the adventures suggested to him by an irresistible urge to acquire power and domination abroad.

It is for this reason that Germany presents to us a virtually indefinable mixture of technical realism and mystical idealism, a mixture that disconcerts the Frenchman, habituated to greater clarity and logic.   A Germany rendered impotent by inadequate synthesis tempts the ambitions of a shifting periphery.   Conversely, a Germany united and therefore strong and powerfully armed takes up the imperial idea once more, and, turning upon all sides, threatens simultaneously all the surrounding nations.

Be it noted that we have here, in both cases, *a breach of equilibrium*.   In Germany, to begin with, either the predominance of particularisms destroys the central power, or the latter destroys all autonomous powers by a crushing dictatorship.   Then, in Europe, either Germany's neighbours take advantage of her weakness or, on the contrary, they feel paralysed by irrational, brutal force.   The thing that Europe has never known is *normal equilibrium*, equilibrium between a healthy Germany and a periphery capable of standing up to her while assuring her the resources she needs.   From the remotest times down to the Reformation of the sixteenth century this destiny reveals itself with astonishing clearness.

The struggle between Teutons and Romans before the barbarian invasions reveals already the Germany I have just defined.   It explains, in particular, why the name of Arminius became, in the eyes of the Germans, the symbol of the union which they needed at all costs to establish between their dispersed energies if they were to succeed in resisting their external enemies.

From the decline of the Roman Empire to the middle of the sixteenth century there followed the slow growth, and then the rise to the zenith, of the "Holy Roman Empire of the Germanic Nation" as virtual master of all Europe.   But, owing to the conflict between the Papacy and the Empire, after the fatal Interregnum, there came the irretrievable ruin of the imperial power, and then the triumph of particularism, until the day when, within the decaying Holy Roman Empire, confessional dualism allied itself with territorial fragmentation and brought about the Thirty Years War that left Germany, about the middle of the sixteenth century, quivering and entirely devastated.

When one attempts a broad survey of that long evolution, and of that of the following centuries, the sixteenth to the nineteenth with the end of the Holy Roman Empire and the nineteenth and twentieth with the Bismarckian enterprise and the Second Reich, one sees entering successively into German history, both on the social and political and on the cultural plane, on the one hand the constituent elements of particularism, and on the other the systems of thought and action in which is strongly incarnated, in the anxiety to overcome fragmentation and the resulting impotence, the will to unity.

Primitive racial components, ethnic diversities dating from a distant past and grouping together, in face of the colonized East, Frisians, Low Saxons, Franks, Bavarians, and Alemanni; a vast world of regional dialects that remained vigorously alive because they were solidly anchored in popular life and customs; territorial States in course of formation and development since the thirteenth century, and afflicted with absolute sovereignty until the eighteenth; diverse confessions that implanted themselves in those States, intimately associating their churches with the civil power; later, after the Vienna Congress, great political parties, under rigorous discipline, real blocks, solidly and massively organized; finally economic, professional, or literary and artistic groupings of every sort—all these are historical factors of which the final result was German *pluralism*. Of this pluralism it may be said that between 1919 and 1932, freed under the democratic régime from the old monarchical shackles, it reached its supreme expression, bringing the ruin of the Weimar Republic and the destruction of the hopes of peace which the old Continent had nursed since the end of the World War.

In face of this spread of particularism, a hotbed for all the germs of anarchy, great efforts were made from the first toward centralization in thought and action. First of all came the incredible effort ventured on by the Merovingians, the Carolingians, and the Ottos to build up what was one day to become the Holy Roman Empire. After the collapse of the Empire, and on entirely new foundations, there came the hard and persevering labour accomplished by the greatest of the *Länder* or territorial States, which by a miracle of brutal force and astute diplomacy succeeded in inducing the other territories to unite.   After Frederick II came Bismarck and the Second Reich. After the timid steps of Weimar toward centralization came the pitiless Hitlerite *Gleichschaltung* or Procrustization.

Parallel with this great social and political effort went the vast unification in language, culture, and thought since the Reformation, the magnificent attempt at German and European synthesis that began in the seventeenth century, leading to the spread of classicism and romanticism, and then the fatal simplification and impoverishment when there came, under Bismarck, the utter downfall of the values proceeding from humanism and the ruthless effacement of foreign influences, until the day when, profiting by the moral and intellectual ravages caused by war and defeat, Nazi propaganda organized the mobilization of men's very thoughts.

The total fragmentation was the reality and the total unity the dream: no one realized this better than Hegel in his youth, at the beginning of the nineteenth century.   From this point of view he was the most authentic representative of his people, the typical German who turned in disgust and despair from a political reality eternally uncompleted and inadequate, and set before himself as a guiding star an ideal State that was alike a supreme aim and a consoling dream.

How can we fail to be filled with admiration by his *Zur Verfassung Deutschlands*, dated 1802?   Never had any German said before him, never did German say after him with such sad sincerity, such despairing lucidity, what was the essential cause of the deep-seated evil that had preyed through all time upon the German community: "The things the Reich does as Reich never proceed from the collectivity but from a group of greater or lesser extent.   *These groups make one think of a heap of round stones trying to build a pyramid though they remain absolutely round and loose.*   The moment the pyramid begins to move toward the end for which it was made, it disintegratete or, at least, proves entirely incapable of offering any sort of resistance. . . . For centuries a situation such as this has coms pelled Germany to oscillate between two desires, that of opposing the existence of a German State and that of being that State."

It could not have been better said.   But this same philosopher, talking at the Protestant seminary at Tübingen with the poet Hölderlin, himself a young man, on the consequences of the French Revolution and the future of Germany, agreed with his companion in the aspiration that the future Germany should be, like ancient Greece, a mystical community, a sort of national, popular Church, a new sanctified Race that should accomplish a providential mission in Europe. Later, in his *Grundlegungen der Philosophie des Rechtes* (1821), Hegel set before Prussia, for her to realize, the model of a perfect State, complete in itself.

2. *The creation of the Holy Roman Empire*

Through the stone, bronze, and iron ages, prehistory leads us to the first encounter, shortly before the birth of Christ, between Teutons and Romans. Before this, one may trace in the primitive Teuton world the lineaments of a national community, *both religious and military*. Its god Odin and his complement incarnated respectively the inspired, violent, warlike aspects and the calm and regulated manifestations of sovereignty. The Teutons also confused packs of semi-animal wild men with troops of warrior champions. We have here a type of *magico-military society* that seems to be specifically Germanic.[1]

The remote origins of this community lead us directly to the immediate present. That militarization assured to the mythology of the Teutons a remarkable destiny: that mythology did not die away with the external forms of paganism; it experienced a resurrection that figures among the essential facts of the nineteenth century. It visibly retained a national religious value. We see it, as M. Dumézil excellently says, "*resuming its hold over the Teutons of the Continent, fighting on their side against Christian disciplines and practices with all the frenzy of an act of revenge.*" It was not, as elsewhere, a question of fine legends recalling a past that had disappeared for ever. For the past century and a half the Germanic legends have been not only re-popularized but *re-created as myths*. They have once more become true myths, since they "produce individual and collective attitudes that have all the characters of the sacred." M. Dumézil notes "the spontaneous movement by which the German leaders and masses, after eliminating foreign conceptions, naturally ran their action and their reactions into mystical social moulds that conformed, in a way of which they were not always aware, with the most ancient organizations and the most ancient mythologies of the Teutons."

This outline may suffice. For it furnishes a point of departure and a point of rest. It admirably justifies the celebrated prophecy

[1] Georges Dumézil, *Mythes et Dieux des Germains* (Paris, 1939), pp. 154 sqq.

of Heine, who showed the French, about 1834, that the Germans, by their piecemeal destruction of artistic and Christian values, were returning to a past that might well inspire them one day to the most violent political revolution the Continent had ever known.

At that remote epoch the Teutons were already divided into numerous clans. This fact constituted a danger for Imperial Rome, since these tribes had a tendency to anarchical violation of the "limes"; and also an advantage for Rome, since it was easy to play off tribe against tribe. Only Arminius and Marbodius seem to have triumphed, and only for a limited time, over this disorder.

The struggle between Teutons and Romans lasted about three and a half centuries, from 100 B.C. to A.D. 250. The phases of this conflict are well known. Those who wish to understand it will seek the basic reason for the antinomy which German thought, at all times and especially from the sixteenth to the twentieth century, has noted between the Germanic world and Roman civilization. If I am not mistaken, it is Rousseau's old antithesis reappearing here under very special aspects, the antithesis between *Nature* and *Civilization*. It governs all German thought about the primitive past.

The Germanic world is thus regarded as *Nature*, that is to say, the reign of spontaneous instincts and violent passions, the association of religious rites with military organization in a community at once mythical and mystical, metaphysically hypostatized in some fashion. The Roman world, on the contrary, is *Civilization*, that is to say, the predominance of an individualist and egoist law, the multiplicity of juridical contracts, the sovereignty of private property, the absolutism of the State, the complicated artifices of a more and more refined culture, desiccating and softening. On one side, *healthy* and regenerative forces, on the other the signs of *decadence* and of *corruption*.

For more than a century and a half German thought has been riveted to this absurd and puerile system. How shall the evil consequences of this system be measured, or the damage done by the misunderstandings it has produced between the two peoples? In his *Geschichte des deutschen Volkes* the historian Friedrich Stieve, who is certainly not a Nazi, declares that the Teutons represented emotion (*Gefühl*) and dynamic energy (*Wucht*) as against the discursive intelligence (*Verstand*) of the Romans. It is an ancient cliché, as stupid and tiresome as it is obsolete, a hundred times revived and repeated. It is also an infinitely dangerous one, since it impresses on German minds the idea that the Germanic Community, in itself superior, rejects for all time the social and political forms and the intellectual and moral traditions of the Roman world and of the European West.

A fateful historic turning point was the migration of the peoples. While among the Teutons larger and more massive units took the place of the sparse tribal communities, a sort of mortal paralysis in the face of danger overcame the immense body of the Holy Roman Empire. After long preparation, the decisive assault came in the latter half of the fourth century. The Rhenish and Danubian dykes both gave way. *The onrush was such that the Germans, haunted for all time by that memory and naturally urged on by the nostalgia of limitless spaces, were ever afterwards incapable of concentrating their attention and their energies on their own national destiny, in order to set limits to it and to achieve it.* That early European conquest harboured the secret germ of their ambitions, their habits, and their later excesses.

About A.D. 450 the Frankish masses burst over the West. Three decades sufficed for Clovis, king of the Salian Franks, to occupy Gaul. When he died, in 511, that monarch left behind him a vast kingdom which, about 550, united Gaul and Germania.

For centuries after this the Teutons mingled with a civilization that had proceeded from antiquity and from Christianity. The German historians are asking themselves to-day whether the Germanic self-awareness was or was not obliterated, indeed destroyed, by this culture, which they call artificial, and particularly by a religion that preached human brotherhood and love. To most of them it seems that the Germanic genius lost some of its primitive spontaneity and heroism.

It is true that since the conversion of Clovis the institution of royalty had rested here on a double basis, Roman and Germanic. Thenceforward its power extended *throughout the kingdom*, however vast. It had now *to create and foster the intermediary powers beneath it.* Toward the end of the Merovingian epoch, Gallo-Frank society had replaced the Emperor, the senatorial families, the farmers of taxes, and the slaves of the Roman era by its royalty, its spiritual and temporal nobility, its free peasantry, and its semi-serf small cultivators.

Here we see the divergent paths which France and Germany took. Why did monarchy consolidate itself in France, achieving

national unity there?   Why did it meet in the German countries
with the insuperable obstacle of feudal, territorial particularism?
It was because under Charlemagne, and especially under Otto I,
the monarchy *made itself universal.*   In this wider framework,
within which the German national consciousness was placed at
the moment when it might have been effectively formed, it was
crushed in advance beneath the weight of Christian universalism,
and the grand tug-of-war began again between the central and
the regional powers.   What was Charlemagne pursuing but the
old Roman chimera of a government both centralized and
universal, a chimera that reappeared here in Christian Gallo-
Germanic clothing?   Universalism preserved the heritage of
antiquity and Christianity, but particularism remained the concern
of the German racial groups.

The Carolingian harmony was but ephemeral.   Scarcely was
the Verdun partition concluded, toward the middle of the ninth
century, when the nobles attacked the very substance of the
royal power.   The grasp of the imperial dignity was feeble
because it was too wide;   the intermediaries grasped more
effectively because they had less to grasp.   When the distinction
between freemen and serfs disappeared, this levelling up added
to the power of the great landowners, on whom the imperial
power also showered secular and ecclesiastical benefices.   Fierce
struggles came in what were later Germany and France.   Royalty
that had not the vision or the power to unite its lot with that of
the people and the middle class was defeated in advance.

From 936 to 973 Otto I had been able to renew the Carolingian
tradition, temporarily restoring its lost prestige.   An immense
and unwieldy officialdom enabled him to effect a certain centralization, to colonize the East, and to widen his external policy.
But, to his misfortune, he tried to surpass Charlemagne.   He
assumed the style and the prerogatives of both political and
religious supremacy.   His Italian ambitions were inordinate.
The edifice he constructed, a true colossus with feet of clay,
grew gradually weaker under his successors from 973 to 1056,
while beneath the surface the formidable alliance between the
Papacy and the feudal lords was in preparation.

Did the three successive empires establish a true culture in
Germany?   Did they effect a happy union between the Germanic
tradition and the ancient and Christian contributions?   The
Teutons possessed little beyond the heroic legend and the elementary art of ornamentation with animal figures.   Their great

legendary florescence had attained its zenith about the sixth and seventh centuries, thereafter fading until it was revived by Charlemagne. In that new heroic legend, dating from the migration of the peoples, the figures of Attila and Theodoric the Great stand out because the Teutons saw in them, rightly or wrongly, the chief founders of their power. Like that literature, the animal ornamentation of the Teutons seems to content itself with the representation of types, but already they are full of life.

Wooed from the East by Arianism and from the South-west by Catholicism, the Germanic world adopted Christianity in the train of Clovis. From this first encounter there arose a number of hybrid forms in which the old Germanic gods lived alongside Christ and the Saints. The old faith defended itself, and, as everywhere else, Catholicism shrewdly adapted itself to it. The ancient elements preserved by Catholicism naturally predominated, thanks to their pagan and polytheist aspect. Popular customs continued to ignore the Gospel and the primitive dogma. This curious syncretism seems to have lasted until the end of the sixth century.

It was from the Anglo-Saxon West that true Christianity, with its monkish asceticism and its missionary energy, came to the Teutons. All the Germanic tribes were conquered simultaneously by it. In the first half of the eighth century there rose, fully constituted, the Frankish Church. What it then preached, with all the fervour that could be desired, was the dogma of sin and redemption, salvation through Christ made man, the severe Christian discipline that imposed humility and long-suffering.

Clearly this Christianity, a religion of rude austerity and of total renunciation, no longer had anything in common with the heroic legend of the Teutons. The old schematic polytheism, impersonal and tolerant, disappeared before it. It was to the individual that Christianity appealed, to the infinite value of every soul and of all human reason; and it assimilated the former gods to diabolical powers. Gone were the barbaric customs of the past. The new morality penetrated the whole of Teuton society. More formal and rigid than at Rome, it progressively modified family life, the position of women, the status of blood-relatives (*Sippen*), the relations between the social classes, law and the State, poetry and art. The Teutons had conquered the Roman and Christian world, but this in turn took its conquerors captive.

What could Germanic art, with its poor edifices of wood and its rudimentary ornamentation, set against the stone buildings of the Holy Roman Empire, and in particular the magnificent architecture of Ravenna? The contrast was so extreme that there could be no compromise, except in pile foundations. At Aix-la-Chapelle, at Nimègue, and at Ingelheim, on the contrary, Teutonism and Romanism were interspersed without influencing each other. As for the churches, they bore eloquent witness to the Romanesque victory. The competition was no less unequal in sculpture on ivory, in the illumination of manuscripts, and in the magnificent Gospel-books of the Ottonian epoch.

Who does not see the reappearance here, in a new and more complex environment, of the problem we stated just now? A well-known historian, Adolf Bartels, did not wait for the Nazis in order to declare that "a Germanic culture, *pagan* and *warlike*, a true culture, furnished with a *virile* and *proud* morality and *with a highly developed poetry*, entered into conflict with *Latin and Christian pacifism*." He adds: "It was the *pacifist* culture that carried the day against the *bellicist* one." [1] He attributes this victory to the lassitude that overcame the Teutons after all their exploits. He laments the destruction of Arianism as a grave "excision" in Germanic development.

In this clash between two cultures Bartels sees, above all, the origin of the distinction established thereafter in Germany between *clergy* and *laymen*, between the *cultivated* class and *popular* customs, a new pretext for the return to the opposition between nature and civilization, between Germanic regeneration and Latin decadence. What could be further from the truth, when the laymen of that epoch themselves recorded in their dialects the teachings and the sacred legend of the Church, when the monkish author of the *Walthariuslied* treated that old Germanic legend in a frankly popular manner, and when in the prayer of Wessobrun, and in the *Muspilli*, the *Heiland* (Saviour), and the *Evangelienbuch* (Gospel-book) of Otfried, codices that succeeded one another in the eighth, ninth, and tenth centuries, we see the Christian inspiration mingled with reminiscences of paganism?

What wonder that German historians have attacked the Renaissance of the Carolingians and the Ottos? They are fond of declaring that Charlemagne failed to attain his purpose of conserving the Germanic heritage while filling it with the Christian spirit. *A true German Renaissance, they say, must be*

[1] *Geschichte der deutschen Literatur*, i, p. 22.

under the sole leadership of the German genius. In both cases, declare Bartels and K. Lamprecht, the German spirit was *sacrificed.* The victory of the Church, they say, imposed on the Germany of that epoch a culture exactly contrary to the heroic traditions of her proud past.

Not that it is easy to pronounce upon such a matter. The essentials, at all events, may be set down as follows.

From the first, kingship in Germany showed an anticipation of the "totality" formula, becoming more and more *religious* and *universal.* Clovis, Charlemagne, and Otto I succeeded in some measure in combining *centralization* with universalism. In each case this was done by a miracle of personal energy and of individual sovereign authority, followed by a profound collapse and rapid decay, until the day when another universal spiritual power, that of the Papacy, united with the feudal powers of Germany against the Empire, which, though a temporal power, aimed at being spiritual and universal.

To identify Germanism with particularism would be to draw the facile conclusion that Germanism had prevailed over the ideas of the classical world and of Christianity—a victory which would have threatened the very existence of kingship in Germany. But the terms of the problem are not so simple as this. In the German territorial States (*Länder*) the ideas of the classical world and of Christianity had penetrated, as though from within, a kingship which, by tradition, was already proceeding from the whole to the parts, itself fortifying the feudal system whose most powerful elements were one day to turn against it.

Thenceforward Germany was the scene and the victim of a fundamental contradiction between a universalism of foreign origin, which secured it no more than an apparent and precarious unity, and a territorial particularism which alone answered to the concrete needs of the national reality. Between the two the possibility was destroyed of any true nation and any real national State. Kingship in France, proceeding from the parts to the whole, followed exactly the opposite course. It did solid work and so vanquished feudalism.

The German failure was not the fault of classicism or Christianity *but of Germanic tendencies which were favoured by the penetration of classical and Christian universalism.* It may be said that in face of that penetration Germanism failed to secure for itself an equilibrium between the central and the intermediate powers. It seems, moreover, to have receded on the cultural plane because it had no cultural resources that could offer effective opposition to the ancient and Christian cultures. Not that it disappeared in consequence. Toward the middle of the eleventh century the whole problem was still alive in the political and cultural spheres. Between these there still existed a certain parallelism. But when the Empire had foundered and the political centre of gravity had shifted toward the North-east and Prussia, the severance between statecraft and culture became inevitable. It became the essential characteristic of German history.

3. *The victory of the Länder*

It was impossible, indeed, for these two to have equal chances in the great struggle that began between the universalism brought in from without and German particularism. When the imperial power had fallen completely into decay, centuries were needed for the restoration of territorial, administrative, and military unity. On the other hand, the influences from without were allowed full play on a plane unlimited by any concern for political concentration; linguistic and intellectual unification was one day to permit Germany to proceed to a sort of European synthesis, giving her culture an original and magnificent breadth.

Thus, by the simple play of compensation, culture gained in cohesion and extension at the times when territorial fragmentation condemned the nation to political impotence. *That is why Germany seems to be condemned to dream herself before giving herself concrete shape.* She has always invoked her great future. In Nietzsche's phrase, she has always been and always will be *of yesterday and of to-morrow, and never of to-day.*

We may follow the progressive decay of both universalist powers, Empire and Papacy, from 1050 to 1500.

The causes of the imperial decay are known—Italian ambitions resulting from temporal universalism; the electoral character of the imperial crown, which had once been hereditary; the fact that all the feudal powers, secular and ecclesiastical, were in league against it; the absence of any effective bond between its policy and the concrete needs of the nation—an instance of which is Frederic Barbarossa's conquest of Sicily; the predominance of southern romanticism over the cold realism of the north; the continual aloofness of the imperial house from northern interests in its egoistic desire to round off its possessions. Since the Empire could neither be attacked nor conquered, it was not subjected, like the kingdom of France, to the salutary test of the danger that was incessantly reappearing to whip up the national energies. It grew lax and incapable of exerting effectual pressure in all directions at once.

Its fall had been prepared between 1002 and 1056. It was then brought about, between 1056 and 1152, by the quarrel over investiture. In Barbarossa's time, in the second half of the twelfth century, the imperial and universalist tradition of Charlemagne and Otto I radiated its last and most sumptuous effulgence. There was one last attempt at recovery, under the Emperor Frederic II, at the beginning of the thirteenth century. Then came the fall of the Hohenstaufen dynasty and the terrible Interregnum, which ended in 1273. The rest of the history of the Empire, down to the death of Maximilian I in 1519, is one of unceasing failure and debility.

The Papacy, too, passed through cruel vicissitudes. On the morrow, of course, of the struggle against the Empire, Innocent III led it to the zenith of its domination. Declaring himself to be Christ's vicar and sovereign over all Christians, kings included, he claimed to unite on his head the crown and the tiara. Boniface VIII shared and even exaggerated these ambitions. But toward the end of the thirteenth century and throughout the fourteenth, the period of the exile to Avignon, the papal authority suffered a grave eclipse. It was from that time that Rome, under the pressure of the need for money, committed the excesses which at the outset of the sixteenth century provoked, not, indeed, the ecclesiastical reform aimed at by the great Councils of the fifteenth century, but the revolutionary schism of Luther.

Behind the crumbling façades of the great universalisms there then came into view new powers, new centres of activity, which were to constrict and to mould more powerfully the body of resistance that the German countries presented to all government.

Since the twelfth century the condition of the peasants had improved in the West, but in Central Europe it had grown worse. This contrast explains the familiar difference between Western Germany and the region east of the Elbe. Not that too much should be made of this difference for the period before the Reformation. The German peasantry of both regions was then in a wretched state, as was proved by the peasant revolts at the outset of the sixteenth century, revolts that were due to the unceasing growth of a sort of agricultural proletariat.

The Orders of Chivalry were constituted during the Middle

Ages. They flourished in the twelfth and thirteen centuries, later falling into complete decay. Chivalry is a more familari subject than the peasantry, since chroniclers recounted its exploits and poets gave minute descriptions of its sentiments. In the social hierarchy its members came after the Emperor, the princes, and the great landed proprietors who were lords of numerous vassals. It had fewer members in Germany than in France or Italy. Its decay started earlier in Germany than elsewhere, about the beginning of the thirteenth century.

With the royal power diminishing, the condition of the peasants still one of impoverishment, and the Orders of Chivalry in decay, the only sound elements of the Empire, a pyramid menaced simultaneously at its peak and its base, were the towns and the *Länder* or territorial States.

The German towns date from before the eleventh century. From the eleventh to the twelfth century the towns gained in importance in proportion to the growth in number and wealth of their inhabitants and to the development of commerce under the influence of the Crusades, and became more and more differentiated from the villages over which the knights still dominated. Then, when capitalism, money, and credit took the place of the earlier barter system, the town became in the west the *burg*, surrounded by fortifications, the market in which the peasants sold their produce, and finally the seat of a tribunal in which the lord administered justice. In the colonized country in the east, on the contrary, the towns were laid out from the start, according to a comprehensive plan, by kings and princes. This contrast between the towns of the west, huddled round their castles or cathedrals, and the regular towns of the east, completes and illustrates that between manorial estates and peasant holdings.

We now see plainly the fundamental contrast between the *North-east* and the *South-west*. The former is the country of ethnically differentiated levels of population, of dominating squires (junkers), of systematically planned towns, of methodical organization, of Prussian institutions and tendencies. The South-west long remained the region of countless territorial sovereignties, of relatively free peasants, of independent towns, and of the imperial policy with its romantic aims. The antithesis between *Prussia* and the *Reich*, so important from its very paradoxy for the understanding of German realities, finds here its clearest origin.

The characteristic that distinguished the German towns from those of the rest of Europe, especially after the decay of the imperial power, was their autonomy. They were sovereign republics, vested in principle with the same powers as princes or prelates. They based their constitutions on a sort of egalitarian Socialism that aimed at distributing work and profit among the inhabitants as fairly as possible. Merchant guilds and artisan corporations formed the framework of the system. The former provided the patricians, the latter the burghers. Soon, with the burgomaster, came the magistracy composed of patricians and the municipal council formed by burghers.

The rise and decay of these towns, following the spread and dissolution of Chivalry, were the dominant facts of the fourteenth and fifteenth centuries. The growth of internal trade, the creation of the Hanseatic League and the development of capitalism; the coming of personal liberty, of juridical capacity and rights recognized for all; the increase of political, administrative, and military efficiency; the spread of literary and artistic culture—these were the essential results of the splendid but brief career of the towns, due to the fact that the imperial power and the territorial powers were unable at that time either to oppress or to protect them. The great importance of their rapid decay to the later destiny of Germany is clear. It began in the fifteenth century. The princes prevented them from allying themselves with the Emperor, and then systematically attacked them and absorbed them into their respective territories. *This enforced integration in the territorial order cost the German people its political education.* Little by little the proud and independent burghers were humbled. Had circumstances permitted, they might have made of Germany *a great modern democracy*.

After this quadruple decay of the imperial power, the supreme ecclesiastical authority, the rural military knighthood of Chivalry, and the trading and cultivated burghers of the towns, there remained only the territories. It was these territories (*Länder*), absolute monarchies united with the orthodox churches, that founded modern Germany. We see here the bizarre grouping of an Empire robbed by decay of its natural greatness and its national functions, above an incredible mosaic of territorial powers.

In that period of growing confusion and general anarchy, the territory seems to have been the *only nucleus of order* on German soil. Neither the Empire nor the nobles nor the patriciate could either ward off the social danger threatening on all sides or satisfy so many new aspirations. *This task fell to the territories.* Out of their expansion were segregating already the cohesion and the strength of Prussia. Numberless relationships of close dependence were taking the place of the great and simple relation between Empire and subjects.

Toward the end of the Middle Ages, Germany thus comprised the ancient Western Germany, situated between the Rhine and the Elbe, alongside regions that had been detached from her—the Netherlands, Franche-Comté, Lorraine, and Switzerland—and the new Eastern Germany, peopled by German colonists and by subjugated Slavs and organized into frontier provinces called *Marks* (marches). The territories were not distributed evenly over this vast surface. In the west there were numbers of small secular or ecclesiastical principalities and free or imperial cities. In the east were powerful principalities with extensive territory and strong authority.

The institutions which served as the structure of these petty monarchies were present from the fourteenth and fifteenth centuries onward—assemblies of representatives, a fiscal system, tribunals with professional judges, and a standing army. Their economic and social foundations were also established—development of industry, division of labour, progress in agriculture, in communications, and in commerce, all the essential elements of the capitalist system. The territorial sovereign, the *Landesherr*, was already able to constitute a really strong government, extending his control and his protection to all hamlets and towns, markets and forests, ecclesiastical properties and social classes. He arrogated all powers to himself. He was assisted by his chancellery and his council, in which the nobles and the prelates shared influence. Although he was *legibus solutus*, above the laws, his domination was set certain limits by the States-General or provincial diets (*Landstände*) of his monarchy.

Already Prussia occupied the front rank among these territories. She had been in course of formation since the twelfth century, and was soon the most modern and the best administered of the absolute monarchies. In the fifteenth century Frederick I founded the powerful dynasty whose military enterprises were brilliantly seconded by the Teutonic Order.

Thus, on the eve of the Reformation, the fundamental data of the future German policy were assembled. On the plane of the territories that had been victors in the great struggle between the particularist powers and the national interests, the centre of gravity was visibly shifting from the fallen Empire toward the Prussian north-east. Soon Lutheran Protestantism installed itself in its chosen positions there, while Tridentine Catholicism occupied in the south the place vacated by the Empire.

4. *Civilization and the arts*

Thus the national idea remained here in suspense, between the Empire that had abandoned it in order to achieve egoistic ambitions, the territorial sovereignties that did not hesitate to betray it for their own satisfaction, and autonomous cities which, no doubt, remained faithful to it, but had no means of giving it concrete shape. The history of German culture from 1050 to 1500 reflects this fundamental opposition. In the twelfth and thirteenth centuries it was inspired by the ideal of Chivalry, heroic or courtierly, and in the fourteenth and fifteenth by the ideal of the burgher.

For the first time since the barbarian invasions, the European world had attained a certain equilibrium and proceeded to determine with some rigour the relations between the countless imperial feudatories pushing their way everywhere and the princes. It was impossible for wars and Crusades to occupy the knights for all time, and the emperors and their great vassals, following the example of the Norman kings of England or of Philippe Auguste in France, encouraged the spread of culture.

This movement was taking place in the eleventh and twelfth centuries, at the time when the union between the Latin of the cloisters and the German of the people was growing closer and closer. Such a poem as the *Ruodlieb*, certain chronicles, and the part played by the wandering poets, reveal the rapid progress of Chivalry. But this vast movement showed a certain hostility to Rome, to the German clergy, and to Christianity in general, and the threatened religious powers tried to organize against the danger. From 1060 to about 1160 the conflict between Pope and Emperor was accompanied by one between prelates and knights.

The Church sought to turn to its profit the sentiments, the passions, and the ideas current in the world of Chivalry; the latter, in turn, utilized the great Christian themes for its own purposes. There resulted a certain syncretism, a mixed literature which, under the influence of the Crusades and the wars in Italy, taught a broad tolerance that admitted Hellenism and Judaism, Islamism and Christianity alike. We seem *to see the emergence of the idea of a German Empire, capable of holding the Papacy in check, which would assure temporal and spiritual government to Europe.* The legend of Barbarossa, which adequately expresses this idea, treats that emperor as the successor of the Roman Cæsars and the august founder of a new universal monarchy. He is often represented *as assuring the salvation of the world.* In face of the current hypocrisy and corruption, the Germans claimed already to possess the secret of intellectual veracity and purity of manners. A moment of unique ecstasy came when—on the very eve of the imperial collapse—Frederic Barbarossa, having triumphed over the Lombards, secured the canonization of Charlemagne!

All the conditions were present here, between about 1150 and 1250, for a true Renaissance to set its powerful and grandiose imprint on letters and the arts. The old Germanic ethic, the memories of the ancient world of Greece and Rome, and Christian teachings, adapted to the current taste, were the principal ingredients of that culture. It shows the more or less conscious conflict between a sort of nationalist universalism, responding to the imperial idea, and Latin Catholicism. It was in epic poetry that this conflict had fullest play. Do we not find in it once more the symbolic opposition that tends to show itself between Low Germany, where the Nordic element necessarily predominated, and the South-west, where Mediterranean influences were paramount? An eternally yawning gulf, which Thuringia and Bavaria tried in vain to bridge.

Proceeding from the north-west, the heroic legend reached Central Germany. Here a relative harmony was able to establish itself between the primitive inspiration and Christian principles. This explains the new level reached by such poems as the Nibelungen and Gudrun sagas, which nevertheless represented the thought and the customs of a barbaric epoch. The epic of court life set profane against religious love. In Hartmann von Aue the taste for the good things of this world and the exigencies of Christian morality are fairly well harmonized. The balance is less happy in the romances of the Round Table, in which an enervating eroticism and a sentimental pseudo-idealism are with difficulty reconciled with the duties of virile heroism and of the struggle for uprightness in a corrupted world. How much more profound and how much truer is the art of Gottfried van Strassburg when he shows the tragic extent to which violent passions can eat into the fragile substance of the ideal of Chivalry!

This mediæval German culture, aiming at a living unity between the national tradition and the civilizing influences of antiquity and of Christianity, finds its fullest and most fruitful expression in the works of Wolfram von Eschenbach and Walther von der Vogelweide.

How distinguish, in the work of the former, aristocratic tastes from popular tendencies, the worldly fervour from Christian morality? Wolfram understood the conflict of his epoch better than anyone—the opposition between aggressive paganism, still alive in the depths of the German soul, and the Christianity, tempered by Hellenism, that brought it measure and moderation. Was the Fellowship of the Grail anything other than a tolerant Church, very Germanic in spirit, independent of Rome, a secret society obeying the eternal laws of the mediæval world, and trying to discover in the universe spiritual powers that would be superior to the papal system because more universal? Wolfram conceives religious and moral life as the passage from an inevitable primitive confusion to the growing clarity and perfection that men can acquire by merit. He does not find an irreconcilable dualism between the children of this world and the children of God. Free enthusiasm, fervent pantheism, universal toleration, and the will to unity—one may find in *Parsifal* the remote first shaping of the religious feeling that was to appear later in Leibnitz, Goethe, and most of the romantics.

The same tendency to turn Christianity in the direction of a sort of candid and tolerant pantheism, absorbed in the beauty of the world, is found in the lyricism of Walther, in which hostility to Rome is so evident at times. This religious feeling engendered, from that period onward, the longing for a German Empire that should be both free and universal. This is evident also in the liturgical drama, the imperial chronicle, and the satirical or didactic writings of the time. From a specifically German state of mind that nevertheless remains strongly imbued with Christianity, this literature seems to pass already to the idea of a national community that should be at once religious and imperial.

Is it in this sense that W. Scherer maintains that mediæval poetry founded German nationality as the *Divina Commedia* of Dante founded Italian?[1] It may be. The great Germans of

[1] *Deutsche Literaturgeschichte*, pp. 230–231.

that period affirmed the spiritual Empire at the very time when the concrete Empire was collapsing. They entertained the dream with fervour. In fact, *statecraft* and *culture* separated. In statecraft the North was beginning to triumph over the South. In culture the South was gaining predominance over the North. Both movements signified the struggle against Rome and the Roman idea.

Nothing is more remarkable in this regard than the judgment concerning the plastic arts of this epoch arrived at by certain German historians, whether they deal with Romance or Gothic architecture, or miniature or other arts. The general purpose is to show that there has always been a victorious struggle for the freedom of the national genius against the forms of Roman Catholicism, which were regarded as too rigid and consequently paralysing. This rigidity, it is often declared, engendered an intolerable asceticism or else an intolerable corruption.

In other words, Germanic freedom grew in proportion as the imperial idea, without ceasing to aspire to European scope, detached itself from Rome and from Catholic universalism. Was this the genesis of a specifically German universalism? Perhaps. Secular in tendency, it adopted the most diverse nuances from the Crusades in the east, the French influence in the west, and the Italian incursions in the south. From this point of view the thirteenth century might be considered as having produced a German Renaissance after both Charlemagne and Otto I had failed. *It remains true that the imperial dream expanded beyond measure at the very moment when the territories began to carry the day and when all chance of the realization of the dream was lost.*

In this struggle between Germanism and the Roman Idea the townsmen of the fourteenth and fifteenth centuries also played an important part.

These burghers were more realist than was Chivalry. They were a new danger for the Church, which once more assembled its troops. Mendicant orders, Dominican or Franciscan, organized its defence. Revision of dogma, popular preaching, protest against the unbelief of the cultivated classes and against the superstition of the masses—such were the aims pursued. Speed was necessary, for the new middle class was rapidly secularizing its thought and its morality, criticizing piety and the ecclesiastical institutions with growing vigour.

It also opposed to them, while yet the Lutheran schism was in the future, German mysticism and humanism.

From a mystical movement of which the origins seem to date back to the middle of the twelfth century, there came in the first half of the fourteenth century the works and the preaching of Meister Eckardt, Tauler, and Suso, followed well into the fifteenth century by those of Dietrich von Freiburg, Rulman Merswin, and Thomas à Kempis. A middle-class mysticism, accessible to all, replacing that of knightly love. It was the cult of the soul's betrothed, the search for the divine slumbering within the soul, the permanent mysterious intercourse between the human spirit and its divine essence. The *Reden der Unterscheidung* of Meister Eckardt contain the first elements of the religious and philosophical terminology which the great German thinkers were later to employ.

Here is revealed one of the most fruitful forms of the religious feeling in which the best of the Germans of that day were to commune. It is the first germ of the Invisible Church, based on one and the same inner experience, which Luther was one day to announce, the first manifestation of a psychological activity that appealed both to the forces of emotion and passion in every man and to the light of the intelligence. It is the first notion and the first practice of the purely inner freedom which each one of us may owe to a purely divine gift of grace, the seat of which is to be found in a higher region of the spirit, distinct, no doubt, but not absolutely separated from the human soul in its normal state. Here, as if by anticipation, was the secret spring of the Lutheran Reformation—the entire self-surrender (*Hingabe*), inner calm (*Gelassenheit*), an attitude of renunciation and humility, but a state that permitted the personality absorbed in God to receive from Him the communication of universal energy and to rise to the most extraordinary accomplishments.

In Germany, as elsewhere, humanism was a very different thing from a simple return to antiquity. It brought about a true scientific Renaissance. This was produced in the universities that sprang up everywhere on German soil in the fourteenth and fifteenth centuries. Mysticism was a philosophical and emotional reaction from scholasticism and the practices of Roman Catholicism. The new science was a protest, of growing boldness, against the pure transcendentalism of mediæval dogma. It went straight to the study of the terrestrial world. Already pan-dynamic in tendency, it treated reality as a system of forces continually created and re-created by the divine energy.

But the new science proved yet bolder. It made alchemy, magic, and astrology fashionable. No less enthusiastic than mysticism, equally alive to the external world, it profited, under the inspiration of Campanella or Giordano Bruno, from the extraordinary progress the natural sciences had made in Germany since the thirteenth century. The true Faust of the epoch was Nikolaus Cusanus. His aim was not only to know by direct experience all the elements of the real, but to reconcile contraries, to perform a work of synthesis, to grasp the organic totality of the universe. After this preparation the movement attained its full extent toward the end of the fifteenth century. Everywhere there rose savants and humanists, such as Rudolphus Agricola (1443–85), who revolted against scholasticism and advocated the substitution for it of the study of physics, of the natural sciences, of ethics, and of philosophy. About 1500, after revealing remarkable strength in Western Germany, the movement penetrated the colonized countries.

But, like mysticism, humanism in Germany took a strongly accentuated national character. At this time the Empire was no longer the Christian magistracy of old. It was tending to become a German State. Its universalism, as we know, had changed in nature. For that reason, as we have seen, the historians of this time devoted their attention to the Germanic past, resuscitating Arminius and declaring that the moral unity of the nation still existed above the territorial mosaic. We are far removed here from the tolerant, international humanism that Erasmus and Reuchlin were later to teach. Everywhere there appeared powerful personalities, men of ardent spirit and fanatical enthusiasm. Ulrich von Hutten among the nobles and Conradus Celtes among the townsmen dreamed of a new and magnificent future for the German Reich.

We see then why literature came closer to the people and proceeded to a critical examination of the established institutions on which the power of the Church was based. Religious poetry addressed itself to the masses, to their deep, elementary feelings. But secular poetry predominated. The poets of the epoch celebrated either the solid virtues of the humble burgher, in particular the love of nature and the freshness of soul that are the true sources of poesy; or the spirit of corporative organization incarnated in the output of the "Meistersinger," true communal poetry, with a local habitation and the support of a local body of singers; or concerned themselves with the most disturbing realities of the epoch, the statecraft of the territorial princes and the great national events.

With Hugo von Trimberg, Heinrich der Teichner, and Sachsenwirt satirical poetry attacked Rome and the great prelates, the higher social classes and the ideals of Chivalry, and the corruption that money brought into the life of the burghers. Manorial halls and town squares saw the birth of comedy and carnival, which in turn humorously castigated the vices of knights and townsmen. Hans Rosenblut satirizes those knights in want of money who mortgaged their castles and stirred up local wars in order to free themselves from their liabilities; the avaricious burghers who refused to lend money to their lords; and finally the unfortunate peasants who suffered from the general corruption. Chroniclers and orators, for their part, initiated the people into the national life. Prose everywhere abandoned Latin for German in attacking the abuses of the age.

This literature carried out a specific mission—to show the social, political, and moral picture of these centuries before the Reformation. It respected or, perhaps, ignored the imperial power, but it was implacable in regard to the Church and the secular powers whose betrayal of trust crushed the poor.

The plastic arts were to profit admirably by this bourgeois movement, which glorified craft occupations and turned naturally to a democratic art consecrated both to the rich Mæcenas and to the people.

But religious architecture gained nothing from all this. Like the scholasticism of the time, the Gothic architecture of the fourteenth and fifteenth centuries, in its purely geometrical combinations, reached its most barren stage. When the burghers took the place of the clergy in church-building they copied the models of the mendicant orders in their simplicity, directed entirely toward the preaching of the Word. In the north-east there rose the brick buildings of the Teutonic Order. Religious architecture thus moved toward the style that was one day to be adopted by the Lutheran parish churches. Only civil architecture progressed in the towns, magnificent buildings rising everywhere, like the sumptuous dwellings at Nuremberg and the picturesque houses at Halberstadt.

More original was the sculpture of the epoch. Independent of the churches, it devoted itself to the representation of individual personality. In its search for expression, its exaggeration of certain gestures or attitudes, its more and more popular outlook, and especially in the teeming figuration of altarpieces or the statuary of tombs, it is a living demonstration of the victory of naturalism. The progress of painting was still more astonishing. It, too, reflected the awakening of individual life. It expressed the mystical emotions of Assisian gentleness, or the renewal of Christian sensibility at the time when the bond was becoming more and more intimate between the believer and the object of his faith, or the taste for nature and realism. The ecstasies of German mysticism and the vigorous naturalism of the scientific renaissance united, for example, about the middle of the fifteenth century in the works of Stefan Lochner, until the time when realism definitely triumphed and art, like all contemporary life and thought, escaped from the Church. Each city sought to be a centre of art. This spread of particularism, and of the anarchy it engendered, assured the predominance of the towns.

From this pre-Reformation evolution there emerge clear outlines of Germany's development.

On the social and political plane it was an immense, desperate effort for total hegemony, followed by a no less total collapse. The German Empire had sought to attain concrete realization, uniting at its zenith the temporal and spiritual powers. Then it lost both. *But the German mind was permanently haunted by the dream, the realization of which was again and again deferred—a chimera that slept like Barbarossa. It was never abandoned.*

Beneath it appeared the realities, more restrained and more solid—social elements in conflict and local powers greedy of sovereignty. Peasants and lords, lords and towns, towns and princes, warring aristocracy and trading capitalists, burghers and the incipient town proletariat—there was general anarchy under the ægis of an impotent Empire and a Papacy that was forfeiting the sympathies of the nation. The only pre-Reformation signs of the future unity were the consolidation of the territories and the growth of Prussia.

On one side was the vision of a great political and religious community, maintained, after the rupture with the Papacy and at the time of the decay of the Empire, by the heroic legend and by court literature, and later by mysticism and humanism. On the other were a literature and an art which, in describing the anarchy that existed, protested against its causes. In the end it became clear that neither the Empire nor the Church was capable any longer of moulding, unaided, materials so diverse and so chaotic.

Two ideas stand out clearly from these fifteen centuries— (1) that of a *common kinship* and a *national religion* that constituted an invisible bond between Germans; and (2) that of a federation or republic of territories and local monarchies out of which Prussia was one day to rise.

Thenceforward the German spirit was divided between a universal culture that extended beyond the territorial limits and aimed at attaining the dream of the Reich or of "*Volkstum*," and the countless local tendencies that gained neither motive for nor means of unification until much later, at the time of the industrial revolution. Such are the outlines of the dualism to which Georg Steinhausen refers at the end of his *Geschichte der deutschen Kultur*. In defining the contemporary crisis he writes that, if the Germans have no true civilization, the fault lies with "the profound opposition that exists among them *between the man with technical or economic activities and the man of the inner, spiritual life*, and, indeed, with the proscription from which the latter has suffered."

Let us go yet further. The two diverse elements sought desperately to rejoin, sought fusion in a common effort. The dream of the Reich to come and the whole culture turned toward "*Volkstum*," and later toward Race. They became *nationalized*, in the special sense Germany gives to that term. On the other hand, Prussia became under Bismarck, by the play of her hegemony, the real Germany, a Lutheran, industrial Little Germany to begin with, until the coming of the Greater Germany dominated by a national religion. The means she prepared— personal, autocratic monarchy, a disciplinary system of legislation, administration, and army—she was one day to place at the service of the national and imperial idea. The alliance between Prussia and pan-Germanism was the true German revolution. Its elements were formed in the course of the four centuries that now open before us. On one side were Luther, classicism, romanticism, and then "racist" pan-Germanism. On the other were the republic of the territories, the conquests of Frederick II, the wars of independence, Bismarck, William II, and Weimar. After this long preparation the Third Reich was a mixture of racial mysticism and dictatorial discipline, a terrible, crushing mobilization of minds and bodies, a façade of formidable appearance but behind which, though we cannot prejudge the future, the *disjecta membra* of German reality have fought desperately for their existence and their autonomy.

CHAPTER II

The Lutheran Reformation and its Consequences
(1500–1750)

THE Treaties of Westphalia divide roughly into two halves the long period from the start of the Reformation to the middle of the eighteenth century, the opening of the modern era.

Between 1500 and 1650 Germanic destinies assumed the revolutionary character which could be foreseen at the end of the fifteenth century. Luther's appeal, first spread by German mysticism, but supported also by the contemporary rebirth of science, resounded throughout Central Germany; its multiplied reverberations continued throughout the North. The schismatic religion took possession of many territories, whose rulers took advantage of it to bind the new churches to the absolute secular power and made of them the most solid supports of their sovereignty. The two great innovations of the epoch, united in a common hostility to Rome, were the Invisible Church, forming a secret communion of believers, and the republic of the princes, in which liberty reigned only between potentates and could not reach their peoples, who were subjected to rigid social, political, and intellectual discipline.

From them proceeded the German nation. It stood out for the first time against the confused and anarchical mass of the decaying Empire. After the Counter-reformation, led by the universalist powers, which were threatened with ruin, and after the terrible scourge of the Thirty Years War, the territories were divided between Protestant and Catholic potentates. Confessional dualism was added to territorial fragmentation. It accentuated the opposition between the South-west, which remained faithful to Rome, and the North-east. Thus there was added to the racial groupings and the territories a third factor of decomposition.

After the terrible ordeal of the war the German countries slowly recovered. The pessimism aroused by so much devastation gave place to a confident optimism. In an entirely changed environment the Reformation bore new fruits. The philosophy of the Enlightenment, introduced from the West, and pietism, the prolongation of a tradition that had continued without break since the sixteenth century, modernized it, penetrating it with logical clarity and enthusiastic fervour. In the first half of the eighteenth century a magnificent philosophical and musical development took place, marked by the famous names of Leibnitz and Bach. Literature and the arts followed only at a distance, but they bore witness to the renewal that was in preparation. The territorial States consolidated and at the same time renovated the absolutist system, while in Prussia an energetic dynasty accumulated the heritage into which Frederick II entered in 1740.

Thus there reappeared at this epoch, in still stronger outline, the dualism of which the elements had slowly formed in the course of the preceding centuries. From Luther to Leibnitz the classic religion was in preparation that was to attempt to unite and to transcend official rationalism and sentimental pietism. The territories gave precision to their methods of government and of education, at the time when the ascendency of Prussia was beginning to impose itself upon them. From these two orders of facts proceeded a literary and artistic movement that was the prelude to the expansion of classicism.

1. *From Luther to Leibnitz*

In 1517 Luther posted up at Wittenberg his "theses" on Indulgences, and in the succeeding decades his thought developed with magnificent amplitude. In 1543, two years before Luther's death, Copernicus published his *De Revolutionibus Orbium Cælestium.*

Two revolutionary dates, two revolutionary acts. In this first part of the sixteenth century a German monk and a German astronomer threw down the greater part of the mediæval edifice. Destroying the illusory unity of the Christian world, they cast it in its entirety out of the security in which it had seemed to dwell, exposing it to new perils and new anxieties. These were two terrible blows struck at the humanism that had proceeded from the ancient world and from Catholic Christianity. For more than a thousand years humanism had maintained the old system of thought in Europe and had delayed the explosion of its latent energies; but in doing so it had consecrated too many errors and injustices.

The monk declared to the Papacy that it could have no claim to any sort of control over the eternal mystery of death. The astronomer revealed to the men of his day the true place that our planet occupies in the starry universe. Neither Luther's protest, of course, nor Copernicus's discovery could challenge the right to exist of the humanities or of Christianity. Græco-Latin culture and the churches that issued from the Reformation continued to fulfil their mission in Europe. But the one outstanding event of that epoch was the conjunction between Luther and Copernicus, between an energetic conception of religion and scientific pandynamism.

Luther's protest was the symbolic act that revealed the German's customary attitude. The monk had carried out with meticulous rigour the commands of the monastic rule. Then, tired by the vain accumulation of efforts and sufferings, he suddenly threw overboard the whole mechanism of Catholic piety. With the intuition of genius, by an act of pure inner liberation, he grappled directly with the mystery of the soul, the region in which divine grace, operating in full sovereignty, frees the believer from his infinite debt, demanding nothing from him but perfect humility and absolute trust in the divine forgiveness.

The tragedy of the evil conscience, ending in the joy of full and free forgiveness, in the certainty of salvation—that is to say, in the exaltation of inner energies suddenly recovered. The Lutheran faith was less a matter of intellectual adhesion than a permanent source of life and activity. To be religious was to believe and to feel, by virtue of direct experience, that the universal Energy is acting in us, provided that we allow ourselves to be directed by it. No more recourse to an external mediator. The universal priesthood, democratic in origin and in essence, abolished at a stroke, in principle at all events, the privileges of the clergy and every inequality in the matter of religion.

An extraordinary message. It made of Luther, almost in spite of himself, a schismatic, a revolutionary, and the founder of a Church. The new ecclesiastical Community was invisible. It was because of that that it grew so rapidly. Its invisibility enabled it to cross the outward barriers of territorial fragmentation. Putting fresh life into the *disjecta membra* of Germany, it wove new bonds between them. The sacred Word, the simple Gospel message, sufficed for all. There was no need for abstruse theology or for exalted mystical contemplation. We may describe it without hesitation as a first spiritual *Gleichschaltung* for the Germans. An extraordinarily simplifying force was that of the appeal launched by Luther in 1520 in his "Address to the German nobility." [1] For, in contrast to the wealth of the Catholic tradition, it carried the visible sign of a psychological impoverishment of which Germany was one day to suffer the grave consequences.

It seems also that the Lutheran Reformation, when reduced to its fundamental affirmation, announced a breaking-away from Western thought.

Already Luther regretted the heroic humanism of Zwingli, which bound up the salvation of the individual soul with the democratic reorganization of the Church and of civil society. More important still was the difference that separated Lutheranism from Calvinism. The French Reformation, heir of the Roman Idea, remained close to humanism, its conception of religion being more individualistic than Luther's. Lutheran individualism was purely religious, purely inward. It was unlimited only within. It related only to the sphere of the soul. The Lutheran found and maintained his inner felicity in the very midst of the troubles of this world. Instead of remedying them, he submitted to them in the name of a social order that was both civil and religious. He was always in danger of passively accepting all things. His Church, a mystical communion of the faithful, *existed of its own accord* and came before the believers. Calvinist justification, on the contrary, stimulated the Christian's activity, urging him to glorify God by his works, to struggle against the blemishes and the evils from which mankind suffers. It directed itself above all else to active voluntary service. The believer came before the Church *because he was its substance*. From this primary difference there proceeded other elements of opposition. Moral, political, or economic, they were later to create many failures of understanding between Germany and the West.

Still more revealing in this regard was the polemic between Luther and Erasmus. While Erasmus was trying to reconcile the sovereignty of grace with free will, Luther made of grace a sort of psychological absolute, an absolutely gratuitous and unpredictable internal grace that directs all things in us, provided that we recognize its unique value. In face of the world of Erasmus, a world of universal tolerance and humanism, of spiritual liberalism and of international tendencies, seeking

[1] *An den christlichen Adel deutscher Nation von des christlichen Standes Besserung.*

behind individuals and nations and epochs the eternal values of human nature, there rose the dark and disturbed universe of Luther. Thenceforward there existed in the latter a division between the active heroism of a directing *élite* and the rigorous obedience of the masses under its leadership. This conception proclaimed the necessity of an authoritarian government—in the name of original sin. It admitted the coexistence of good and evil, and declared conflicts and wars to be inescapable. Nothing could any longer bridge the gulf between Luther's capricious God and the divine wisdom as conceived by Erasmus.

The influence of Melanchthon and certain later developments whittled down the primitive Lutheranism. Its original heroic mysticism, its belief that Christ inspires in the Christian acts that are not "habitual," was modified. Justification was reduced to an act of reconciliation that consoled the believer, faith constituting a sort of merit that brings us salvation. From these premises proceeded the dull and conservative dogmatism that adapted itself to new needs of felicity and engendered the pedantic orthodoxy of the territorial churches. Between 1550 and 1650 Lutheranism lost its original accent, at the very time when it had to struggle against the Jesuitism of the Counter-reformation and the high policy of Richelieu.

Not that mysticism had entirely disappeared from the official churches. It never ceased to lead a secret existence in them. It even reappeared in some strength in the first half of the seventeenth century, inspiring the fervour shown by the hymns of Paulus Gerhardt or the "Passion" of Schütz. Men re-read St Bernard, Tauler, and the *Theologia deutsch*. Between 1606 and 1609 appeared *Das wahre Christentum* of Arndt von Ballenstedt, which was followed between 1610 and 1650 by a whole succession of religious works leading straight to pietism.

When, about 1770, the new literary *élite* looked back, with Goethe, to the sixteenth century in order to discover there the sources of a true national culture, it found not only Luther and the Reformation; it discerned also the pandynamism of the Renaissance, which, under the inspiration of the Copernican revelation, had established a new conception of the living universe.

The connexion with mediæval mysticism and with the thought of Nikolaus Cusanus seems clear. The ideas that dominated the movement, of capital importance to the future of German thought, were three in number.

The universe, it was said to begin with, is an infinite Unity. This is the most striking and the most powerful idea of all three, the idea that gives the most exact measure of the abyss that was suddenly to open between the new scientific conception and mediæval anthropocentrism. Nikolaus Cusanus had already deduced from it, well before Copernicus, that the earth, the sun, and all the celestial bodies revolved round the axis of the universe. Thus, in infinite space every point had the same value as every other. This infinity of the universe proved that God is himself of infinite power and perfection. His creative ability is eternally manifested. The imperfection of the individual human being was, as it were, corrected and compensated by the infinity of the universe. The world was no longer a vale of tears. The life we lead in it was a gift of God.

This being so, the spirit and Nature were closely united, instead of being antagonistic as Christianity declared. From the inferior beings up to the highest manifestations of life, said Paracelsus, there was an ascent that obeyed eternal laws. Consequently there existed a fundamental analogy between all beings. The microcosm was united with the macrocosm by a certain identity of structure. The stars, like men, were living beings governed by laws that were applicable to human life. The acts of the stars were models for our existence and our morality. The same fundamental phenomena were produced in individual life, in society, in history, and in the universe.

The third idea was owed by German thought of the sixteenth century to Giordano Bruno. He declared that beings are endowed with a relative independence. They exist and count by themselves. They form *continuous* series in a hierarchy. Every creature has its place in the scale of beings. Here there appeared, before Leibnitz, the idea of the monad of monads. From this point of view pantheism and theism were equally true. Within each monad the external vision was analagous to the internal vision, intuition coming always to complete the observation of nature.

These fundamental ideas, which were one day to reappear, transformed and broadened, in Leibnitz and later in Goethe, received but a naïve formulation in the sixteenth century. But their importance is no less clear than that of Lutheran dogma.

We may go further—a bond was established at that time between Lutheranism and these scientific ideas. A first modernization of Christianity was here in preparation. Men had begun to integrate Christianity in an historic whole in which, like the earth in relation to the sun, and the sun in relation to the universe, it became an historic fact among historic facts. The metaphysical acts of salvation and the dogmatic system deduced from them no longer appeared in the category of a reality fully existing and accomplished once for all. It was possible, then, to conclude from this that Christianity was nothing but a sort of vast historic symbolism by means of which was manifested the relation between God and man, which must be based both on the eternal divine nature and the eternal nature of man.

This shifting of perspective produced in the course of time a new mysticism. We find its first elements, in the middle of the sixteenth century, in Sebastian Franck and Schwenkfeld, who figured among Luther's first and most enthusiastic disciples. Frank saw in God an active Goodness freely lavished, a productive Energy that worked in all creatures. The divine revelation was thus permanent and universal. It illumined us everywhere and at every moment. Christ and Adam, the good and the bad principle, lived in us and through us. Their conflict was eternal. The original Fall was reproduced permanently in us, and redemption equally so. The Bible was nothing but a vast allegory that showed that this alternation between fall and regeneration is the very breath of our life. Valentin Weigel, who lived toward the end of the century, showed himself still bolder. Reviving Paracelsus, Giordano Bruno, and the whole philosophy of the Renaissance, he drew from them a pantheism that claimed that we could understand the universe because between it and us there was an identity of substance and of structure. Just as we knew the physical world because our body was the quintessence of all substances, so we comprehended spiritual realities because our soul took part in the divine life from which it had issued and because it received nourishment from it through the sacrament.

Jacob Böhme resumed this effort of thought in the seventeenth century. Associated through his origins with Christianity, Anabaptism, and mediæval mysticism, he was the complete theosophist of the epoch. He was as much poet as prophet, and enriched the religious and philosophical terminology which Meister Eckardt had elaborated, and which modern German thought was later to develop. He had Luther's longing for salvation and for its glorious certainties. Like Luther, too, he delved into the problem of good and evil, asking himself whether

they could be united in God, and adopting the view that in Him
light and shade must be opposed to each other as complementary
phenomena, since the one could not exist without the other.
But, considered in His essence, God was neither good nor evil,
neither light nor shade. It was outside Him that this fundamental opposition became the law of the universe. It was we
who lived and were constrained to live between the infernal
kingdom of Wrath and the celestial kingdom of Goodness and
Love. It was in our power, however, to leave this intermediate
position and to assure the victory of the celestial world over
the evil world. That was the true aim of existence. That
permanent struggle of the good against the evil would one day
transfigure the world.

The Christian tradition renewed by Lutheranism and Tridentine
Catholicism, a naturist pandynamism based on the science of
the times, a theosophical religious outlook giving the freest
interpretation of the Christian dogma—in these we see amalga-
mating in the crucible of German thought, between 1500 and
1650, the essential elements of the mediæval heritage. Even
before the eighteenth century a characteristic religious system
was forming in the German lands. It was, no doubt, the first
expression of the profane piety (*Weltfrömmigkeit*) which, breaking
with ancient and Christian statism, was intoxicated with the idea
of a world in which all would be strength, power, and sensual
delight. It substituted for the old beliefs a restless dynamism
and is to be explained by the immense upheavals of the epoch
and by the general insecurity resulting from them. It put the
problem of evil and of redemption in terms of *decay* and *regeneration*. Instead of absorbing the universe in Christianity as the
Middle Ages did, it placed Christianity within universal life and
history, which it regarded as emanations of the divine Energy.

In that epoch German thought began to follow its natural
bent, and adopted an attitude that it was never after to abandon.
It enclosed Christianity, which was regarded as transcendental
and universal, in a sort of universal immanence which was
regarded as of German inspiration.

The century from 1650 to 1750 reaped the heritage of that
immense effort. In other words, the modernization of Christianity took place in Germany thanks to the action of rationalism
in the form of the philosophy of the Enlightenment (*Aufklärung*),
thanks to sentimental pietism, and thanks above all to the
synthesis effected by Leibnitz, at the end of the seventeenth

century and at the beginning of the eighteenth, between those two movements. The first wave of the *Aufklärung*, the first awakening of the pietism that culminated in the creation of the Moravian community, the great system of Leibnitz, the effects of which were to be felt when his *Nouveaux Essais sur l'Entendement humain* appeared posthumously in 1765—such were the three stages of that evolution.

Religious thought in Germany, of which we have just seen the first manifestations, thereafter underwent considerable development. It was still moving in the orbit of the instituional churches, but for all that the victory of naturalism was certain. That victory was achieved by the middle-class spirit. For the middle class was beginning to realize and to enter into possession of the inner wealth of human nature, wealth that had remained unexplored in the earlier Christendom. On the other hand, scientific discovery and invention brought to men new power over the forces of nature. There was a sudden abundance of inner wealth and of material wealth, so great as to burst the old limitations of thought and action.

Thus the antithesis between nature and civilization existed already in men's minds before it was formulated by Rousseau. Ancient thought and Christianity, the pillars of the old humanism, had closely associated nature and reason, physics and logic. In Greek wisdom and Christian morality they had created a sort of fixed model, a veritable *order of salvation*. Now, between the sixteenth and eighteenth centuries, this order began to crumble. Rationalism and pietism attacked it from within and without. Yet there was certainly no radical opposition in Germany between these two first manifestations of the modern spirit. They were connected by endless distinctions and transitions. But the antinomy was no less definite between the methods of rationalism, which engendered utilitarian individualism, the reign of the social conventions, and the taste for exact science and technology, on one hand, and on the other the passion for irrational and obscure realities, instinctive or mysterious feelings, and violent instincts and ambitions. Rationalism and pietism confined their attack, however, to Christianity.

Goethe has given a marvellous definition of the spontaneous and profound character of the rationalism of that epoch. Nature, he writes in his *Memoirs*, has endowed everyone, according to his needs, with a certain good sense and certain intellectual directives. It is possible, therefore, to emerge from the narrow

Christian tutelage, to gain knowledge of oneself and confidence in oneself, to grapple directly with reality and to think freely, working in a determined sphere. But the rupture with Christianity could not be as radical as this in Germany. The philosophy of the *Aufklärung* remained strongly tinged by the confessional spirit. It endeavoured either to retain those elements of Christianity which were in conformity with reason, or else to demonstrate that there was no absolute contradiction between Christian data and the demands of reason. It admitted only *a natural revelation* that implied the autonomy of thought. It sought the meaning of life *before death*, relating humanism to the idea of a purely terrestrial progress and perfection. Thus it made of Christ the divine model, one model among others. Such ideas spread through the patrician class and through the upper ranks of the middle class. This was the period of the foundation of a large number of learned societies, and of the fresh start given to university study by the teaching of Thomasius and of Wolff, insufficient though it was.

Pietism made its appearance at the same time as the *Aufklärung*, toward the end of the seventeenth century. It attained full development between 1700 and 1750. Like the *Aufklärung*, it did not break with official Lutheranism. Its aim was rather to effect a separation between ecclesiastical orthodoxy and the personal experience of life, between intellectual belief and religious feeling, in order to restore to fervent piety its normal rôle. Here we enter the individual, emotional, sentimental, and irrational domain. The metaphysical Christ of orthodoxy was to become a living reality close to us. He was to be the soul's betrothed, a principle that should fructify spiritual life and action.

In his *Collegia pietatis* Spener, the founder of pietism, insists on the necessity of the conventicles, of biblical exegesis, of the universal priesthood, of the cult of the family, of fervent preaching, and of acts of piety. Another founder of the movement, Francke, places the emphasis on radical, sudden conversion; but, whatever nuance is in question, the inner miracle, the new birth, the action exercised directly by Christ on the Christian soul, in brief, religious subjectivism, renewing the Lutheran idea of the communion of souls and the Invisible Church, represented the common, essential element. In his *Bekenntnisse einer schönen Seele* Goethe was the perfect analyst of this movement, which is of absolutely capital importance to the understanding of German classicism and romanticism. Pietism made its stand in relation to Church and State less in order to correct social and political abuses than precisely to resuscitate the Invisible Church within the official churches.

In 1722 Count Zinzendorf founded the first Moravian community, that of Herrnhut; in 1727 he drew up its constitution. Moravianism was the most precise and the most suggestive form that pietism took in Germany. The Moravian's soul lives in close communion with the Christ of the Passion, the suffering Christ. Christ is the supreme Friend of that soul, which is consumed with love for Him. This feeling, created by the most intimate experience, floods and illumines the believer. Such love is proclaimed to be superior to all science and to all knowledge, to preceptual morality and to official piety. For that reason Moravianism broke with the Church more radically than pietism in general. From the moment when each soul enjoys Christ in its manner and, by the celebration of communion, personally partakes of His flesh and His blood, that experience has its true value. Souls also communicate their experiences. From these spiritual exchanges there resulted a particular *Geselligkeit* (companionableness) which, once secularized, was to play an essential part in the classic and romantic periods.

Orthodoxy, rationalism, pietism were all tendencies or systems between which transitions were not lacking, but which remained irreconcilable with each other. It needed a genius to attempt to master them by a synthesis. That genius was Leibnitz.

Leibnitz died in 1716, but his true thought remained unknown until 1765, when the *Nouveaux Essais* appeared. Seen as a whole, his immense work is virtually an effort to reconcile the rationalism and the sentimentalism of the epoch. Thus it was a perfect expression of the progressive, dynamic humanism which European thought was elaborating at the same period.

Leibnitz's theory of knowledge is rich in meaning. Placing man between unconscious matter and Divinity with its perfect consciousness, it forms a hierarchy of the individual monads according as they possess more or less apperceptive virtue and clear consciousness. The first knowledge, called inferior or obscure, proceeds from the direct experience of the senses, from the products of our contact or our unconscious communion with the universe. Pure empiricism, but nourishing and fruitful. From this experience, both rich and sincere, the spirit rises, working through reason, to clear and eternal verities, to the

higher knowledge. For the intelligence exists for itself, and
its representations are subject to laws proper to it. It is because
of that that it acts on the first knowledge, purifying and clarifying
it. The uniting of experience and intelligence, of feeling and
reason, of fervour and technique, is the whole man. He who
is familiar with German thought is able to declare that the
nucleus of the whole of it is to be found in this theory of
knowledge.

The monads are perfect in proportion to their realization of
this union, participating by that fact in the divine power and
clarity. Among them there is a natural hierarchy based on a
more or less high degree of synthetic perfection. Salvation
lies in the permanent conquest of a perfection always growing
and never exhausted.

The *Théodicée* of Leibnitz, one of the works most widely read
in the Germany of the seventeenth century, drew from these
premises a new interpretation of the Christian dogmas of fall and
redemption: *man passes from one state to the other as from the least
to the highest perfection.* Christian dualism thus lost the elements
of the tragic and the inexorable that it possessed in Lutheranism.
An enthusiastic religiousness was born of this optimistic conception. Independent of the orthodoxy of the territorial
churches, it became the essential element of German culture.
What wonder that Leibnitz had dreamed of a religious organization of the world, and that the cosmopolitanism of a genius so
European knew no limits? It may be admitted, with Troeltsch,
that this was the German philosopher *par excellence.*

2. *From Dürer to J. S. Bach*

The religious and philosophical movement of this epoch led
to Leibnitz; the movement of letters and arts led to J. S. Bach.

Two currents may be distinguished in the German literature
of 1500 to 1750—one of strictly religious and particularly
Lutheran inspiration, the other of secular tendency, but with
main preoccupations that came very close to religion. This
was entirely natural in that period, when the religious life and
the profane world were inextricably intermingled in all culture
just as State and Church were intermingled in the territories.
The Christian religion was thenceforward to be in Germany on
one hand an object of lofty objective speculation and of personal
mysticism, and on the other a rigorously disciplinary system

imposed on populations by the ruling power (*Obrigkeit*), effecting the close subordination of every individual to a collectivity in which the civil and ecclesiastical authorities reigned in concert.

Religious literature, properly so called, begins with Luther, with his translation of the Bible, his treatises, his sermons, his hymns. That very fact brought it close to music. It announced the complete triumph of music in the seventeenth and eighteenth centuries.

Considered as a literary phenomenon, the Reformation was equivalent to a rupture with Rome and Italy, with the Mediterranean tradition. In this it was in opposition to the Renaissance. Beautiful as was the language of Luther in itself, it ran the risk of falling back after him into barbarism. The Reformation thus considerably retarded the coming of classicism in Germany. But it bore fruit. Indeed, it never ceased, as a manifestation of positive religion, to enrich by its many developments the whole of German literature, and particularly classicism and romanticism.

If the Word of the Bible was the foundation of the Invisible Community, if it had to be received by all as divinely inspired, if the sacred Book was superior to the letter as faith was to the works it engendered, then the relation between *spiritual fervour* and *the language that incarnates it*, the source of poetry in general, became the principle of modern German poetry. Even when, in 1541, Luther published the complete translation of the Old and New Testaments, he proceeded from the sacred Book to the living language of the people, to a sort of vigorous, positive, limited vocabulary that re-created the national idiom by a literary miracle of the first rank. It might be said that the German language became conscious of its original value and its intrinsic power through its encounter with the most universal of all books. The Lutheran Bible became a national book, authorized for church services, the basis of education, and the foundation of practical morality. It was imposed even on German Catholics, who were compelled to make acquaintance with it in order to refute the Protestants. This translation was, moreover, the culmination of an immense effort in biblical translation that may be traced in Germany from the middle of the fourteenth century. Finally, by imposing High German on Low Germany, the Reformation attenuated the opposition between the Protestant Germany of the North and the Catholic Germany of the South.

Luther's sermons and treatises, though widely read in the sixteenth century, have not the same national significance. The sermons taught the Word, and were thus no more than a direct commentary on the translated Bible. Here again there was a balance between inner fervour and practical intelligence. The treatises, for their part, were an anticipation of modern subjectivism. They were the work of an agitator who had written them as propaganda. He addressed himself to thousands of people at once, varying his tone according to the public he was addressing, and attacking rather than discussing. In this he was a worthy successor of the pre-Reformation popular preachers, of Frater Berthold or Geiler von Kaysersberg. The vigorous language, lively and forceful, imaginative or sententious, often led into excess by wrath or contempt, the art of dramatizing situations, the employment of abuse, of dialogue, of violence, passion, daring—all these aspects of Luther's literary genius reveal his personality, even better than the translation of the Bible or the sermons; they reveal it by relating him to the enormous pamphleteering literature of the epoch.

Luther's work was continued alike by his partisans and by his adversaries. Whether it proceeded from Anabaptists or Catholics, this controversial literature was inspired by the great problems of the day, dealt with them in the German language, and addressed itself to the mass of the people. Thus it propagated not only the dogma itself but the language into which the religious truths had been translated. The case of Thomas Murner is typical. Murner had been Luther's chief enemy. He is never lacking in vigour. He proceeds by fiery poetic improvisations that make easy play with the difficulties of versification. He continues the tradition of the fourteenth and fifteenth centuries, presenting the whole social picture of the epoch. He attacks the vices of the times—the avarice, pride, ambition, and luxury of the middle class. When he criticizes the Church he provides fuel for the partisans of Luther. When he turns against them he reinforces the Catholic polemic. Combative by nature and conviction, he ends by turning upon both the opposing camps at once.

Luther had broken with the tolerant internationalist humanism of Erasmus; he did not disown the German humanism of such men as Ulrich von Hutten and Pirckheimer. In 1514, before the Reformation, Hutten had collaborated in drawing up the famous *Epistolæ obscurorum virorum*, attacking the Inquisitor Hoogstraten, and showing violent hostility to Rome. What Hutten wanted was to return to the German past, to the old neglected customs, to a purer *and therefore more Germanic* Christianity.   He attacked Roman law and scholasticism, the jurists and the theologians.   When the Reformation came, he ranged himself at once on Luther's side.   This time he wrote no longer in Latin, but in German, handling the pen as he had handled the sword.   Programmes, discourses, invective, indictment— any form served him for this vehement protest against the Papacy, the clergy, the courts, and the various social classes. He reproached all of them with betraying their German country, the Fatherland whose first hero was Arminius.

Hutten died in 1523.   Pirckheimer at once took up the glove. He became the great adversary of Eck, the Catholic theologian who was attacking Luther.   As for Hans Sachs, he, too, took Luther's part, but, in his four Dialogues of 1524,[1] advised conciliation.   How many forgotten names we might quote, how many works, what a wealth of curious correspondence would have to be resuscitated to show the spirit of that time, the dimensions the anti-Rome polemic then attained in Germany —Eberlin of Günzburg, Nikolaus Manuel, with his prose dialogue *Krankheit und Testament der Messe* (1528), and so many others!   These were the beginnings of a true journalism.   We may add to them the employment of the *Meistergesang* and of the *Reimpaare*, biblical translations in verse.   Extraordinary was that efflorescence of prose religious literature in those thirty opening years of the sixteenth century!

Lutheranism also drew near to the people in its religious verse, its hymns.   Luther revived that tradition, which had been formed in the fifteenth century.   He borrowed largely from the Psalms, but did not neglect the wonderful canticles of the mediæval Church or the old German *Lieder*.   His best productions saw the light in 1523 and 1524.   The qualities that assured them a place of their own in German poetry, their virile tone and their power of expression, show well that there was nothing subjective about this versification.   What Luther set out to render was the state of the believer's soul.   And it was this same state of soul, but in more complex forms, that the music of J. S. Bach affirmed in its wealth, by new means.   Luther was not alone in the writing of hymns.   He encouraged his friends to follow his example.   The Hymnbook of 1528 included forty already.   From 1528 to 1550 there was an unprecedented outpouring of hymns.   Not that they were all original by any

[1] Notably *Disputation zwischen einem Chorherrn und einem Schuhmacher.*

means. But they always drew strength from their great themes. What they rendered was the ideas and feelings common to the members of the Invisible Church. Religious singing was one of the great things of the Reformation. It represented the contribution each one could bring to the general edification. It served also as a bond between the territorial churches in process of formation. Its unifying action extended to private life, to family devotions and domestic piety. For it was the poetic form of the collective prayer. For that reason every pastor and every teacher felt it to be his duty to compose hymns for his parish.

This religious literature fell into decay in the second half of the sixteenth century. Polemicism grew as Lutheranism gained safe positions. Little by little it changed into political conflict. It may be said also of the hymn that it had already exhausted its material, running through every shade of religious feeling; as it followed the evolution of Protestant theology it fell into pedantry or mystical primness. Its thought weakened and its form lost simplicity. The diminutive suffix *lein* and the adjective *süss* (sweet) constantly made their appearance in this over-sentimental poetry. It was improved on from 1560 onward by the reformed Psalms of Marot and Bèze, set to music by Goudimel.

But the tradition of the Lutheran hymn did not die out either during or after the Thirty Years War. The day came when pietism was to renew it. Paul Gerhardt composed hymns as late as 1676, almost reaching the time of Bach. It was necessary, indeed, for the Lutheran hymn, preserved by orthodoxy and rejuvenated by pietism, to be still living at the end of the seventeenth century and the beginning of the eighteenth, in order that Bach should draw from it every shade of its meaning with such delicacy and power and richness.

The profane literature of that great epoch remained second-rate. The scientific movement contemporary with the Reformation no doubt exercised considerable influence over German prose. But there is little to be said about the fable and the short story, still less the novel, which scarcely existed at that time except in the form of translations from French or of the Faustian legend. The drama was more successful. The Reformation favoured didactic drama. It made use of religious drama for the propagation of the new truths. At Nuremberg, especially, with the dramas of Hans Sachs, which appeared from 1513 onward, the dramatic vein seems to have had more persistence. But the work of Hans Sachs, whose immense production covers almost the whole of the sixteenth century, was still entirely consecrated to the problems of the time, and developed in the shadow of the Reformation. We find in it also the echo either of pandynamist pantheism or of the conciliatory tendencies that showed themselves at that time.

It may thus be said that German literature was of religious inspiration throughout the sixteenth century. The Lutheran Reformation took up the Catholic tradition of passion plays. No doubt three novelties were seen at the time—the Carnival festivities, the learned dramas imitated from antiquity, and the companies of English comedians who played Shakespeare and Marlowe. But Fischart himself, one of the most spontaneous geniuses of the sixteenth century, moved in the atmosphere of the Reformation. He attacked the preaching Orders, the Roman hierarchy, monasticism, the whole of the scholastic teaching, and the retrograde bourgeoisie. He was, perhaps, after Luther, the most ardent of the partisans of the Reformation. It is difficult, indeed, to distinguish the profane from the religious in the literature of the sixteenth century. The independence of culture did not yet exist. It was entirely subordinated to the doctrinal quarrels of the epoch.

The arrival of a secular literature virtually dates only from the beginning of the seventeenth century. On the very eve of the great war there came a revival that showed what a development might have been taken by German culture if that long struggle had not devastated and exhausted the country. Works of considerable importance appeared between 1600 and 1618. Learned or literary societies were started everywhere. When the war broke out, this movement came to a sudden end. But the germs it contained developed later when the war was over.

Toward 1650 the direction of the literary movement passed to the classes that had suffered least from the war, the aristocracy of the courts and the patriciate of the towns. Literature also developed on the periphery of Germany, which had suffered less than the centre of the country. This explains the learned and artificial character it assumed, in contrast with that of the Reformation. Opitz, in his *Deutsche Poeterey*, defined it in 1624: the essential thing was to have a thorough knowledge of the models and the rules of the art. Eyes were turned to the ancients or to Italian Marinism, and later to Boileau and the

French theoreticians. At the end of this period, between 1730 and 1750, the struggle between Gottsched and the Swiss came to assure the triumph in Germany of a more fruitful æsthetic. It must in any case be recognized that such men as Opitz and Gottsched, by purifying the taste of their contemporaries, prepared, in their way, the great literary epoch that lasted from 1750 to 1815.

The evolution of poetry was exactly parallel to the preceding movement. It was still penetrated by religious and popular elements until about the middle of the seventeenth century, but later became more and more erudite and conventional. Hofmannswaldau and von Lohenstein tended to Italianism. The work of Christian Weise had more sincerity and vigour. On the other hand, French influence, which overcame Italian influence, purified taste, while the art was enriched by the contributions brought to it by the new culture. This explains the efflorescence of poetry between 1700 and 1750. Its importance has been too long overlooked. The scholarly verse of Brockes, Hagedorn, Zachariä, Gleim, Uz, and Goetz, expressed profounder ideas and feelings than is generally supposed, whether in connexion with the optimist and sentimental religious feeling of the period, or patriotism, or love. Above all, after this too patrician and still stilted art, there came a generation that bore already the marks of the spontaneity of genius, that of Christian Günther in Silesia, the true forerunner of the *Sturm und Drang* movement, and of Ewald von Kleist in Prussia, of Ramler, of von Haller, and of Klopstock at the very outset of that movement.

Drama remained visibly behind lyric poetry. Gryphius, in the seventeenth century, certainly had the sense of the tragic and already represented in Germany the Shakespearean vein which the Thirty Years War was to help to develop. From 1700 to 1750 Gottsched preached the imitation of the French and helped to spread the taste for composition and for form. Other more vigorous and original temperaments announced the revival, in particular J. Elias Schlegel, who was inspired by the ancients or by Shakespeare, and Felix Weisse, who in his dramatic works combined the French art of construction, the themes and the lyric effects of Shakespeare, and finally a certain German realism.

In Moscherosch and Grimmelshausen the novel of the seventeenth century drew upon the Thirty Years War. This time it was with the middle class that it was occupied, because that class, with the peasantry, had suffered most from the great disaster. It is no exaggeration to say that *Simplicissimus* was a remote anticipation of Rousseau and Herder. But the first half of the eighteenth century produced but poor fruits in this field. The new individual and social psychology had not yet come. At most we may point here to Wieland's initiative.

Consider German literature as a whole from 1500 to 1750, and you will say that, while it was above all religious in the sixteenth century and until the middle of the seventeenth, it then tended to free itself from ecclesiastical influence and to come under that of the neighbouring cultures. It announced, with growing precision and amplitude, the civilization that was to spread after 1750. But at this period it played but a secondary part when it was not moving in the atmosphere of the Reformation and of doctrinal polemic.

More important was the growth of art. After the wonderful rise of the plastic arts in the first half of the sixteenth century came the no less admirable rise of music, with Schütz, Handel, and Bach.

The rise of painting began in Germany in the fifteenth century. From 1520 onward, like literature, it entered the orbit of the Reformation. It turned away, accordingly, from the too ascetic religion of the Middle Ages and the fifteenth century, as well as from the too external or subtle religion of Rome. It gave expression to the great problems of the hour, the distress of the plain man in time of revolution, the depth and strength of popular feelings. It was a powerful art of revolt, despair, and anguish. It was by no mere chance that, toward the end of the fifteenth century, Dürer engraved his scenes of the Apocalypse, a true Bible for the poor, and a warning to all classes of society. A youthful and ardent art, with plain Teutonic clumsiness, greater in philosophic and religious intention than in formal perfection. Death, the plague, falling stars, the struggle of all against all, the unloosing of evil forces—such were the scenes depicted by the artist. It was indeed the expression of systems swallowed whole and of dogmas accepted in advance! It was pure desperation that had to be rendered, the sense of general insecurity and of permanent danger that was one of the essential elements of Lutheranism at its outset. The fight between angel and demon, the struggle of light against darkness. It ended in a nature and society at peace, but the peace had been won at the cost of hard struggle.

Four times Dürer represented Christ's Passion. Again for the people. His Christ at Gethsemane is the Man of the supreme decision, of the acceptance of the most terrible suffering, and of the acceptance of this world such as it is. A true peasant is his kneeling Christ. At first he appeals against the destiny reserved for him; then he resigns himself to it. All that had most profoundly affected that epoch is in these pages, as in the language of Luther. There was man's solitude in face of destiny, that of the resolute knight, that of Jesus consenting to drink of the cup, that of Saint Jerome in his hermit's dwelling, happy to have the opportunity for the concentration which alone gives strength to the thinker, the solitude of the Melancholy that cares nothing for astronomy and all its instruments, knowing that they will not enable it to probe nature and life to their depths, and finally the solitude of the Madonna and her Child, the most moving of all those solitudes because the most fruitful. Such was the truly new experience of Luther and of the Reformation— to be alone in the face of destiny, of suffering and death.

Grünewald, too, turned to the crowd. He installed his Madonna and Child in the intimacy of their natural environment, with the cradle, the manger, and the stall. Over this scene of maternity the heavens spread an entirely natural light, for truth is in nature and not in the sumptuosities of the Church, which the painter represents close by. The same vision of simple humanity appears in the Passion. Fearful is the face of that plebeian Christ, livid, close already to decomposition. A tragic representation of the fate in store for men. The *Memento mori* takes the place of the Last Judgment. All hope of the life beyond must be abandoned. The macabre dances of the period show that death had as much reality as life. Life, then, must be lived to the full, while recognizing in the midst of all that lives the infinite value of the human soul. That is why Holbein installed Death in a smiling, sunlit landscape. Death was a terror only for those who transgressed the laws of life. Before it we were all equal, the lovely young girl of Baldung and the great ones of this world painted by Holbein.

Whether in the colourists like Grünewald, Cranach, and Baldung, who softened the rigour of contour and line, or in idealist art such as that of Holbein and Dürer, all this painting gravitated round the central theme of the Reformation, as finally expressed in the Apostles of Dürer.

Do we find other accents in the admirable sculpture of the

same period, when it spread in the South with Veit Stoss, Adam Krafft, Riemenschneider, Peter Vischer, and Flötner? Less expressive, certainly, is the architecture, which was passing from a flamboyant Gothic, a truly baroque Gothic, to the baroque of the Italian Renaissance. In its chaotic confusion it was beginning, at all events, to free itself from ecclesiastical tutelage. But it tended to reflect the sumptuous life of the castles, of the great towns, or of the mansions of wealthy burghers.

From 1650 onward, painting and sculpture fell into decay like literature. The progress of territorialism substituted for the strongly personal and popular art of the Reformation a courtly and aristocratic art aloof from the people and responding only to the aspirations of the higher classes. These courts, especially in the South, were open only to Italian influences, and on the eve of the Thirty Years War Germany no longer had a national art. This time it was architecture that profited from the rise of the territories. Great buildings were erected by the wealthy burghers in the South at Augsburg, Nuremberg, Rothenburg, Munich, Stuttgart, Heidelberg, and Aschaffenburg, and in the North at Brunswick, Danzig, and Posen.

After the Thirty Years War the baroque style conquered the South and even the North with lightning rapidity, insisting even more than in Italy on the *decorative* element and on the *picturesque* effects that were obtained by the abandonment of the straight line and the abuse of rounded forms. But Italian influence was succeeded by imitation of the French. The art of Versailles and the rococo style became German styles between 1650 and 1750.

From all this literary and artistic evolution the conclusion is to be drawn that German art was of real significance only in the epoch of the Reformation. The Thirty Years War was to let loose a sort of fury of Italian and French imitation, for the religious struggles resulting from the Reformation had produced a sort of vacuum in men's minds, which for the time could only be filled by foreign influence. It was not in this domain that Germany was great between 1650 and 1750; it was in music that her true genius reawakened, rising, with Bach, to the height of the European dream of Leibnitz.

Like literature and the arts, German music in the first half of the sixteenth century had been almost exclusively religious. The Middle Ages had passed from the simple plainsong of the Church to counterpoint, thus constructing a vast architectural tone-system, completed about 1300, which subsequently grew until it attained the extraordinary virtuosity that characterizes the music of the sixteenth and seventeenth centuries. With the Reformation, while in Italy profane music was already flourishing in the form of the madrigal, the Lutheran chorale made its appearance in Germany. It became for some time the essential form of the national music. The chorale, far from breaking with counterpoint, utilized it for vocal harmonization. The novelty lay in its building up of this harmonization with given melodies, which as a rule were popular melodies. The four-part hymn was thus one of the most authentic fruits of the Reformation. On the other hand, the instruments began to be perfected and diversified. The organ, the harpsichord, the violin and other instruments acquired thus a sort of new in-dividuality. Finally, and above all in Italy, the human voice revealed and developed all its wealth of expressiveness. Thenceforward the forms of collective and personal music were continually developed.

In the second half of the sixteenth century the Lutheran chorale made further progress, adopting the form of the motet; on the instrumental side the organ achieved excessive predominance, with the result of a certain orchestral backwardness in Germany. But after 1650, a little before Handel and Bach, the Italian *dramma per musica* renewed the musical possibilities of the time. Dramatic action with musical interludes—this form, well suited to a music both collective and individual, made its appearance in Germany at the opening of the seventeenth century. The first Italian opera, translated by Opitz and reshaped by Schütz, was played in Germany in 1627. The German courts seized upon this foreign innovation. German opera itself developed almost solely at Hamburg, between 1680 and 1750. But that was no more than an aristocratic episode. The important development was that of the music of the Protestant churches, under the influence of Italian opera. Heinrich Schütz, a century before Bach, threw open fresh perspectives for this music in the seventeenth century, in the drama of the Passion, with the Italian forms of chorus, recitative, and arioso. These were fruitful borrowings, but they did not prevent organ music from attaining at that time, with Buxtehude in the north and Pachelbel in the south, a magnificent expansion. Toward the end of the century, in the year 1685, that saw the birth of Handel and Bach and the appearance of the *Pia Desideria* of Spener, the founder of pietism, the progress made by vocal and instrumental music was to bear its finest fruit.

Handel began to conduct Italian opera in London in 1720. He created the grand oratorio, a first compromise between the profane art of Italy and the religious art of Germany. With a broad, sovereign objectivity, his music rendered magnificently the great episodes of Hebrew history. From 1720 to 1741 there came his incomparable series—*Esther, Samson, Israel in Egypt, Belshazzar, Judas Maccabæus,* and then the *Messiah,* a glorious hymn celebrating the incarnation of the divine in the person of Christ. In the classic but sublime solemnity of these master-pieces expression is given to an essential aspect of the German genius. And is it not Germany herself that is seen again in the destiny and the messianic hope of the Hebrew people?

Bach rendered yet more adequately, like Leibnitz, the spirit of that great epoch, with its concern for European synthesis. His comprehensive religious outlook, orthodox, rational, and pietist at once, close to primitive Lutheranism, is explained by a musical sense in which are admirably wedded the German genius and the Latin genius. He certainly wrote his best works at Leipzig, at a time when the secular culture or the scholarly art of the courts and the patriciates had begun to carry the day in Germany. But, none the less, Bach remained until his death in 1750 the most representative artist of the time. Dürer rendered in line and colour the revolutionary drama that was to lead Germany into the Thirty Years War; Bach symbolized the era of systematic innovation that came between the last period of the Middle Ages and modern times.

His was an art both collective and individual, rational and senti-mental—profane and religious at one and the same time! A music that set its sovereign seal upon the passage from the old mediæval and Lutheran music to the new music that Mozart and Beethoven were soon to create. It was the epoch in which bourgeois individualism declared its first offensive, still timidly, against the absolutism of the territorial States. Men's souls sought emancipation from traditions too burdensome for them. They were in love with liberty. A balance was established between an extremely rigorous social order and these individual aspirations, which found their natural outlet in philosophy and music. The masterpieces of Bach convey the incomparable impression of massive solidity, ardent fervour, or deep and quasi-cosmic emotion, that corresponds so well to the spirit of that civilization. The rigorous architecture of their construction is very happily united with the emotional power of their conception.

Johann Sebastian Bach, descendant of an extraordinary line of excellent musicians, continuing from 1550 without break, had great difficulties in the towns in which he lived, and especially at Arnstadt, Weimar, and Leipzig, with the civil and ecclesiastical, communal and princely authorities. He did not always submit to their masterfulness or their pedantry. He boldly freed himself from them each time the circumstances enabled him to do so. His portraits reveal the vigorous temperament, the energetic character, the frankness and firmness, the robustness of genius and the perfect integrity that made it possible for him to serve his art in his profession and yet to resist the powers that menaced the free growth of his genius. Bach had the forcefulness of the great natures, sovereign in their art, that refuse to bend the knee to those who are sovereign in the political and social order. His destiny was the most symbolic of all. It marks the passage from the age of strict subservience to the era of individual liberties.

Considered as a whole, Bach's production may be divided into two distinct groups. His music celebrated Christian mysteries and dealt also with secular subjects. These two aspects are united by clear relationships that correspond exactly to the bonds which at that time united the religious and the profane, State and Church, in the territories.

Bach's religious music took advantage of every possible form of his day—the chorale harmonized for choir, the organ chorale, the motet or small cantata, the cantata proper, which Bach modernized by introducing homophonic elements; the oratorio, a veritable cycle of cantatas; the *Passion*, a vast cantata-oratorio consecrated to the death of Christ; and finally the *Mass*, conforming to the plan of the Latin Mass and enabling him to present the universal Christian truths. Nothing could be richer or more complex than the processes of musical rendering to which Bach had recourse. His religious subjects turn upon three great themes—the life and death of Christ on earth; the piety of the believer, based on the Lutheran faith; and objective dogma. In them orthodox belief is intimately allied with the most spontaneous manifestations of individual religious feeling.

Alongside the religious life was the secular existence, the political and social life in the territorial States, and the family life with its domestic activities. Bach's secular cantatas treat of certain events in the humble career of the musician, municipal festivities or princely ceremonies and anniversaries. There were frequent exchanges between religious and profane cantatas. Bach made use, for instance, of the same means for expressing the majesty of God and the glory of the prince. His instrumental work set an analogous problem. Its themes are often of religious origin. They deal always with fundamental human attitudes or emotions in which the traditional religion was closely intermingled with the new psychology. Works for organ, music for harpsichord, pieces for violin, violoncello, or other instruments are not mere exercises in virtuosity but the deeply emotional expression of eternal sentiments.

Thus the whole of that epoch is condensed in the music of Bach. Drawing from the actual sources of the Reformation and of primitive Lutheranism, utilizing all their later developments, and resorting to fruitful imitation of Italians and French without the least loss of its own individuality, this music occupies a central place in the history of German culture.

3. The Länder and the rise of Prussia

Considered in themselves, the thought and the art of this epoch attained their full scope, at the end of the seventeenth and the beginning of the eighteenth century, in the philosophy of Leibnitz and the music of Bach. Of unequalled breadth, reconciling differences both within the nation and on the European plane, these two manifestations of the German genius dominated at that time the whole intellectual life of Europe.

But on what social and political foundation did this culture rest?

Scarcely had the religious schism become inevitable when Luther turned to Frederick the Wise in order to organize the new Church with him. What did this prince, this German "Landesherr," do? *He enlisted in the support of his still precarious sovereignty the fresh and abundant energy that the Reformation brought to him.* He applied these energies to an ecclesiastical reorganization on a grand scale which should serve as a model for the Protestant princes. He demonstrated to the Pope and the Emperor that religious and moral discipline and order and solid political institutions would thenceforth be found not in the Roman Church or the decadent Empire, but *in the territory*, the "Land."

We have just been considering a great fact of the *spiritual* order—the birth and growth of the Lutheran Reformation and the new science, foundations of the Invisible Community which was thenceforward to unite Germans; they were destined, moreover, to expand, in the course of two and a half centuries and after the worst of sufferings, into a great philosophy and a great music. Now we are faced with the *temporal* fact of a new civil power, whose absolutism drew strength from the very multiplicity of the territories in which its methods of government were to be applied. *At the very moment when they were beginning to be united spiritually by a common language, thought, and art, the Germans were split up on the practical plane by the consecration of the territorial order.* The republic of the princes, in which freedom reigned solely between sovereigns and could not reach their subjects, who were at the mercy of the many authorities (*Obrigkeiten*) of the epoch—such was the other face of the German Revolution of the sixteenth century.

Does this mean that, since the territories occupied the forefront of the social and political scene, the idea of the Reich had passed out of men's minds? Far from it. The humanists remained nationalist, that is to say, faithful to the Empire. They retained the enthusiasm that was to be noted already in Luther, and especially in the pandynamist philosophy of the time. Among them the nobles had the independence of position and the aristocratic confidence that permitted them to give characteristic expression to the essentials of the national ideas of the time. Ulrich von Hutten dreamed of the Reich of the morrow, its future extent and glory. He resented the opposition of the Venetians to German penetration in Italy. He adjured the Empire to defend itself against the Turkish peril. He thought of a new Europe in which a regenerated nobility would play a leading part. It was on his advice that von Sickingen tried, though in vain, to move the German nobles. Von Hutten declared himself in favour of the full independence of the Germans. Among the bourgeois humanists, savants such as Wimpheling, Beatus Rhenanus, and others sought to restore its true meaning to the national history and to the struggle against Romanism. The Erfurt group of humanists whom Luther often visited, and who later gave him their support, knew, with Luther himself, that the Reformation must mean above all the progress, consolidation, and broadening of the national consciousness.

Was not Luther the disciple of German mysticism and of the *Theologia deutsch*, the disciple of the Gabriel Biel who subordinated universal reason to the will to power? Luther addressed his great appeal to "the German nation." He was in revolt against the particularism of the princes, the pretensions of the nobility, the egoism of townsmen and peasants; he assimilated the honouring of the Gospel to that of Germania. It was "his dear Germany" that he was determined to obey. In his thinking he visualized the spiritual and moral unity of the Germans. He went so far as to reconstitute the image of their Race: "*We Germans are Germans and wish to remain Germans.*" And the Reformer traced the idealized portrait of the German, less gracious than the Italian, less eloquent than the Frenchman, but more straightforward, more loyal, more attached to his traditions, more faithful in marriage, more laborious and disinterested, more frugal—in brief, "purer" and "simpler" than the people of the West. Germany was for him "the best of all countries and the finest of all nations." Luther wanted Germany to be *foremost in the spirit.* Certainly he was not thinking of anything but spiritual primacy when he dreamed of a vast educational reform and of a school that should be both Christian and national and thus capable of endowing Germany with men and women worthy of her.

At the very base of Lutheran thought was the irreconcilable opposition between the Germanic genius and the intellectualist legalism of Rome and the West. This opposition, latent in the fourteenth and fifteenth centuries, *broke out* with the Reformation. The German laid down that, for him, religion lay in the inner feeling, in the full spontaneity of nature, while the Latin preferred to place it in rational faith, in a system of constraint that bound individuals in the name of the Law. The Germanic nation, said the Germans, must not be a "slave" to that civilization, juridical in its essence. Accordingly the German Emperor, the princes, the clergy, the townsmen, and the peasants were grouped together against Rome. The *Gravamina* of 1518 showed already that, in spite of the existence of the territories, Luther had at his back a whole people, with all its constituent elements.

The famous "Address to the German Nobility" (*An den christlichen Adel deutscher Nation*) is nothing but a complete programme of religious and political nationalism. Germany is to be *liberated* from the fiscal administration of the Curia and from the spiritual tutelage of the priesthood. Let her thereafter be united *directly with God,* by the means of a *common consciousness,* founded in theory on the pure Gospel, in practice on Church and School. Luther did not repudiate Christian œcumenicalism or transcendentalism. He invited the princes to convoke the Council and to reform the Universal Church. It was only the resistance of Rome that threw him back more and more on a *German* Reformation. "It is for you Germans," he wrote in 1531, "that I seek salvation and sanctity." He wanted to nationalize the liturgy. Words and music, the outward and visible material of the new faith, must be German.

Luther thus entertained a dream of religious supremacy. He seems to be transferring to the Protestant faith and to the politico-social order it implies the ambitions once cherished by Otto I and Barbarossa. God is addressing himself to Germany through his Word translated into German, *and therefore through Germany to all men. Universalism comes after the nation.* "The Word descended upon the Jews. Saint Paul carried it to Greece. Rome and the Latin countries received it in their turn. *But Germany has been visited, illumined by its grace with an incomparable richness, superior to that of all nations.*" Had Germania already, in Luther's thought, a providential mission; was she to build the Kingdom of God on earth?

Luther substituted the theology of intuition for that of dialectic. But intuition may at any time be confused either with individual sentiment or with national consciousness. If intellectualism is considered the seat of error, internationalism may then find itself menaced in its surest and oldest positions. If reason signifies sin, if the criterion of truth is now only in inner experience, where will be the bond between nations? A universal faith is not to be founded on feeling. Only the intelligence engenders the universal. Lutheran religious feeling plainly determined the anti-intellectualist attitude which German thought was thereafter to assume, even when it was visited by the philosophy of the Enlightenment.

It was clearly seen in morality when the religion supposed to be of "love" was opposed to the morality alleged to be "of precepts and of constraint." Then, in the name actually of religion and of nature, the Germans destroyed all the disciplines established by others than themselves. They conceived freedom only as absolute release from legality. *The only thing that was truly free was the sovereign will, the will to pure power, acting without any sort of limitation, without concern for any distinction between good and evil, without concern for any law.* Such was the sense of the *De Servo arbitrio,* published by Luther against Erasmus. Threatened by an excessive rationalism and a pedantic morality, the German took refuge in intuition and feeling, accusing other peoples of trying to impose on him an insupportable rule which, in point of fact, he himself invented.

This new national consciousness, which seems to have fluctuated between the idea of the Reich and that of the national State, could not agree in principle with pure territorialism. It may even be that it was in relation to the narrow territorial disciplines that a national consciousness with conceptions so vast and so ambitious was formed. It is here that the opposition appears between the *spiritual* and the *concrete* plane. The lofty culture that culminated in Leibnitz and Bach was soon to lead Germany to Goethe, to classicism and romanticism. On the other hand, while German thought developed with a rapidity accounted for by the freedom it enjoyed relatively to the social and political institutions, these had scarcely changed. For centuries, while the Western nations were being modernized and transformed into true *national States,* Germany remained divided between aristocrats, peasants, and the poorer townspeople, and riveted to agrarianism and to a complicated economic system that was broken into fragments by a thousand barriers. *Instead of being a national State, she was a great collection of tiny territories that dreamed of being an Empire vested with hegemony.* That is the supreme German paradox.

The politico-social conceptions of the Reformation, and in particular Luther's ideas concerning the relations between Church and State, are convincing evidence of it. Luther's doctrine led him to absorb the Church in the State. He opposed his invisible and purely spiritual Church to those "purely human" institutions the Papacy, the Councils, the episcopate, and the whole system of canon law. The Church must not be essentially a juridical organization. The evangelical message was in radical conflict with laws and constitutions. The Church was a community made up of pure "inwardness." It was formed in and by suffering. It was hidden in the mass of the "wicked," a mass proceeding from original sin and unceasingly oppressing it in principle and in practice.

But the State was the form in which, under God's will, this evil world lived. It was thus a system of necessary constraints. The Kingdom of Souls was a totally different thing from the political world, which, with its schemes and intrigues, was simply a consequence of sin. Separated from politics in its capacity of Invisible Church, the visible Church, considered as a "human organization," had all the more need of the State since its destiny was precarious. If it remained alive, so much the better. If it grew spiritually impoverished, it would then be nothing more than the State's affair. In relation to the Church, which is the machinery of salvation, the State was a material society that embraced both Christians and the wicked. It had power only over persons, things, and property. It was based solely on law and the sword. All in all, it was simply *an organization against evil*, an organization that represented order, that did justice and injustice, and disposed of full sovereignty in order to cope with so many associated egoisms. Its sword was in the hands of God. Those whom it ruled had no recourse against its power. This authoritarianism was based primarily on the existence of original sin. Later it was transformed into enlightened despotism, the prince being the first servant and therefore the first legislator of the State.

Thus the equilibrium between Church and State was broken to the detriment of the Church. Luther had conceived his State Church from the outset. He lost no time in inquiring into the positive forces that should serve as the armour of the new religion. He grasped the significance of the territory, and at once availed himself of it. If the ecclesiastical institutions were but the work of man, then the State had the right to make them its own. No doubt Luther only asked for the help of his prince against Catholicism, the Papacy, and external legal claims. But in the end he left to the prince authority over persons, consistories, parishes, and pastors, over the form of the religious service, over dogma, and over ecclesiastical properties. It was the princes and their magistrates who decided such issues as the Confession of Augsburg or the Articles of Smalkald. Soon the prince was the *summus episcopus* of the territorial Church. That was the reason for the transition, between 1520 and 1555, from the Invisible Church to politico-ecclesiastical territorialism. Luther, certainly, remained faithful to his true and great thought. For him, the Invisible Church and the temporal State had to be guided in concert by the Divine will. But when the Church had become merely visible she tended to be immersed in the State, in the superior authority (*Obrigkeit*) that took the place of all the powers of the old hierarchy.

This first outline of the German nation was (1) a Republic of monarchies of greater or lesser extent, in which the zone of liberty existed only on the monarchical plane, between the decaying Empire and the populations; (2) a collection of territorial units in which the civil and the religious power were amalgamated, the *Landesherr* or territorial prince incarnating their union in his episcopal function; (3) the sum of the *Obrigkeiten*, comprising jurists, officials and officers, theologians and pastors, and finally the savants of the universities. Legislation, administration, the army, the clergy, and science imposed the political, social, and religious direction of these *Obrigkeiten* on the subjects (*Untertanen*). A horizontal mosaic had succeeded the former vertical hierarchy. Germany had become simply a juxtaposition of police States (*Polizeistaaten*).

Such was the framework sanctioned in 1530 by the Confession of Augsburg. In it the individual was free only in the measure in which he was part of the Invisible Church. In relation to the State and to the visible Church he had only to obey, since obedience was equivalent to conformity with the *divinely appointed* authority. Alongside the superior minds that thought for the Reich or for mankind, we had this good average type, the Germans whom Charles Andler describes as "enemies of dreams, with small horizons, each specializing in his trade," and in no way concerned to direct the destinies of the Fatherland.

In the territory (*Land*) thus conceived, the *function* (*Amt*) played the essential part. The prince appealed to the jurists of the universities to propose laws in accordance with the "Christian" spirit, to the theologians of the same universities to interpret the biblical Word, to the officials to apply the laws, and to the pastors to teach religion, and finally to the officers and the army to defend the territory. A strange nation indeed! In its state of fragmentation it left its thinkers and its devout souls absolute freedom—freedom to throw themselves open to influences from without. But, by the very play of its original institutions, it shut itself in and imposed upon itself an austere and dreary discipline.

In this way, since 1520, the religious Revolution and the territorial Revolution had interpenetrated each other. After it had won the towns, the Reformation rapidly conquered a series of territories. The princes easily gained the upper hand, having to deal only with an absent Emperor, living in Spain, with nobles whom the Sickingen enterprise had left in impotence, with a town bourgeoisie that was growing weaker, and with rebellious but resourceless peasants. Lutheranism, popular and democratic in its origin, had allied itself with the monarchical powers. In 1555 the Peace of Augsburg marked the imperial defeat and the decline of the towns, while consecrating the coexistence of Catholic and Protestant *Länder*. Germany had finally lost her territorial, political, and religious unity, as well as the political-mindedness and the political education of her townspeople.

This victory of the territories was confirmed between 1555 and 1618. The princes consolidated their positions and perfected their administration. From the bourgeoisie they demanded service alongside the nobility, thus imitating Burgundy and France. They developed religious and secular culture. Protestants and Catholics kept watch on each other. The Protestants, at first in an excellent situation, grew weaker through their internal divisions and through the conflict that began between East and West. The old imperial Constitution remained in existence. Tridentine Catholicism took up its position. In 1608 a Protestant League faced a Catholic League. During the Thirty Years War the cause of the territories, facing the Papacy and the Habsburgs, was united with that of France. The treaties of Westphalia consecrated the federation of sovereign States, which in 1648 comprised 8 Electors (of the Emperor), 69 ecclesiastical princes, 96 secular princes, and 61 towns, in all 234 territorial units. One sole territory in this curious mosaic, Prussia, grew great and outlined her future rôle. Toward the middle of the seventeenth century she was already by far the most powerful unit in northern Germany. And she was beginning to stretch her antennæ toward the western regions.

It was between 1650 and 1750 that the territorial system was constituted and spread and grew to historic significance. A fundamental opposition also set at grips with each other Austria, the premier *Catholic* State, and Prussia, the *Lutheran* State by definition. It could be seen already that Prussia would have the advantage.

Small as they were, the German courts at this time were all in pursuit of absolute independence. It was the zenith of *particularism*, of "*Kleinstaaterei.*" But let us beware of the injustice the historian may easily do to the German courts in condemning them for having imitated Versailles. The truth is that the territories did excellent work as States in Germany, setting up a solid administration within their limited areas. *By a curious paradox, administrative perfection was a function of particularism.* The same progress that other States had made thanks to absolutism and to mercantilism turned in Germany against national unity. The system marked also the decay of the town bourgeoisie. That bourgeoisie was, indeed, preparing its own renewal and the elaboration of the great German culture. But that culture was so largely "highbrow" that it had little effect on the masses. They still lived in wretched conditions. The contrast was immense between the magnificent mediæval mansions and the homes of the poor in the seventeenth and eighteenth centuries.

The Reich had fallen into utter impotence. The Emperor, the Reichstag, imperial justice, and the imperial army had lost all prestige. The Empire was *irregulare aliquod et monstro simile corpus*—something unique, almost a monstrosity. Pursuing ends more and more alien to German interests, this old political rubbish-heap, for all practical purposes little more than a fiction, was superposed on very concrete and real absolutisms. Who can fail to see that in such a situation *a great modern State was impossible in the Germany of that day*? No doubt, in passing from the formula of patriarchalism to the formula of enlightenment, absolutism was drawing closer to the bourgeoisie and appealing to its fresh energies. But the aristocracy and the clergy intervened with determination between Empire and bourgeoisie. In reality the prince did what he liked and acted just as he thought fit. He was the monstrous Person of whom Schiller speaks in a celebrated scene of his *Don Carlos*, who absorbs in himself the persons of his subjects.

This is easy to see on the theoretical plane. Since 1650, absolutism had tended to separate from its confessional origins. Everywhere, with the *Aufklärung*, the idea of the Social Contract had penetrated, the idea that men who are virtually free and equal delegate to the sovereign the power that nature has given them. But on the territorial plane neither democracy nor aristocratic oligarchy was possible. The only practical possibility was monarchical absolutism, though divested of all divine right. This was the system that Bodin defended in France and Hobbes in England. Pufendorf inferred that if the prince is sovereign, he should nevertheless be constitutionally limited in the exercise of his power.

This was but doctrine. In reality the Lutheran Christian

State remained in existence. Where its foundations seemed to have been shaken, the prince continued to profit by the very diminutiveness of his territory. He considered himself to be a landed proprietor, administering a mediæval estate. It was an out-of-date system, accounted for by the devastation of the Thirty Years War. Not until Frederick II came do we see applied in the greatest State of Germany the theory that the prince is servant to the State. In fact, the prince of the seventeenth and eighteenth centuries possessed omnipotence through his means of constraint, omnipresence through his bureaucracy, and omniscience through his archives and his universities; finally, if he wished, he was omnibenevolent toward his subjects.

So retrograde an absolutism could not escape, in the long run, from coming into conflict with the new society, and particularly with the middle-class forces, of which the first manifestations began to be visible at that time. Until about 1720 German society offered the spectacle of dynasties, nobilities, and patriciates rigorously dominant over a peasantry and a middle class both of whom had been ruined by the Thirty Years War. All this ruin, together with the numberless territorial barriers, the decay of the great international route through Germany since the discovery of America and of the Indies, and the fidelity of the churches and of monarchical absolutism to the old economic principles of the Middle Ages, had perpetuated a state of things that favoured absolutism itself.

Between 1720 and 1750 the picture changed to some extent. Agriculture began to revive. A new rise of commerce was on the way. The Continental routes recovered their importance. Where they crossed stood Leipzig and Frankfort. Immigration, especially of refugees driven from France by the revocation of the Edict of Nantes, stimulated German economic and industrial activity. The material liquidation of the Middle Ages began. Both in Central Germany and on the periphery the birth was witnessed of a new bourgeoisie representing the upper strata of the masses subjected to absolutism. Sons of craftsmen and merchants, of officials and of people with small private incomes, these bourgeois were the intellectuals and the artists of the new generation. They brought to German culture their fresh outlook and their enthusiasm, their love of nature and their ardent passions, their simplicity of dress and habits, and a certain creative idealism. These were the makers of *Sturm und Drang*, of classicism and of romanticism. They were less tolerant of the methods of absolutism than their elders had been. But they tried in vain to modify the rigidity of its forms and practices in order to carve for themselves a place in a wider society.

Absolutism faced them invincibly with the rigour of its system, and especially with the multiplicity of its powers and its forms. Wherever a State possessed fairly ample territory and a certain internal cohesion, a double victory was achieved. The potentate won the day against regional particularisms, and also against the privileged classes. In order to assure dynastic unity, he gradually ruined the aristocracies and the patriciates. It was by this method that the *Landesherren* built up their bureaucracies and their armies, their economic organizations and their fiscal systems. They applied all liquid capital to the service of the State. Through their efforts mercantilism installed itself everywhere in place of the various systems of the cities. If the territory grew rich in the process of internal standardization or of shutting itself off from the outer world, the prince was able to dispose of the whole of its resources. This was the heyday of protectionism and of subsidized export. If any attention was paid to the peasant, it was in order that he should pay taxes, should serve as a soldier, or should be turned into a poorly paid industrial worker.

This system, furnished since 1650 with the revenues from more and more rigorous taxation, enabled each prince to finance a strong central administration and a powerful army. The officials were directly dependent on the potentate, regarding their employment as a particular favour that demanded in return the most absolute sense of duty. The reigning power invoked Roman law in order to exercise severe control over the landowners and the towns. The army was built up on the mercenary system. This created a difficult problem, which only the great territories were able to solve; they set up standing armies or made of the army a sort of instrument of State placed immediately under the sovereign control of the prince.

Thus the officer was simply an official of another order. The administration and the army were the essential pillars of the whole edifice. They were the means by which the *Landesherr* reduced his subjects to tutelage, acting on their behalf and asking nothing of them but to attend to their trades and occupations. He alone ruled his territory. No doubt it was an immense success for the absolute power. What chance against it had a young bourgeoisie beset by so many new aspirations, most of them sentimental? How destroy this hundred-headed hydra? The very serious counterpart of this too easy political success, this too well established domination, was a considerable economic backwardness and a total commercial failure. What a difference between the proud pre-Reformation bourgeoisie and the poor "subjects" of the seventeenth and eighteenth centuries! What a contrast between the privileges of those who lived in the shelter of the ruling power and the poor existence of the rest!

In the background of this all-conquering territorialism we see standing out two great States, Austria and Prussia. Prussia began to gain the advantage over her rival, thus preparing the way for the second great disciplinary concentration from which was one day to proceed the Frederician kingdom, and then the Bismarckian Empire. Between 1650 and 1740 Austria grew steadily weaker while Prussia continually advanced. With its seaboard, its intercourse with neighbour-States, and its opportunities of international commerce, the North was assured of gaining the advantage. Brandenburg left Brunswick and Hanover in the shade, and made herself the centre of attraction, beginning also to turn to the north-west, which until then had been more closely associated with the Rhineland in the south.

Between 1640 and 1688 Prussia was transformed into *a military State*. Between 1688 and 1740 its monarchy consolidated its positions, resisting Polish pressure and Swedish designs of hegemony. While Austria was busy absorbing heterogeneous territories of too vast extent, Brandenburg systematically digested her successive acquisitions. The State was sovereign ruler, Prussian absolutism standing head and shoulders above all other absolutisms. Nowhere were the official and the officer more docile instruments in the hands of the prince. The Prussian army attained a strength of 80,000 at a time when all France had but 160,000 men. A greater demand was made on the peasant than anywhere else as taxpayer and as soldier. But, to be just, it should be noted that more attention was paid in Prussia than anywhere else to the town bourgeoisie and to industry.

Such are the fundamental lines of the picture presented by Germany between the Reformation and the middle of the eighteenth century. We see her as a country in which vast intellectual or musical syntheses were being shaped, but where in practical life strange hesitations were showing themselves. Germany had ventured on the first ecclesiastical Reformation. But, unable to develop from it its democratic consequences, she had stopped midway, freeing men's souls only on the inner, mystical plane, and confining men as obedient subjects within the multiple framework of her burdensome absolutisms. Her thought oscillated between the old Christian positions and the boldest visions of the new science. Her music was an admirable compromise, on an immense scale, between mediæval polyphony and the homophony of modern times. A certain individualism found a place in her culture, manifesting itself in rationalism or in pietism.

But this individualism had not the strength to gnaw at the actual structure of her institutions. It confined itself to "subjectivism," to its inner dreams. It was incapable of influencing the social and political order. It contented itself with the conception of a sort of spiritual hegemony, a Kingdom of Souls, an Invisible Church in which all Germans should be communicants. How could it realize its conception in a Germany cut up for all other purposes into an infinity of territories? Thus the national idea remained diffused. It tended to mingle with the religious feeling that was beginning to form above the confessional churches rigorously bound to the territories. There was no vigorous Third Estate capable of controlling Governments or representing its grievances, and of giving a little freedom to the mass of the people. A certain militarization was preparing on the territorial plane, but there was still no sign of any national or racial mysticism. The Empire was in decay, the new imperial idea was not yet born, and all that existed was the sentimental basis of a vague and impotent cosmopolitanism.

Leibnitz dreamed of a religious organization of the whole world. Bach brought within his prodigious work every form of the past and all the germs of the music to come. As yet tendencies to hegemony had established themselves only on the plane of thought and in the realm of music. But in face of these vast syntheses there was being slowly developed the hard Prussian nucleus. Its constituent elements were the administration and the army.

These two orders of facts remained apart. Their association was to be the work of the future.

CHAPTER III

From Cosmopolitanism to Pan-German Nationalism
(1750–1815)

In the whole history of German culture there has been no more
memorable epoch than that which embraced the second half of
the eighteenth century and led from pre-classicism and from the
coming of Frederick II to romanticism and to the Congress of
Vienna. It marks the end of the territorial Germany formed by
the Middle Ages and the Reformation. It also marks the decline
of the Holy Roman Empire that served as its historic framework,
at the time when German thought, making a *volte-face*, passed
from cosmopolitanism to pan-Germanism and substituted for
the imperial relic a precise conception of a community at once
national and religious. Thus, a little before the Bismarckian era,
the two factors took shape which were thereafter to determine
the destiny of Germany—Prussian hegemony and the dream of
a new Reich.

For the purpose of a rational classification of facts and of the
search for a general interpretation, some notice must be taken
of the French Revolution. The half-century that preceded it
led, in spite of its own wealth, to two essential facts—the
secularization of Christianity and the Frederician policy. While
German thought was establishing its governing positions and
finding its natural mould in a language which beyond any
question was the most beautiful and the most harmonious ever
written by a German, Prussia, at the death of the great king,
revealed herself as the State with a strong political armour that
could brave the Napoleonic tests.

The twenty-five years that separate 1789 from the Congress of
Vienna form a whole. This time the French Revolution and
the French Empire, with the wars that accompanied them,
produced the sudden oscillations that threw France from the
monarchy to the Republic and from the Republic to the imperial
dictatorship—a process that in the eyes of contemporaries had
the dimensions of a cosmic phenomenon, producing in Germany
apologias and above all passionate condemnations. These upheavals proceeding from the West gave Germany the consciousness of her existing impotence and of the strength that could be

hers if she could recover cohesion. While the romantics intoxicated themselves with magnificent visions and dreamed of a national religion which, in face of the juridical and political French State built on the principles of 1789, should create the Germany of the morrow, at last unified and regenerated, Prussia, which had fallen into decay between 1786 and 1806, and had been cruelly humiliated at Jena, recovered and led on the Continent the coalition that was to defeat Napoleon and put an end to French hegemony.

Immense was the distance that German thought and Prussian power had covered in so short a space of time! These events throw a strange light on the outstanding importance that the problem of the relationship to be established between Prussia and the Reich was to assume in the future.

We see, then, what was the exact nature of the German Revolution that was in the making. We have already noted, between the sixteenth and the middle of the eighteenth century, a fact of the *spiritual* order and a fact of the *political* order. This original dualism of German history showed itself in clearer outline and in ampler measure between 1750 and 1815. *Germany became "revolutionary," that is to say, capable of overthrowing the old Continental order, when the strength of Prussia and the aspirations towards a national community that were summed up in the word " Reich" were united.*

To give Prussia the command over an anarchical federation of sovereign States, and to complete the restricted reality of Lesser Germany by that of a material and spiritual hegemony—such was in future to be the preoccupation of Germany's rulers.

1. *Revolutionary symptoms and Classicism*

In the course of the last four decades before the French Revolution of 1789 there was completed in Germany a process without the knowledge of which no interpretation of Germany's course is possible: the secularization of Christianity. This took place on different lines from those of the corresponding process in France. The difference is of capital importance, and the two neighbour nations could not devote too much thought to it.

Catholic France, after almost smothering the Calvinist Reformation in its infancy, made a sudden *volte-face* when, faced like the other European nations with the problems of the foundation of a lay culture, she broke up in the eighteenth century into a

Catholic and a free-thinking community, into the supporters of the Roman religion and of laicism. The existence of these two enemy brothers was due to the fact that Christian natural law had itself engendered the secular natural law that was one day to culminate in the principles of 1789. Both sides declared, with the same emphasis, the infinite value of human personality. But while Catholicism invoked original sin in order to justify the divine right of kings and the authoritarian methods of monarchy, free-thought, proclaiming the natural goodness of man, simply invoked the imprescriptible rights of the individual in general.

In Germany, however, Lutheranism held a position with which it is impossible to compare the part played by Calvinism in France. The Counter-reformation had won the day in the West and the South, so that confessional dualism had been established on German soil. The two confessions had consequently been compelled, especially after the treaties of Westphalia, to fit themselves into the territorial frameworks which had split them up into territorial Churches. Although they were of œcumenical tendency and the heirs of Christian transcendentalism, they had become associated, by the force of circumstances, with more or less narrow regional and local interests. The bond was the more indissoluble since in each territory the distinction between the civil and the religious power tended to be lost.

Confessional territorialism favoured the development of the most rigorous orthodoxy, the most disciplinarian control of morality, and a pedantic pedagogy. All this constraint could not be satisfactory to the best Germans, men either of fervent piety or of lofty intellectuality. Most of the territorial Churches began, as it were, to wither. In compensation there tended to be superposed on the Christian confessions a semi-Christian, semi-profane religiousness, as a sort of indispensable mysticism.

This is explained by the very natural aspiration of thinking Germans to see the end of confessional dualism. It could only disappear, however, before a religion which should be a *national* religion—a religion incapable of identification with traditional Christianity. This diffused religiosity, to which the Germans gave the name of " *Weltfrömmigkeit*," because it was a curious mixture of theism and pantheism, Christian universalism and earthly enthusiasm, associated itself with cosmopolitanism before 1789, and then with nationalism or " *Volkstum*." Here we reach the heart of the problem. Here we see the specific origins and the true nature of German nationalism.

Undoubtedly this was a direct consequence of the Reformation. On the one hand the Reformation awakened and at the same time satisfied in German souls a thousand new aspirations of the sentimental, religious, or intellectual order. But it also produced the Lutheran State Church, the Church that governed and exerted constraint. By uniting its destiny with the territorial States, Lutheranism limited needs and held in check demands of which it favoured the free growth elsewhere. The territorial Churches adopted Lutheranism for their own profit. In reality they took the life from it and, so to speak, transferred its living substance to profane culture. If Lutheranism, like Calvinism in the West, had promoted a movement of ecclesiastical freedom and independence, public feeling in Germany would have joined hands with Lutheran Christianity. The bureaucratic character of the official Churches destroyed the free play of religious forces, which were compelled to emigrate to the neighbouring sphere.

That is why in Germany the secularization of Christianity retained a religious tinge. The mystical instinct of the Germans turned away from territorial confessional Christianity to other activities, until the day when the Reich turned to its own advantage all these values of sentiment and faith. All the hopes and expectations which the Churches were disappointing turned to world civilization. There resulted a religious way of regarding the world.

Another cause intervened in this strange process. So long as the territorial Churches remained small, they were able to attract believers owing to the intimacy and the fervour of their religious life. They were struggling against Rome, against the Empire, against all universal powers, in the name of the Lutheran faith, in the name of the Invisible Church that served as a refuge from so much despair. But later the Lutheran State Church changed in character. And it was especially in the larger States, and above all in Prussia, that it drew away from primitive Lutheranism.

Here the Prussian problem reappears with new nuances. In that authoritarian State the politico-ecclesiastical institution quickly became a crushing burden. A phenomenon of repression was produced here under the action of the bureaucratic system. The individual counted now for little. Prussian Lutheranism was the opposite of Anglo-Saxon Protestantism. Its machinery broke its subjects. That which in Catholicism had appeared natural became absurd and intolerable in Protestantism.

This explains the religious indifferentism of the Germans. It was indifference only in regard to the churches. The religious instinct of the Germans, disappointed and deceived, turned to science, or to art and literature, or, finally, *to the nation conceived as an imperial community*. Science, literature, art, and imperialism profited by this curious transfer. But imperialism increased the breach between *politics* and *culture*. No doubt Lutheran sentiment favoured the spread in Germany of a universal philosophy, music, and literature. Only, since it became incorporated in the territories, it was opposed to the unity of the nation. Through that fact it deprived the individual, and in particular the middle class, of all opportunity of broad political activity such as would provide political education for the citizens.

Between a family life inspired by an out-of-date patriarchalism and a State not so much patriarchal as authoritarian or despotic, there was no outlet, as a rule, for the middle-class German except in associations of minor importance. That is why in Germany the bourgeoisie remained politically weak and impotent while in Britain and France, where it took a growing part in public affairs, it developed towards a very active Third Estate, keen to control the acts of the Government. Hence the origin of the German "Michael," the little man on whom the nationalists poured boundless contempt.

We can see, then, why religious indifferentism merged, in Germany, into political indifferentism. Men prided themselves in the past on being "*apolitisch*," unpolitical. It was because he loved private life too well that in the end the German lost it. The German revealed this indifference in regard to all that was "public," whether of State or of Church. The very structure of Germany was an incitement to the German to withdraw into himself, to live apart from the confession in which he had been brought up by disciplinarians, and from the bureaucratic machinery with which a petty State bore down on him. For all these constraints he found compensation in his professional activity, or in science and culture. The immense advance of German culture after the middle of the eighteenth century had no other cause. What was there for a man of intelligence to do in the territorial State and Church? In emancipating himself from that tutelage he gained the freedom of spirit, the broad outlook, the passion for the universal which were just the things that gave German culture the cosmopolitan and European character that it retained down to the end of the eighteenth century. *But this cosmopolitanism, shocked by the notorious impotence of the nation in its fragmentation, turned to nationalism, and that nationalism became the most terrible of all European nationalisms, precisely because it was religious and fervent, while unlimited in its ambitions. Thence came pan-Germanism.*

Such is the explanation of the most curious original features of German life. The imponderabilia that govern the mentality of that enigmatic people, in which so many tranquil and benign individuals are in a state of eternal fury, the mixture of incredible indifference and of political irritability that characterizes it—in short, the traits that most disconcert the Englishman or the Frenchman—all these matters of surprise are accounted for by Germany's religious and territorial history. During the periods in which political life was nothing to him, the German brought to the sciences, to philosophy, to literature, or to art the implacable gravity and the almost total lack of humour that are native to him. But let political activity come into the foreground, let the German be given the opportunity of a nation or a Reich, and he became terrible. Heine's celebrated prophecy was entirely true. Pan-Germanism was nothing but *a misplaced religion* which, for national reasons, because Christianity had too faithfully adjusted itself to territorial forms, had broken with Christianity itself.

Thus German culture presents itself, from this point of view, as a sequela of a confessional religion compromised by territorial fragmentation and by the State Church. To understand that broad fact is to understand Germany. At the end of the eighteenth century, and at the beginning of the nineteenth, the German middle class created *a culture with the stamp of religion*, which turned more and more to philosophy, a grandiose philosophy of global and synthesizing character, a truly "romantic" philosophy in the most exact sense of the term. A lofty and admirable culture certainly, since it emanated directly from the absolute liberty which the great middle-class intellectuals of Germany created for themselves in the vacuum between the territorial States and Churches and a Nation almost non-existent. But a culture that remained without foundations and without political consequences until the day when, faced with the events in the West, it suddenly turned into pan-German nationalism.

The forty years that preceded the French Revolution saw the

accomplishment in Germany, especially after the appearance of the *Nouveaux Essais* of Leibnitz (1765), of a modernization of Christianity. This secularization was produced by means of rationalism and pietism, culminating in the classicism of Herder, Goethe, and Schiller.

The process was analogous to that of 1650 to 1750, but on a larger scale and with broader consequences. In the second half of the eighteenth century rationalism and pietism both entered on a new phase of their existence. The former, more and more penetrated by sentimental elements and represented by such philosophers as Mendelssohn and Garve, ended in Kantism, that is to say, religion within the limits of pure reason. As for pietism, it passed beyond Moravianism, which in that epoch had formed so many great spirits, to culminate in a sentimental philosophy without which the literature of the time remains unintelligible. Hamann and Claudius, Lavater and Jacobi, Klopstock and other poets, are celebrated names that mark the course of that movement.

The more we penetrate the intimate recesses of pietism, the more we are able to understand why, once it had abandoned the Christian dogma, it was transformed into pantheist fervour. What else did such great thinkers as Herder, Goethe, and Schiller, to speak only of those three, do but recommence, after Leibnitz, the synthesis between reason and feeling? It was from that immense effort of universalism that there was born the religious feeling *sui generis* that was and remained theirs. A feeling new for their epoch, and of irresistible influence on their contemporaries, a feeling still entirely penetrated by the ancient Hellenic and Christian humanism, but united especially with the restless humanism of the Renaissance and the Reformation.

After its first appearance in Germany, the *Aufklärung* ran the risk either of withering there and of degenerating into the worst scepticism, or of taking on certain nuances of sentiment. That is why Kant, after returning to the theory of knowledge, attempted to restore the primacy of morality, basing it on a categorical imperative, and to save from the Christian heritage that which appeared to him to be conformable with practical reason so conceived. Current rationalism contented itself with the affirmation that there is agreement between human thought and the order of phenomena. Kant took up again the position of Leibnitz. From the outer world we receive impressions. But in what respect does our judgment modify them? Kant replied, with Leibnitz, that the reason and the intelligence have an ordering function, since they arrange our impressions according to certain categories in space and time. He only added that the reason acts on sensibility and its workings in an *a priori* manner and without waiting for reality itself.

Kant thus performed a Copernican act. The individual subject becomes the centre of an awareness relating to itself, but of which it does not know whether it corresponds to reality. The subject is the norm of knowledge, but a norm that has no guarantee of absolute objectivity. That is why the supreme truth established by Reason will be an object of faith, not of demonstration. The practical Reason is there to complete what is lacking to the theoretical Reason. The regulative principle of our will is the moral law, is duty. We have to act in the universe, and in conformity with a universal truth.

If, then, faith results not from knowledge but from a will conforming with the moral law, the existence of the moral law signifies that God exerts action upon us, that He legislates in us and through us. Such is the explanation of the Kantian conception of so-called "natural" religion, the nucleus of all positive religion. Religion is of value only in so far as it induces us to carry out the moral law. Christ can here be no more than a great model, a model that is in our reason but lived on earth. Kant restores in his own fashion the divine image, morality inscribed in men's hearts. To believe in Christ is to imitate His august example. It is in imitating Him that men believe in Him. No more mediators, no more means of grace. How far we have wandered here from orthodoxy! It is still, no doubt, the Lutheran sovereignty of God over the soul, but without the Bible and without Luther's dogma.

The secularization of pietism was of still more importance. It was accomplished between 1750 and 1790, by such thinkers as Karl Philipp Moritz, Jung Stilling, and Jacobi. Pietism considers Christ as the living, fruitful Principle, as the soul's Betrothed. Christ is here something very different from a simple model to be imitated. The whole abyss that separates pietist mysticism from Kant is revealed in this formula. Kant's subjectivism is at all times of the rational order. *The subjectivism that proceeds from pietism admits that a Principle of universal life governs the soul.* Let the theocratic basis fall, cease to believe in the dogma of original sin and of redemption through Christ's sacrifice, and you will have, as a Principle living in us and in nature, the direct inspiring action of the Divine. That is pantheism. God is discovered in the very centre of the universe, of all our psychic activities, of our feelings and passions. That is what Hamann, proceeding from the purest Lutheranism, one day declared. Passion, passion freed from every rule and every precept, is divine. It is the breath of genius, the proof that a God acts in us. *That is to say that feeling, in its very ignorance, is the condition of knowledge.* To know is before all else to feel and to live. Everything comes from the personality, from its intimate and direct communion with the universe, with that Energy in action which is God. The day was to come when Catholics like Princess Galitzyn and L. Stolberg were to say the same thing. Jacobi believed in the intuitive Reason as one believes in the witness of one's eyes. Men can perceive suprasensible realities. Religion resides in the mysterious "*Sinn,*" the direct apprehension of the Divine that guides the world. The antagonism between Jacobi and Kant is evident. It showed itself plainly about 1790. Kant never admitted that there was the slightest analogy between his critique of the demonstrative proofs of the existence of God and Jacobi's. Kant considered only that to be true which was demonstrated. He rejected the claims for emotional truths. In his view Jacobi and Claudius were simply dangerous mystics.

Here, in its exact terms, is the antithesis between rationalism and the *Schwärmerei* (zealotry) of which the eighteenth-century German talked so much. It was over this that the classics, following the example of Leibnitz, tried to triumph. Herder, who had followed the doctrines of Hamann and Kant, proceeded from Leibnitz and aimed like him at uniting feeling and reason. He also returned to and renewed the religious effort made by the great philosopher between 1770 and 1790, when he (Herder) was pastor of Bückeburg. The story of salvation and the Christian acts had only symbolic value for him. The miracles had historic meaning only in so far as they symbolized ideal and therefore eternal verities. Herder kept equally distant from an arid rationalism and a facile mysticism. The Bible was undoubtedly the divine Word. But, like all the great books of Humanity, it was also the word of men. Being the source of eternal life, religion was always springing forth. It was dogma that paralysed its divine spread. Christ offered us a divine experience which everyone could know and reproduce. Like Leibnitz, Herder thought that man, in raising himself to perfection, could gain a progressive victory over matter and over evil.

This religious outlook recalls that of Rousseau, that of the Savoyard Vicar. Goethe goes farther than Herder, while Schiller remains close to Kantian moralism. Goethe entirely secularized Christianity. He was the true creator of the new religious outlook. He knew from direct experience all the forms of Christianity of his day. His pretended paganism was full of Christian echoes. He was the forerunner of the union which, after him, Hölderlin and the romantics tried to establish between Hellenism and Christianity. Whatever the differences that existed between the three great classics on the eve of the French Revolution, they had at least in common a conception of the universe that requires definition.

They seem to have retained from Kant the truth that, if man is no longer the centre of the universe, as men had believed before Copernicus, he has at all events the right to consider and to know the universe. With Kant and Leibnitz, they admitted a fundamental duality in man, a lower nature facing a demand, also natural, for higher things. It was still a question, as in ancient and Christian morality, of a fundamental opposition between spontaneous nature and the moderating reason, which man must bring to a vigorous synthesis.

The classics claimed to know by experience and to apply in practice to individual and social life all the *energy* and *legality* in the universe. This energy and legality were attained by intuition, by direct feeling. Finite individual beings must, in their structure and their activity, be such that there was *analogy* between them and the universal Infinite. Knowledge and action had a mystical basis, even apart from all positive religion. For the old Christian dualism, the radical opposition between sin and redemption, they substituted the secret play between nature as perceived by the senses and the higher organization of our creative forces. The classics were not content with the Kantian certitude, with the over-simple Kantian conception of duty. They regarded that as a poor substitute for the abolished Christian certitudes. They wanted something more and better.

In face of the modern mechanization with which man is threatened, they must build, they thought, the kingdom of the soul. The intuition of genius was sovereign. Whether in connexion with external nature, with the individual soul, or with history, the true man avoided empiricism, rationalism, and pure speculation.   The essential thing was the living relation between object and subject.   That strange epoch, immediately preceding the French Revolution, recovered both the spirit of primitive Lutheranism and that of the pandynamism of the Renaissance. Fervour of soul must preside over our acts as the Lutheran faith presided over the works of the Christian.   But that fervour drew its virtue from our communion with the universe, from creative images within us, from the coincidence between men's ideas and the original phenomena that are at the root of all liberty.

There we have the true mysticism of Goethe, a mysticism that made no difference between external nature and the inner life. A revelation of the true life took place within us, owing to the action of the universe or of God in us.   That revelation was permanent and eternal.   God was the immanent cause of the world, and the world was a totality of active forces.   Intuitive knowledge, as Goethe conceived it, avoided alike the abstract universalism that identified all beings and the relativism of pure contingency that led to nihilism, and it sought the universal realities common to all beings.   Goethe's religion, his piety, was the sense he had of all that is sacred in nature, in man, and in existence.   It was the idea of a fundamental agreement between the three teachings lavished upon us by the starry universe, the terrestrial globe upon which nature and history are manifested, and the entrails of the earth itself.   The poet who drew these lofty lessons was a creator as well as a worker.   He brought his inner fervour to the labours and the professional technique without which there can be no work of art.   But the work of art is the symbol of all creation, divine or human.

There is no more complete example, no more living demonstration than the work of Goethe, for anyone who desires to define the German religious spirit.   Goethe was at the very centre of that truly unique period in the history of the German mind and the European mind.   The term *Weltliteratur*, applied to the immense work of this poet, corresponds exactly with that universal religious spirit.

It was that religious feeling that provided the essential themes of the literature of the epoch, whether that of the first precursors of *Sturm und Drang* or that of Goethean classicism.   That conception of the person, considered as an organized assemblage of inner forces which, by their very harmony, should be in intimate communion with the universe, nature, and society, was the central preoccupation of all that literature, whether æsthetic, lyric, dramatic, or fictional. It was the cult of Nature, the passionate feeling, in which optimism and pessimism were so strangely mingled, of the plenitude and the grandeur she manifests alike in her elysian aspects and in her most infernal works of destruction. It was the sentimental apologia for friendship, which made friends throw themselves, weeping with emotion, into each other's arms, and which Goethe so exactly expressed in his odes to the ladies of Darmstadt. It was the fervent celebration of love between the sexes, with its inexpressible felicities and its tragic dangers, of love considered as a cosmic power which human beings were unable to resist. It was finally the broadened conception of a Humanity in whose bosom irreconcilably diverse peoples and cultures could dwell alongside each other, to their mutual enrichment. Such, in a few outlines, was the content of German literature between 1750 and 1790.

Already the precursors, Klopstock, Wieland, and Lessing, in spite of the bonds that united them with pietism or rationalism, were announcing *Sturm und Drang*. But what else was *Sturm und Drang* but a recommencement of the Lutheran Reformation, a new protest of the faith of genius against works that did nothing but repeat or imitate, a return to the grand Paracelsian dynamism? This strange movement brings us to a vast classic expansion, to the Goethe of Weimar and of Italy, between 1780 and 1790. Between these three phases the transitions and the nuances are delicately drawn. From Klopstock, Wieland, and Lessing there proceeded directly, through the play of the profoundest influences, the first *Sturm und Drang* period, from 1770 to 1780. Here we are in the midst of classicism with *Egmont, Tasso, Iphigenia*, and the fragments of *Faust*, at the very moment when Schiller, ten years younger than Goethe, was writing his revolutionary hymns and dramas.

What is the true notion of the Beautiful? We assume that in art the national work of genius cannot be born of imitation of foreign cultures or of an exact knowledge of the rules and recipes, the "canons," deduced from masterpieces of the past. We assume that in the domain of art as elsewhere there is no abstract universalism, no code with which it would suffice to comply in order to produce. Artistic creation is the supreme mystery. *The work proceeds from faith.* It is the daughter of amorous fervour, which is itself an emotion of the cosmic order, an individual communion in which the inspired artist lives with the universe. The ardent centre of our soul corresponds with the sun, the ardent centre of our world. The sun lavishes heat, energy, and enthusiasm on the creature, but only if the creature directs its own radiation to the sun. The work of art is born like the child, for it is the fruit of a fecundation and carries with it the structure proper to it.

In order to reproduce the movement and the rhythm of universal life as they pass through us, the work of art must have its technique and must submit to rules, but rules that are freely chosen. This æsthetic, preluding that of Paul Valéry, sees in art a fervour which, in order to be productive, bows spontaneously to certain necessities.

The poetry of that period, as revealed in its works from the odes of Klopstock to those of Goethe and to his pure master-pieces of the Weimar days, reveals in itself all that contemporaries dreamed and lived. We have only to compare it with the poetry of the first half of the eighteenth century in order to measure its marvellous advance. The scholarly poets among the patricians of the towns voiced their emotions and their impressions within measures provided for them and conscien-tiously imitated, though these emotions and impressions may have been more sincere than is generally thought. Klopstock renewed at a stroke the content and the form of German verse by demanding of the German that he should express through his own resources *the pietist conception of Christianity and of the Passion, and the new feeling for nature* which, since Rousseau and the spread of English influences, had revealed itself everywhere. Here was a secularized religiosity that emanated, fresh and full of youthful ardour, from pietist quarters. But Klopstock contented himself with almost official collective emotions, with sentiments still nebulous or conventional and not the objects of direct experience.

Goethe was still to come, with his youthful poems, those of the *Leipziger Liederbuch*, already so full of ripened and fruitful germs, the adorable poesy of Sesenheim, and finally the magnifi-cent odes that followed one another between 1770 and 1775, and his first Weimar works, still so quivering with youthful vigour and spontaneity. Nothing was better suited to the mystical feeling and the naturistic pantheism of the time. From then on Germany possessed a literature that was truly lay and secular but in which, under the influence of the most intense poetic emotion, classic religious feeling exhaled its best qualities. Schiller's youthful poems have not the same accent of sincere passion. They remain more abstract, more forced. But they treated of the great themes of the period in the special pathos that so exactly characterized the mixture of Hellenism and Christianity that was then found among the loftier spirits.

The dramatic art of the *Sturm und Drang* period and of the earliest of the classics has a still more precise significance. The writers of the day understood their tragic destiny. They knew themselves to be revolutionaries, but only "within," impotent to remove the formidable obstacle of the absolutisms around them. Isolated from the amorphous masses, they knew only an inner freedom, an activity of poets and enthusiasts. They felt condemned in advance by a social order that would mercilessly turn against them if they dreamed of fomenting revolt. And they were not unaware that, after the violent liquidation of the old methods, their works would be in danger of remaining inchoate, and their personalities, reputed of genius, would risk destruction amid the conflict of passions. They knew the evil of the times, and found an irreconcilable conflict between the individual and the social conventions. Their rather over-simple psychology was unable to conceive the Ego otherwise than as a force in itself unlimited, great alike in good and evil, of which the very extravagance provoked the inevitable collision with social demands. The dramas of the *Sturm und Drang*, still so much alive, exclaim to us that the German collectivity gave no support to genius, whether genius manifested itself in criminal disorders or in legitimate protests against the established order.

There have been those who found in *Götz von Berlichingen* an echo of Luther. They saw repeated in it the tragedy of the Reformer, victim of his own superior qualities, of the generosity and the courage that led him to revolt against an order which he regarded as evil, at a time when that order was still supported by respected traditions. But the enemies of genius, those who made use of the established order to satisfy their egoistic ambitions and passions, themselves suffered chastisement. *Egmont* is the drama of inner freedom, of the unconcern of genius, deliberately ignoring fateful political and social forces in order to remain true to itself. The *Urfaust* is the spirit that wishes to know all life, the drama of the too violent passion of a love that breaks with convention and ends in inexcusable crime.

Better even than Goethe had done, because their author had directly experienced the tragedy of absolutism, the youthful dramas of Schiller express, with an accent which German dramatic art was never, perhaps, to recover, the double conflict, the crumbling alike of the generous spirit of reform and of egoistic ambition. Carl Moor and Posa claimed to correct the established order in the name of genius—the former by fire and sword, the latter by clumsy intrigues. Both perished, victims of their dreams. There is no finer scene than that in which, in *Don Carlos*, Philip II, before the dead body of Posa, tells of the desperate daring of the dead man and of the relentless insistence with which every traditional régime pursues its career, until its sun goes down. Ferdinand and Louise, in *Cabale und Liebe*, are condemned to die through the fatal course of a love that defies convention. But Franz Moor, Fiesco, and President von Walther suffer no less the penalty for their criminal designs. *Order* avenges itself upon the *genius* that disturbs it either to build it up or to take undue advantage of it, and so it hastens its own decay.

This dramatic art was both revolutionary and conservative. It began by writing of rebelliousness of soul and of its social dangers. Goethe took up this theme at Weimar, in his *Torquato Tasso*, a drama that summed up Goethe's experience at court, and a work scarcely less pessimistic than *Egmont*. But *Iphigenia* and *Faust* are works of moral reconstruction, visions of triumph won and defended at a heavy price. Here we see the affirmation of an idea of material and moral organization, individual and collective, that was later to govern the destinies of the nation that was coming into existence. Iphigenia is the woman who, like Rousseau's Julie, restores the social order in the hour of danger, evincing the loftiest morality and the inner heroism of which only great souls are capable. In that entirely spiritual world conflicts are assuaged. Over the criminal Orestes, the lying Pylades, and the brutal Thoas, over every aspect of masculine evil, the pure virgin triumphs in abandoning the sanctuary in which she regards her existence as useless. Through a symbolic act she cures Orestes—whose only thought was of death and who thereby proved the absolute sincerity of his remorse—of his stain and his suffering by the very method which Luther employed. Like the sixteenth-century Reformer, Goethe thought that the soul, on the one condition of being true to itself, could in any circumstances free itself and recover full sovereignty. Divine grace and natural grace—are they not at bottom one and the same, given the spontaneous manifestation of "pure humanity"? The voice of Iphigenia, the sister who has remained immaculate, recalls to Orestes that he has the right to live *as if he were free of blame* and to return to active existence.

He thus perceives the mysterious reality that is beyond good and evil; and at the same time he discovers his parents reconciled among the shades of Elysium.

There is nothing that Faust, a new symbol of the masculine destiny, does not know of real life, of the scandals that break out in courts and aristocracies, of the intrigues and wretchednesses that rage in art and literature, of the meannesses and horrors that disfigure the world of the common burghers. Goethe had condensed this picture in his *Hexenküche*, which was first produced in 1790. Faust was educated as a *true poet*. For true poesy is *heroism* and *labour*. His effort never ceases. It penetrates the whole of reality, recoils from no spectacle, searches the dark entrails of the earth for Beauty, the true beauty that is revealed to us only at fugitive moments and yields itself up only to unceasing effort.

An uncompleted work, no doubt, is this first *Faust*. But Goethe's novels, the only ones of that epoch that count, *Werther* and *Wilhelm Meisters Lehrjahre*, reveal more fully and with more precision the double destiny of man and woman in the society of his day. Everything that is to be said has been said of the causes of the suicide of Werther and of the psychological and social aspects of the evil that gnawed at him. Werther is a *Saint-Preux*, a Saint Valiant, who kills himself because, in a world that does not seem to be shaped to fit him, he is unable to satisfy his love and his legitimate ambitions. But in *Wilhelm Meisters Theatralische Sendung* the social environment, described with more care and objectivity, plays a more important part. There is no longer any question of a vain revolt against it, ending in a useless catastrophe. On the contrary, one has to carve oneself a place in it, after gathering full experience of the elements that enter into its composition, by the judicious choice of a profession. Here was the future of the new bourgeoisie.

Such was the grandeur and such were the limits of German culture in that epoch. Transcending that of the preceding period, it followed it in taking refuge in philosophy, in religious and moral thought, and above all in a lay literature lifted at a stroke by an enthusiastic pantheism to the most thrilling sublimities and to supreme perfection. Alongside these disciplines the plastic arts scarcely counted, important though the place was that Goethe accorded to the experience of them. Only the evolution of music, from Gluck to Mozart, gives an idea of what that time was. But, as always, music was less advanced than the civilization around it.   We have to wait for Beethoven, whose first original productions date from after the French Revolution, for the translation into music of the thought of the *Sturm und Drang* period and of the first classicism.   Not, it is true, that the modern music created by Gluck, Haydn, and Mozart does not constitute an immense achievement, in itself as remarkable as the *Sturm und Drang* and Goethe's classicism.   For music, too, freed itself from ecclesiastical tutelage and also from Italian opera, which had fallen into decay, and from the elegant style cultivated in France. But it still expressed a world of feelings and ideas that remained behind the great literature of the epoch.

The best operas of Gluck fall exactly between 1760 and 1780. They were *Orpheus, Alcestis,* and the two *Iphigenias.*   There is close agreement between words and music.   The words indicate and the music expresses the emotional content.   *Bel canto* is not entirely abandoned, but it has ceased to be cultivated for itself. These were bold initiatives, which were one day to lead to the art of Wagner.   Although they were behind current thought, Haydn and Mozart admirably rendered the change that had come in men's minds.   They passed deliberately from the old style, rigorously polyphonic and objective, to the homophonic style and to melody, so well fitted to express the soul's joys and sorrows.

Haydn, who was already twenty years old in 1752, created the classic symphony and the quartet.   But his art, perfect as it was, still drew its inspiration only from the light and charming material and *motifs* of eighteenth-century Austria.   Mozart alone dominates the whole epoch with his instrumental, dramatic, and religious music.   He had first imitated the Italians; then he turned to Gluck, and later he discovered all the depth and solidity of Bach.   Like Bach, he is truly a European genius. He is Austrian in tendency and close to the influences of France and Italy.   His immense work dates from 1770 to 1790.   In it is all the charm, the inexpressible charm, of the end of the eighteenth century, together with his marvellously solid classical construction, so well arranged beneath the diaphanous veil of a lightness and resiliency that exclude neither tenderness nor passionate emotion nor mystical depth.   This music, which aims above all at lifting the soul out of its natural sluggishness, is intermediate between the deeply religious mood of Bach and the restless subjectivity of Beethoven.

Mozart triumphed in the melody that expressed individual

feelings; he went beyond Gluck, whose music responds always to a collective action and to sentiments of a general order. Mozart's characters are individualized. In the domain of religious instrumental music he can voice his exquisite sensibility and his gravest thoughts. Nevertheless, his music, like Haydn's, is absolutely pure, free music, an art sufficient to itself, with a wholly Racinian nuance that modestly veils the secret thrills of emotion. Each of his works constitutes a completed whole, admirably balanced and coherent. Mozart reveals the triumph of naturalness, of a gracious, ordered, often deep naturalness, the triumph of rational and formal mastery, with the perfect ease and spontaneity of inspiration. It all culminates in *Die Zauberflöte*, in the apotheosis of the Enlightenment, in the victory which eternal truth and wisdom gain over the Kingdom of Night. This is certainly a step toward subjectivism. But the form, the grace, and the sprightliness, aiming at entertaining, are dominant. We remain in the days before *Sturm und Drang*, and especially before the pre-1789 classicism.

Such were the essential aspects of German culture on the eve of the French Revolution. A new surge had been made in the direction of rationalism and of pietism, followed by a progressive broadening and a gradual secularization of the Christian tradition. Then, with the *Sturm und Drang* movement, there had come the sudden outburst of an ardent religious feeling, a lyrical enthusiasm, and a tragic sense, which seemed to fuse in the pantheist crucible all the heritages of the past. From a civilization governed by Lutheran Christianity there was a transition to a definitely secularized culture that sought its models in Græco-Latin antiquity as in France, but retained its close bonds with Lutheranism.

It was, on the whole, a period of marvellous equilibrium between the contrary tendencies which were to separate and to fight each other from 1790 to 1815. German classicism was strongly distinguished from romanticism, which it finally engendered, because it fused the *abstract* universalism of the eighteenth-century West with the universalism of *composition* which, after Herder's time, was its own most original discovery. From one point òf view it admitted man, the human person, and gave him as substance the moral conscience that seems eternal and identical at all times and in all countries. That was why it admitted not only Hellenic and Roman culture, not only the Christian preoccupation with the individual's salvation, but also

the rationalist idea of *progress*, the Leibnitzian notion of a universal
attainment of perfection, men being equal at law and in principle
in the nation, and all peoples having a mission to accomplish—
that of contributing their share to the perfection of all mankind.
From another point of view, German classicism insisted on the
original traits of individuals, peoples, and cultures. It even
thought that individual temperaments were mutually irreconcilable, and national mentalities equally so. This was the characteristic that distinguished it the most clearly from French classicism.
Nevertheless, it did not fall into absolute relativism or into
nihilism. It was far from affirming the eternal struggle between
men, or between peoples or races. "Pure humanity," it considered, should have sufficient intrinsic power to restore harmony
when it was momentarily lost, or at least to impose it by main
force, to appease disputants and finally to rediscover *that Greek
mother-country* that was the object of so much nostalgia.

In the course of those ever memorable years, German culture
thus prepared and finally achieved the synthesis between the
old humanism, nourished by the ancients and by Christianity,
and the new humanism developed between the sixteenth and
the eighteenth centuries. Beauty, friendship, love, universal
progress, such were its familiar *motifs*. It was, no doubt, a
more restless humanism than the earlier one, because it was
haunted by the idea of hostile forces at work in nature and society,
and was conscious of its limitations, of the needs of the individual
and of society in order to conquer the forces of disorder that
are permanently at work in nature and among men. It was also
a more comprehensive humanism than the Western type. That
humanism, heir of Shakespeare and of many English influences,
heir also of Rousseau and Diderot and so many other French
thinkers, had been able to enrich by those fruitful contributions
all that was most original in the mind and the culture of the
Germans.

German culture had also attained a balance between a certain
irrationalism and the governing tendencies of the *Aufklärung*
or Enlightenment. This was the Leibnitzian synthesis, but
broadened, subtilized, and humanized, between feeling and
reason. Reason here took a less logical than *analogical* significa-
tion. It was "*Vernunft*," reasonableness, and not "*Verstand*,"
intelligence. The German obstinately sought in the human
spirit the Idea, not the concept, the Idea that corresponded to a
universal reality and would permit the finite man to know the

Infinite by a sort of mysterious apperception, to grasp the eternal within the limits of the moment, to enter into living communion with that universe in which destructive and creative forces are indissolubly intermingled, since Nature creates beings whom she destroys and ceaselessly destroys the beings she creates.

Nowhere, in this grandiose epoch, was there nationalism or imperialism in the vulgar and brutal sense of these terms. No doubt there was produced around Klopstock and the Bardites a curious movement that seems to foreshadow the pan-Germanism of later days. Such currents are absent from no period of German culture. But this very limited effervescence, at the end of the eighteenth century and especially before the French Revolution and Napoleon, had no importance and no grave consequences. The better German no longer thought of the principality, even though the greatest geniuses of the time had lived and worked in a petty court. He scarcely had a conception of the German nation or Reich. He affirmed the originality of the individual, or the originality of German culture, that was all. He had no settled hostility against Western thought, and not the slightest against the *Aufklärung*. Never, perhaps, had the most essential elements of Anglo-Saxon Calvinism and of French free-thought so strongly affected the religious outlook in Germany.

In this atmosphere of perfect spiritual liberty, thus constituted above the territorial barriers, the German genius, made fruitful by the Lutheran Reformation and its extensions, but moderated and pruned by influences from the West, produced its finest fruits. It addressed itself to the whole world. The time was near when England and France would have the sudden revelation of that Germany anterior to the French Revolution. The liberal rationalism and the passionate sensibility they had lavished upon Germany were to be repaid a hundredfold, within a truly European framework, in the form of a magnificent culture which is one of the purest glories of the old Continent. Leibnitz and Bach, Goethe, Herder and Schiller, Gluck and Mozart—an incomparable efflorescence of genius! This in face of a multitude of petty principalities, within which, however, was rising already the edifice constructed by Frederick II, the legislative, administrative, and military Prussia, conquering and daring, of the king who died in 1786, only a little before the French Revolution.

2. *Romanticism*

It was now that the wars of the Revolution and the Empire, coming from the West, profoundly shook Germany. The Germany of 1790 to 1815 was no longer the Germany of classicism: she had entered the *romantic* period.

Not that the classic tradition disappeared immediately after 1789. It was prolonged until the death of Goethe, Schiller, and Beethoven. All three passed through all or part of the romantic period without being infected by it. Klopstock and Herder died in 1803; Schiller in 1805; Beethoven in 1827, and Goethe, last of all, in 1832. This classicism remained, through so many vicissitudes, admirably faithful to itself. Preoccupied with man in general, with man conceived as a person and an organized Ego, it was inspired by a certain moral system that placed the individual within society but still gave consideration to his own value, his attitude as bourgeois or aristocrat, and the world of feelings and passions and possibilities that he represented. But it was just with this personal system of morals, which German classicism had gloriously constructed, mingling with it the Lutheran religious sense and the influence of the West, that romanticism was to break.

Goethe does not seem ever to have deviated from this profound individualism, which led necessarily to cosmopolitanism. It has been claimed that in his last works he sacrificed the individual to the community. This is a grave error, falsifying the interpretation of Goethe's old age. Goethe's view was that the individual and the community should be guided in common by the divine Norm, by the eternal laws of Nature, laws of "mobility," which teach change and progress, laws in virtue of which we should know how to die in order to "become." Goethe had unceasingly broadened the Leibnitz tradition, the idea of a growing perfection which the individual and consequently society would acquire through a permanent effort, through the struggle against the trials that threaten them from all directions.

Goethe's last works have one element of Christianity—they all gravitate around a theme which is none other than that of fall and redemption. Or, better, *decay* and *regeneration* of the secular individual and society, since Goethe is concerned only with life on this earth and admits human merit. Since, moreover, he takes the point of view of man's intrinsic value, he does not proclaim any people superior in principle to others. He shows no trace of nationalism. On the contrary, he does not believe that the Germans could ever form a nation. Goethe sees neither why nor how *Weltliteratur*, his universal dream, should be confined within Prussian, Austrian, or even German limits.

The same may be said of Beethoven. From his very beginnings to his last masterpieces, his music is the direct echo of *Sturm und Drang* and of the classicism of the days befo.e the French Revolution. It is impossible to see what element of the romantic it could have. Beethoven must, indeed, be dissociated from the romantic legend, which distorts him. His music is itself a sort of morality in action. Certain convictions came to Beethoven from the *Aufklärung*. He belonged to the eighteenth century. Contemporary criticism took great pains to prove it. Beethoven devoted his later life to giving expression to the revolutionary aspirations of his youth, that richer and more concrete conception of human personality, and to the emotional aspects of human nature. Inspiring influences had passed over Europe. The dogmas and forms of Christianity had been shown to be obsolete. The intelligence, on the other hand, was no longer considered the original principle of the human spirit. The individual life, with its fervours and its depressions, was concentrated, it was thought, in the soul. To some young revolutionaries who were to become classics, the soul was before all else emotion and will, but both tempered by a living reason, an inner mastery of which that admirable age ardently sought the secret. It was known— Spinoza had taught it—that the passions must be utilized by making them converge towards a focus of permanent inner energy. The rhythm of Beethoven's life and of his compositions was that of an epoch which was not romantic. A strong allegro opening, a lament in the slow movement, the brightness of gaiety and humour in the scherzo, an heroic or lively finale—such was the plan.

Beethoven maintained throughout his life his individual passion and morality. He was a fighter, and at the same time a character of great simplicity. At the centre of his conception of life was the notion of *resistance*. Nothing could break him. He triumphed over the world, like Schiller, thanks to heroic dignity (*Würde*) and sprightly grace (*Anmut*). He believed in Providence, but in a Providence that helped men only in proportion as they deserved it through their own efforts. He believed in an heroic Christ who showed us the true way of life by his own sacrifice. It was in order to translate that attitude and those convictions

that he played havoc with the whole musical heritage that had
come down to him, writing works now tense, now smiling.
Constantly advancing, he symbolized in his way the increasing
perfection that had been the religion of Leibnitz and Goethe.
His compositions culminated in the ode to joy, the hymn to
universal love, and the *"Es muss sein,"* formula of entire
renunciation, of his last and supreme triumph.

Classicism thus remained, with Goethe and Beethoven, faithful
to itself; nevertheless, between 1800 and 1805 fresh nuances
made their appearances in certain classics. They had lived long
enough to suffer from Napoleonic oppression. Before his death
Schiller wrote his *Wilhelm Tell*, a drama symbolic of Germany's
destiny. Above all, he wrote the ode *Deutsche Grösse*. The
drama was the rising of a people, begun by the organization of
regional energies in a vast conspiracy, which, however, only bore
fruit in effectual revolt through the individual initiative of Tell,
who was forced to murder the tyrant in self-defence. The ode
dates from 1801. It contains already, a curious thing, all the
essential themes of the future pan-Germanism—Germans de-
spoiled by the English on the seas and humiliated by Bonaparte
on the Continent; the Anglo-French spirit corrupted by
materialist scepticism and base utilitarianism; Germany stamped
with the seal of a special destiny, explained by her communion
with the universal Spirit and by her practice of a timeless culture;
the Lutheran Reformation considered as a guarantee of that
mission; reserves of freshness and renewal accumulated by a
Germany behind the times but called to piece together the image
of mankind which until then had been dispersed in scattered
fragments.

Herder had long broken with the *Aufklärung* and its idea of a
necessary and continuous progress of human civilization. Each
being, he thought, and each civilization carries within itself the
law of its own existence. This law is thus "willed" by God. At
an earlier time he had repudiated Frederick II and had expressed
the fear that Germany would one day be crushed between Russia
and France; he now considered that a Greater Germany uniting
Prussia and Austria had become necessary. In his ode *Germanien*,
published after his death, he sang the sacred union of all Germans.
If, finally, we recall certain patriotic tendencies evinced around
Klopstock and the *Sturm und Drang* movement, it will be seen
that since about 1790 external events had had their influence on
classicism itself. Did not the *Messiade* celebrate a fatherland

called to high destinies? Did not Klopstock discover in the *Edda* a whole assemblage of ancestral traditions to which it was necessary to return? Somewhere he claimed Ossian for Germany; the inhabitants of the British Isles were "the descendants of the bold navigators who had sailed the North Sea in the past." Finally his historic drama, devoted to Arminius, created a Germany of pure fantasy, in which he imagined that he saw perfect racial purity, the signs of clear superiority to classic antiquity itself, and a sort of new freedom proclaimed in face of Latin civilization. As for *Sturm und Drang*, originally, especially at Strasbourg, it was an exaltation of Germanism.

These were but symptoms. The movement that carried Germany toward nationalism bore fruit only in romanticism.

Romanticism was a continuation of classicism. But in the process it marked much more strongly the original positions of German thought. A philosopher-historian, Ernst Troeltsch, was able to declare in 1932 that the true elements of German thought come "solely" from romanticism. On the other hand, he contended that romanticism was simply "a classicism developed and prolonged indefinitely." It was really, be it said to correct Troeltsch's interpretation, *an unlimited universalism enclosed within nationalism.* Was it, as an outcome of the French Revolution and of Napoleonism, a German Revolution? Troeltsch declares, following Heine, that it was. Romanticism, according to him, was "*a revolution against the bourgeois spirit born of respectability; against a universal morality that should be the same for all; above all, against the scientific spirit of Western Europe, based on mathematics and mechanics; against the natural law that mixes together utilitarianism and morality; against the pale, cold abstraction of a universal humanity in which all men are equal. The Western idea of natural law had, as it were, exploded, and it was that idea that produced the well-known revolutionary upheavals.*"

Such was the negative aspect of romanticism, according to Troeltsch; here is the positive aspect:

"German romanticism was more and more consciously *a conservative revolution, contemplative and mystical, which turned to the multiple phenomena and the wealth that life brings us, and sought to isolate the deep forces underlying them and to see how there proceeds from them the magnificent world of the creations of the human mind.* From this point of view, German romanticism is logically associated with historic traditions, not with the theological or scientific currents that tend to glorify natural law, *but with the mystical and poetical doctrines which at all times have remained alien to natural law.* German romanticism loved organic, positive realities. *It saw in life, above all else, a creative Power that continually engenders the new. It celebrated the organizing Spirit in the universe that makes use of plastic forces superior to individuals.* It took pleasure in assembling those isolated individuals in *spiritual communities* incarnated, so far as the political order was concerned, in particular institutions."

Thus, in its negative aspect, romanticism was a criticism of the Latin and Western world. This criticism, we know, was latent already in Lutheranism. Between the Thirty Years War and the French Revolution it seemed to retire into the background because during that epoch Western influences, that of the France of Voltaire and Rousseau and that of Anglo-Saxon individualism, were powerfully at work in Germany. The struggle carried on by Lessing and later by the *Sturm und Drang* movement against the imitation of France was, we think, more an adjustment than a real liquidation. The formal perfection of the first classicism and its obedience to the famous rules of the unities prove this. But with romanticism the criticism became more detailed and more violent; also more unjust.

What is, in fact, *Kultur*? It is undoubtedly civilization, but civilization decked with certain religious nuances. We come back constantly to *Weltfrömmigkeit*, to that fervour for earthly life that is characteristic of the superior German. We know that we also find in it certain special tendencies of Lutheranism. Lutheranism has always sought to project the faith as it conceives it, a faith that is a comprehensive attitude of men in regard to life, to the realities of this earth, to family life, to men's trade or occupation, to the State itself. Earthly life was thus consecrated to religion. Man serves God either in gaining a living for his family, or in performing his everyday duties, or, finally, in conforming with the authority of the State. Work is thus, here below, a holy thing, the opposite of sin. Nothing prevents the individual from devoting himself entirely to his work and so acquiring a certain religious independence. He will thus remain indifferent to politics. His religious life will above all be his *private* life, his *inner* life. There was indifference in Germany to politics and to the Church, precisely because the two were too closely united. Calvin, on the contrary, placed the Church above the State. He regarded as holy the work done *for the Church and for God.* The Lutheran sought to sanctify the secular life, life outside the Church. He extended religion over everything. He did everything *with religion*, to quote Schleiermacher's formula. Here doctrinal Christianity took second place. There was substituted for it a religious life on a grand scale, which drew apart from the churches in order to throw itself into culture, later into politics, and finally into industry. Hence the fundamental *paganism*, of vast scope, of which Nietzsche and Marx were the greatest heirs.

Romanticism declared war on those *frères ennemis*, Roman Catholicism and the philosophy of the Enlightenment. It grasped the profound reason for their solidarity. The *Aufklärung* was, in the final analysis, simply a secularized Catholicism. The principles of 1789 had liberated the individual from the State in Church matters and from monarchy "by divine right." The Renaissance, the Reformation, the national State, parliamentarism, natural law, and the natural sciences had culminated in that liberation. But rationalism was at one with Catholic Christianity in affirming *the absolute dignity of the person*. On one side was authoritarianism relying on the doctrine of original sin and on the other the doctrine of liberty as a natural human right.

Territorialism, however, cut Germany off from these two European currents. It set obstacles in the path of the liberation of the middle class, thus separating Germany from the West. The ideas of the *Aufklärung* were unable to strike root in Germany either in politics or on the economic plane. Did the great rationalists, Frederick II, Lessing, or Kant, ever awaken deep echoes in the German countries? The German *Aufklärung* remained, moreover, confessional, penetrated by Christianity. The true preponderance belonged here to the Lutheran religious outlook. This, whether it were that of the Church or of the lay world, led to romanticism, to a romanticism that had drawn its inspiration from Rousseau through the classics, a romanticism that made the opposition between nature and civilization the favourite theme of its mysticism. At bottom Germany never saw in traditional Catholicism and rationalism more than the fruits and the symbols of the Roman Idea. She sought always to get free from them in order to find herself again in her integral Lutheranism or in her pagan pantheism.

Let us not forget that the epoch of the rise of Westernism coincided with the epoch of German decay. That is why Western individualism has never figured among the essential traditions of the middle class beyond the Rhine. Catholicism was isolated

from the rest of the nation. It was able to take up its position
both against the Evangelical Church and against modern industrialism. At bottom it is still a negligible quantity. Its
only possible reaction to the pantheism around it is to shrink into
itself. How could it participate in a culture that was inspired by
Protestant ideas and was nothing but a secularized Lutheranism?
How attack a world secular only in appearance? In spite of the
attempts at Germanization, Catholicism was to remain always an
exile. Lutheran Germany was to remain absolutely hostile to
the three great forms of Westernism—Roman Catholicism,
rationalist liberalism, and Anglo-Saxon individualism with its
Calvinistic tinge. Never would Germany break a lance for
freedom or progress or international solidarity, *because these were
values in which she had no share.*

Classicism had affirmed, especially through Goethe, that the
evil that gnaws at individuals and societies and kills them is dreary
inactivity, stagnation, paralysing conservatism, or, conversely, the
lack of balance due to passionate desires, the anarchy, the revolution, which has no positive aim and seeks only to destroy. The
romantics took up this idea and outlook. They generalized it,
applying it particularly to the France of the old monarchy, of the
Revolution of 1789, and of Napoleon. It was that immense
oscillation that disturbed them, that they found unpardonable.
They saw in it *a blow at the laws of life.* They, too, readily accepted
the Renaissance, the Reformation, the new science and religion.
They did not dream of denying the progress made since the
sixteenth century. They were keenly alive to the incredible
diversification of values, the national differentiations, and the
immense wealth of European life. They were well aware that
the mediæval unity was bound to end at some time because it was
too poor to satisfy so many needs and aspirations. But they
were afraid of the menace of anarchy, afraid of the dissolution of
culture.

They then charged the Renaissance and the Reformation with
having been too favourable to that dissolution. The continually
increasing mechanization of life, the maintenance of separation
between individuals, the atomization of society by the destruction
of its natural groups, the suppression of all living communion
between men and the universe—all this was *ruining faith*, faith
as the German romantics conceived it, the fervent religious
feeling we have described. That was what they could not
forgive in the Roman Idea, in French liberalism, and in Anglo-

Saxon Calvinism. *This, beyond all doubt, was the beginning of the great German protest against modern mechanization.* Classicism had first uttered the protest. Romanticism made the protest its own. Germany began to blame the West for all the troubles from which she suffered through her own fault; she sought to pin the responsibility for them on the English and the French.

She carried this criticism of the Roman Idea, in the forms of Catholicism, free-thought, and individualism, into philosophy, ethics, and politics. It was a condemnation from which there was no appeal. It led Germany far, simply because she was so ready, in the very vehemence and injustice of her criticism, to confuse certain blemishes of her own with those she alleged against the outer world. All this embittered argument, in which ignorance mingles with disparagement, is to be found assembled in Thomas Mann's *Betrachtungen eines Unpolitischen,* published in 1917.

Read, for example, the third of Schleiermacher's discourses on religion, and it will be seen that his attack is directed less against the *Aufklärung* in itself than against the *Aufklärung* in the forms it has assumed in Germany. He attacks it as a false science that is spreading everywhere and, in his opinion, killing the religious spirit, the spirit that brings us into direct and intimate communion with the Infinite. Abandon, he said, arid geometrism and rationalism. Grasp, by intuition, the whole man and the whole universe, and then set them into relation with each other. Is there not in feeling a spontaneous reality that cannot be regulated in advance, that refuses to submit to the tyranny of external laws, of conventions and precepts?

Poor men, imagining that their petty activity exhausts the possibilities of life! Schleiermacher has in view, in these pages, the narrow and paltry philistinism that had been spread throughout Germany by a misinterpreted rationalism. Why should young souls be killed by the abuse of analysis and the search for superficial explanations? How long were unsullied minds, made for the intuitive knowledge of divine things, to be kept from them? How long were they to be driven simply into eudemonism, towards a science of earthly happiness, towards a utilitarianism that ruined in them all spontaneity and all disinterestedness? This pamphlet needs to be read in order to understand the full violence of the romanticist protest. And Schleiermacher is not unaware that that arid rationalism throws many weak intelligences into the opposite extreme, into a false mysticism and a thousand emotional and intellectual aberrations.

The criticism is just in itself, but it goes too far.   It is directed against the Western cultures in order the better to glorify the Germanic spirit, to which a sovereign mission is assigned, that of regenerating the world.

For this criticism is primarily metaphysical.   Fichte simultaneously attacked Latin and Jewish thought, charging them with a sterilizing intellectualism.   This is the explanation of his hatred of the eighteenth century, of his idea that Frenchmen, Italians, and Spaniards speak only a dead language, and that, in particular, French philosophy is decadent because it is occupied only with inert concepts.   Hegel is more moderate than Fichte, understanding the importance of Kant and of 1789, of the broad universalism that exerted so profound an influence over Europe. But he charges him with abstractness and with leading to pure individualism, which enables him to claim for Germany the right and the duty of saving the old Continent.

This criticism is still religious because, Protestant and Lutheran in inspiration, it glorifies the German Reformation and disparages Roman Catholicism, free-thought, and Calvinism, sources of the modern dissociations.   But let us not forget that it also, in such Catholicizing writers as Novalis, F. Schlegel, and Görres, sets the Germanically inspired neo-Catholicism against Latin or French Catholicism.   The latter is charged with having passed from Gallicanism to ultramontanism, thus provoking, moreover, the rupture of 1789.   Mystical and theosophical, harsh and scornful, this criticism has its origin in the religious fervour which, returning to Christianity, utilizes it for the dream of a national German religion.

On the social and political plane, attacks were multiplied against France, which, through the wars of the Revolution and the Empire, had profoundly shaken Germany.   Her oscillations were considered unpardonable.   She was blamed above all for having twice sought to impose on Europe her clear, rational, centralizing genius.   It was not 1789 *qua* Revolution that demanded the mocking attention of the romantics.   In their early youth they had all shared the revolutionary enthusiasm of the first days. What they reproved with growing horror was the logical character and the fixed principles of 1789, its passionate egalitarianism, its ideas on universal progress.   And they were no more indulgent to Napoleonism, though they secretly admired it.

So many wars and very legitimate reactions created an abyss between conquering France and the Germany awakened by

romanticism. In face of the French State and of the English constitutional monarchy the romantics, as is well known, set up
the organic State, a living synthesis of unitarism and federalism,
of monarchism and republicanism, a State already "totalitarian."
A society that aimed at perfection, to be realized by Prussia within
the Lutheran fold, by Austria in the Catholic environment, and
finally by the future Reich in a system still vaster. A well-
balanced State because it would introduce so-called "natural"
groups between the nation and its individuals. This conception,
an admirable protection for the privileged classes, who made use
of romanticism to save their traditional positions and to destroy
the principles of 1789—this conception of the State merged into
the earliest pan-Germanism.

It is evident why pre-1815 romanticism aimed at the regeneration of Europe. Read Novalis' *Die Christenheit oder Europa*.
From the moment when the decline of Germany and of Central
Europe began through the Enlightenment, from the moment
when the latter set itself against any synthesis between emotion
and reason, it became necessary for Germany, by establishing that
magic bond, to regenerate the Continent by regenerating herself.
How to establish a precise distinction between healthy or legitimate romanticism and an arrogant romanticism, ready to turn
toward pan-Germanism? The protest was of importance only
in so far as it concerned Germany. The attempt at salvation
similarly concerned her alone. But on both sides there was an
extension of the conflict.

Romanticism was claiming, in the last analysis, what the
German classics had demanded already on the basis of a broad
cosmopolitanism. It was talking in its turn of *salvation* and
regeneration. But whereas the classics had written at first solely
from the point of view of individual morality, later proceeding to
social or political considerations, and in doing so had invoked
nature or had chosen ancient Greece as model, the romantics
proposed the entire regeneration of Germany and Europe under
the modernized and secularized Christianity they themselves
followed. But modernization and secularization meant simply
and purely Germanization. A Germanic Christianity, superior
to the old confessions—such was their common dream. It is
the dream of the Hitlerites of to-day. The German romantics
believed they had discovered true Christianity. Only the
Germans, they thought, could comprehend it, and restore the
knowledge of it to a Europe thirsting for universal religion after

so much aridity, after the great anarchy that had sown dissension between Catholics and free-thinkers and theosophists, and brought the various national cultures into collision. To return to a new mediævalism, to re-create Catholicism in such guise that it should be German, to restore the unity of the past in the German style, the union between temporal and spiritual—such was the programme. A free and bold Catholicism, bound already to the Austrian reaction that was to follow the Congress of Vienna. Alongside it, Prussian neo-Protestantism, claiming that Lutheranism alone is in conformity with the Gospel and will one day create a Universal Church of the German Nation.

While the Protestants proceeded from Christ to the Church, and declared that individual piety is the solid foundation of religious universalism, the Catholics, in Schleiermacher's formula, proceeded from the Church to Christ, declaring that in their renewed Church they would make room for the demands of the subjective conscience and piety. For Novalis this was *the true German Revolution*, which must oppose and obstruct the work of the French Revolution as well as of Protestantism and mediæval Catholicism, both of which had degenerated. Germany, he said in his pamphlet of 1799, must not allow France to be alone in having a European programme, that of Western rationalism. Germany was imagining in her turn, and poetically creating, her political, social, and religious Gospel. As the country of true poetry, she was forming the exalting vision of the political order of the morrow. The mediæval City was ended. Sixteenth-century Protestantism had brought the decay of religion. Science and the Enlightenment were corrupting men's minds. There remained regeneration by romanticism, the *Concordantia Catholica* of the future, a sort of Teuton Peace!

A strange mixture of cosmopolitanism and nationalism was this dream of Novalis'. He wanted a new clergy and nobility, fighting together for the Church which, with a reconstructed Papacy, should dominate the national States. The schism of the sixteenth century had destroyed the mystical Community of aforetime, loosening the stones of the edifice; it had confined religion within the limits of the State, had exposed the Bible to all sorts of interpretations, had dissolved the ecclesiastical institution into sects scattered over the surface of the Continent, and had assured the triumph of a mechanistic science: German romanticism would rise and *re-establish the bonds destroyed*.

His book thus closed on the idea of a German Revolution, a true vision of Ezekiel: life was to be infused into the bones scattered over the plain. From this point of view, Germany was *ahead* of the other peoples, it would be said, because she possessed the secret of the true life and the true thought. She would give birth to the higher culture that would assure her an absolute preponderance over other nations. *She would be the country of the great Conciliation. It was she who would make the Saviour visible to believers.* A strange vision, prelude to that which Richard Wagner, in the midst of the Bismarckian Empire, was one day to envelop in his enchanting music, the vision of Parsifal, of the German Parsifal, who should heal the kingdom of the Grail—that is to say, Europe—of all the ills from which it suffered.

All romanticism and all pan-Germanism are there in a nutshell. To Germany were to be confided the United States of Europe. She, she alone, would create them.

In the philosophical domain to begin with. Fichte, who opposed German philosophy to Western thought, believed himself to be the supreme representative of that philosophy. To reconstruct Humanity, to inaugurate a universal era, was not that to be, after Jesus and Luther, the third liberator? For the Germans, he said, lived only for that higher aim, of the *mythical* order, which individuals, when they are members of a true community, represent collectively and feel to be above them. This image alone awakened true liberty in men. Germany was the people of peoples because she knew that truth is taught *by constraint* and *by education*, thanks to the reign of the Wise.

Hegel, too, lived the drama of his time. His dream, since his youth, had been of a popular, national religion, created by Germany, excluding all Jewish intellectualism. That spiritual power would mould the amorphous mass charged with a high mission. An enlightened despotism of a new model, claiming to found true liberty. *Germany had the right and the duty to project her national image over all Europe.* The premier people was the ripened people, authentic representative of the universal Spirit (*Träger des Weltgeistes*). For Napoleon, substitute *Bonapartism of the German type*, which understood the mystery of the organizing intelligence.

This thought was thus religious. The effort toward mystical, mythical, and theological reconstruction made between about 1800 and 1820 by Protestants, Catholics, and theosophists beyond the Rhine was immense. In that synthesis there was a healthy and fruitful element. We owe much to Schleiermacher, Möhler, and Baader. The Christian confessions and theosophy sought mutual completion. A sincere enthusiasm here evoked new horizons. But the national preoccupation is visible everywhere. Fichte said that Germans alone could understand Christian liberty, that the Germanic soil was the only one on which the divine seed could bear fruit. After Luther, all Germany had lived in the noble anguish for eternal salvation, individual and collective. For Hegel the Reformation was an entire spiritual revelation. For Görres the Germans were the chosen people because they had "new blood and divine ideas." A sort of racialism, religious and not yet biological like that of the present day, was already exercising men's minds.

Thus the social and political vision was mixed up with the religious and ecclesiastical programme. Certainly that ideal of collective organization claiming to combine monarchy and republic, centralism and federalism, did not lack grandeur. The romanticist State had for its sole foundation German philosophy. It was its direct expression. The Divine Spirit, it was said, was on the verge of incarnation in the concrete form that was being prepared for it by Germany in travail with unity. *This creation would be both liberal and conservative.* The component parts of the nation would have a certain degree of liberty and autonomy, but under the control of the central authority. A relative liberalism would deliver the individual from the old absolutism and would regenerate the politically and economically impotent middle class. On the other hand, a conservatism, also relative— Protestant and Prussian, Catholic and Austrian—would succeed in maintaining the monarchy, the clergy, and the nobility, while granting to the people its indispensable prerogatives. Germany would thus build up the total Reich, the model Society. Thus we can understand why, half a century later, Marx confided to the same Reich the mission of carrying integral Socialism into practice.

Nowhere did the romantic spirit show itself more fully than in art and poetry. Here it was able to construct visions entirely independent of reality, to express by symbols or allegories a philosophy which was itself nothing but an exalting dream. To renew concrete institutions, that is to say, Churches, States, the Reich, the whole political and social body, was more difficult.

In this æsthetic reconstruction the plastic arts did not play a leading part. The abstract and symbolic character of romanticism lent itself with difficulty to pictorial representation and offered little inspiration to sculptors or architects. One need say no more of the work of such men as Cornelius, Overbeck, and Schnorr von Carelsfeld. On the other hand, poetry and music were fully represented. The first romantic school was the beginning of a movement that carried with it almost every writer and every type of literature. Weber, Schumann, and Schubert expressed in music a little later the most original aspects of romanticism. The year 1813 saw the birth of the man who was to incarnate those dreams and that ideology in his marvellous music —Richard Wagner. He thus prolonged German romanticism until near the end of the nineteenth century. He caused the whole substance of it to pass beyond the frontiers of Germany.

Romanticist poetry aimed very consciously at being the complete image of reality or, if you like, to be reality organically represented and restored to the mind by the magic of art. That was the theme of Friedrich Schlegel in the Jena "*Athenäum.*" The work of art was to be "organic," like life itself. It was Goethe's lesson, but taken up anew, expanded, and made into a system. All life must be *poetized*, in order to do away with the abyss that commonly separates prose from poetry, the daily existence from its eternal ends. Render poetry living, and life poetic. Goethe had said this already when he compared poetry to the true *labour* that extracts from the entrails of the real the hidden treasure, the precious solid metal, the eternal wisdom which the earth infallibly teaches us.

Romanticist poetry was thus poetry "of progressive universality." All true poetry was for that very reason romantic. Conversely, all true romanticism was poetry. Science, poetry, and art were indissolubly associated. The poet disposed of the whole universe. He treated it as he chose—by philosophy, by science, or by pure poetry. He *organized* it or, what amounted to the same thing, he brought it into harmony with his own spirit, which, thus floating above all things, experienced infinite freedom. This was romanticist irony, in its deepest significance. It made us penetrate into the mystery of the world, which was at the same time the mystery of our spirit, into those irrational realities which the most rigorous analysis could not exhaust. It was by this irony that we absorbed all reality into poetry, that is to say, into an organic vision that simplifies it by distilling from it the best of its substance.

The poet had the power to discover and to reveal these aspects of life, through which it expressed an eternal verity. He had the right to apprehend it and to render it symbolically. The romantics took up Goethe's phrase, "All that happens has but symbolic value." But they insisted on the term "symbol." Where Goethe introduced into his works the most concrete and the most plastic visions, mingling them with the most living and the most profound symbolism, the romantics absorbed the real in the symbol. The *Ofterdingen* of Novalis is in this respect the unequalled model of the type. The hero of the story sees his whole life, as though in anticipation, in an initial dream that makes the "Blue Flower" appear to him. This is nothing else than the magic power that is given us to reduce reality to a dream. In the *Hymnen an die Nacht* illusory images and acts of the Day melt into the august and benevolent Night. Day hardens the elements, separating them from one another. Night alone is guarantor of our absolute communion with the universe. In *Die Lehrlinge in Sais* Novalis dreams—that is to say, poetically reconstructs—the whole life of nature. And, in *Die Christenheit oder Europa*, does not Novalis poetically build up the New Society, the New Church, the union so greatly desired between the spiritual and the temporal, between the ideal and the real?

All avenues had thus been traced, whether for æsthetics or for the various literary types, by the first romantic school. The literature of this period pursued them all to the end. Inspired by its principal prophets, it dreamed of nature, man, love, society, and the State. It transposed into its own keys the essential themes of the *Sturm und Drang* and of classicism. It lived and made its readers live in the wonderful, in a sort of perpetual miracle, in a special, magical atmosphere through which were sensed or perceived bonds between things and beings, bonds that remained unknown to the common herd, to thought that lacks subtlety, and to reasoning that lacks concentration. In this field the philosophy, the religious outlook, and the literature of romanticism were a conscious and permanent *organicism* which, transcending the hardening illusions of the normal senses and reason, claimed to discover and at the same time to create a world of marvels into which only the initiated could penetrate.

Novalis had himself declared that this poetry was music, music both of the soul and of the universe. Here again, music made its appearance rather later. But had not Tieck and Wackenroder defined in anticipation the new rôle it was to play? Had they not mingled it intimately with their harmonious prose, writing almost "in music"? The days were near when Wagner was to translate into music the *Märchen*, the romantic short story. To unite the dance, mimicry, poetry, and music in the comprehensive work of art, to represent the permanent and organically complete human tragedy by bodily gestures, by the linking of verses and situations, and by the resources of the singing voice and of orchestral harmony, was to bring romanticism to its completion.

That is why pan-Germanism took shape in Germany at that time. The external conditions were favourable to its birth. The shock which the wars of the Revolution and the Empire had given Germany was severe. On the other hand, German thought was ripe for this creation, since union was about to be achieved between the secularized and theosophical Christianity of the Germans and their apologia for *Volkstum*, for the religious and national Community. On a closer view it will be seen that the main lines of the later pan-Germanism were traced in this period.

We noted certain nationalist tendencies in the classics. Romanticism went far beyond them. Philosophical pan-Germanism made its appearance with Fichte and with the works of Hegel that were published before the Congress of Vienna. For Fichte, Germany was the Nation *par excellence*, and consequently had the right to achieve the foundation of her nationhood by *force* and *to use further force and also trickery* to assure its hegemony, even though it should resort to the craftiest Machiavellism. Hegel, in his youthful works, appealed for the *strong Master who should mould the German masses*, which had remained amorphous. To be free in the German sense was *to be capable of leading the world by thought*. Only the German Mind, incarnation of the Universal Mind, knew how society and the world should be rightly organized. Hence its right to pre-eminence. Schelling said almost the same thing, and his whole philosophy taught, alongside the hegemony of conscious thought, the concrete hegemony of the future Reich.

Religious pan-Germanism, for its part, announced Germanic Christianity. It desired inter-confessional unity, to be achieved in a national religion. This was once more Fichte, conceiving himself as a third Revealer after Christ and Luther. It was Hegel, declaring that the Teutons were an unsullied aspiration, a great will, ready for a thousand possibilities, and that the German people was predestined to achieve true Christianity. The Catholics spoke almost the same language, and, all in all, their *Concordantia* was simply a restoration of the Holy Roman Empire.

The idea of Race appears here already.   Jahn, in 1809, declared
that the Germans were the nationality that most perfectly expressed
pure Humanity.   If Germany was at the moment in mourning,
let her be consoled, for one day she should reign over Europe.
She was the Holy Race, which would succeed the Hebrews and
the Hellenes.   Hegel did not hesitate to pronounce her pure from
all admixture.   This racialism remained religious.   It had not
yet the biological resonance of to-day.

The geographical or historical demonstration was already at
hand.   Arndt supplied it in 1803, when he showed that each
State must fight the neighbour States when they rob it of the air
and light it needs for development.   Here, fully armed, was the
notion of *Lebensraum*!   The partition of Poland and the annexation of Holland and Switzerland—all these seemed to Arndt to
be natural conquests.   Hegel loaded himself with historical
arguments.   The "Germanic Moment," he thought, followed
the "Roman Moment,"   The Reformation proved it.   "Since
the Germanic Empire," he said, "is the empire over the whole,
we see clearly repeated in it all the earlier epochs."   Here were
the first outlines of the continental programme, to say nothing
of the colonial programme!   The movement continued thereafter
without interruption.

Between 1790 and 1815, with romanticism, *Weltfrömmigkeit*
turned into *Reichsfrömmigkeit*.   The old classic religious outlook
had become the religion of the Holy Roman Empire of the
German Nation, the dream of a future Reich which would not
forget that it had existed historically in the past.

3. *Frederician Prussia and the Länder*

While German culture and thought, inspired by a secularized
Christianity that was gradually turning to paganism or to a new
theosophical conception of religion, advanced to the conception
of the nation and traced the lines of the future Reich, outward
events in Germany, between 1790 and 1815, took the form of
grave upheavals.   The old Holy Roman Empire, the territories
(*Länder*), and Prussia underwent profound modifications which
culminated, after the Vienna Congress, in the Germanic Confederation, with its forty States dominated by Prussia and Austria,
Prussia being certain one day to gain the upper hand.

First of all came the complete and final crumbling of the Holy

Roman Empire. The signs of this dissolution were evident between 1750 and 1790; only the territories counted any longer. Never had the Empire appeared in a more pitiful guise; it calls to mind irresistibly the admirable pages devoted to it by Goethe in his *Memoirs*. Was not the coronation of the last Emperor the final effulgence of the imperial institution before its extinction? Did not the magnificent procession that emerged from Frankfort Cathedral symbolize the visions of extraordinary and melancholy sumptuousness that immediately precede the end of great historic forms? Already at Wetzlar, as at Frankfort, Goethe had realized the extreme decrepitude of the Empire. He gives a marvellous description of the *Reichskammergericht*, in which so many cases were piling up, and in which all the juridical instruments of the past lay in disorder.

When the French Revolution broke out it brought the end of the Holy Roman Empire. The first stage in its destruction covers the years 1792 to 1797. Austria and Prussia, out to restore the French monarchy at the instance of the French *émigrés*, were beaten at Valmy. "A new era is opening!" exclaimed Goethe. The legitimism of the East had been conquered by the republicanism of the West, the army of mercenaries by that of the people, the pursuit of heterogeneous ends destitute of idealism by an enthusiasm sure of its methods. The victory of France was confirmed after 1793. She acquired the right bank of the Rhine. With the Rhine lost, the Holy Roman Empire lost all reason for existence. Already Prussia and Austria were seeking compensation by means of the secularization of the ecclesiastical territories. And between 1797 and 1799 there came the appalling deals of the Congress of Rastatt.

The second coalition led, in 1801, to the Treaty of Lunéville. This time the victor was named Bonaparte. His plan was very simple. After destroying the Holy Roman Empire he would make Prussia and Austria neutralize each other. He would do this by creating smaller States strong enough to defend themselves against either Austria or Prussia but not strong enough to carry on a high policy of their own. Above all, they would be able to assist France with their troops. The ordinance of February 25, 1803, suppressed by a stroke of the pen a hundred petty territories. At the same time it set Catholicism free and made it a popular reality. The States of Hesse, Nassau, Baden, Württemberg, and Bavaria saw the light. Austria, however, gained nothing. She was considered to be sufficiently provided for. Prussia received enough territory to be able to consider herself thereafter as powerful as her rival.

After the third coalition, on August 6, 1806, Francis II abdicated the imperial dignity. This time the end had come of the Holy Roman Empire. Thereafter Prussia and the other German States acted together in freedom from all historical fetters. The Empire was dead. Long live the Empire! The whole thought of that epoch, we know, kept the idea alive.

It was not enough for the Empire to fall. Its area was transferred now from two hundred and thirty-four to forty territories (*Länder*). This territorial simplification is the second important historic act of that memorable epoch. The process was completed in two successive phases. In the first, on the left bank of the Rhine, ninety-seven territories were suddenly amalgamated into four *départements*; in the second, a hundred-odd territories were reduced to a dozen new States. An admirable stratagem, invented by Napoleon. Prussia had every interest in favouring a regrouping that enabled her to unite Protestant with Catholic territories. On the other hand, the smaller States could feel nothing but lively gratitude toward Napoleon, since the disappearance of municipal, aristocratic, and ecclesiastical *Länder* was complete. In its early days the dynasties had saved the Lutheran Reformation. Then, in the seventeenth and eighteenth centuries, they had adopted in Germany, though on the territorial plane, the principles of French centralization. From 1803 onward they added to them those of the Revolution and of Bonapartism.

From these territorial upheavals and concentrations there issued, in 1815, a Germany greatly simplified and modernized. It comprised: (1) the States of the north, spread over the plain, all of reduced size and reactionary tendency, with their old dynasties and their traditional social classes; (2) the States of the south-west, more modern because created by Napoleon, States almost without a history, centralized like France, bureaucratic in structure, and relatively open to Western influences; and finally (3) Prussia, hesitating between East and West, between the conservatism of the former and the modernism of the latter—eminently the country of compromise. What wonder that there came promptly into the mind of Baron vom Stein the idea of a new nation, a Greater Germany comprising Prussia, Austria, and the States of the south-west?

At the time of the third coalition, in 1805, it had been precisely the smaller States that had profited from Napoleon's victories. As they supplied troops to the Emperor, he installed his creatures at their head and conferred on them full sovereignty in return. Bavaria and Württemberg became kingdoms. Baden was transformed into a grand duchy. Napoleon knew how to utilize egoism everywhere. He created the Confederation of the Rhine, of which he became Protector, a true *Staatenbund* or federation for defined purposes of otherwise independent States, the first beginning of the Germanic Confederation. Abandoning the imperial rubbish-heap, sixteen German princes proclaimed their independence and promised 60,000 men to Napoleon. Napoleon assured them the most absolute liberty of action in home affairs and demanded from them the most complete submission on the European plane. The princes knew that the second clause would not last for ever, and made sure before all else of the first one. Never had territorial egoism reached such heights as at the very moment when the outlines of the future unity were beginning to appear. Never had national humiliation been so deep, through the princes' own fault. Napoleon was imitating the Papacy of the past in allying himself with the German particularisms.

France had thus provoked in the German countries a true territorial revolution. It may be asked whether Germany would have undertaken of her own accord so drastic a reduction. It needed the enthusiasm of the revolutionary armies and the Napoleonic troops to drive her to it. On the morrow of Jena, the German States were no longer associated. Prussia was beaten and Austria had lost contact with Germany. From then on the opposition between North and South-west was accentuated. In the North, old methods and obsolete institutions predominated. The smaller the territories, the more tenaciously the past system was adhered to. All aspects of absolutism were represented there—court absolutism in "electoral" Hesse-Cassel, middle-class oligarchy in the Hansa towns, and oligarchies of nobles in Saxony, in the States of Thuringia, in Hanover, and in Mecklenburg. Everywhere the most effete Lutheran spirit reigned. The old privileged classes and the tradition of absolute monarchy were maintained here in full.

The States of the south-west, on the contrary, were endowed with Napoleonic constitutions. Drawn up on the Western plan and following the French model, they were to some extent inspired by natural law. Their system was based on the separa-

tion of powers and on a constitutional régime. Montesquieu
and the Constitution of 1791, with the modifications Napoleon
had introduced into it, served as their sources. The entry into
force of this system was facilitated by the fact that Napoleon
impressed on it the seal of imperial absolutism. From 1805 to
1815, in the preparatory decade, the whole Confederation of the
Rhine obeyed his orders. There was less insistence in the smaller
States on parliamentarism than on administrative centralization,
and on the employment of the prefectural system which had been
elaborated in France by the monarchy, the first Republic, and Bonapartism. Here were united the elements of a political system that
was *both absolutist and liberal*. They were established in the German
South-west by France. They bore fruit later under Bismarck.

All this was quite apart from what Prussia herself owed to
France. The fall of the Empire and the territorial simplification,
which set face to face the northern States and those of the south-
west, gave full significance to her future destiny.

Between 1740 and 1786, just at the time of the great advance of
German culture, Prussia had been formed and aggrandized by
Frederick II. She had already been steadily rising between 1650
and 1740. Under Frederick II she became the great State whose
firm framework was to prove indispensable for the coming
unification of Germany.

The external policy and the territorial conquests of Frederick II
assumed a definitely *revolutionary* aspect in his own day. On
this essential point it was once more Goethe who, in his *Memoirs*,
showed the true significance of the phenomenon. In a few years
Frederick II had overthrown the whole of the old territorial
order. He was not content with establishing the predominance
of Prussia over Austria. He showed himself much the greatest
and most powerful among the German princes. In a few
pregnant lines Goethe recalled that public opinion had divided
into two camps in face of the policy of the *accomplished fact*, of
the incontestable victories of Frederick II. Some refused to
accept this violation of public order. Others saw in it, on the
contrary, more or less clearly, a revolutionary phenomenon of
vast importance to the future of the German countries. It was
in every respect a triumph of the colonization of the German East
over the older but much less coherent colonization of the West.
And, above all, in the East itself, the preponderance of the North
over the South was assured for all time by the conquest of Silesia.

The external policy of Frederick William I had proved feeble:

that of Frederick II had been violent and decisive.   His ambition had been to transform Prussia into a European Power, so as to utilize every opportunity of action.   It was a vain dream, Prussia not being able to play the part of a great Continental State by herself.   But it was a fruitful dream as regarded the part she was to play in the building of German unity.   Frederick II knew in 1740 that Austria was in a wretched situation and that Maria Theresa, in spite of her personal qualities and her strength of character, was very inexperienced in politics and was ill seconded by her husband.   The first Silesian war and the opening of the war of the Austrian Succession between 1740 and 1744;   the second Silesian war and the end of the war of the Austrian Succession between 1744 and 1748;   the Seven Years War from 1756 to 1763;   the alliance with Russia and the first partition of Poland between 1764 and 1776;   finally the League of Princes in 1785, a year before Frederick's death—all these were events and exploits that contributed not a little to the prestige of Prussia and opened surprising perspectives for the future.   At the end of his life Frederick could flatter himself that he had accomplished a great task.   He had exerted decisive influence over German history, considered in relation to contemporary European history.   In making Prussia into a strong State, he had modified the whole European constellation.   He had laid the foundations for a reconstruction of Germany.   The French Revolution and the Napoleonic wars themselves contributed greatly to the territorial simplification of Germany, but it was plainly to Frederick that the credit for it was mainly due.

The internal reorganization of Prussia was of no less importance. It began between 1745 and 1755, during the decade following the Treaty of Dresden.   It was at that period that there was formed in Frederick's mind the curious conception of the State and of the monarchy that he owed to the philosophy of the Enlightenment, a conception that favoured, to some extent, the birth in Germany of a political liberalism *sui generis*.   Frederick did away with monarchy "by divine right," but left monarchical absolutism intact.   He saw in the prince simply the first servant of the State. He thus prepared the way for the conception which, at the opening of the nineteenth century, was to place both parliament and the monarch under the Constitution (*Verfassung*).   The supreme duty of the prince was to procure for his subjects the maximum of well-being and of culture.   He allowed a certain play to individual initiative.

The upshot was that it was the king's task to govern. Consequently Frederick proceeded early to a first attempt at administrative and judicial reform and to an economic effort that claimed, under the mercantile system, to favour manufactures and in particular the silk industry. A further object of his was increased unification in communications and increase of the external commerce of the Prussian State. Agriculture was also the subject of special attention. As for military organization, Frederick had little reason to alter anything in his heritage. After the Seven Years War he sought to heal the wounds the State had suffered. He carried out a vast programme of reform. He worked for the re-establishment of his kingdom by personal visits, on which he took note of all its needs. The finances were not in a bad state, and the king was able to venture on a restoration on a grand scale that benefited all classes. The consolidation of the public finances, attention to industry, the re-establishment of a balance between industry and agriculture, the practice of the broadest tolerance, in religion and education, for the various confessions, the most careful attention to schools and universities —such were the steps that might be expected of a victorious monarch.

It is difficult, however, to judge these internal reforms. It is known that Mirabeau, who was in Prussia in 1786 and 1787 and published two volumes on the state of the kingdom, predicted the early ruin of the Prussian State and the rapid decay of Fredericianism. The years that followed seemed to justify his prediction. But how can we leave out of account the incalculable consequences of that historic phenomenon? Mirabeau's criticism was directed especially to economic problems. It was inspired by the ideas of the Physiocrats and the Free Traders. On that point the French writer was right. It was when mercantilism was abandoned that the efforts of Frederick II bore fruit.

To reconstitute the public fortune and finances, to place the necessary resources at the disposal of the executive power, to risk an ambitious population policy, to centralize the administration of the State, to create in it a uniform commercial domain, to develop exports and to attract capital to the country, to support industry without neglecting agriculture, to accord to the nobility sufficient privileges to make sure of its services, and thus to create the aristocratic, bureaucratic, and military Prussia, adding to borrowings from France institutions of Lutheran origin—this was assuredly a grandiose task.

Nevertheless, the great mistake, the mistake truly fatal for Germany, had been made. The great king had neglected the middle class. The towns remained cut off from the countryside. Frederick II weakened them in order to set limits to their independence, thus compromising the political education of his best subjects, paralysing the spirit of economic enterprise, and creating a momentous and permanent hiatus in German political life. Never did Frederick dream of extending the benefit of the Enlightenment to the so-called lower classes. He enforced absolute obedience on the masses, especially the peasant masses. They were given only the rudiments of education, at a time when compulsory education was already beginning. In short, Frederick contributed more to the material improvement of the lives of his subjects than to their cultural advance. The lasting element of his system was the idea of "service," of social service as a duty of princes, nobles, and officials.

Under Frederick William II, from 1786 to 1797, Prussia grew considerably in extent. She acquired in 1791 the margraviate of Anspach and Bayreuth, in 1793 part of Poland, namely Danzig, Thorn, and a large part of Posen; in 1795, after the third partition of Poland, she received new territories in the east. But these aggrandizements did not consolidate the Prussian State. They did not even guarantee the power it had acquired under Frederick II. Frederick William II was succeeded by the weak Frederick William III, a monarch of the best intentions but entirely lacking decision. His neutrality in regard to Napoleon alienated many sympathies. He did nothing to correct administrative abuses. The organization of the Cabinet Council separated him from his ministers. The army remained stationary in every respect. There were too many old officers. Too much attention was paid to parades. An antiquated absolutism and a meddlesome bureaucracy stifled in Prussia the sense of duty and the readiness to make sacrifices for the State. The Polish acquisitions, which made of Prussia a semi-Slav State, enervated it. Everywhere was the corruption which Mirabeau had already seen so clearly. This was internal and external decay. It ended in the defeat at Jena in 1806 and the Peace of Tilsit in 1807.

Thus it was again through Prussia that the passage was to be made, as in culture, from cosmopolitanism to nationalism, this time under the brutal pressure of the Napoleonic dictatorship. All the German patriotism of the epoch, called forth by the wars of the Revolution and of the Empire, turned to the Prussia of

Frederick II. Between 1807 and 1813 Prussia was the scene of a momentous recovery well known to historians. A curious alliance is, however, to be observed there between the Prussian institutions of the Lutheran past and the principles of the *Auf-klärung* (Enlightenment) or of the French Revolution. This alliance was, indeed, in the tradition of Frederick II. Hardenberg and Stein realized, in fact, that it was impossible to raise Prussia from her ruin and her humiliation without politically modernizing her, that it was impossible to have the support of a people devoted to the patriotic cause and ready for the indispensable sacrifices without giving the people an interest in public affairs.

Hence the idea was born of the abolition of peasant serfdom and the grant of administrative autonomy to the towns, the rural districts (*Landgemeinde*), the *Kreise* embracing a number of districts, and the provinces. Hence, too, came the institution of the *Reichsstände* or consultative councils drawn from the professions.

Stein achieved only the first two reforms. The abolition of serf-dom naturally provoked a violent reaction among the privileged classes. It was not genuinely achieved until much later. Stein also modified the Government, replacing provincial ministers by ministers for special administrative branches who were responsible for the whole country. He installed at the head of the Govern-ment a Prime Minister who had direct access to the king, and finally he separated the judiciary from the administration. Hardenberg completed this reform on the financial and econo-mic side. In 1810 and 1811 came the introduction of free enterprise (*Gewerbefreiheit*); in 1812 Jewish rights were recognized. The edifice was crowned by army reform. The system of mercenaries was replaced by that of obligatory service. Finally the University of Berlin was created and substantial efforts were made for the moral regeneration of the people. There followed, in 1813 and 1814, victory.

Thus Prussia, which had not followed the example of the South-west, but had remained faithful to its traditional organiza-tion, endowed itself, by adopting certain Western principles, with a restored administration, a broadened Government, a freer urban middle class, a peasantry that was beginning to emerge from serfdom, and even a rudimentary form of parliamentarism. From now on it appeared a *model State*, a sort of ellipse—the Constitution to come—with two foci, one of them the monarchy, disposing with its governmental organs of the executive power, and the other the representation of all social classes. The shadow of Austria still stretched over Prussia, hindering the realization of Stein's ideas. A further half-century, and the obstacle was removed.

In 1815 Austria found herself assigned territories that turned her from her traditional policy; Prussia rounded herself off and prepared to link up East and West. She had had the good fortune to lose the Polish regions that had been exerting too much Slav influence over her. Thereafter she was composed of two distinct groups—the old provinces of the east, with some Polish elements, and on the west Rhineland and Westphalia. It had been hoped to weaken her by multiplying her frontiers. In reality the gap between the east and the west of the northern plain was closed. Thus Prussia was able to accomplish the mission of hegemony that destiny seems to have held in store for her.

The great problem that then demanded universal attention was that of *union between Prussia and the Reich.*

Under the compulsion of misfortunes which opened new economic perspectives for Germany while modifying the ancestral relations between the social classes, Prussia, as she passed from defeat to victory, had had to strengthen her political, administrative, and military framework. At the same time, romanticism, which had proceeded directly from classicism, elaborated a vast programme of national regeneration. Prussia, however, while adopting a certain measure of the innovations of the French Revolution and Empire, opposed to them her ancient monarchical and territorial traditions. And we see detaching themselves from a confused and tormented background, at a crucial stage in history, on one hand *the Prussian effort* and on the other *the renewal of imperial ambitions.* On one side was a very definite legislative, administrative, and military system, and on the other the flamboyant myth of future greatness. In 1815 *Bismarck* was born, in 1813 *Richard Wagner,* the most authentic representatives of the two great forces by which Germany was impelled.

The bonds that could unite the German Reich and the Prussian State were of an exceedingly complex nature. That is the great paradox of German history. Prussia is too often forgotten in speaking of Germany, and Germany in speaking of Prussia. It is the gravest of mistakes.

Prussia was not a State within a State. That expression has no meaning in this connexion. Prussia was a State *alongside* other

States within the Reich.   It was the *greatest* of the States included
in the Reich.   But the Prussian State and the Reich were not of
the same nature.   The former, under a very old tradition, had been
formed in the course of centuries on the principle of the most
drastic centralization.   The latter, which had existed in the
Middle Ages, was no more than a simple possibility, since the
Holy Roman Empire had just disappeared and no new empire
had succeeded it.   Prussia signified the German State of which
it could be foreseen about 1815 that it would unify, with the
exclusion of Austria, the still existing territorial conglomerate of
the Germanic Confederation.   The Reich was nothing more
than a name, but a name round which crystallized all the aspirations of the growing pan-Germanism, all the dreams of greatness
in which Germans were indulging just when they saw themselves
to be most impotent, though on the eve of the first victory won
by Prussia against Napoleon and France.

*Here the idea had as much importance as reality and reality as much as
the idea.   But the idea of the Reich and Prussian reality did not and
could not coincide.*   The Prussian reality was the solid nucleus
round which were to arrange themselves one day the elements of a
Reich that was in principle unbounded and vastly exceeded Prussia.
Here there was no common measure, though there was necessarily union.

Thus the existence of a great Prussia was both an obstacle and
a means to the realization of the national and political unity of
Germany.   Prussia was the most strongly particularist State of
all, and at the same time a most vigorous protagonist of unity.
We may see this already in examining the history of the problem
toward the end of the eighteenth century.   *At that time the
Prussian State was not a nation and the German nation was not a State.*
This was still truer between 1790 and 1815, with the disappearance
of the Holy Roman Empire.

The distinction between "State" and "nation" plays here an
essential part.   The Prussia of 1814 was a State furnished with all
the necessary attributes and provided, in spite of the geographical
dispersion of its constituent elements, with a tradition, a dynasty,
a bureaucracy, and an army.   If that State, tottering in 1806, had
suffered defeat, as we know, it had nevertheless shown itself to
be capable of recovering with astonishing rapidity, had shown
incredible vitality.   But where was the Reich, where was
Germany, on the morrow of the fall of the Holy Roman Empire?
Where could one point to it as a political body?   Where was
its centre, where its unity?   Its existence could neither be

affirmed nor denied. The German nation rested then only on a certain unity of language and culture assured by classicism and romanticism, and in particular on that extraordinary unanimity of thought that was the essential mark of romanticism. Never were the antithesis and also the necessary union between Prussian *statecraft* and German *culture* more evident.

Without that nation, the Prussian State would never figure in modern Europe as a Great Power alongside the Western nations that had long been unified, or alongside Austria in the south and Russia in the east. If she did not enrich herself with the whole of the national culture then in full growth, she would be nothing. She had feared it since Jena. On the other hand, what would become of the vast Germanic body without a centre of political crystallization? How would it emerge from its fatal fragmentation if it had neither the will nor the power to become a State, a State like other States, with definite contours and a definite structure?

Plainly that meant that Prussia and Germany were indissolubly bound together, that the Prussian State demanded the German nation and the German nation the Prussian State. The Prussian State must move over the Germanic waters if it was to endure. But who was to pay for this alliance between matter and form? Would Prussianism absorb Germanism, or would it be the other way round?

It is important to establish a clear distinction between *Prussianism* and *pan-Germanism*. After the period here under consideration we must neither confuse them nor separate them. It might have been imagined in 1800–15 that neither of the two would ever amount to anything without the other. The proof of this is that the first pan-Germans were already utilizing the Prussian edifice as a sort of foundation for their dreams of the future. But we must analyse the two terms and carefully define them. This definition explains in advance the whole Bismarckian century, which opened in reality about 1815 and ended in 1918.

Pan-Germanism possessed from the outset all the characteristics it was to reveal later. In its essence it was a sort of revolution— a revolution of the German pattern, opposed to the French Revolution whose guiding principles it rejected. It aimed at a European universalism, but one commanded by Germany. It affirmed its bellicose hegemony in relation to that of Napoleonism. German universalism, which aimed at collecting under its domination or "protection" all the various elements of the

European periphery, in order to reduce them to servitude, opposed itself to French abstract universalism, monarchical, revolutionary, or Napoleonic in form but always enthusiastic for common principles for the various peoples. The Germans set up as their principle, for their own profit, *their ideal of organization*. They proceeded to an unceasing criticism of what they called Western and Latin mechanization and of the great French oscillation. And they dreamed of a Germany both one and multiple that should be able to reconcile in a vast living synthesis the elements in conflict elsewhere.

How could a dream of this sort be realized, how could all these aspirations be canalized, how could clear, visible, effective form be given to that demand, both *universal* and *German*, which was clearly a transmutation of the earlier cosmopolitanism into a mystical nationalism? Here it was that Prussia intervened, the Prussian State, the State which, on the morrow of Jena, silently rebuilt itself under Stein, Hardenberg, and Scharnhorst, slowly achieving the union of its parts, so as to be able soon to assure the indispensable interdependence of the agricultural East and the industrial West.

"It is possible to be a people rather than a State." So Dahlmann was one day to write. Beyond question that was an exhaustive definition of Germany. The consequence *was that Prussia was destined to become Germany*, or that Germany, in the formula used by Bismarck, was to be simply *the prolongation of Prussia (ein verlängertes Preussen)*. A grave problem and a weighty preoccupation for the future Pan-Germans, when they asked themselves whether it was possible to graft a true German culture on the disciplinary, military, conquering Prussian State.

In the eighteenth century the great German writers had been cosmopolitans. They did not separate the future German nation from Europe. They passed without any transition stage from the territorial fragmentation of Germany and its many States to the great federation of cultivated peoples. No doubt they did not see clearly, in spite of Goethe and his *Memoirs*, what the work of a Frederick II was to mean for the Germany of the future. The Prussian State demanded *the whole man* for its defence and its conquests. Its concrete basis was a sort of popular patriotism, the only force that exercised any coherent action in the Germany of that period. Did not certain Prussian officials talk, before 1786, of uniting *the Prussian State* with *the national civilization*?

It was a strange antinomy that thus set face to face the State ruled and administered by officials and soldiers and the universal dreams of cosmopolitan, nationalist, or pan-German thinkers. German culture made too large a suit for the lean body of Prussia, sound though that body was, and on the way to entire recovery. From the Prussian State and the German culture there issued of necessity the German nation-State.

Germany of the revolutionary and Napoleonic epoch presents, in fact, a paradoxical spectacle. A tumultuous flood of new aspirations and ideas was flowing over her whole surface. But she was not yet a political State, and when she sought to define herself she did so by turning to the Prussian State. That State might explode if it allowed itself to be too suddenly penetrated by that influx of obscure forces. On the other hand, it was certain to become stunted and degenerate if it did not draw sustenance from that overflow. *What was to be done but open the floodgates to avoid destruction and dismemberment, and to preserve the framework built by the labour of centuries, simply in order not to perish from atrophy within the out-of-date forms of the eighteenth-century territorial State?* Prussia's essential preoccupation became to *modernize* and *defend* herself simultaneously, *to be the nucleus of the future unity without sacrificing herself to the Reich.* Such was to be thenceforward the play between the political Prussian State in process of expansion and the German nation, which was not content to be a vast culture but wished to become in its turn a political State.

Fichte admirably grasped the problem when he expressed the hope that the head of the Prussian State would one day be the head of Germany, *but in such a way that Prussia should be absorbed in Germany.* Niebuhr, on the contrary, hoped *that Germany would sacrifice herself to Prussia.* Actually neither of these two solutions materialized. Each of the two elements eternally menaced the other with absorption. Such was the living form of the dualism between *culture* and *statecraft* in Germany. We know the reasons for it.

The meaning of the term Revolution now becomes clear. The German Revolution was more and more identified with the march *toward national cohesion and European hegemony.* The German Revolution was a *political* fact—the transformation of Prussia, the Prussian State, into a German State by the play of hegemony; and a *spiritual* fact—the construction of the Community organized on the *religious* or *racial* principle in virtue of a mythical mentality.

At the outset the Bismarckian Empire left these two forces to pursue their ways separately. It united them only in view of a coming war, which it lost in 1918. The Hitlerite State united them afresh in view of a new offensive, a new *irruption* of Germanism into Europe. It is this that should be termed the German Revolution.

BOOK II

THE BISMARCKIAN EMPIRE

CHAPTER IV

THE ERA OF COMPROMISES (1815–71)

IN 1863 Bismarck remarked that the whole life of a constitution is nothing, and can never be anything, but a series of compromises. No one, I think, has ever formulated a more accurate definition of the Second Reich. Now a compromise presupposes contradictory terms, antinomies which, since an exclusive choice is impossible, must be reconciled by a complex interplay of reciprocal concessions. Such was in fact the very principle that underlay Bismarck's creation. We have already discovered the explanation of this in its remote historical origins. It is undeniable that this conflict of opposites left a particularly deep imprint on the history of the Germanic Confederation.

From this period Germany, geographically the centre of the old Continent, began to play the rôle of the "middle country." Since the First World War her most distinguished writers have displayed a certain affection for this phrase, which represents actual fact. In a country like Germany, Western ideas, born of the English Revolution of the seventeenth century, of the monarchy of Louis XIV and of the French Revolution of 1789, and finally of the Napoleonic Empire and the institutions which it imposed on the German States, came at every turn into conflict with social, political, and intellectual conservatism (which in the North took a Lutheran and in the South-west a Roman Catholic colour); for in virtue of their most rooted traditions both Prussia and Austria were authoritarian and monarchical States. As was natural, Western ideas entered through the smaller States of the South-west. The new ideas were tinged with German conservatism; on the other hand, conservative States allowed themselves to be invaded by liberalism. Between the reactionary conservatism of the one extreme and the revolutionary liberalism of the other, there arose every variety of intermediate system, a fact that makes this period peculiarly difficult to study.

The design which history presents to our gaze is none the less clear-cut. From 1815 to 1850 opposition makes its appearance in every domain of public life. It reached its zenith and displayed its full significance between 1848 and 1850. Then, after ten years of ruthless reaction, the year 1862 saw the rise to power of the man who was to make it his mission to substitute the most necessary and the most urgent compromises for the irreconcilable conflicts of the past. Bismarck succeeded in negotiating the first three of these compromises between 1862 and 1871. He united Prussia and the other German States into one Empire; he formed an inextricable blend of unitary and federative institutions; and lastly he installed alongside monarchical rule a national Parliament elected by universal suffrage. Not until after 1871 did he attempt three further compromises: he sought to reconcile the new Empire with Catholicism, to organize its relations with Socialism, and finally to satisfy the demands of industry and agriculture.

Thus, between 1815 and 1871, was prepared the great social, economic, and political drama the course of which was determined by the new unity and the Industrial Revolution. The reader will feel no surprise that this drama should have had its repercussions on the plane of thought and culture, where during this same half-century of almost complete peace the moral and intellectual crisis was brewing which preluded the first world war.

1. *The social and economic transformation*

Round about 1815 the States of the Germanic Confederation were still poor, thinly populated, and agrarian in structure. Compared with the industrialized States of the West they were at least a century behind the times. Excepting the artisans and the cultivated *élite* there existed no social strata between the aristocracy and the peasants in the countryside, or in the town between the remains of the patrician bourgeoisie and the first proletarian elements. The new spirit began, however, not without some violence, to penetrate this still stagnant society. From 1815 to 1850 and beyond, Germany proceeded to a partial liquidation of this old mediæval system. While the feudal aristocracy was drawn into large-scale agricultural enterprise, and even into the related industries, a whole new urban middle class arose: big capitalists, members of the learned professions, and public or company officials. The example of their Western neighbours, and above all the immense territorial unification produced by the Zollverein (Customs Union), lured this new-born bourgeoisie toward free enterprise. Finally, a new agricultural and industrial proletariat made its appearance. Freedom of movement, the development of means of communication, and recent inventions combined to speed up this modernization, which, despite violent political reaction, continued to make progress from 1850 to 1860. Industrialization made its first appearance toward the middle of the nineteenth century, and yielded its first results between 1860 and 1870.

What was Germany, from an economic point of view, at the outset of the nineteenth century? A country paralysed by territorial fragmentation and the most out-of-date methods of material activity. Everywhere there were differences between the legal systems, everywhere there were Customs barriers. Everywhere were unfree peasants, debarred from initiative and from gaining technical knowledge. Everywhere was severe trade-guild oppression; everywhere were home industries. Everywhere communications were in the most lamentable condition. The Germans of those days were humiliated at the sight of the Western nations, amongst whom new ideas and new forms of economic life had come to birth. Here, too, the entire Germanic body had need of the prodigious shock which was administered by the French Revolution and the French Empire. It is well known how greatly some of Napoleon's measures, especially the blockade of 1806, stimulated a resurgence which was to produce such formidable consequences half a century later.

Until 1850 Germany remained an agricultural country. The liberation of the peasants, carried through by Prussia (which in this as in other domains served as an example to the other German States), met with formidable resistance and provoked a conflict which lasted until 1870 between the great landowners and the well-to-do peasantry, a conflict which, however, did not prevent the junkers east of the Elbe from maintaining their position. Under the stimulus of agricultural experts like Thaer and Liebig, German agriculture began about 1820 to make great progress, and perfected itself with incredible rapidity. When the sugar-beet industry made its appearance in 1830 German agriculture quickly turned to new activities. After 1850 modern mechaniza-

tion was widely developed.   And it is safe to say that until
1875 German agriculture sufficed unaided to meet all the food
requirements of the population.

Home industries survived in Germany till about 1830, though
England, since 1810, had installed a considerable number of
steam-driven machines.   Until 1840 Germany's introduction
of industrial machinery was very slow.   But her exploitation of
her mineral wealth, especially coal and iron, made more rapid
progress.   In 1850, 208,000 tons of iron were produced; in 1860,
1,391,000 tons.   Inventions and discoveries multiplied, and when
once the Zollverein had been extended to cover almost all the
territories of the Germanic Confederation, no further obstacle
impeded the enormous growth of German industry.

It was between 1816 and 1850 that Germany constructed her
first network of roads and a postal organization worthy of a
modern nation.   The building of railways scarcely began before
1835.   In 1840 Germany had 469 kilometres of line; by 1850,
8556; by 1860, 11,088.   These figures speak for themselves.
But German trade remained backward until 1850.   We have to
wait till 1850–70 to see the expansion of Germany's internal and
the birth of her external trade.

In the days of the Fuggers and the Welsers capitalism was
already flourishing in German lands.   But the Lutheran Reformation, the Thirty Years War, and the disastrous subdivision of
territory destroyed the very foundations of capitalism.   No less
than two centuries had to pass before capitalism was able to
develop once again, thanks to the encouragement of some
intelligent rulers and the rise of the middle classes.   In the
sixteenth century it was mainly commerce that took on a capitalist
form, agriculture and industry lagging behind.   By contrast
the mercantilism of the seventeenth and eighteenth centuries
favoured industry.   Finally, in the nineteenth century capitalist
evolution drew both agriculture and industry into its ambit.   But
it is not until 1848 and the discovery of gold in California and
Australia that we see the Germans captured by the capitalist spirit.
German banking organization hardly existed before 1850–70.

Who can fail to perceive the importance of these elementary
data?   It is scarcely possible to speak of a German industrial
system before 1850; the system assumed no real importance
until Bismarck had founded the Second Reich.   More rapid and
much more striking was the progress of economic theories and
ideas between 1815 and 1871.   Up to the end of the eighteenth

century, religious and in particular Lutheran conceptions of economic and financial activity had drawn their inspiration from the Middle Ages. Moreover, though from the sixteenth century onward mercantilism had reserved its favours for industry, since 1750 the Physiocrats had confined their attention almost entirely to agriculture. Adam Smith was the first to formulate a comprehensive system of economics. His ideas took final shape at the very moment when the French Revolution broke out, and they exercised a decisive influence in Germany. For Adam Smith demonstrated *the equal importance, on the plane of production, of agriculture, industry, and commerce.* In particular the idea of economic freedom and free enterprise, and the demarcation established between the State and the sphere of private interests, profoundly modified the German outlook.

So thorough was this modification that in this curious and complex transitional period, when all Germany seems to have been slowly turning to free itself from the apathy and paralysis of the past, and to welcome the most large-scale economic modernization that any European nation has ever undergone, *economic liberalism assumed for it more importance than political liberalism,* especially in the form the latter had assumed in the West. In order to preserve their own power the German monarchies, and later the imperial monarchy, deliberately kept the middle classes away from public affairs, permitting them no political education. Their attention was thus diverted into economic channels. This is why materialism suddenly took possession of the bourgeois masses, who were still almost entirely without intellectual tradition when the Industrial Revolution overtook them.

It should be noted that although Adam Smith's doctrine spread rapidly in Germany from 1800 to 1850, and although the legislation initiated by Stein and Hardenberg between 1807 and 1811 embodied Adam Smith's principles, these innovations came into conflict with State Socialism, which made its appearance in France between 1800 and 1830 and developed in Germany from 1830 to 1850, growing still stronger between 1850 and 1870. In the name of romanticism Adam Müller had already taken up arms against Adam Smith's individualism. But Friedrich List's protectionism, later reinforced by the theories of Rodbertus, assured a great future for State Socialism. So it came about that German capitalism was destined to be always official, corporative, and authoritarian.

This same half-century witnessed a similar transformation in the German social structure.

At the beginning of the nineteenth century German society as a whole was divided into three principal classes: the nobility, the educated bourgeoisie which called itself "the middle class," and lastly "the people." This last term is necessarily somewhat vague, because it includes all strata below the bourgeoisie: that is to say, peasants, artisans, traders, servants, and a rudimentary proletariat. Apart from the privilege conferred by noble birth, class feeling was still embryonic. The differences that counted were those of culture, religion, and profession. This state of affairs remained unchanged till 1850. Only the extraordinary development of industry and capitalism created two opposing classes: the Haves, including nobility and bourgeoisie, and the Have Nots—the proletariat.

It is true that the nobility lost some essential privileges in 1848. From then onwards it can scarcely be considered a class apart, except for the higher aristocracy, that is to say the group of noble families who in 1806 belonged to the imperial nobility, had the right to sit and vote in the Reichstag, and counted among the ruling and mediatized families. These families were the pillars of throne and altar. From 1850 to 1860 they favoured reaction and sought by every means in their power to recover their privileges. Until 1872 the junkers of the East and the upper middle-class landowners retained police control and the right of jurisdiction over their peasants. To this class still belonged after 1850 the army officers, the high officials, and the great landowners. In Bismarck's time the monarchy favoured this class by regularly nominating members of it to the most important administrative and military posts. In the eyes of the law the bourgeois was the equal of the noble, but he was not his equal in social prestige or opportunity of professional preferment. It is certain that the position of the nobility was more secure in Germany, and has remained so to this day, than in France.

As for the bourgeoisie, round about 1850 it became the great possessing class. It was almost exclusively devoted to economic activity. It is true that the constitutions of the time, especially the Prussian Constitution of 1850, secured, in principle, to the bourgeoisie access to public life and politics. But, as we have seen, the monarchies of the day, and later the imperial monarchy, deliberately diverted the middle classes from politics, directing their attention solely to industry and finance. In the eighteenth

century the middle classes had been brilliantly distinguished by
their culture, and Goethe had shown in his great novels what an
important part they ought to play alongside the nobility in the
conduct of the State. But industrialization was destined to make
the wealthier section of the middle classes a sort of new nobility,
an aristocracy of wealth, an economic oligarchy exercising an occult
and almost irresistible influence over the nation through its
concentration and accumulation of immense capital resources.
The less prosperous section of the middle class was partially
converted to liberalism between 1820 and 1848. But political
liberalism came to grief. It quickly turned into the sort of
economic and national liberalism that easily came to terms with
the monarchy.

In opposition to these middle classes there arose an immense
proletariat which increased steadily in numbers after 1850,
especially as the population grew and German soil no longer
produced sufficient food to feed its peoples. The exodus from
the country to the town and the consequent rapid urbanization
of Germany began early. A Prussian law of 1816 authorized the
large landowner on the death of a small landowner or the expira-
tion of a tenant-farmer's lease to expropriate the family. This
is why such large numbers of disinherited peasants found their
way into the large modern cities. They were the most active and
the hardiest elements of the population. Their flight from the
land deprived their native soil of the strength with which their
toil would have enriched it. While the middle classes devoted
themselves to economic activity and to their own unique variety
of liberalism, steeped in aggressive nationalism, the working
masses of the towns gave their hearts to a moderate Socialism,
reformist and in no way revolutionary. So much was this the
case, that toward the middle of the nineteenth century a certain
political apathy overtook the social classes which industrialization
was creating and leading in the direction of parliamentary life.

It is easy to see that everywhere the mode of life was rapidly
changing in this Germany which the Industrial Revolution had
transformed at one blow. It is only necessary to recall the
eighteenth-century German family, as we know it from both
sacred and profane literature, with the characteristics it owed to
Lutheran patriarchalism and paternal authoritarianism, or again
to the influence of rationalism and pietist sentimentality, or finally
to the many foreign influences to which Germany was subjected
from the seventeenth to the eighteenth century. It will be

enough if we recall what this family life was like from 1815 to
1850, the period which is known as the Biedermeier age—
untranslatable word—with its profound consciousness of the
bonds uniting its members and of the incalculable value of these
bonds to the intimate personal life of the individual.   Life was
peaceful.   People were relaxing and resting after the wars of the
French Revolution and Empire.   Many innovations, it is true,
crept in after 1835 to disturb this idyllic picture and announce
the changes that were on their way.   But the reaction of 1850 to
1860 restored the German family as it had been: small towns
mediæval in atmosphere and appearance; lives enclosed within
four walls; simple dwellings; dress and manners somewhat
rudimentary.   We are still far removed from the great industrial
cities, from the future rhythm of life in an over-industrialized
nation.   If we are to realize the shock to which the German
people were subjected in the Bismarckian epoch we must grasp
what German life was like up to about 1860.

The main lines of the picture are extremely simple.   The
Germany of the Germanic Confederation, still divided into some
two-score separate States, seemed to be hesitating between the
past and the future.   She was slowly emerging from the Middle
Ages in which she had continued living despite the revolutionary
and imperial wars, and despite the great culture of the eighteenth
century.   Her people, who had preserved the manners and
customs of olden days, scarcely roused themselves to face modern
life and political struggle.   The chosen few who were conscious
of the drama to come lived a life apart, and were incapable of
arousing national feeling in these little States, still slumbering
under those monarchs of whom Heine wittily said that he could
hear them snoring.   But no sooner had the Zollverein and
political unity forged by Prussian hegemony created the possibility
of rapidly exploiting the resources and methods of modern
industry, than the sleeping giant woke, stretched the limbs which
had for centuries lain numb, and thenceforward left no peace to
Continental Europe.

2. *The political transformation and the origins of the
Bismarck régime*

The Holy Roman Empire and the Napoleonic Empire both
vanished between 1806 and 1815.   In the north the States of the
Prussian plain represented Lutheran conservatism.   In the south

the eight provinces of Austria were the traditional stronghold of Catholic conservatism. In the south-west a block of seven States, rejuvenated and enlarged by Napoleon, cautiously welcomed Western influences, especially between the two revolutions of 1830 and 1848. Finally Prussia, with her four eastern and two western provinces, picked her steps between the conservatism of the one side and the liberalism of the other. Since the German States of those days each enjoyed full sovereignty, and were bound one to another only by a few conventions, she had plenty of room to move.

And this ample space, in the middle of a Europe reorganized by the Congress of Vienna, served as the stage for an historical drama of vast scope and of supreme significance.

On the one hand, the system of the Holy Alliance, with its particularist, monarchical, and anti-liberal principles, exerted heavy and persistent pressure on the German States. On the other, the disunited western nations proved unequal to giving a political lead to the States of the Germanic Confederation. The situation was grave, and burdened with heavy responsibilities. The diplomats of the Congress of Vienna had founded their peace on the balance of power between East and West. But in the west there was Franco-English dissension and in the east Austro-Prussian rivalry. From the moment therefore that Russia joined the eastern block, it was inevitable that German unity—*whether it were to take the form of a Lesser or a Greater Germany—should come to birth under the ægis of conservatism.* With England satisfied and France defeated, the initiative could in fact come only from Austria and Russia. Austria and Russia needed only to combine their efforts to be sure that absolutism would triumph. Though these two nations had been rivals between 1815 and 1818, while Tsar Alexander was everywhere supporting and Metternich everywhere hunting down the liberals, the Congress of Aix-la-Chapelle, and later the famous Carlsbad decisions of 1819, proved that under the pressure of well-known events an Austro-Russian entente had superseded the rivalry between these two great eastern nations.

We thus see developing, between 1819 and 1823, a formidable intervention policy, punctuated by four great congresses and sealed by Metternich's memorandum on the causes of the Revolution. Too long the western Powers tolerated this intervention. It required the affair of the Spanish colonies and the Eastern question to rouse Canning's England to seek approach to Russia and from 1823 to 1830 to oppose the proceedings of the eastern Powers. This is the reason why from approximately 1830 to 1836 the western nations reversed their procedure and worked together to counterbalance the Holy Alliance. Unfortunately about 1840 the Eastern question again divided England and France. In 1846 the affair of the Spanish marriages created new difficulties. The Concert of Europe was destroyed just at the moment when the Revolution of 1848 broke out.

Preparations for a French Restoration were in progress from 1848 to 1852, until the Second French Empire came into being, an Empire which was to serve as a model to Germany in her effort to reconcile ancient traditions of government with the liberal aspirations of her peoples. To summarize the curious, clearly defined alternation of political trends that ceased only when Bismarck came to power, we note the first wave of liberalism (1816 to 1820), a violent reaction (1820 to 1830), the second liberal wave (1830 to 1833), a fresh reaction (1833 to 1845), a third liberal movement (1847 to 1850), and lastly a desperate reaction (1850 to 1860). This same great conflict, which we have just defined on the plane of European politics, is exactly reflected in the German society of the time when, on the social and economic plane, the old mediæval traditions clashed with the most modern innovations.

The Germanic Confederation was the very embodiment of political reaction. Its Constitution forbade any close union between Prussia and the States of the south-west. Austria considered any such *rapprochement* contrary to her interests. This constitution could only consecrate particularism since all the German States claimed full and complete sovereignty and recognized no other bond between them than the contract, entered into with an eye to their internal and external security, mutually to defend each other's selfish interests. The generai will of the Confederation was, of course, something other than the sum of the separate and particular wills of the individual States. But the Diet of the Confederation required the unanimous vote of all its members before reaching any decision. This was a permanent and irremovable obstacle.

As for internal security: what the reactionaries wanted was to combat liberalism, unification, in short every new aspiration or institution. Thus the decisions of the Confederation disastrously emphasized the alternation of political trends that we have just tabulated. These decisions were always upheld by the eastern

Powers, always directed against the constitutional movement, against parliamentary activity, against every manifestation of cultured youth and the cultured middle class, against every effort toward social reform or economic progress, against every step Prussia took to lead the German States towards unity. It is therefore no matter for surprise that Austria, after the upheaval of 1848 and the humiliation of Prussia at Olmütz, supported every reactionary measure taken by the German States between 1850 and 1860—little suspecting how near was her own crushing defeat at Sadowa.

But it must not be supposed that Prussia was the champion of liberalism. It was above all in the economic field that Prussia was ahead of Austria. She did also, it is true, introduce a shade more liberalism into her political institutions than her rival. Nevertheless she wrecked the 1849 Constitution of Frankfort, whose immense significance lay in its antithesis to the Constitution of the Germanic Confederation, that cause of political paralysis and death. The draft of the 1849 Constitution gave admirably clear and precise expression to all those aspirations of the day which sought to make of Germany both *a unified and a democratic State*. It was of course only the draft of a Constitution which never came into force. Nevertheless, when Bismarck, between 1867 and 1871, was planning his constitution for the new Empire, he could not afford to ignore it. How could he? For the Frankfort Constitution was the fruit of the three liberal upheavals that had somewhat violently shaken Germany between 1815 and 1850.

Vehement criticism of the Germanic Confederation; the birth of the Burschenschaft or youth movement; the Wartburg festival of 1817; the murder of Kotzebue in 1819; the parliamentary movement in the south-western States; the infiltration of liberalism into the North after 1830; the Hambach festival of 1832; the Frankfort affair of 1833; the rise of liberalism in Saxony; the appearance of social and political radicalism after 1840; the intellectual and doctrinal ferment created by Western ideas—all these were historic events of far-reaching significance and of identical origin. The Frankfort Charter, with amazing audacity, solved in its own way the six great problems of the time. It dismembered Prussia to absorb her in the Reich, similarly sacrificing the other States to the new Empire to give more weight to centralism than to federalism. It created a two-chamber Parliament, one chamber federal and the other national, a Parliament which would soon override the personal government of the future Emperor since it was to have the decisive voice in matters of finance. The Charter boldly separated the Churches from the State and from the School. Finally it smoothed the way for free enterprise and for social reform while safeguarding the essential liberties of the individual. The Charter took the line of its own choice; it launched the country on a voyage towards a clearly defined and stable destiny. But this admirable Constitution was the product only of an intellectual *élite* and lacked the backing of a self-confident, eager, and resolute people. It was shipwrecked by the King of Prussia's refusal to accept the crown tendered him by the Frankfort Assembly. This refusal doomed the Frankfort Constitution to remain a mere paper scheme without the slightest hope of ever being carried into effect.

Political progress had to take place within the States themselves. It could only be slow. It was bound to lean, not towards a bold solution like that formulated at Frankfort, but toward compromise, toward that curious blend of traditionalism and liberalism which was one day to characterize Bismarck's Empire. Bismarck had not a blank sheet on which to sketch his own design for the policy and Constitution of 1871. It was precisely by accepting the teaching of the political evolution of the several German States between 1815 and 1860 that he showed his realism.

Positive creative activity was at this time the monopoly of the south-western States. The little northern States were later and much slower in modernizing themselves. Between the two groups Prussia, shortly before 1848, worked out the formulæ and institutions of the future liberal Empire.

The States of the south-west were the first to risk compromises between the two worlds symbolized by the great constitutional statutes of 1815 and 1849. The Constitutions of Baden and of Bavaria in 1818, of Württemberg in 1819, and of Hesse-Darmstadt in 1820, all had this feature in common: they were Charters graciously granted to his subjects by the monarch or *Landesherr*, an hereditary ruler whose powers nevertheless derived from the Constitution itself. All these Constitutions provided for a bi-cameral Parliament or *Landtag* (one chamber for the aristocracy and one for the middle class), exercising a certain control over the budget. In ecclesiastical matters they took a strictly impartial line, giving equality to the two Christian Churches. Lastly they granted all citizens equality before the law and all essential liberties. It is clear that their chief anxiety was to unite all elements and all social classes in their respective territories into one organic and coherent whole.

The little States of the north also made an effort to reorganize themselves. But they did not begin till after 1830 and then with leisurely caution; besides, they cancelled by outbursts of sudden and violent reaction such progress as they achieved.

Prussia, who gradually imposed her Customs Union as well as improved means of communication on the other German States, proved less liberal than the Constitution of Frankfort or the south-western States, but also less conservative than the other States of the north which separated her various territories. After her reorganization of 1806 and 1807 she set out to devise a constitutional reform. Her programme in reality did not differ in essentials from that of the South-west. But between 1820 and 1830 a mood of reaction swept away all her good intentions. Prussia got only as far as introducing Provincial Estates. Between 1830 and 1840 the Zollverein alone made real progress. Not until the accession of Frederick William IV was study of the constitutional programme again resumed. The new King of Prussia was distrustful of parliamentary institutions, but anxious on the morrow of the Cologne affair to reconcile the Catholics with the Prussian State. He therefore united the Provincial Diets into one *Landtag*, a body which met twice, in 1845 and 1847.

This new assembly was full of able deputies, among them Otto Bismarck, but was swept by all the currents of the time. Under the pressure of the circumstances which accompanied the Revolution of 1848, determined also, no doubt, to preserve at any cost the cohesion of Prussian territory, the King granted a Constitution to his people. This emphasized the unity of all the territories of the Crown, defined the fundamental rights of the citizens, granted wide liberties to the religious communities, recognized a certain degree of ministerial responsibility, assigned to the Crown all executive power, and established two Chambers: a *Herrenhaus* (House of Lords) and an *Abgeordnetenhaus* (Chamber of Deputies). This constitutional document is undoubtedly more important than the Frankfort one for an understanding of Bismarck's Constitution of 1871. From 1850 to 1860 every effort was made by the reactionaries to undermine the foundations of this Constitution. But the sole result was to arouse such excitement in the *Abgeordnetenhaus* that in

1862 Bismarck had to be called to the rescue to avert serious disturbances.

To sum up, the data on which Bismarck had to build were the following: the preservation of Prussia's territories; the devising of one uniform constitutional formula to suit both the south-western States and Prussia; a statute for the Churches; and finally the success of the Zollverein—all questions of primary importance to a moderate German policy.

We thus see how the doctrines and the parties arose by which Bismarck was confronted. Protestant conservatism and Catholic conservatism roughly corresponded to the attitudes assumed in practice by the northern States on the one hand, and on the other by Austria and by the Germanic Confederation in general. The radical liberalism imported from the West, with its theories of the sovereignty of the people, republican democracy, and parliamentary institutions, was the antithesis of these conservatisms. Between the two opposing extremes, most of the German States developed a doctrine, or, rather, a vague state of mind, which was an odd blend of conservatism and liberalism: *either conservatism coloured by liberalism or liberalism coloured by conservatism.* There was room for every variety of shade between those who represented the old absolutism and those who represented the republican idea.

Almost everywhere, even at the Frankfort Assembly, the supporters of most doctrines proposed the continuation of the monarchy. Alongside it, however, they set up a special parliamentary body consisting of two chambers, one to represent the former privileged classes and one to represent the classes that were acquiring culture and a new economic activity. This was the German interpretation of constitutional monarchy. Its hesitations and complexities are explained by the fact that the conception of a *living organism* coloured the whole political ideology of the day and was felt to demand a *synthesis of authority and liberty.*

In proportion as men's minds shook themselves free from the old absolutist conceptions on the one hand and from Western radicalism on the other, they turned spontaneously either towards a *tempered authoritarianism,* primarily based on the Churches and their traditions but according a certain degree of liberty to individuals and constituted groups, or towards a *diluted liberalism* which, while anxious for innovation and reform, was careful to avoid a breach with the past, with monarchy and its original institutions. The differences were simply a question of the degree in which one or other tendency was more or less dominant.

This curious fluctuation between two extremes explains a fact which is in my opinion vital to an understanding of modern Germany's political history. Though Western liberalism penetrated into all the States beyond the Rhine, it took on peculiar shades there; and served various purposes almost unknown in France or England. Just as, in the eighteenth century, the philosophy of the Enlightenment which came from England and from France assumed in Germany more ponderous forms and a religious bias more marked than amongst the Western nations, finally leading to nothing more than a compromise between Christianity and rationalism, so now between 1815 and 1860 political liberalism applied itself to singular tasks. *Though the south-western States provided themselves with parliamentary institutions, they did so only in order to consolidate their territories, artificially united by Napoleon, and in order to represent in their two chambers all the social elements that had to be satisfied.* If the monarchy in Prussia posed as more liberal round about 1848, that again was only *because a Prussian Parliament appeared to be a bulwark against a threatened dismemberment of the Prussian State.*

Religious politics showed similar traces of this strange blend of conflicting doctrines and attitudes. The Centre assured Rome of its loyalty, and progressively organized itself in dependence on the Papacy. Simultaneously, however, it carried on noisy campaigns for the liberty of the Church in the German Community. It made liberalism the excuse for demanding a certain degree of autonomy. Liberalism in Germany was thus being pursued not only territorially but *corporatively*. Yet the liberals themselves made strange concessions to the conservatives. It would be a mistake to see in Stahl's philosophy of a Christian State (the model which Bismarck was later to imitate) simply a return to the absolutism of the seventeenth and eighteenth centuries. Roman Catholic doctrine also aimed at keeping on good terms both with monarchy and with democracy, unwilling to take a definite step either to right or left. No supporter, moreover, of any of the doctrines failed to assert that in the State of the future the parts and the whole must be *organically* bound together. But some insisted on the *coherence* of the whole and the *subordination* of the parts, relatively autonomous though they might be, and some on the *liberty* and *relative independence* of the parts in relation to the central power.

This is why we cannot speak of political parties before 1850. Metternich in Austria, Frederick William III in Prussia, and the Germanic Confederation were all on the alert to prevent the development of "factions" in the German States. There were no well-defined programmes, there were no organized political groups. There were at that time only *doctrinal tendencies*. None the less, an attentive observer can already detect amid the general confusion the first germs of the future German parties.

The Protestant conservatives, whether of the northern States or of Prussia, already formed the solid nucleus of the future conservative party from which one day the Free Conservatives were to branch off, converts to the ideas and methods of Bismarck. National Liberalism was born of the bourgeoisie who were preparing for an economic revival based on the Zollverein and on industrialization. This National Liberalism was essentially opportunist, concentrating by preference on economic realities and Free Trade, not on parliamentary institutions in so far as these sprang from doctrinal liberalism. Progressive Liberalism was the natural prerogative of the cultivated middle classes, the professors and jurists, in love with Western ideas and ready for any constitutional innovation. As yet only the general outline of the future Social Democracy could be perceived. It was in 1848 that the first Workers' Congress met at Berlin and the first trade unions and co-operatives were founded. Finally the Centre, with its Right wing and its Left wing, began to take shape, a party adapted to every sort of bargain and every sort of compromise: the real Germany in miniature.

Between 1850 and 1860 the groupings of forces, parties, and programmes began to become more clearly defined. A new spirit of *political realism* (Realpolitik) came to birth, the policy of positive interests which Bismarck was to adopt, though he was by no means its inventor. The term *Realpolitik* simply defines and denotes the spirit of the time. In view of new opportunities and new perspectives, hitherto unknown in Germany, "principles" were in fact gradually superseded by brutal "realities." But faced by the fanatical reaction which conservatism organized for the attack on modern institutions, a fanaticism that conferred on conservatism a cohesion previously lacking, the liberals rallied to the defence in their own way, trying to consolidate their old positions and above all to conquer new ones by harmonizing their doctrines with economic realities.

Naturally, it was in Prussia that this procedure was most clearly and fully developed. The doctrinaire democrats or liberals, confronted by the three-class electoral system, permitted the formation of a Chamber in which the moderate liberals formed the Left in opposition to a Right twice as numerous as they. The conservatives, now masters of the parliamentary field, set themselves to liquidate the entire pseudo-revolutionary tradition, every reform, every innovation. The great landowners asserted their material interests, while maintaining the principles of the Holy Alliance. Everywhere, in Prussia and elsewhere, the old liberalism found itself attacked, weakened, and compelled to leave the direction of political affairs to the governments and to the Right. In due course it abandoned its principles of the past. In 1859, when the Austro-Italian war broke out and danger threatened Prussia, the Nationalverein was formed under the direction of Bennigsen. This was the nucleus of the future National Liberal Party.

The same fundamental realism actuated Catholics and Socialists. The Prussian Catholic "fraction" (Parliamentary group) aimed solely at correcting the Prussian State, which it reproached for not integrating the Catholic provinces of the West. It sketched out the future confessional programme of the Centre—preservation of the Constitution and of the essential Catholic liberties, Catholic primary schools, individual right and equality between the Churches, and the search for a middle way between the absolutism of the past and the sovereignty of the people. It was at this point that German Catholicism adopted a social policy. After the beginnings of industrialization German Socialism abandoned Western principles and turned toward legal, parliamentary, and practical solutions, while the trade unions and the co-operatives made their triumphal entry into its ranks.

Thus it came about that Bismarck in 1862 found a *political milieu ready-made*. After passing through a free-thinking phase, he remained conservative and Lutheran. He desired a Christian State, a monarchy by divine right. Now "Christian" implies *compromise, synthesis*. In the name of Stahl, Bismarck violently attacked the whole of Western liberalism, the English tradition (inapplicable in Prussia), and especially the Assembly of Frankfort and the Constitution of 1849. After his service on the Diet of the Germanic Confederation, however, Bismarck revolted against the paralysing conservatism of Austria. Then in Paris he studied the liberal Empire. This dual education, both conservative and liberal, made Bismarck the *man of compromises* that he became. With his whole soul he hated the Diet of the Germanic Confederation in Frankfort. He conceived that every compromise was possible on a Prussian basis. He saw in Prussia the coherent State which should be upheld by a minimum of federalism, a State capable of creating by its hegemony the unity of the future Reich and breathing into the whole German body its own legislative, administrative, and military spirit and its own organizing genius in the social and economic fields. *Bismarck understood the contribution that middle-class democracy tempered by German conservatism could make to a nation rapidly forging ahead.*

Subjected to influences from East and West, *Germany did not choose, could not choose, between them.* She *combined* and *blended* them. Her sure instinct rejected the Constitution of Frankfort as too centralizing, democratic, and liberal, too daring and arbitrary for her taste. But at the same time she liquidated the Germanic Confederation with its Diet as being, by its own admission, too particularist, reactionary, and absolutist. And it was to Prussia that she entrusted the task of achieving that *equilibrium* of which she had never ceased unconsciously to dream.

Like all compromises and all syntheses, Bismarck's creation was bound to be unstable. From the moment of its birth it bore within it the seeds of death. Bismarck began by winning in the Prussian Chamber an overwhelming victory over the liberals. Its immediate fruits were the military triumphs of 1864 to 1871. Thereafter he was in a position to formulate his three most urgent compromises and to embody them in the Constitution of 1871— the union of Prussia with the other German States; the balance between centralism and federalism; and the synthesis between monarchical and parliamentary government. But it was *only thanks to industrialization* that he succeeded. It was only in virtue of the formidable phenomenon of the *nineteenth-century Industrial Revolution* that alliances of interests arose in Germany and, taking the form of *new social classes* and *great disciplined political parties,* sketched out their programmes and defined their methods with increasing precision.

To make such alliances possible, certain forms both of liberalism and of conservatism had to be liquidated, and the attempt had to be made to associate the Imperial Government with the Prussian Government, and with the people, represented in the Reichstag thanks to universal suffrage, in the common task. Now at last Bismarck was freed, in appearance at any rate, from the conflicts which had weighed so heavily on public life from 1815 to 1860. The new monarchy was free to devote itself to politics and the new social classes to economic activities. The Catholic Centre and the Social Democracy were the two pillars of this unique parliamentary structure, whose duty was to collaborate with the Prussian Government invested with imperial hegemony. The central power established over the head of the German States made Germany a Federal State (*Bundesstaat*), neither a Confederation of States (*Staatenbund*) nor a Unitary State (*Einheitsstaat*). As for the dynasties linked to the Prussian royal house, the aim was, without leaving power in their hands, *to organize a synthesis of national energies.*

The charter of 1871 was therefore an incomplete charter born of the exigencies of the moment. It specified the twenty-five territories which were to compose the Reich of Lesser Germany. It entrusted the central power to the Emperor and to the Chancellor, who remained at the same time respectively King and Prime Minister of Prussia. It set up the Reichstag over against the Federal Diet. Finally it divided legislation and administration between the Reich and the dynastic States.

The paradox is obvious. It leaps to the eye from the text of the Constitution. In all that concerned the relations between the Reich and the States, *centralism* definitely preponderated. On the plane of government, *monarchism* was no less definitely preponderant. *Bismarck created a Monarchy, Prussian in origin and centralizing in its tendencies.* The tragedy of Bismarck is inherent, however, in this formula. For on the plane of the victorious principle of centralization conflict was bound to break out between the Imperial Government and the Reichstag, and to develop with ever-increasing acuteness until the day came when, under a feeble Emperor, personal government would fail, while effective parliamentary government was as yet unborn.

Bismarck set out to achieve national unity through monarchy and at the same time through parliamentarism. Hence he failed to establish an organic bond between authoritarianism and democracy, between the German monarchical tradition and institutions imitated from the West, between ruling Prussia and a business bourgeoisie supported by opportunist Socialism. His creation could not stand the test of time.

3. *The beginning of the intellectual crisis and the idea of a national religion*

Here was a great and formidable reality: a territorial, economic, and social organism, entirely renewed by the Zollverein, in which, for the first time in Germany, the national energies called forth by the most modern technique were to work harmoniously together. Big business, the middle classes, and the proletariat, all dedicated to material labour and constrained to manufacture feverishly for export in order to pay for indispensable food and raw material imports, found themselves enclosed in and directed by an all-embracing political system. And this political creation had set itself the task of both directing and unifying this multitude of released ambitions and related efforts. Political and economic crisis was forthwith begotten of this creation itself and of the abnormal conditions or emergencies in which it had been designed and carried out.

But there was the germ of yet another crisis, an intellectual and moral crisis, dormant in the evolution of German culture between 1815 and 1870.

If in nothing else, this epoch would be great in virtue of its negations. The reproach is commonly levelled at it that it was the period that saw the collapse of liberalism as understood by the Western nations. That is a narrow and superficial view. German thought during these years had begun to attack the values, all the values, of Western humanism. Heine's prophecy contained an invaluable warning of what was to come. He had but recently arrived in Paris when, in 1834, he called France's attention to the immeasurable significance of the work which philosophic and religious thought beyond the Rhine was silently accomplishing. Little by little it was undermining and destroying the essential bulwarks of Christianity. In so doing it was breaching the dams which had hitherto restrained the Furor Teutonicus. Once let the ramparts of Christianity and of Christian values be breached, once let the various national energies, so long divided, coalesce, and there would follow a German Revolution beside which the French Revolution of 1789 would seem to have been an idyll, a children's game!

"Historism" was already beginning. Geology, and above all geography, had developed during this half-century with ever-increasing speed and scope. It was between 1845 and 1858 that Alexander von Humboldt's *Kosmos* appeared. Conceiving

Nature as a unity and a totality moved and animated by internal forces, Humboldt seemed to be resuming in the light of recent studies and discoveries the essential theses of Renaissance philosophy and to be deducing from the Copernican vision of the world all its implicit consequences. German historians had long since turned away from purely pragmatic history. Romanticism had strangely widened their horizon. They even went so far as to treat all the mental sciences from the *historic*, that is to say from the *evolutionary*, point of view. In due course even Law lost a large part of its normative value, since it was conceived as having slowly evolved during the course of centuries, and as representing first and foremost the customs and the potentialities of human societies.

All the seeds which Herder had sown in the eighteenth century here found fertile soil. If history was made by great personalities, it was also simply the succession of great human cultures which had become incarnate in representative individuals of genius. And if cultures thus succeeded each other in time and space, was not their value *relative?* Where were the eternal standards that govern this unending process of becoming? If God "creates himself" by inscribing his works in Time, could men recognize his immortal essence, could they hope to share in his Eternity? Assuredly the German still believed in the destiny of Humanity as a whole. But what was this destiny to be in an epoch of industrialization, of technique, of specialization? At that moment the historical view of life laid hold not only of the mental sciences but of all literature and art. It would almost seem that German science set itself in desperation to take stock of the whole heritage of human history at the very moment when its faith therein was lost.

It is impossible not to see that the conception of Greek and Roman antiquity had been revolutionized by the vast body of research, excavation, and discovery, which revealed Prehistory and at one blow revised all preceding methods, standards, and teachings. As early as the end of the eighteenth century the "Sturm und Drang" School and Hölderlin had drawn a picture of a violent and combative Greece, a Greece that had been but one human "culture" amongst others, a culture born of blood and battle—a picture to which Goethe reverted in the light of the revolutionary and Napoleonic wars when he wrote the classic *Walpurgisnacht* of the Second Part of *Faust*. The Greek people became the dazzling heroes of an historic picture in which the distant scenes were strangely sombre, painful, and dramatic. Curtius, following the lines of Hegel and Jahn, was before long to demonstrate that the German people would one day be inheritors of the same destiny. Roman history, interpreted in the same way, yielded, under Mommsen's hand, an analogous comparison. What had become of the Greece of Socrates, of the "canonical" Greece of Winckelmann and the æsthetic connoisseurs of the eighteenth century?

By treating in the same manner the history of the Hebrew people and the history of Christianity, it was possible to restore them to their place in the universal evolution and thus to cast a doubt on their absolute normative value. Undeniably, the great period between 1815 and 1870 was one of immense religious revaluations, and it would yet seem that at no time had the Christian ideal, whether in its Catholic or Lutheran form, exercised a more compelling power over German minds. It would be a fallacy to attribute this to the ultramontane reaction that followed the supreme theological and ecclesiastical efforts of the years 1810 to 1850 or the revival of orthodoxy and pietism in Prussia during the same period. Here Christianity was subservient in the one case to the aims of Prussian conservatism, in the other to the conservatism of Austria and the Holy Alliance, and hence of reaction. What is more, Christianity tended to merge into a purely national ideal and to become indistinguishable, as we shall see later, from pan-Germanism.

In the German universities of the time, Christianity was subjected to the most violent and devastating attacks. Between 1830 and 1840 German theology breached the strongest ramparts of the Christian dogma. Hegel, of course, in his lectures on the philosophy of religion, strove afresh to reconcile science and faith. He did so by representing religion as the science of the Absolute Spirit within the limited spirit of man. He still recognized Christianity as the supreme revelation. David Friedrich Strauss, however, in his *Leben Jesu* (1835), interpreted the life of Christ and of his Apostles as a myth born of the common thought of the earliest Christians. He saw the biblical Jesus as the product of a sort of reflection which Mankind as a whole might make concerning itself and its symbolic destiny. Strauss entirely swept away the ancient dogma and in his last work, *Der alte und der neue Glaube* (1872), sought to substitute for it a positive conception of the world based on materialism and the natural sciences. Bruno Bauer and Arnold Ruge went further and treated the dogmas of Christianity as free and fantastic inventions. A large number of clergy allowed themselves to be borne along by the irresistible current of this total scepticism and destructive criticism.

In 1841 there appeared Feuerbach's *Das Wesen des Christenthums*, the first philosophic system unreservedly to accept atheism and materialism. Feuerbach denied all the so-called "transcendental" values, that is to say everything that postulated a world beyond physical humanity and visible Nature. Hegel still recognized the World Spirit. He considered Germany the most complete incarnation of that Spirit. This conception Feuerbach rejected. In his eyes, heaven, salvation, and the other world were nothing but inventions of the human mind. For him nothing was real except what the senses could perceive, and thought itself was nothing but an organic function.

This mania of philosophic and theological destructiveness reached its height before 1850. The triumph of the exact sciences and the brilliant progress of industrial technique from 1850 to 1870 could not fail to foster it. True, the Christian Churches stood firm. They even reacted vigorously and defended themselves by re-emphasizing the most essential postulates of their respective creeds. Many phenomena bore witness to the vitality of the Christian Churches: Stahl's doctrine and his conception of the Christian State, the new orthodoxy and the Home Mission in Prussia, the wave of ultramontanism which was to lead in 1870 to the acceptance of the Vatican decrees by almost every German Catholic. But from this time onwards indifferentism unmistakably gained ground, especially amongst Protestants. For the time being the sole enemy of the Churches was a theoretical scepticism. They were not yet faced by a species of State Religion bent on eradicating them from German life. Yet we cannot now fail to detect in the religious polemics of the years 1830 to 1870 the preliminary skirmishes of the battle of to-day.

This battle, fought against doctrinal and rationalist liberalism, was all the more acute because it represented the vital choice which Germany had to make between her own traditions and those of the West. We may fairly say that the period between 1850 and the Franco-Prussian war decided that dramatic choice. At no other time did Western liberalism—in particular French liberalism—win so many minds in Germany. At no other time was it so bitterly opposed. The struggle was above all a political one.   We have seen clear proof of this in the transformation undergone by the structure of Germany.   To appreciate how deeply liberal ideas had been able to penetrate into the Germany of those days the student must read the "Political Dictionary" (*Staatslexikon*) of Karl von Rotteck and Theodor Welcker.

Not indeed that this political and philosophical liberalism remained consistent from 1820 to 1870 or was enshrined in one unchanging formula.   Even in Rotteck and Welcker it was more often than not allied with monarchism.   Between 1830 and 1840, under the influence of the July Revolution, it veered definitely toward France and cosmopolitanism.   After 1840, however, when France under the ministry of Thiers showed signs of casting covetous eyes on the left bank of the Rhine, German liberalism tended to merge into the national movement aiming at territorial and political unity.   This nationalism had not as yet assumed an extreme form, certainly not in the Frankfort Assembly of 1848 and 1849, for the Greater Germany of which in those days professors and jurists dreamed was to be a democracy under the cloak of a highly centralized constitutional monarchy.   For the rest, the liberalism of this spacious age was not confined to politics.   It inspired all the literature of "Young Germany," coloured all the work of Heinrich Heine, and gave birth between 1840 and 1848 to a body of political verse that bore witness to the extraordinary radicalism of the time.

Everybody is well aware of the hatred with which German liberalism was pursued during this half-century by the dynasties, by the Churches, and by the hostile political parties.   This ruthless battle began as early as 1819 with the decisions of Carlsbad, assumed new intensity after the Revolution of 1830, and died down between 1840 and 1850 (the most decisive decade of German history), only to be unleashed afresh from 1850 to 1860. This time it was complete rupture with Western rationalism and the principles of the French Revolution, complete rupture with the West.   Thenceforward there was to be no bridge across the gulf that separated Franco-British from German political thought. It was no longer a question of the romanticist protests against the Enlightenment, made in the name of a new sentimental education. *This time, two political systems were arrayed one against the other.*   The liberalism which found itself a niche in Bismarck's system had nothing in common with Western liberalism.

Socialism suffered a similar fate.   Before the days of Marx and Lassalle, Socialism in Germany had been the direct heir of

Western Socialism, from 1820 to 1850 it had been primarily inspired by Babeuf, Saint-Simon, Fourier, Louis Blanc, and Proudhon. With Lassalle and Marx it had speedily nationalized and Germanized itself to the point of losing the international direction it had originally taken. The development of Social Democracy in the course of the years 1850 to 1870 was curiously akin to the development of the Catholic Centre. In the one case social interests and the interests of the workers came into play, in the other the interests of the Church. In both there reigned the spirit of ponderous corporative organization which by degrees inevitably stifled early enthusiasm and was fatal to all live contact with social or religious internationalism.

Taking account of the immense development of the exact sciences after 1850 and the remarkable success of scientific and popular materialism, the student can, and even must, recognize that *the intellectual and moral crisis in Germany began not only before the World War but even before the three victorious wars of 1864, 1866, and 1870-71.* These three military triumphs completely transformed a public opinion already exposed to so much mental ferment, already so willing to accept the postulates of the most unbridled nationalism. Thenceforward the pan-German variety of nationalism appears as the complement of the spiritual crisis that destroyed all ancient values and left empty the German soul. The vacuum was filled by a vision of might that gradually took possession of all classes of society.

From the fact that the new-born German unity was the product of a memorable series of victories won in ever wider fields, it naturally followed that the Second Reich, completing the work of the Germanic Confederation, must achieve the final triumph of centralization. It was equally necessary to it that its land and sea forces should together form the best organized military power in Europe. This double effort was destined, as we know, to protect and foster an economic renaissance which, powerfully assisted by the territorial unity prepared by the Zollverein, was to secure for the Empire the sudden prosperity that Europe so greatly admired, and to darken the whole world with the threat of an apparently unlimited imperialist expansion.

Thus Prussia was thenceforward to play a lone hand in her great game. Sadowa had long since eliminated Austria. She continued, of course, still to exist in Europe—from 1867 under the guise of a Dual Monarchy—and to pursue her aim of pacific synthesis, the supreme hope of the last federalists in the old

Continent.   And of course the Reich lost no time in concluding an alliance with this Dual Monarchy.   Without unduly anticipating future events, we may recall that when the two Central Empires, Germany and Austria-Hungary, went under in the World War, it was a greatly *reduced Austria* that emerged from their tragic defeat, an Austria divorced from the other partners with whom she had been united under the Habsburgs.   Rejected by the Allies after the armistice, the Greater Germany with its two foci, Potsdam and Vienna, the dream of 1848, was for the moment doomed. The brutal annexation of March 11, 1938, seemed, temporarily at least, to have given that Greater Germany the *coup de grâce*.   For this was not merely the end of Austria, *it was Prussia usurping the hearth and home of ancient Austria, it was the total ruin of one form of Germanism.*

These reflections enable us to determine what exactly was, from 1815 to about 1870, this dream of Empire, this vision of a species of religious Community whose hegemony should supplant that of the French Revolution and should govern a securely unified Europe.   At a time when they appeared to repudiate so many values, and were obviously preparing for an early break with the West and the international order, many distinguished Germans voluntarily abandoned themselves to this vision of future Empire. Until the emergence of the Racial Myth at the end of the nineteenth and the beginning of the twentieth century, this vision was the compensation they discovered or invented for the bitterness of so much ruin and collapse.

At the very outset of the period we are now studying, from about 1820 to 1830, three outstanding minds devoted themselves in very divergent ways to this problem of Empire: Goethe, Hegel, and Friedrich Schlegel.   Comparison of the three is instructive.

Goethe remained impenitently cosmopolitan.   Even on the morrow of the Congress of Vienna he never believed that the Germans were capable of becoming a nation.   He refused to imprison his thought in a national frame.   The imagined Reich did not yet exist; the Germanic Confederation was nothing more than a very loosely knit federation of sovereign States; he refused to look whether to Austria or to Prussia and expect that either, as a State, should realize a political or social ideal to which he for his part could do homage.   He could not abandon the point of view of universal literature, that of a disinterested religious devotion entirely free from any national preoccupation.   His kingdom was not of the German world. Goethe entrenched himself in simple anticipation. He kept vast perspectives open before German eyes to prevent his countrymen from plunging into a too narrow nationalism.

Hegel was South German and a Protestant; his thoughts were of Prussia. Schlegel was North German and a convert to Rome; his thoughts were of Austria. Hegel's *Philosophie des Rechts* appeared in 1821. Friedrich Schlegel delivered his Vienna lectures shortly before his death in 1827. Each of these philosophers expounded a new theory of the State for the benefit of the two Powers which were at that time the true pillars of the Germanic Confederation. But they did so in the name of the *whole world*, as witnesses and prophets of a religion and a system of thought *deliberately universal*.

What did Hegel see in the State as conceived by Frederick II? He saw in it the State of Reason, the supreme Rational Principle. Prussia implied for him more than merely the Prussia of his day. He saw it as the foreshadowing of an imaginary society, of a self-sufficing State, "totalitarian" therefore, in which both liberty and authority would be safeguarded. Not that Hegel's horizon was in fact bounded by Potsdam; his outlook was always that of the Universal Spirit. But for the moment he wanted to concentrate attention on Potsdam. A philosopher whose thoughts are of the Eternal must have either a genuinely total Empire or else an imperfect State which he can believe to be a *necessary stage* on the road leading to the ideal. Prussia might be narrowly circumscribed in space, but for Hegel she was, and could not fail to be, but a halting-place in the progress of limitless Time where Universal Logic reigns. It was enough that the principle was total. Hegel deified one particular, indeed particularist, State. With him, Germany's political and religious thought, which but a short time before had hovered over all her territories, had, as it were, alighted on the most important of them, before taking possession of the Reich itself. Here it found the *Military State par excellence*. It spiritualized it and made of it an Absolute: an instructive example, a terrible example, the lesson of which was not to be lost in time to come.

Though less well known, Friedrich Schlegel's attempt was in no wise less important than Hegel's. In Prussia it was taken for granted that the days of the Habsburg Monarchy were numbered. Then Schlegel came and bent his knowledge and his talent to endowing Austria with a universal significance such as Hegel

had lent to Prussia. It may of course be objected that Austria
lasted well beyond Schlegel's time. It also remains true that
with one single interruption fourteen separate peoples lived in
peace under her ægis for no less than a century. We might
therefore fairly consider her, too, as an anticipation of the future,
a future of comprehensive federalism which from the totalitarian
point of view was to be accounted indispensable for Europe.
While Prussia represented simply the *Staatsräson*, the requirement
of the State, Austria was a *relatively comprehensive totality*. Her
existence, thoroughly irrational as it was, presented most striking
historic contrasts. In her were preserved the remains of an epoch
that had lasted a thousand years. She was herself *a miniature
Europe* whose history seemed to be a compendium of the essential
phases of the history of mankind.

Schlegel could not avoid seeing in Austria the *Catholic* country
par excellence. Inevitably he dreamt that she was destined to
revive a universal monarchy. It was for her that a writer like
Schlegel was bound to preach the *Concordantia Catholica*. Just
as Hegel consecrated the existence and the significance of the
Prussian State from the totalitarian point of view, Friedrich
Schlegel took up again and made real again, in the name of
Austria, the idea of the Reich. And in his mind this Reich
remained a Christian Empire in the Catholic sense of the
word, as Hegel's Prussia remained Christian in the Lutheran
sense.

Another step brings us to the ideas of Paul de Lagarde and of
Constantin Frantz. They resumed and amplified the conception
of the Reich as *the great national German Church*, whose mission
was to subject Europe to its direction.

Paul de Lagarde was a disciple of Fichte. He sought to
rekindle in Germany the enthusiasm of 1813 because this
enthusiasm had been religious and in accordance with Germany's
true mission. Even at the time of the military triumphs of 1864,
1866, and 1871, he declared himself dissatisfied. He resented
Bismarck's remaining content with a Protestant Lesser Germany
instead of taking responsibility for the whole religious future of
the German people; his casting Austria out of Germany, and his
failure to take more territory from France and Russia. These
seemed to him inexplicable blunders. Why? Because his great
passion was *to create the Religion of religions, the New German
National Religion, superior both to traditional Catholicism and to
traditional Protestantism*. What he wanted was to divine the

faith of the future, to discover the eternal religious impulse of which the German people, the *Chosen People*, should be the incarnation for Europe and the world.

What *is* the essential of religion? Paul de Lagarde took refuge in Fichte's mysticism. Religion was an inner life, a regeneration, a personal communion with God. But religion was not narrowly individual. It was the feeling of being *surpassed and dominated* by a great reality, of submitting to the divine command *as member of a nation itself charged with a divine mission*. For nations, like individuals, had *moral personalities*. They were of divine origin. The Germans relived and carried out the Gospel in their own way. The nations were to be regenerated by contact with this Germanic Christianity. This lofty spiritual existence must be clothed in an adequate terrestrial reality. *That is why Paul de Lagarde wanted Germany to strike down France and Russia once and for all.* Was Germany to be deprived of the means of her own salvation and of the consequent salvation of the world? The Germans should colonize Hungary and the Slav regions of Austria. *If necessary they should have recourse to deportations.* They should build up a Central Europe worthy of so lofty a destiny. *For the German Empire was foreseen in God's design* and Germany had the *right* to use the *force* necessary to accomplish her mission. The German people should be accustomed to the idea of the Great War which was to come.

Constantin Frantz, disciple of Schelling, was no less hostile than Lagarde to Bismarck and to his master Stahl. He reproached Stahl with having no conception of a Christian State save Lutheran Prussia, the antithesis of genuine Christianity. Frantz early began to dream of a vast Central Europe with a unified economic system, of a Confederation comprising Prussia, Austria, and the small European States, a Confederation *naturally directed against France and Russia.* As a Saxon, he was hostile to Prussian predominance, and he sought to limit it by the inclusion of Austria and the Slav States. He craved a new Imperial Germany that should be mistress of Europe after he dismemberment of France and Russia. This new Germany should be a *new Holy Roman Empire*. Such, he thought, were the principles of a sound policy, at once *German* and *Christian*. The Middle Ages had not been truly Christian. Europe, dominated by Germany, would be.

It would be easy to find similar ideas in Görres and other writers, but these indications suffice. We are now in a position to cast a comprehensive glance over this period extending from the Congress of Vienna to the Franco-Prussian war.

What had it brought to Germany? Three new prerogatives which destiny had hitherto seemed to deny her: *a territory economically one*, which opened up a thousand opportunities for her agriculture, her industry, her internal and external trade; an Empire of Prussian inspiration, *limited as yet in extent but militarized and strongly administered*; and, finally, *the vision of the Future Reich, the Central Europe* which would assure the domination of the Continent to a Greater Germany embracing Austria and the Slav South-east. From this time forward Germany constituted a menace to the European West and to Russia. Only by destroying them could she fulfil what she believed to be her destiny.

By destroying them or by destroying herself. For the history of Bismarck's Empire is the tale of a gigantic crisis which it is our task to analyse if we would explain the collapse of 1918.

CHAPTER V

UNDER THE SIGN OF BISMARCK AND OF THE INDUSTRIAL
REVOLUTION (1871–1914)

THE century between the Vienna Congress and the armistice of November 1918 opened with the victory of the coalition Powers of the east, aided by England, over Napoleonic France, and ended with the triumph of the western Entente over Bismarckian Germany. It was cut almost into halves by the military clash of 1870–71 between France and Germany. Prussia, Germany unified by Bismarck, and the union of the Central Empires conducted operations against France in three stages.

This series of offensives, of growing extent and violence, strongly impressed all men's minds. It presupposed on the German side an almost boundless increase of power, which was certainly the dominant fact of the nineteenth century. This renewal of energy in a continually widened attack was owed by Germany to two new factors with which destiny endowed her— a *central power* over the German States, based by Bismarck on Prussian hegemony, and *industrialism*, which made her economically the first nation of the old Continent. But these brutal affirmations of Germany's strength were accompanied by a terrible collapse of values that was to lead her to nihilism.

1. *Prussia and Germany*

This process, formidable in itself, and watched at all times by well-informed contemporaries with mingled astonishment and anxiety, took place in three distinct phases.

The first, as we have seen, was that of the Germanic Confederation set up by the labours of the Vienna Congress. It lasted from 1815 to 1867, the year that saw the old federal association of 1815 replaced by the much more rigid union of the northern States, a system to which the southern States adhered in 1870-71.

The second period was that of Bismarck. It opened on the elaboration of the fragmentary Constitution of 1871, a vigorous but incomplete programme, the fruit of a tenacious labour of genius. This period ended with the fall of the Chancellor, dismissed in 1890 by a young emperor who had come to the throne in 1888. It included two dissimilar decades, but was a period of incessant struggles, in the course of which the extraordinary personality of Bismarck was at grips with all the particularist elements to which the achievement of national unity was anathema.

Finally came the Empire of William II, covering the quarter of a century immediately before the world conflagration and the four years of war.

These three phases were closely bound up with each other. It is impossible to understand Bismarck without the political events and the economic innovations of the half-century of peace between 1815 and 1864. However great he might be, a statesman unprovided with certain guarantees of success would have failed to galvanize a human collectivity which until then had remained divided and impotent. Anyone who carefully studies the social and political history of the German States and of Prussia at that period readily comes to the conclusion that, under the action of similar circumstances, there were coming everywhere into view in the wide territory of the Germanic Confederation the governing features of a system that was in future to be applied to the Reich. Remote as they were from a centralizing militarism, the German States submitted themselves more and more to political or administrative standards common to them all. They had also material resources and material interests in common. This half-century saw the triumph of the Zollverein (Customs Union), started by Prussia in 1818, which about 1860 made of the national territory a homogeneous commercial domain in which the free movement of persons and of goods was possible. In this more favourable internal situation, Bismarck turned his attention abroad, and welded together the elements of the Reich by means of three victorious wars: against Denmark in 1864, against Austria in 1866, and against France in 1870–71.

During the succeeding twenty years, from 1871 to 1890, the Germans aimed for the first time at *a common existence*. But this common existence was possible only through the powerful personality of the Iron Chancellor—who showed himself, however, in spite of that fallacious appellation, to be the most astute of diplomats, and the most moderate as well as the most resourceful of statesmen. It will surprise nobody that Bismarck, to quote his own phrase, saw in the difficult political material that he had to mould "a rich orchestra" to be organized and conducted. He aimed at forming his country less by fidelity to the letter of the constitution than by a vigorous activity in establishing and maintaining "a series of compromises."

But in order to carry out this programme he found himself compelled to battle with territorial dynasties acutely conscious of their decay, with strongly organized and increasingly energetic political parties, with the religious denominations, and with sectional interests of every sort. He had to conquer his adversaries group by group, without any certainty that the conflict would not break out again on the very morrow of the settlement. Internal difficulties grew with economic prosperity itself, the social classes and the rival material interests engaging in incessantly renewed conflicts. Bismarck's task was easier in foreign policy, where new machinery, entirely independent of parliamentary control, patiently created the Triple Alliance in the centre of the old Continent.

It was to be feared, however, that once the great miracle-worker had disappeared, the edifice so hastily constructed would crumble. The process of disintegration continued unmistakably throughout the reign of William II, until the First World War. Political crisis, economic crisis, diplomatic crisis—such were the three aspects of the deep-seated malady from which the Reich was suffering on the eve of hostilities, and which brought about its collapse. So long as Bismarck had been there, able himself to defend the compromises upon which the edifice rested, it was possible for the immense construction that had so rapidly been achieved to hold together. But, once his guiding hand was gone, there came sinister signs of trouble everywhere. The executive power tossed to and fro between personal rule and the parliamentary institution, the incessantly accelerated rhythm of an economic production that had grown incredibly but lacked foreign outlets, the dismemberment of the Triple Alliance under the menace of war, discussions between Austria and Italy—such was the spectacle presented about 1914 by the Bismarckian creation. The administration and the army were its only tolerably solid cement. There was a desire for war, not only for the extension of the Reich on the Continent or in the colonial domain, but also in order to consolidate its tottering internal power and to get its rulers back into the saddle.

A disturbing and difficult situation, beyond question. But it in no way prevented German thought from returning to the dream of future greatness. It was in the nineteenth century that pan-Germanism spread. There is an exact parallelism between its development and that of Prussian hegemony. Between 1815 and 1870 ideological conflicts were still of some importance. It was the period in which the influence of Western liberalism was disappearing, after the hopes to which it had given birth on the eve of the Revolution of 1848. On the other hand, with Friedrich List, Constantin Frantz, Paul de Lagarde, and Richard Wagner, pan-Germanism dwelt again on the themes romanticism had bequeathed to it. The Zollverein, however, and the creation of the Second Reich, turned public attention away from it, for the time at all events. The leading part was played by Prussia. The situation was the same between 1870 and 1890, when the pan-Germans, ardent advocates of Greater Germany, would have nothing to do with Bismarck. But under William II, when the political machine was beginning to be thrown out of gear, biological racialism made its appearance. The universities undertook to establish it geographically and historically. The Continental programme of *Mitteleuropa* and the colonial programme took on a new and boundless extension. In the offensive of 1914, an attack on a grand scale against the West, the means of action forged by Prussia for the Reich were united with the renewed myth of Germanic might.

This brief summary, reducing to its elements the history of the Second Reich, throws full light on the great importance which the problem of the cohesion of the national forces had assumed for the Germany of Bismarck. *But it was cohesion for cohesion's sake*, not any political or social principle to be established in the European world. And it was through that defect that the Bismarckian Empire was to perish.

Why did not Bismarck achieve Greater Germany at the first attempt? Why did he rest content with Lesser Germany? The reason is that the latter was itself simply a compromise, the key to all the other Bismarckian compromises. This was the central problem of German politics. The terms of the compromise were *the national State and the Idea of the Reich*.

It was not, in fact, a question of establishing a simple mean between the dynastic pretensions of Prussia, Austria, and the other German States. What was needed was to take account of two fundamental but irreconcilable aspirations. The Germans wanted to be a true national State, provided with a normal political, administrative, and military organization, on the natural basis of a population speaking one and the same language. They wanted also to be an Empire, an Empire that could unite in Europe all the German-speaking populations.

Now, taken as a whole, the Germans could not renounce either of these two pretensions. The difficulty came, in Bismarck's time, from the fact that it was impossible fully to satisfy both aspirations in a State which was an Empire embracing all Germans and which at the same time continued to possess a solid political framework, the essential attribute of a State. Bismarck realized this difficulty. He solved it in his characteristic way, by a compromise.

Nobody denied the necessity of superposing upon the German States a central power, a common legislature, administration, and army. The evolution of the German States since 1815, moreover, justified that aspiration. Everywhere there came into existence within the various constitutional frameworks the same fundamental relations between Crown and Parliament, the same concern for social and economic unification, the same search for an equitable settlement for the two Christian confessions. From this point of view there was nothing to prevent Bismarck from bringing Austria into his Empire.

But was it possible at such a time, without war, to sacrifice Vienna to Berlin or Berlin to Vienna? Submission to Berlin would have been for Vienna a renunciation of her most authentic traditions. Austria remained a Catholic Power. She was the

State that until 1806 had dominated the Holy Roman Empire of the German Nation; she was the seat of Apostolic Majesty and the centre of a federation of peoples, a federation of international, universal tendencies. The future German State, on the contrary, the German nation that was to be built on a definitive basis, was inspired by the principles of the Lutheran Reformation. Only Protestant Prussia could give to the future Reich, through the exercise of her hegemony, the internal framework it lacked.

Here we have the entirely typical conflict, running through all German history, between *nationalism* and *internationalism*. Such States as France and Britain are nations boldly and precisely delimited and able not only to exercise great international influence, through the spread of the political principles that inspire them, but also to found and maintain colonial empires of vast dimensions. *The German countries, on the contrary, claim to be at one and the same time a nation and an inter-nation.* They want to be a nation, that is to say, to possess the necessary internal cohesion, in order to become thus a super-nation, such as was the Holy Roman Empire. In other words, they are led by the influence of their history, and of the geographical and racial conditions imposed on them, to *identify the international order essential to Europe with their own Continental hegemony.* They seem incapable of integrating themselves in a league of peoples provided with a power capable of imposing, if not an arbitrary will, at least *common standards* upon nations which would sacrifice part of their sovereignty in order to accept them and to comply with them. The imperial ambitions of the Germans, based on their special position and their history, lead them *to exclude Internationals* that seek to impose themselves on them *from without*, and to substitute for those Internationals a nationalism that inevitably changes into an *internationalisme à l'Allemande*, that is to say, into *hegemony*.

It is not sufficient to state that the historic past must be invoked. No German statesman can in reality arbitrarily dissociate himself from the imperial aspirations, or, on the contrary, entirely lose himself in them. If he abandons them, he betrays one of the most deep-rooted traditions of his country. If he tries to realize them in full, he is doomed to come into conflict with the whole European periphery.

The truth is that the *political* frontiers and the *racial* frontiers of Germany are not the same. This strange paradox is adequately expressed by the term *Volkstum*. In 1871, long before Hitler's annexations, it was impossible to deny that outside Germany there were not only German minorities, but true racial or political German entities.   Switzerland, Austria, the Sudetenland, Alsace, the Netherlands, and Flanders represent to a German view transitory forms between Germany and the West, between Germany and the European periphery.   This is what has nurtured Continental pan-Germanism throughout its existence.   Was it not against the Holy Roman Empire, with its claims to universal hegemony, that such nations as England and France took their stand, in order to save their independence, their liberties, and their advantages?

Bismarck was too intelligent, too good a diplomat, not to sense the distrust aroused all over Europe by the Empire he had created.   That was the supreme element of his political wisdom. Whence, indeed, did this instinctive hatred come, this hatred that showed itself everywhere?   It was explained by the fact that *Volkstum*, the German racial principle, could not, as such, form an integral part, a component, of the Europe of the nationalities. That Europe, formed by the centuries that had followed the Middle Ages, had justly maintained the German countries in territorial fragmentation, and consequently in complete political impotence.   Europe had feared for her stability.   She could not return to the conceptions and the dominations of the Middle Ages, the epoch anterior to the nationalities, and still less achieve suddenly the true solution, *the United States of Europe*.   She clung to the nations, *and superposed upon them, as yet, nothing but an abstract humanism*.   It was of that abstraction that in our day the League of Nations died.

Europe was caught in a terrible dilemma.   If she maintained the principles for which nationalities are founded, she could not refuse to the German *Volkstum* the right to apply them to itself and so to proceed to a sort of territorial revolution of which we see to-day the manifestations and the effects.   On the other hand, if she did not maintain them, if she returned to the forms of the past, she denied the very foundations of her juridical organization.   As she was not ripe for the United States of the Continent, the only form that could rationally be conceived for the future, she remained face to face with the dilemma, divided between *mistrust* and the principle of *justice between nations*.

That was what Bismarck felt.   Consequently he adopted only a restricted and moderate solution, that of Lesser Germany.   Not that he thus suppressed the difficulty, which was explained by the very structure of Europe. But he was able to *secure acceptance for his creation*, and so to maintain the new Germany, and consequently Europe, in relative tranquillity. When the First World War broke out, the hostilities and the treaties that ended it revived the problem in its full acuteness and its full dimensions.

But Bismarck secured acceptance for his creation by *limiting* it, not by *justifying* it before Europe. He installed at the very centre of the Continent, in creating the Lesser Germany under Prussian hegemony, *a Great Power without a political idea*.

Why? It is impossible to have a thorough grasp of the problem without returning to the political evolution of Germany between 1650 and 1815. At the very time when the French nation was constituting itself a citadel of Catholicism and of the free-thought that is its complement, and when the English nation represented political Protestantism, the German Empire was in entire decay, terminating its existence in 1806 and giving place to a Napoleonic creation with little probable duration. In the same period there had grown great, with Frederick II, the Prussia-Brandenburg which, vanquished at Jena, was reconstituted with incredible rapidity to carry on the anti-Napoleonic campaign in 1814. It is easy to see why, within the worm-eaten Holy Roman Empire, the political centre of gravity had shifted from Vienna to Berlin. This shifting meant precisely the victory of Lutheran Protestantism on the political plane. But nothing more. *That victory largely shut Germany out from Western political influences, from the influences which Puritan practice or the principles of the French Revolution might have exerted over her.*

Thus it may be understood why Bismarck, in creating Lesser Germany on the Prussian basis, directed Germany's whole future policy into the path traced for her by the tradition of the Protestant territories.

The German nation was born in the sixteenth century. It was founded on a sort of alliance between Lutheranism, which was indifferent to political issues, and the territorial monarchy ruled by patriarchal or enlightened despotism. That despotism, that politico-ecclesiastical direction (*Obrigkeit*) imposed on the people, was clearly contrary to liberty as conceived by the West. In the Western view the State must always respect the sphere in which individual life moves. Humboldt maintained the same theory later in Germany. Germany was thus condemned to an entirely territorial policy, limited to a narrowly monarchical region that was incapable of even conceiving, to say nothing of bringing into actual existence, a State that would protect the liberties of its subjects. This policy Prussia, owing to her extent, her importance, and her colonizing traditions, carried to extremes. We know her conception of monarchy by divine right, her strictly bureaucratic organization, and the strength of her military machine. This policy could do nothing but develop in the various German populations discipline, submission, and obedience.

Thus shut in between the remote or impracticable idea of the Empire and the policy of territorial sovereignty, Germany was unable to develop into a truly modern State. The Prussian State had the form and the functions of a national State. It possessed the attributes of political life and activity. But it had not the true substance of either; it had not a great political idea of strong originality such as could be imposed abroad. Prussia, thanks to Bismarck, became the Reich. But that Reich was not and could not be anything but *a fragment of a nation*. It was a Great Power without a political idea.

Such was the defect which, from its origin, weighed on the Bismarckian creation. Such was the destiny of which Bismarck was himself to be one day the victim. If a Great Power wishes to be recognized, adopted, and tolerated, it is absolutely necessary that it shall justify itself *in the order of ideas*, that it shall represent a human principle and a value in itself. Otherwise it engenders by its very creation and its very existence nothing but *fear* and *mistrust*. The rise of Prussia never promoted any other reaction in Europe than this. There was no appeal to the imagination of peoples, to a hope for the future, to any such thing as faith in mankind. Here was a collection of psychological motives exactly the opposite of humanism. It was Prussia for Prussia's sake, the Reich for the Reich's sake, cohesion for its own sake, force, domination for its own sake. The State was everything. The individual was absorbed in the service of the collectivity, of society. Public tasks devoured individual liberties.

It was for that reason that, after having been Prussian for the sake of being Prussian, the German became *German for the sake of being German*. Nietzsche realized that danger when he wrote: "Nothing could prevent me from here becoming insolent and proclaiming to the Germans some terrible truths. Who should do it but I? I speak of their impudence *in historicis* . . . before all else they want to be 'Germans'; before all else they want to be a 'Race.' Only then, they think, will they be able to distinguish between values and non-values *in historicis*; only then will they be able to discover the true values. 'To be German' is an argument. 'Germany, Germany above all' is a principle."

Well—if there is nothing of higher quality than the German, then every value of transcendent order is denied and all humanism becomes impossible. If the German-Prussian works only for himself, he no longer serves any supranational ideal, though claiming to play the part of a European. He is absorbed in himself, in the community of which he is a member. His argument is that of pure existence. Working only for the collectivity of which he forms part, the German can do no more than busy himself within the State, purely for the State; *he can show the world only the spectacle, certainly a grandiose one, of his collective achievements*. But by that very process he frightens and disgusts the whole world. He inspires the same horror as certain financial successes of the Jews. When Germany followed her industrialization by Americanization, Europe could no longer tolerate her. The problem left in suspense by Bismarck led inescapably to war.

Such is the explanation of the three crises through which the Bismarckian creation passed in the nineteenth and twentieth centuries—an *economic* crisis, a *political* crisis, and a *moral* crisis. We must grasp their secret springs, if only in order to understand why the German people is the most vulnerable of the European peoples.

2. *Economic and social crisis*

To study only the play of Bismarckian politics is to see only one aspect of Bismarckism. The capital fact was the industrialization of Germany, which in the nineteenth century assumed the character of a veritable revolution. Historically German industrialization is explained, as we saw, by the great economic and social liquidation that took place in the first half of the eighteenth century. That liquidation was necessary—there is no need at all to prove it. The territorial fragmentation was the *cause* of too much backwardness for the progress made between 1790 and 1815 not to make its effect felt at once.

We have already seen what a transformation agriculture, and especially industry and commerce, underwent between 1815 and 1850, thanks to political unitarism, to the Zollverein, and to the perfecting of political and social doctrines. The Revolution of 1848 failed because the forty States of the Germanic Confederation were not ripe either for unity or for democracy, and still less for a *unitary democracy*.

They made, nevertheless, considerable progress in the relations between the nobility and the middle class. Here culture had exerted very powerful influence. From the beginning of the *Sturm und Drang* period the middle class had suddenly risen above its former level. It was precisely in the light of that culture that the social injustices had appeared in tragic colours. Moreover, the two classes had met in the pietist conventicles. The courts themselves, especially that of Weimar, had readily associated nobles with middle-class persons of superior quality. Until his death, in 1832, Goethe pondered on the problem of the relations between nobility and middle class. The middle class, moreover, did not remain passive. It did not rest content with its defence against aristocratic prejudices,—it attacked the nobility itself. No doubt the horrors of the French Revolution had put a stop to the process of emancipation and had served aristocratic reaction. But Prussia, in order to reconstitute her army after 1806, had had no choice but to associate officers of noble and of middle-class extraction.

It may be added that the Jewish question had received a more satisfying solution. Terribly oppressed since the Crusades, the Jews had profited by the *Aufklärung*. Under Frederick II the wealthy Jews had made important contributions to the progress of literature. Moses Mendelssohn (1729–86) had worked all his life for the integration of Judaism in German culture. The *salons* of Henriette Herz and of Rahel Levin played a leading part in the history of romanticism. This Jewish emancipation was to have incalculable consequences.

When the industrial revolution began in Germany, about 1850, a strange contrast showed itself between the extreme fidelity of some to the old principles of Prussian policy and the implacable realism of others in economic matters. This gave the process an appearance of cynicism which has often struck the foreigner. The reason is simple. *The German saw in the State not an idea but a regulative mechanism.* The habit of strict subordination and the rigorous accomplishment of duty, virtues which were eminently Prussian, were reconcilable with the conceptions, the ambitions, and the demands of the great capitalists. Thus, when German unity and industrialization came, the German middle class devoted its whole attention to economic achievement and its rewards.

As this middle class was divided in the religious field into several confessions, and as on the other hand it had no political ideal of its own, except those of Lutheranism and of national power, it proceeded to throw itself unreservedly into material achievement. The qualities required for bureaucracy and for industry were such as it had long possessed.

It was for that reason that it was so easily and so rapidly *Americanized*. No room was left for rest or for the simple pleasures of life. This middle class, whose energies had been accumulating for centuries and were now united for the first time on the national plane, spontaneously created a dynamism impossible to moderate, so great were its passion for work and so wide its ambitions. In this strictly realist Bismarckian Reich, in this State where the most important thing was to be "German" and to bring about the cohesion of individual efforts, there was displayed an uneasiness, an agitation, a nervousness unprecedented in Europe. At an early stage Bismarck's Germany was like a sort of childish giant, aware of his faults and failings, but imagining that he could make up for them by the most intensive propaganda.

It is possible that Germany never understood that nations recommended themselves to foreigners more by indolence, carelessness, and gracefulness, by spending their leisure time beautifully in pursuit of a real culture, than by the exaltation of toil and the apologia for output. The pride of Germany was her effort to be *at the same time attractive and very powerful*. Richard Wagner understood and described excellently, in his *Ring des Nibelungen*, this opposition between Power and Love.

Germany found ahead of her the privileged nations of England and France, both capable of exercising great influence in all directions. She was too late in the field, and became both jealous and exacting. So, in her lack of calm and moderation, she threatened to upset the whole European apple-cart. She suddenly became a strange mixture of *Prussianism, romanticism,* and *Americanism*. She subordinated her habits of discipline to the satisfaction of the most sweeping ambitions, and applied the most austere toil in the service of her visionary romanticism.

A Germany merely Prussianized in accordance with Bismarck's formula and with his moderation might have come to a lasting agreement with Europe. *A Germany that was simultaneously Prussian, romantic, and Americanized could not do this*. She was bound to play the part of a spoil-sport, a universal disturber.

What troubled Europe, before both wars, was not the recognized exercise of those Prussian virtues which, as Oswald Spengler has shown, arise solely from the sense of social duty, but *the fact that these virtues were brought to the service of boundless ambitions.* It is possible for Bolshevik Russia, in the system she has adopted, to unite Slavism and Americanism with the mobilization of certain spiritual energies. But Germany was struggling simply for her own existence and her own greatness. That is why, from 1914 to 1918, Western propaganda easily got the better of her. Her argument that she was struggling for simple existence and for a place in the sun made no appeal to other countries. It only excited fear and distrust.

Now comes a question of paramount importance. The Germans accused the English and French of disguising the selfish satisfaction of their interests under the phraseology of the great principles inspired by humanism. That is too simple. Western humanism might be found mixed with base interests that compromised its prestige and its credit. That happened, in truth, often enough before, during, and after the last war. But humanism had an independent existence outside such interests. Its attraction remained great because it had behind it very ancient traditions and values felt to be eternal. Germany, on the other hand, could make play with nothing but her interest in national cohesion. If she spoke of material issues, she had no thought beyond them. If she spoke of nationalism, she had nothing in mind but the German nation. She had no great idea to warm men's hearts and gain sympathies for her.

When the industrial revolution was brought about in Germany, after half a century of preparation, she headed straight into it without any spiritual tradition that might have protected her against certain excesses. We have seen that her political and religious history explains why she remained entirely aloof from the formation of the great modern States. She had not acquired, like France and England since the sixteenth century, a real style, a rule of life worthy of the name. Why? Because she had been unable to find her way to her own religious and national equilibrium. While around her the sense of nationhood was growing everywhere, together with political and religious individualism, capitalism, and a whole cosmopolitan civilization that displayed the most profound indifference to monarchy by divine right, Germany, boxed up in her 234 little monarchies, remained immobile. She acquired neither a great political tradition nor a culture in harmony with her politics. Britain and France, on the other hand, passed from the Middle Ages to modern times through the philosophy of the Enlightenment and through their revolutions, attaining completion and self-expression through their fecund genius. Meanwhile Germany looked askance at that stupendous movement. Nevertheless, instead of growing prematurely old, she remained young, husbanding her reserves: she had at her disposal immense forces which had too long been unused. In her case, there was something of Freudian repression.

The romantics had carefully noted this peculiarity. Nietzsche also referred to it when he asked, in his last philosophy, to what nation in Europe the future belonged. This was one of the most important arguments of pan-Germanism. We know how it ran. Germany was clearly behind Britain and France. But she had avoided the period of liberal intellectualism, which had exerted its influence on her only from abroad, where it had been transformed into a shabby utilitarianism that must be got rid of. Thus Germany had the future in her favour because she possessed, well into the nineteenth century, inexhaustible reserves of energy, reserves which the territorial fragmentation had kept intact simply by preventing them from acting in Europe with concentrated force. The nineteenth century was to be eminently the German century, the twentieth still more so.

These are the real origins of German *economic romanticism*. Held back by the fatality of history in her territorial cells, Germany had not been able to create for herself a culture that could give direct expression to her national policy. The great classical and romantic literature did not emanate from the political and religious activity of the territories, but, as we saw, was its counterpart, almost its negation. Confined within his little fatherlands, the German had indulged in dreaming. His thoughts had become uneasy. Disciplined in character but tumultuous in spirit, he would have had no need of so much militarism and discipline, so much professional feeling, so much method, so many collective and public organizations, if he had not had ingrained in him that uneasiness, at once metaphysical and practical, which he himself called problematism. While life in the territories induced disciplined toil, culture developed a breadth and universality of ideas that transcended territorial boundaries. When that diligence and that vastness of outlook or of ambitions met on a new and concrete terrain, the German problem assumed its real significance for Europe. That phenomenon occurred at the time of the industrial revolution, from 1840 onward, for the phases of the phenomenon ran strictly parallel with those of the political evolution of Bismarckism.

In the course of that period, as is known, the traditions of the past and the humanist values were destroyed. With Græco-Latin antiquity and the divided Christianity that had proceeded from the Reformation, progressive liberalism found itself threatened. As the Germans had received classical culture, Christianity, and liberalism merely as imports from abroad, they were not only lacking in tradition but even *ready to understand the very absence of tradition*. They rejoiced in a kind of pure liberty in regard to the past and the future, in a superabundance of fresh and untamed energies, in short in *barbarism*; for there was something barbaric in the sudden development of industrialism under Bismarck.

The nineteenth century brought innovations. In the space of a few decades, inventions and discoveries related to life and economic activity multiplied. Everyone knows the remarkable description of modern mechanization which Walter Rathenau essayed to give. This formidable process burst the normal bounds of human existence. The great changes of the sixteenth and seventeenth centuries were not yet concerned with the technique of daily work in town or countryside. But that which was preparing after 1750 and which burst out after 1850 was the *revolution of labour*.

Industry had become dynamic; production had to be increased and at the same time new outlets had to be constantly found for the product. There was no longer any static solution, except for the problem of what would pay. Markets were multiplied by creating new needs. Indissolubly united, economic and technical activities together formed a power which, set in motion by a pitiless logic, destroyed the equilibrium of human existence. A terrible process, devoid of intellectual or spiritual quality, and crushing the traditional values of those orders. Man became at once master and slave of material things. He could no longer be anything but producer or consumer. He perished of wealth which became a matter of indifference to him. He was thus reduced to mere existence, to methods of calculation and instrumental intelligence. He believed neither in progress nor in evolution nor in his own rights. He wondered whether the power thus acquired was any compensation for the moral bankruptcy engendered by mechanization and for the loss of liberty which it implied. It was from economic liberalism that the fourth form of humanism, the vision and hope of social justice, directly proceeded. But who believed in that justice? Men saw, in the very destruction of the world economy, the abyss opening between liberalism and proletarian Socialism.

Why did Germany suffer from this crisis more than other peoples? The answer is simple. She had had no experience of liberalism as practised in Britain and France. She underwent the industrial revolution without preparation, without transition, and without resistance. She had never believed in political progress, and with the set-back of 1848 the last remains of Westernism in Germany had crumbled. She adopted with the more eagerness and confidence the simple belief in material progress arising from scientific and industrial specialization. This specialization was thereafter confused with her intellectual substance. Full of vital and creative energy, Bismarck's unified Germany was carried away by an infinite hustle. She literally jumped at the entirely new opportunities which territorial unification and technical progress offered her. For a long time she had believed in nothing beyond life on earth. But as she had never been liberal, she made her industrial effort in the names of Prussianism and pan-Germanism.

This was how the German middle class of the Bismarckian epoch saw things. It saw in the Reich ruled under Prussian hegemony nothing but a guarantee of economic progress, and in the national unity nothing but the essential condition for certain bureaucratic and military achievements. Its ideal was reduced to one of mere power, an ideal imposed even on its Socialists and sapping the foundations of a borrowed humanism. And what happened? The romantic heritage was added to the dream of economic expansion of the employers and to the Socialist hope of the proletariat. *It was industry, and not the State or politics, that absorbed the intellectual tradition.* While the middle class was attending to business in complete indifference to politics, the masses of the workers were rejecting the Bismarckian State with their thoughts on the liberties of the morrow, or accepting it in so far as it promoted their welfare. Germany passed from her former idealism to complete materialism. She thus became *the most vulnerable of European nations* because the coming economic crisis would affect *her sole asset.*

This crisis came long before the First World War.

Germany, industrialized from 1850 onwards, had a couple of decades in which to prepare on the economic plane before

Bismarck's creation of the Reich. From the same epoch date the completion of the Zollverein, begun in 1818, the renovation and consolidation of the Prussian army, and finally the advent of that realist spirit which was the work not only of Bismarck but also of the political parties and of all the organized groups.

The smoking chimneys multiplied, the towns grew like mushrooms; the urbanization of the rural masses proceeded with lightning rapidity, and new inventions enabled the townsmen to indulge in growing comfort. Everything did violence to nature, at the very moment when the natural and technical sciences were invading the universities. Capital piled up. Enterprises sprang up all over Germany. These tendencies favoured territorial and political unification, and that in turn promoted them powerfully.

This immense economic development, from 1870 to 1890, was a real miracle. Germany's population increased from a total of forty million inhabitants in 1871 to fifty millions in 1890. The freedom of traffic in this rapidly growing population had the aspect of a veritable revolution. While the means of transport rapidly came into existence, the Press, better equipped than formerly, poured out instruction and appeals to the masses. So many novel facilities and the search for better conditions of life, in a country in which nature and the soil were far from generous, produced immense social displacements, with a drift from the agrarian East and South to the industrial regions, attaining its maximum between 1880 and 1890. This urbanization presented certain advantages. It mixed the racial components, strengthened the national sentiment, partly levelled religious barriers, increased the influence of the towns and of their culture, and also expanded the home market. On the other hand it had a terribly levelling and an excessively rationalizing effect on an industrious and docile people, condemned to mechanized production.

At the beginning, after Germany had pocketed the French indemnity, this evolution had proceeded at a catastrophic pace, becoming a veritable debauch of hazardous speculations and business ventures. About a thousand joint-stock companies had sprung from the ground almost overnight. The crash of 1874 was, however, nothing but a sort of growing-pains. Economic activity in the Reich afterwards assumed a more normal rhythm. But Germany lived thereafter by her commerce and industry alone. In the Bismarckian Reich more than anywhere else, modern enterprise accumulated capital, extended its plant, employed millions of workpeople, and produced a growing mass of merchandise. The mining, metal, and chemical industries grew to fantastic dimensions. The credit establishments were legion. This neo-capitalism destroyed the old forms of home industry, the handicrafts, and antiquated corporations and organizations. The tide was so powerful that it irresistibly carried away all isolated enterprises. Commerce reached such a development about 1890 that in this sphere Germany took the fourth place among the European Powers. Consequently she lived increasingly on her external trade and on purchases abroad. Thus work and the opportunity to earn were *the only safety-valve* for a country with a swollen birth-rate and a reduced mortality.

With industry, commerce, and transport assuming such dimensions, agriculture was bound to suffer. The era of its great prosperity had lasted from 1830 to 1870, even extending to nearly 1880, that is to say to the moment when Europe was to meet the competition of the new countries, when foreign cereals were pouring into the home markets at falling prices, and when, as land and rents dropped in value, real estate acquired a crushing load of debt. Accordingly Bismarckian statecraft tried, between 1880 and 1890, to restore agriculture and to favour it at the expense of industry. Agricultural prices were raised, railway rates for home produce reduced, schools of agriculture set up, credit organized, in order to protect the farmer in the face of the unhealthy growth of commerce and industry.

At the same time, the structure of the social classes became profoundly modified. While the old landed aristocracy retained its reactionary and anti-capitalist spirit and its feudal and patriarchal customs, it nevertheless modernized itself in so far as the junkers came to consider their property as a source of safe income, or organized rural industries in which they associated themselves with the capitalist system. The most active element was the aristocracy of enterprise, the captains of industry. They judged men solely by their capacity to make profits, their success, or their wealth. They constituted a special caste, strong and independent, much stratified, and dominated by high finance, which imitated the nobility, adopted its ways, and gained access to the Imperial court.

Alongside this small oligarchy came the middle class of the propertied and the salary-earners. They gained in importance as the Reich grew in extent, but too much divergence of interest prevented them from organizing themselves. Lastly, in numbers equivalent to the middle classes, the proletarian masses organized themselves more and more solidly from 1875 onwards. The Social Democracy, their great political party, grew from 113,000 votes in 1870 to nearly 1,500,000 in 1890. Behind it stood already the great trade unions and the co-operatives. This social evolution substituted for the old categories, founded on differences of social function, divisions based on variations in income. But incomes tended to become equalized, and the danger of being forced into the proletariat was soon weighing on the unorganized middle classes, caught between the economic oligarchy and the proletariat with its strong unions.

Under William II the crisis assumed an enormous extent. It was the direct consequence of this too rapid development. A miracle was needed to avoid, within this capitalist system, destitution for a nation that had trebled in numbers. Between 1890 and 1910 Germany increased by yet another fifteen million people. About 1907, of every 1000 people 427 were working in industry and 131 in commerce. Two-thirds of the population were living in the towns and the other third in the country, the reverse of the proportion in the past. The disproportion between agriculture and industry had become so great that Germany might be compared to a house in which the ground floor, finding itself too small in comparison with the first floor, was forcing the upper floors to find external supports.

The great industries were all in a state of crisis from 1890 to 1914, because they had expanded too rapidly. The farmers, who could no longer feed the whole population, groaned about their mortgages, about the abuse of speculation, foreign competition, and their dependence on the industrialists, since exportation had to pay for foodstuffs coming from abroad; about bad harvests, and finally about the dearness of clothing, of machinery and tools, of implements and manures, to say nothing of taxation, of the scarcity of labour, of rural Socialism, of succession duties, and of the difficulty of getting credit. It was a vicious circle, or an endless screw. The more the agricultural workers forsook the country, the more it was necessary to import, and consequently to manufacture and export, and that at the very time when Europe's external markets were beginning to dwindle. There was already talk of the *restoration of German agriculture and of economic self-sufficiency*.

Industry, commerce, and transport were in no better case. Workshops, factories, businesses, and banks were undoubtedly performing prodigies, accumulating capital, extending their plant, concentrating armies of workpeople at vital points and producing enormous quantities. But the system was obviously being pushed beyond the sane limit. The process attained its culminating point between 1895 and 1900. This was the period when Germany passed definitely from the agrarian type to the industrial. In 1907 the industrial and commercial population represented 50 per cent. of the total. And a number of foreign industries, in Switzerland, in Italy, in Spain, were being turned into branches of German industry.

This formidable growth brings out clearly the original aspects of German capitalism. There would be no greater mistake than to confuse it with Western capitalism. A strange association was formed here between the habits of German labour, organized with the strictest discipline, and the economic or technical requirements of modern production. In Germany, a strongly organized employing class, with an unusual audacity and breadth of view, ruled a proletariat no less disciplined than the masters, thanks to its political party and to its trade unions. This time the Germans concentrated their disciplined energies on activities of a nature to ensure their expansion in the world. They tended, by a natural movement, toward the *concentration* of capital, of machinery, of men, and of efforts, rather than toward competition of the Anglo-Saxon type. At an early stage their capitalism was to be *authoritative* and *corporative*.

This capitalism inherited, in fact, feudal and patriarchal traditions that brought it close to the landed aristocracy, which was itself attracted towards agricultural enterprise of the industrial type. Is it surprising that, in this Second Reich, syndicates and cartels of employers multiplied alongside the great working-class organizations? Nowhere was there closer collaboration between factories and banks. Nowhere was production more scientifically conceived, the mass of foreign innovations utilized in a more wholesale manner, university teaching more definitely directed to immediate applications.

This means that the old social disciplines, the heritage of the Prusso-Lutheran tradition, showed themselves capable of a prodigious yield. It explains the immensity and the startling rhythm of German production. *It was the plant and the personnel that here controlled the rhythm, not the demand. The creative activities were carried away by their own dynamic quality.* This economic world became a sort of monstrous entity that seemed to exist for its own sake. There was action and reaction between repetition work and accelerated production; hence the inevitable over-production. The country was being suffocated by superabundance, the equilibrium between the national production and the capacity of absorption of the markets having been upset. The combines submitted to such formidable discipline that they became an oppressive menace, not only to the small or moderate-sized industries, but also to foreign production and commerce.

The banks did their best to promote this deliberate, systematic expansion. The incessant renewal of plant obliged the Germans to employ in their industries capital which had to be remunerated at all costs. Joint-stock companies assumed crushing obligations, because their shareholders demanded large dividends, 15, 25, or even 35 per cent. Besides this, the millions of workers employed had to be paid. With their numbers their rates of wages increased, by reason of the growing power of the trade unions. Faced with the triple demand from employers, shareholders, and workers, the German banks became deposit, credit, and commercial banks, or great financial companies. They occupied themselves with the concentration of capital. Above them, the Reichsbank wielded a dictatorship of increasing severity. There was a veritable mobilization of German wealth for the creation of credit. All savings in Germany were roped in by industrial and banking business. Moreover, Germany attracted foreign capital, and this capital in turn encouraged the national over-production. Thus the obligations of the German banks often exceeded their liquid assets.

While the landed aristocracy and the middle-class oligarchy were carrying on vast enterprises in agriculture, industry, banking, and commerce, the Prusso-German State came to their assistance, accomplishing the mission it had always claimed. It protected and encouraged that formidable activity all the more easily because, in virtue of the old territorial tradition, the Germans readily accepted administrative tutelage and official interference. The Government of William II thus exercised a fairly vigorous sort of economic dictatorship. Methods of the past reappeared, applied to a much enlarged system, the dynamism of which disturbed the whole world. On the backs of the disciplined working masses, the Imperial State and the great economic powers, in accordance with the excellent formula of the German economist Friedrich List, concluded a formidable alliance that made *Germany a kind of social monster*.

Carried away by the movement which it thus promoted and animated, the State became constantly more industrial and commercial. It no longer attached so much importance as in earlier times to the balance between industry and agriculture. The Empire, Prussia, the States, and the local authorities, all the wheels of the machinery, collaborated in the task of the common expansion. This Empire was, moreover, an excellent customer in its capacity of railway, military, and naval Power. Its multifarious orders eased over the crises. It nationalized the cartels while providing the working masses with a very complete system of insurance. Its diplomacy, its consular officials, and its fleet made their contribution to the commercial expansion. But at the same time the Reich was the sport of all the forces released. It hesitated between Free Trade and Protection. It constructed as well as it could the parallelogram of German forces in a world more and more uneasy or hostile.

The restriction of outlets thus menaced this congested world with a veritable collapse. Vast crises, shoals of bankruptcies, resounding crashes multiplied as the date of the war drew nearer. With a people of such precarious destiny, innocent causes could provoke formidable panics or collapses. The crash of 1874–75, the crises of 1892, 1901, 1902, 1907, and 1911 were so many symptoms foreboding a more universal upheaval. In this too rapidly enriched population there was no relation between the increase in private fortunes and that of the national revenue. Germany suffered equally, on the local government plane in particular, from an excess of public expenditure and of unproductive wealth. The economic and the financial crises were closely associated. In the end the country found itself in the position of a rich man who has committed himself to an over-grandiose enterprise and sees that it needs more capital than he possesses. How would William II's Germany hold out if war came?

Too much science, too much toil, too much purely material activity. Private and collective life were both in danger. Large-scale capitalism took its definitive form in Germany, with all the consequences implied by its extraordinary development. It was a revolution, one which affected the very foundations of German society, as of humanity in general. In Germany more than anywhere else everything was reduced to a *system*, a *method*, with a complete indifference to all religion, to all morals, to all belief in progress or in human improvement. The German nation, preoccupied above all with its success, knowing the power it would have the day it secured the necessary cohesion of its energies, sacrificed its liberty to this dream of greatness. It began to bind the individual German, usually so devoted to his private life, to a social order hostile to life and to liberty. It became dehumanized. In following the methods of modern industrial technique it saw only the *functional* side of the individual. On the other hand, if a crisis came, it risked losing everything. And the result of this long malaise, on the eve of hostilities, was precisely the extreme *vulnerability* of the German people.

3. *The political crisis*

Considered from the point of view of its political structure, the Bismarckian Empire was what Guglielmo Ferrero called a "demo-monarchy." An evil-sounding term, but one which defined in a perfectly adequate manner the system which was developed in the German countries between 1815 and 1860, and which served as the framework of the Second Reich.

It is easy to see the curious compromise represented by German centralization when we set its resulting federal State (*Bundesstaat*) between the federation of States (*Staatenbund*) of the Germanic Confederation and the centralized State (*Einheitsstaat*) devised by the admirable Constitution of 1849, which never came into force in Germany. Bismarck vehemently opposed the constitutional ideal of 1848; but when, after 1850, he had accumulated valuable experience at the Diet of Frankfort, the principal organ of the Germanic Confederation, he realized that Germany could not stop at a loose formula of federation. The original bond between Prussia and the Reich was the very thing to give him the desired solution. In order that Prussia might continue, as she wanted to at any cost, to exist as a "State" inside the Reich, it would be necessary to retain a certain federalism, that of the twenty-five Bismarckian States. But as it was no less indispensable to superimpose upon those States a strong central power armed with the required authority, that power was confided to that same Prussia, thanks to the personal union between Prussia and the Reich. This combination was proposed by the Reichstag and accepted by Bismarck. The Prussian monarchy became imperial, in the Bismarckian sense of the term. The first Minister of State of Prussia thus became Chancellor of the Empire.

This system, though certainly complicated, did not succeed

badly. From 1871 to 1890, dynastic particularism did not offer Bismarck the opposition he seemed to fear. The successive rapid triumphs of centralization, on the other hand, inflicted a decisive defeat on the old federalism. Centralization had in its favour the majority of the political parties, and therefore the majority of the nation, which felt instinctively that the future belonged to the unification of German energies. National Liberals, who stood for the free circulation of goods and for economic centralization; Progressives who, faithful to the principles of 1848, sought political unity without on that account neglecting material unity; Social Democrats, who were interested in standardizing the condition of the workers in Germany—all these elements formed a large majority over the Prussian Conservatives, the Catholic Centre, and the Democrats of the South, all more or less federalist.

As, on the other hand, the normal play of the Constitution tended to aggrandize the legislation, the administration, and the competence of the Reich, the central power did not scruple to draw profit from these prerogatives, which could be extended at will. The process of unification carried out in Germany between 1871 and 1914 was of a striking character. But it is easily explained. A nation that arrived so late at this relative degree of political integration would try by every means to make up for lost time. All social classes, all organizations, all interests were drawn into this extraordinary whirlpool. Parliament legislated with feverish haste to satisfy the growing needs of the nation in its rapid advance.

Officially or tacitly the Reich, in extending its legislative competence, made rapid progress in the spheres in which it had the exclusive or the relative right to make laws, so that every legislative advance brought new means of control. It encroached even on those domains in which the States were supposed to be alone competent to legislate. Naturalization, the means of communication and transport, currency, the banking system, the civil code, all fell into its hands. On the administrative plane the sections of the vast imperial machine multiplied in consequence, with the formation of the immense army of officials of the Reich, the States, and the local authorities. The powers of the Emperor and the Chancellor increased similarly and supplanted those of the Federal Diet. The imperial offices, the germ of future Ministries, were grouped around the Chancellor, who tended to delegate a part of his responsibility to them. As for military unification, a great idea of Bismarck's, there was nothing in its way but the feeble obstacle of certain rights reserved to the States. Compulsory service was extended, and also served to unify the population of the Reich.

This craving for unification extended to the States themselves, which, to settle various questions, entered into conventions of military import in regard to railway rates and in regard to judiciary administration. Even the Federal Council, which favoured these agreements, furthered the aims of centralization. While Prussian particularism tended to absorb the little particularisms of the country, the Reich integrated in itself all the particularisms at once. Federalism maintained its positions in the financial domain alone.

The States lost of necessity what the Reich gained. But this implied no danger to the future of the régime. The victory of centralization assured, in fact, that of Prussian hegemony. How would Bismarck's Germany have been able to develop without the permanent spread of Prussia's influence? Not that Prussia could govern the Reich as she liked. Still, no one in Germany could push Prussia in a particular direction or prevent her from acting as she pleased. Prussia applied to her rule the principles of Stein, fought against the preponderance of the bureaucracy, and tried to gain more elasticity and liberty through the play of administrative autonomy. She even sought to show as much consideration to the wishes of the toiling masses as to those of the aristocracy and the plutocracy. Bismarck was able to force the junkers to make concessions. It was because Prussia, at once strong and supple, thus prepared herself with an eye on her mission that she was able to maintain a balance between federalism and centralization. The King of Prussia, as Emperor, had control of the army and navy. The personal union and the prestige of the imperial function did not hurt Prussia, which could not be put into a subordinate position by centralization, having all the means of resistance.

Prussia, therefore, could not forgo leading Germany, though nothing constrained her to assume the leadership. Even when the central power developed considerably, she retained a large share of it, without effectively ruling the other States. Her hegemony amounted strictly to the total of the principles and institutions thanks to which she was impregnating the reconstituted nation with her juridical, administrative, and military spirit. The laws of the Reich had a Prussian aspect, and the

German code was only a prolongation of the Prussian. The control the Reich exercised over the States was a control of the Prussian type. The fate of the States was indissolubly bound to that of Prussia as well as to that of the Reich. The Reich was, in fact, a "Prolonged Prussia." Prussia exercised a regulating influence. Not that there was a perfect organic liaison between her and Germany from the political and economic point of view. It was mainly the administration and the army that profited by the Prussian hegemony. By this method the former absolutism could be applied to the Second Reich under relatively modern forms.

There was nothing unnatural in this process, which seemed inevitable, since the Empire was behind its neighbours. The strangeness began with the consequences of this unification on the political plane. The real threat to the régime was the play of political forces, the permanent conflict between Parliament and the Government.

From 1815 to 1918, parliamentarism in Germany simply used its opportunities to work for unification. That was its distinctive feature, or, if preferred, the place it logically occupied in the Bismarckian system. Coupled with the centralization it favoured, it proved to be a sort of mean between the system the Germanic Confederation had tried to introduce and the system sketched in the Constitution of Frankfort. It in no way excluded the rule of the Crown and its personal servants. It left them all their executive authority. On the other hand, it entirely abandoned the sovereignty of the people in the Western sense of the term. It was the instrument of which the monarchy made use in order to find out what interests were at stake, to manipulate them, and to dominate them by setting them one against another. This amounts to saying that the Bismarckian Reich was a State without a political idea. That is why the Bismarckian institution of the Reichstag, which so surprised the Germans in 1867, is explained only by the history of German parliamentarism between 1815 and 1860. Bismarck, in fact, merely summed up and applied to the Reich the experience which had been gained by the forty States of the Germanic Confederation. And, as is known, the paths which German parliamentarism followed in this first period of its history show perfect regularity.

From 1860 to 1864, Prussian parliamentarism tried to seize power and to limit the rights of the Crown. When Bismarck, Prime Minister of Prussia from 1862, intervened, he took the mean between the opposed tendencies, and prepared, thanks to three victorious wars, the solution of 1871.

We know that that solution, once it had arrived at maturity, provided on the one hand for a federal Council which included the plenipotentiaries of the dynasties, which still retained a measure of sovereignty, and on the other hand for a monarch who was at the same time King of Prussia and Emperor, with a national parliament or Reichstag superposed, as it were, on the Prussian "Landtag" and on the parliaments of the twenty-five States, and elected, like all the rest, by universal suffrage. If we add that it was the Reichstag itself that wanted to see the King of Prussia assume the imperial function, it will be understood that there was at an early stage a kind of solidarity between the two unitary organs, Emperor and Reichstag, in face of the federal organ. What was then bound to come about, under Bismarck himself, was the substitution for that initial solidarity of a permanent conflict between the two central organs, particularly between Bismarck as Chancellor and the parties represented in the Reichstag.

It was a strange delusion that Bismarck cherished from the beginning of this period. What he had feared above all was resistance from the dynasties. But the rapid unification and the very prosperity of the Reich, which were at once the condition and the consequence of unification, had the result not so much of producing federal difficulties as of giving new courage to the political parties and rendering them difficult to manage. Bismarck expected an always docile majority from a Parliament which he had organized as a simple State college and had deprived in advance of all authority of its own. This docile majority he never had. The imperial power, the Prussian power, and the secondary dynastic powers were all interested in agreeing together, in order to save for the old monarchism all that could be saved. But the parties and the Reichstag, swelled, as it were, from within by the progress of the Reich, stood in the way. The federal Diet, whose meetings were secret and whose members were entirely out of touch with the people, effaced itself before the Emperor and the Chancellor as before the Reichstag. The very progress of centralization prevented the Emperor, the Chancellor, and the Diet from controlling the Reichstag.

The parliamentary institution saw its importance and its prestige continually growing through the very force of circumstances. The three years between elections had been converted into five. The Prussian Landtag (Diet) and the other parliaments vegetated in the shade. The collision became permanent between the Chancellor, representative and creator of a monarchical absolutism mitigated by liberalism, and a Parliament indispensable for the work of legislation, but not sovereign. There was flagrant and irreconcilable strife between a power that was Prussian and monarchical in origin and spirit, and a people in which the conservative aristocracy, the big-business men, the middle classes, the proletariat, and the Catholic elements could not by themselves find the means of creating a new centre of political crystallization. Prussia superimposed upon the Reich her legislation, administration, and army, in accordance with the method consecrated by the old territorial traditions. But the Reich, having grown too large, struggled wildly in the net and threatened to break it.

Undoubtedly the divisions between the parties permitted a Chancellor as vigorous as Bismarck to govern after a fashion, all the more because foreign policy was entirely in his hands. But even in this sphere these divisions made things awkward for him. It is said that Bismarck invented "Realpolitik," a term used to veil the emptiness of German statecraft. And each party practised "Realpolitik," even the Catholic Centre. Each of them *socialized* itself, disciplined itself, and formed a compact block behind which the great trade-union organizations could be discerned. Bismarck fought the Centre on the confessional plane, the budding Social Democracy on the social plane, the Conservatives and the National Liberals on the economic plane, the Progressives on the political plane. But these struggles made him the prisoner of his own creation. No law could be voted without the assent of the Reichstag. But Bismarck still imagined, as he had done in 1862 and in 1864, that legislation could be reconstructed by agreement, by compromise and collaboration between the Crown and Parliament. Consequently, from 1871 to 1890, conflict between Chancellor and Reichstag was continually breaking out. Bismarck even wondered, a little before his fall, whether the underground work of the parties would not destroy his Constitution, and he was considering an anti-parliamentary *coup d'état*. But it was he, and not the Reichstag, that quitted the political scene.

It was a tragic fall which, under the rule of William II, left the Reich without firm direction. On the one hand, the Reichstag was no more able to seize and organize power than it had been in the past. On the other hand, the imperial Government lost

in Bismarck its surest defender and its best guarantor. The
Germany of William II presented more and more, as the First
World War approached, the spectacle of a nation which, though
toiling with fervour, developing widely, and extending its positions throughout the world, was none the less *badly directed*.

The constitutional mechanisms no longer worked. The
successors of Bismarck, the new Emperor and his numerous
chancellors, were neither the equals of their former master nor
equal to events. How could they exercise with authority a
power that Bismarck had cut to his own measure? As for the
parliamentary institution, it was troubled, in Prussia and the
Reich, by the critical problem of the franchise and of the real
representation of the masses. How could it constitute a power
capable of remedying the failings of the imperial monarchy? The
Prussian franchise was antiquated, and the universal franchise
of the Reich did not work properly. The more the central
power extended its legislation, its administration, and its army,
the more it seemed to be disabled in the face of the release of
the energies and the magnitude of the interests represented
by the Reichstag parties.

The Germany of William II was bound to oscillate more than
that of Bismarck between authoritarianism and liberalism.
Trying to reconcile two contradictory terms, it passed from the
one to the other without coupling their forces in a really organic
manner. Bismarck had conferred a power truly too great on a
monarchy too weak for it, and at the same time he had prevented
Parliament from seizing it. It may, indeed, be doubted whether
that Parliament, the radical impotence of which was demonstrated
after the war by the Weimar Republic, could have exercised
power if it held it, so badly were its political fractions articulated
with one another. The Chancellor, weakly supported by the
Emperor, had to content all parties, to satisfy at once the middle
class and the workers, the farmers and the industrialists,
Protestants and Catholics. As the Catholic Centre, the pivot
of the whole system, could move to right or to left with equal
ease, the equilibrium of parliamentary coalitions proved incurably
unstable, while the Chancellor was urgently in need of it. This
explains the oscillations of the imperial policy. Either William
left the Chancellor to govern with the parties and depended on
the Reichstag, or, on the contrary, he governed with him against
the parties.

The powers, certainly considerable, of the imperial institution were in the hands of a weak monarch, ignorant and nervous, impulsive and verbose, and above all in bad hands, who was incapable of a consistent policy. As for the chancellors, Caprivi, Bülow, and Bethmann Hollweg, they merely weakened their own office. On the eve of the war, the Chancellery was visibly in decay, as well as the Federal Council.

In face of the machinery of government, the Reichstag and the parties vegetated in the worst of confusion. Thus parliamentarism lost all its prestige, and became more and more suspect. And since the opportunity of reforming the Constitution was missed about 1908, when a Ministry with actual collective responsibility might have been created, and a constitutional and parliamentary monarchy introduced by uniting in an organic manner the two great forces of the Reich, the political game was lost.

It has even been said that on the eve of the war *Germany was no longer governed.* The power was slipping from the feeble hands of the monarchy, while the Reichstag could not exercise it either constitutionally or in fact. Five chancellors and eighty ministers succeeded one another between 1888 and 1912! The parliamentary coalitions suffered no less vicissitude. *Only powerful armaments seemed to be able to curb this seething nation.*

This statecraft *without an idea, this policy of cohesion for cohesion's sake,* ended in incoherence. It revealed the secret weakness of the Prussian hegemony. By the operation of this hegemony, in fact, the aristocratic, bureaucratic, and military coteries had tried to *lead* a people whom its own parties merely had to *represent* on the parliamentary plane. This old-Prussian oligarchy, even when reinforced by big business, had nothing progressive about it; it hindered. The new Germany was the creation of the middle class and the proletariat. All that the Prussian hegemony could do was to throw the deceptive veil of administrative and military prestige over the reality of an anarchy that was no doubt brought about by too rapid economic development. It no longer had any hold over the democracy of capitalists and workers, which was itself increasingly uneasy and agitated, but incapable of ruling. Not being able to choose, William II's Germans preferred to allow power to fall to the ground between the two institutions under consideration. Thus the country no longer had a real government.

The internal disquiet was complicated by a diplomatic crisis pregnant with grave consequences.

From 1815 to 1860, the Holy Alliance, with its monarchical, particularist, and anti-liberal principles, exercised persistent pressure on the Germanic Confederation. But it is well known how rapidly the Austrian preponderance declined.

It was dead when Bismarck came to power, four years before Sadowa. In order to succeed, the Chancellor had to interest the Germans, with their many parties and groups, in the Empire. Under the Constitution he was absolute master of the diplomatic sphere, and he played on the European chess-board a game both prudent and forceful.

Between 1871 and 1878, while Italy and Austria-Hungary were consolidating their quite recent unity, Bismarck was preparing the Austro-German alliance, and concluded that of the Three Emperors, soon to lead to the Triple Alliance. The Alliance of the Three Emperors (Germany, Austria-Hungary, and Russia) collapsed in 1878 at the Congress of Berlin. The Triple Alliance, prepared from 1879 to 1882, and founded in 1883, was consolidated between 1883 and 1890. But in 1891 came the Franco-Russian accord. No sooner had Bismarck installed a powerful group in the centre of Europe than the Triple Entente appeared on the horizon. Bismarck had wanted to isolate Russia from France, with England as a benevolent neutral. It was the exact contrary that he obtained. Moreover, the Triple Alliance soon betrayed its weaknesses, for it was only of a defensive character and was hardly popular in Italy. Bismarck had condemned Europe to unstable equilibrium, and from this arose the Triple Entente.

The years that preceded the First World War saw the breakdown of the Wilhelmian diplomacy.

Threatened with dissolution, the "brilliant second"[1] was a source of perpetual worry to Germany. As for Italy, she came to an understanding with France, which in 1902 allowed her to take possession of Tripolitania. From that time, the Triple Alliance went to pieces with disconcerting rapidity. In the same year Roumania broke away from it. The Italian defection, which was in sight after Algeciras, was an accomplished fact between 1912 and 1914. Italo-Austrian relations were more and more strained. It may be said that on the eve of the general conflagration the two countries were in a state of latent war. Relations between Austria and Germany deteriorated after the Bosnian crisis. Von Tschirschky, the Ambassador at Vienna, asked

[1] The Dual Monarchy.

himself about 1913 why Germany had hitched her destinies to a sinking vessel. The two last renewals of the Triple Alliance, between 1900 and 1914, gave rise to the gravest discussions.

While the Triple Alliance was rapidly falling to pieces, the Triple Entente was gaining scope and strength. In 1891, on the very morrow of the fall of Bismarck, the Franco-Russian alliance had risen above the horizon, as a retort to the Bismarckian policy of keeping France and Russia apart. In 1904 the idea of the Entente Cordiale was forced on Britain and France by the Anglo-German rivalry. But the event that most surprised the Germans, who were poor psychologists at this juncture, was the Anglo-Russian agreement that immediately followed the Russian defeat in the East. Next, after the Kaiser's visit to Tangier, came Algeciras. In spite of great difficulties, the Triple Entente made rapid progress between 1907 and 1914.

The comparative history of the two groups is thus easily summarized. The years 1900 to 1904 were a period of uncertainty and transition. The Triple Alliance was not yet irremediably damaged and the Triple Entente existed only potentially. Germany could still feel that she had the ball at her feet. That was why between 1904 and 1908 she pursued the Moroccan dispute, in order to break up the Entente Cordiale. By this one move she lost most of her chances. At the Algeciras Conference the Entente Cordiale was consolidated and signs of the Anglo-Russian agreement began to show themselves, while Italy and Austria pursued an exceedingly dangerous policy for the Triple Alliance, which was already being called in some quarters "a broken vessel." Still more ill-judged and still more fatal than the Moroccan move was the Bosnian affair of 1908 to 1912. This time Germany, manœuvred by Vienna, lost her control of the Triple Alliance. Russia's reply came promptly, and Bulgaria's independence was proclaimed. The Triple Entente brought the Balkan States over to its side. The war between Italy and Turkey weakened the Alliance, set Germany and Austria at variance, and ruined German credit in Turkey.

Finally, after so many mistakes, the Agadir affair set Germany once more at grips with Britain and France, as though to do everything possible to consolidate the Entente. The European conflict spread to the Far East, where the United States took the side of Germany and the Alliance, while Japan played the game of the Entente. There was no longer any choice for Germany. Either she must suffer a distressing diplomatic disaster, or fight a world of enemies. The game had been lost. The idea of "encirclement" entered German and Austrian heads. The Central Empires must either increase their military and naval armaments without limit, at the risk of producing in the Reich an unprecedented social and financial crisis, or make the plunge before it was too late and while military superiority seemed to be theirs. The Central Empires were thus constrained to go to war. On whom did the responsibility fall for that constraint, if not on those who had played their game badly?

The parallelism is clear between this foreign policy and the intestine divisions within the Reich. Over the greatest nation on the Continent there hung a grave menace, to be accounted for by an economic prosperity more sudden than was healthy, by the immense scale of land and sea armament, by the unjust distribution of military burdens, by the more and more dubious relations between the army and the nation, by the progress of democratic and reformist ideas among officers and soldiers, by the impotence of Parliament and of the Kaiser's personal rule, and finally by a dreadful succession of diplomatic mistakes, almost all irremediable. Certainly Bismarck had transmitted a crushing heritage to his successors. But they had stultified his policy. To endow oneself with an organization that demands the unceasing conquest of new markets abroad, to maintain the strongest army in the world and a formidable navy, and then to blunder from one diplomatic failure to another, with the result that the rival Powers are brought together by a common sense of being menaced—all this is to be irresistibly tempted to resort to force.

In resorting to force the Central Powers simply precipitated their own ruin. The Dual Monarchy is now no more than a memory. The Second Reich succumbed in defeat.

During the war the internal crisis in Germany reached an unprecedented acuteness. After the famous national union (*Burgfrieden*) the abyss yawned wider than ever between the embarrassed Government and the people, whose parliamentary groups debated incessantly, abusing the Chancellor with growing outspokenness. The monarchical and military elements grew weaker, and parliamentary anarchy assumed unheard-of proportions. The war gave tragic meaning to the political drama witnessed under Bismarck and William II.

The army of 1914 possessed every quality that could be provided by technical organization and discipline. In this respect it was an emanation from the Prussian military aristocracy, which had made of it an incomparable machine but one that was overstrained. Like the nation, it lacked good leaders, especially at the very top. Von Moltke, who wrecked the Schlieffen Plan and who failed to encircle Paris, was responsible for the irremediable defeat on the Màrne. It was both a military and a political defeat, the final condemnation of the system in the name of which, by the very agency of Prussian hegemony, an Emperor and King of Prussia had thrown Germany into a hopeless war, while depriving her of leaders worthy of her and equal to the struggle they had to face.

Moreover, dictatorship soon put an end to the normal régime. From 1916 on, under Ludendorff, it assumed both a military and a political character. It roughly thrust the Kaiser aside, so destroying the traditional bond between the King of Prussia and his officers. By 1917 the impossibility of victory in a war on two fronts was evident to the well-informed. No doubt Ludendorff organized defence excellently. But as a politician he was pursuing an unattainable and chimerical aim, that of winning the peace. The army was exhausted and the fleet powerless. The nation had obtained obvious military successes, but *no decision*. The Russian front had collapsed, it was true. But the coalition of the Western nations, Britain, France, the United States, and their allies, was perfectly capable of beating Germany without Russian aid. Such was the supreme consequence of the mistakes accumulated by the Bismarckian and Wilhelmian system. The Kaiser's power and the prestige of the military nobility were ruined for all time. One last effort, the offensive of 1918, and the great system, ill-led, and broken by the final and inescapable disintegration of its forces, collapsed, vanquished and humiliated.

The responsible leaders had no sooner been overtaken by defeat than they began to accuse the people of having betrayed them. The people had known nothing of the truth, of the risks it had been running and of the defeat knocking at the door. In those hard years the middle class and the proletariat had shown themselves less able than ever to seize and exercise power. All they had been able to do was to criticize the Kaiser and especially the Chancellor. It had been of no avail for the Social Democrats to vote the war credits ever since August 1914, to stand for national unity, the famous *Burgfrieden*—all this had meant nothing but *passivity, inertia, and uninformed laisser-faire*. At the very outset of the war, the members of the Reichstag had abdicated leaving the conduct of the war and of public affairs to a Government that soon effaced itself before a military dictatorship. Thereafter the people was simply under orders, subjected to a state of siege and to censorship, reduced to the situation of a docile instrument. There was nothing of the firmness shown by the Western democracies. There was no freedom of opinion, no reliable information, no criticism. It was just when Prussian direction had suffered complete disaster that the people, amorphous and apathetic, and entirely without political education, suddenly found itself charged with the rebuilding of the Reich. The tragedy of Weimar was implicit in that political collapse.

Nobody in war-time Germany had a workable plan for integrating the middle class and the mass of the workers in the Bismarckian constitutional framework and for associating the people with the fortunes of those who were leading it. In face of those two oligarchies the aristocracy and the industrialists, the other classes gave their work and their lives for the supposed defence of the Reich. It was indeed the old *police State* that carried on the war. The function of its leaders was to command, that of the people to obey. The blockade, the economic difficulties, and suffering of every sort, provoked within the masses a discontent that grew steadily as the war continued. Suppressed popular fury grew against the officer, the administrator, and the war profiteers. But this fury was dark and elementary, without fixed purpose or political application. And the people remained divided in face of a gang of men who continued to entertain wild illusions and to elaborate an absurd programme of annexations that appealed to the ignorant masses.

Effective political power remained in the hands of the officers, the junkers, and the industrialists, all under the protection of G.H.Q. The Reichstag parties were in a state of complete deliquescence. Neither the Centre nor the Social Democrats and Independents nor the middle-class parties were able to unite with their neighbour parties for action. Meanwhile Ludendorff, installing himself in the Chancellery, left to the Chancellor the apparent responsibility for affairs but threatened to resign when the Chancellor did not do what he wanted, in order to induce the Chancellor himself to resign. *In fact, Germany at this stage in the war was without either a monarchical or a democratic power.* She was *in the hands of a General* who held the *totality* of power. The Reich had to deal not with the Government but with G.H.Q.

It needed Erzberger to make the attempt to give Germany a coherent majority.

In 1917 Erzberger saw that the game was up.   He was able to take some sort of action, as he had the support of the Centre Party and the Social Democrats.   But he made two irremediable mistakes.   He dared not denounce G.H.Q., and he did not base the eventual government of the country on a parliamentary majority.   Ludendorff knew that the parliamentarization of Germany was not popular, and profited from the fact to reinforce the military dictatorship.   But neither this dictatorship nor the claim of the Reichstag agreed with the Bismarckian Constitution, and still less the mediation of the Crown Prince.   The Reichstag contented itself with the famous peace resolution of 1917.   It called for the peace of *conciliation* of the *poor* in place of the peace of *annexation* of the *rich*.   The nation was *cut into two*.   It could not win.   Once more the Reichstag left all initiative to the Generals. It gained power only from the defeat of Germany.   And once the Republic was created, it was pitilessly fought once more by the old ruling oligarchy.

The story of the Weimar Republic was the pathetic epilogue to that immense political failure.   Under the cover of democracy there reappeared the relentless struggle between the German people and its leaders.   The leaders themselves made an end to a democracy that had had the misfortune to inherit all the divisions that had tormented Germany.   In order to lead the people to what they believed to be its destiny, they appealed this time to a political and military Cæsar, to a Leader furnished with absolute power in every sphere, leading a community which, like the Germania of the past, was of a *mystico-military* nature.

CHAPTER VI

THE INTELLECTUAL AND MORAL CRISIS

In the century that preceded the First World War, the economic and political crisis in Germany was but the outward sign of a spiritual malady of which it is necessary to grasp the profound causes.   It was during that interval of time that German thought, turning away from the traditional humanism, moved toward racialism and authoritarian biologism.

This tragedy of the spirit was not purely German. It was
European. But Germany was its principal focus. When
Nietzsche, in his last philosophical works, defined European
nihilism, he had been reading French works. He knew Paul
Bourget's *Essais de Psychologie Contemporaine*, and from it he
borrowed the term "nihilism." Bourget, who had found everywhere the traces of that malady, but especially in the greatest
creative minds of the nineteenth century, had written:

"From end to end of Europe, contemporary society presents
the same symptoms, slightly varied from race to race. . . .
Slowly but surely the belief is taking shape that nature is bankrupt.
This promises to become the sinister faith of the twentieth century,
unless *science* or *a barbarian invasion* saves a too reflective mankind
from weariness with its own thoughts." He notes "the march,
step by step, of the different European races toward that tragic
negation of all the efforts of all ages."

1. *General causes*

In the Bismarckian epoch German nihilism exceeded neighbouring nihilisms in its scale. We need to know the reason.
Was it not from Germany that the new style of barbarian invasion,
of *Völkerwanderung* ("migration of the peoples"), of which
Europe was the theatre, seemed to be coming?

The Western nations had passed through the process of
industrialization well before Germany. But they had not been
affected so suddenly or so violently. They had been able to offer
resistance to its progress, to set a brake on it. Not that the
methods of the great capitalists did not exert determining influence
on them. They preserved, however, greater calm and stability
in face of modern mechanization. To read the principal publicists
and writers of the two Western countries, such as Balzac, Zola,
Dickens, Darwin, and Herbert Spencer, without forgetting the
French and British Socialists, is to be convinced of this truth.
Why was it so? *Because those nations had had experience of rationalism and had drawn from it elements of quiet strength and of normal
progress.* Healthy religious, intellectual, and political traditions
had prevented them from allowing all spiritual values to be
brutally swamped by industrialism, as happened later in the
Bismarckian Empire.

In this connexion Germany brings to mind North America.
The United States found themselves with immense territory and

gigantic mineral resources to exploit.   Sectarian Puritanism, with its energy and optimism, had no natural counterpoise in any political tradition.   It had no links either with a civilization long established in the country or with any political, administrative, and military State that could have set limits to its effort.   That is why it threw itself with such fire and so little restraint into large-scale capitalism.   We had to wait until the end of the nineteenth century to see the Americans, who were before all else colonists and pioneers, modify their mentality and acquire the political sense which the First World War and the events that succeeded it developed in them so astonishingly.   When she had become a great federal State, North America, in spite of her vastness, her power, and her subjection to economic forces, remained faithful to the ideas and principles that had been her original political basis.   Christianity, the idea of progress, the sense of humanity and of international realities, the love of freedom, all these values are recognized even by the American of the Middle West, and he is still ready to fight for them when he sees them menaced.   The old independent Protestantism has here constituted a magnificent tradition of which the strength and the constancy were proved right up to the present war, in face of Hitlerite misdeeds, by Mr Roosevelt's speeches.   From this point of view the United States are a mean between Germany and the nations of the west of Europe.

In the second half of the nineteenth century Germany was a true *terra nova*, as America had been earlier.   When industrialism was implanted in Germany, with the rapidity and energy that are well known, it not only found there a favourable soil and a terrain duly unified by the Zollverein, but found still existing the loose federalism of the reactionary absolute monarchies.   There existed no general idea or general political structure.   *The Empire of Bismarck's creation came after industrialization.*   It was industrialization that was the great innovation, the determining fact.

No doubt Germany had certain traditions, that of the administrative bureaucracy and that of her army.   But the former, which was purely territorial and Prussian, affected the Reich as a whole only after 1871.   The latter, too, was purely Prussian and became applicable to the Reich as a whole only through the play of Prussian hegemony.   Both were thus derived from the existence of the old *Länder*, or territorial States, and after Bismarck's unification of the Reich they were profoundly modified, challenging in the process the habits and the privileges of the nobility and the bourgeoisie. Bureaucracy and army were thus only able to impose themselves on the Reich after relative transformation or decomposition, so as to play the part of cement in the new edifice. The official and the officer were to be in the Reich, as they had been in the *Länder*, the pillars of the social order, the animaters of the great mechanism. There was not the slightest question of any political or spiritual principles.

We may still see the historic tradition of the Holy Roman Empire, the Empire that after slowly decaying through centuries finally collapsed in 1806. Bismarck did not restore it. It remained a great historic memory; to its past existence and its structure might be attributed, however, all the evils that had fallen upon the defenceless Germany. In its influence on the future, on the contrary, it was but a vague dream of a vast community of members, a dream of which Bismarck seems to have realized the danger for Europe, and which he brought only partly into reality through Lesser Germany, lest he should alarm the European periphery beyond measure.

To sum up, there was no semblance here of any great intellectual and political tradition. The cosmopolitan humanism of the classics had become but a cultural treasure piously preserved by a restricted *élite* of the learned and the literary. Romanticism and its dreams were kept within political bounds by Bismarck's limited creation; they found an outlet only in economic activity. After 1871 there flourished in Germany a terrible industrialism of upstarts; a new bourgeoisie with no roots in the past grew in numbers and wealth with inconceivable rapidity, remaining apart from politics and, after 1848, deliberately kept away from it by the territorial monarchies and later by the Reich. It was expressly directed toward material activities alone, toward maximum production.

Thenceforward the dynamic and Darwinian spirit of the Germans could apply itself freely to economic development, but not to the political Empire conceived and constructed by the great Chancellor. The combination of Prussian discipline wisely rationalized with the boundless romantic imperialism that is the German spirit did not find in Bismarck's Empire sufficient food for its unchained ambitions. It was natural that Prussian hegemony should communicate to the whole body, to the twenty-five States united by Bismarck, its juridical, administrative, and military spirit. But this small-scale political play could not in itself satisfy so many aspirations of universal scope. These showed themselves on the theoretical and visionary plane in pan-Germanism; on the practical plane in the unleashing of economic activities. Under William II, after Bismarck had gone, there certainly came an expansion in the political field. The future Reich was more freely defined; this explains the sudden extraordinary development of pan-Germanism at that time, the natural bond that was established on the eve of the war of 1914 between the ideas of the intellectuals, the activity in the economic field, and the military preparations.

The distribution of parts was thus effected in Bismarckian Germany between a restricted political system, narrowly Prussian in inspiration, and a vast deployment of economic activity on a totally different scale, an activity which the innate romanticism of the Germans was to animate with its breath. The common element was the taste for disciplined work and for perfect technique. This distribution of parts corresponded exactly to the great difference that existed between the bureaucratic and military nobility, on one side, and on the other the industrial middle class and proletariat. The nobility remained conservative, in the Prussian sense of the term. It possessed also the ideal of social service that bears witness to a certain greatness and an undeniable moral solidity. In face of it the middle class, from the captains of industry to the poorer section, had inherited the romanticist ideal on the economic plane alone. The revolutionary hopes of the proletarian masses were also inspired by that ideal in so far as the German working masses renounced Marxist universalism, limited their Socialist aspirations to the success of the Reich, and subordinated their cause to that of the imperial monarchy.

Thus the implacable realism of one element had its counterpart in the economic romanticism of the other. The Germans satisfied simultaneously their need for political cohesion and their Gargantuan appetite for commercial expansion. Of necessity culture and religion, with their disinterested universalism and their intense desire for the inner life of the spirit, suffered cruelly from this. How could that country, at that epoch, give birth to a radiant original culture? Not that Germany had then liquidated the whole heritage of her past and sloughed off all that she had of vigorous humanism. Never, apparently, had she been under so many or such diverse foreign influences. But thenceforward she was incapable of making of them, as in the seventeenth and eighteenth centuries, a European synthesis. The collapse of spiritual values and the growth of biological racialism made rapid advance at the expense of healthy conservatism.

This strange separation between political activity, reserved for a body of higher and lesser officials specialized under the Prussian ægis, and a middle class devoted, in concert with the proletariat, to a sort of business romanticism, was curiously manifested in the architecture of the period, a period much darker and much more tormented than it seems at first sight. Nothing was more striking to the foreigner living in Germany about 1900 than the style of its new towns, in which the ancient centres were surrounded by modern sections. I said style, but should have said *absence of style*. That middle class of upstarts, which had formed in no more than a few decades, was installing itself in accordance with its taste. It thus revealed to view its true mentality. Nietzsche poured maledictions over those builders of villas. Those *nouveaux riches* were desperately in search of a tradition they did not possess. They drew at random from the heritages of the past.

Naturally they imagined themselves to be fairly close to the urban civilization that had preceded and accompanied the Reformation in the sixteenth century. Hence the poor style of odds and ends, without either certainty or strength, a feeble substitute for the lacking traditions. Anyone who looked at those efforts in pure imitation and that bizarre anarchy could see that that class, with all its wealth, had little idea what lead to follow in culture and art. It was a class that had no political ideas and was carefully excluded from any part in public affairs, and it suffered from its unexpected enrichment, due to the methods, until then unknown, of industrial capitalism. It was the victim of that extraordinary collective prosperity for which all Europe of that day had unreserved admiration. Nobody knew his true place. Everybody sought precedents and criteria in past history. The best of all terms for that state of perplexity is the German word *Ratlosigkeit* (not knowing which way to turn). *Down to 1914 nobody knew what historical moral justification to invent for the existence and the sudden rise of that new-made nation.*

This also explains the part science was to play in that disconcerting half-century. Under the action of historicism, specialization, and relativism there was produced an almost entire decomposition of the mental sciences, in spite of the apparent prestige they then had in university teaching. As for the natural sciences, applied to economic and technical activity, they, too, thanks to the rise of biology, provided an "Ersatz" for the values that were adjudged obsolete.

Nobody will be surprised that Greek humanism, which interpreted the universe solely in relation to man, was the first to suffer. The Greek had always seen in purely biological and physical reality an impure, crude incarnation of the Spirit, of the very idea of Life, with its eternal and universal attributes. The "nous" was introduced into the concrete only by approximation. Nothing was more hostile to the relentless biologism of the Germans than Hellenic thought. If it was the Spirit that controlled matter, it was of that that it was necessary to have knowledge. Not that the Greeks were ignorant of the opposition existing between the idea of the eternal Spirit and material Nature, which incessantly threatens the Spirit with temporary or apparent destruction. But they always tried, either through rationalism or through mysticism, to escape from pure biologism in order to gain access in one way or another to the Absolute. This attitude, which corresponded adequately to the Platonic view of the world, had been manifestly upset by the Copernican discovery.

But that was no reason for making of science the sworn enemy of Hellenism, for thinking that Nature conditions the Spirit, that life and the spirit depend solely on physical laws. That was a dangerous conclusion at a time when in education the Græco-Latin humanities saw rising by their side, especially in a Germany industrialized to excess, modern technical instruction. That half-unconscious ruin of the Greek Idea in men's minds remained as yet veiled. It simply marked a reversal of terms. Men sought, moreover, in Greece herself the Dionysiac side and the combative aspects of her culture. The belief in the eternity of the spirit and in its superiority to nature was abandoned and a conception adopted that made of it the subordinate of the physical existence.

This destruction prepared the way for that of Christian supernaturalism. Christianity would not accept the Revelation and the Incarnation if it did not itself believe in the eternity of the spirit. Upon Christ's mediation through his death on the Cross it had built an immense edifice that raised itself in its tragic grandeur against nature. It was the strongest refuge that man had ever built for himself in relation to a universe that passed beyond him and menaced him on all sides. Man was declared a "child of

God." All that mattered was his salvation, his integration in the divine life. The demands of nature were neglected, even paradoxically violated. Life on earth seemed here to be sacrificed to the realization of a transcendental ideal and a transcendental City.

The influence exerted by Christianity over Germany, in its three forms of Catholicism, Lutheranism, and Calvinism, was of unequalled scale and power. But nowhere has the criticism of Christianity been carried so far. The rooted hostility of Germanism to Rome is an historic fact to which there is no need to return. Once Catholicism had become a minority religion, that enmity was manifested in the eighteenth century by a strong effort at nationalization, by the most absolute territorialism, and by a temporary separation between the German episcopate and the Papacy. It reappeared in the nineteenth century in the great theological struggle between German and Roman thought, in the *Kulturkampf* and the various forms it assumed. Finally, in the last twenty years, there came the relentless struggle that Nazism itself carried on against the Catholic Centre party and against the whole Roman Catholic institution.

The Protestant problem was more complex. While retaining its links with œcumenical Christianity, the Lutheran Reformation turned Christianity toward Germanism, and, above all, bound it in the territories to the despotic powers of the monarchies. Calvinism suffered a similar fate there. It is true that in the seventeenth and eighteenth centuries Protestant life in Germany was not entirely absorbed in the territorial Churches. But the diffused religious feeling that characterized it progressively whittled away the Christian dogma. It tended to make of Christianity either *a natural revelation* or a *romantic mysticism*. A process of the same sort, but still more marked, took place during the nineteenth century. Under Bismarck, historical criticism attacked Christianity with implacable perseverance and logic. The State Church had lost its prestige, and the population remained indifferent to religious issues; philosophy and theology largely ruined the traditional faith. The idea that collapsed in a thousand different ways in most men's minds was that of eternal salvation historically achieved once for all outside nature and ourselves, in a metaphysical world entirely inaccessible to human vision.

But could rationalism, the Enlightenment, the liberal faith in progress be saved? Germany began soon a merciless struggle against that form of Western humanism. This time, her attacks were directed less against Rome than against France. France at that moment was for Germany both an intellectual and a political menace. The centralizing monarchy, the philosophy of the Enlightenment, and the Revolution of 1789 followed by Napoleonic despotism—what an accumulation of causes for complaint! In the eyes of the Germans of the Second Reich, France represented the Catholic and Latin tradition, incipient Calvinism, and especially free-thought and Socialism—in short, all the forms of the Roman Idea so detested. With romanticism and Hegel, the Germans had still believed in the universal Spirit. But historicism was to destroy that conception, which had itself ruined the Christian faith. Kantism and neo-Kantism upset the belief in the objectivity of knowledge and taught relativism, denying universal progress. Everything became problematical. Positive scientifism and extreme specialization invaded every domain.

In Germany the mental sciences, with tranquil and imperturbable courage, denied their own principles, cutting off the branch on which they were resting; they dismissed progress, reason, and liberty. In a Germany grown more and more restless through her own industrial megalomania, the hatred of clarity of thought and of the Western peoples that owed to it their providential stability spread in all quarters. Progressive intellectualism foundered there because it was not supported as in the West by a truly cultivated middle class, morally educated and genuinely immersed in politics.

If only there had still, in default of rational criteria, been historic criteria! But this middle class, in full pursuit of industrialism, without traditions or style, was wedged, as it were, between Prussianism and dynamic business romanticism. The Socialist proletariat was in the same case. The industrial revolution appealed simultaneously to the technical intelligence and the imagination. *As Germany had little or no belief in universal progress, she was disturbed only about her own, and the more so since she was behindhand.* A wild Darwinism served as motor for the activity Germany displayed everywhere. Historicism let loose its furies in the universities. It was the keenly sought intellectual "Ersatz." The theme of decadence, the doctrine of the selection of the fittest, facile and flattering comparisons between Prusso-Germany and Greece or Rome, conceived as vast systems of domination, all this comfortable and fallacious eschatology intoxicated men's minds. *There remained for the German nothing but specialization and nationalism, nothing but mass production and pan-Germanism.* He imagined that human cultures, linked with races and peoples, form fixed nuclei, mutually impenetrable. The continuity between past and future was broken. This was the moment when biology, anthropology, and sociology took possession of the universities.

Add to this the growing protest against England, against her capitalism and her plutocracy, and against economic liberalism in general. So it was that the liquidation everywhere of liberal rationalism was completed. The struggle of romanticism against the Enlightenment, the final defeat of political liberalism in 1848–50, the destruction of progressivism by historic relativism, are so many causes of the sapping in men's minds of the very foundations of Western belief.

There still remained Marxism. Karl Marx, certainly, scarcely shared the optimism of the Englightenment. His conception of culture was not very remote from that built up by the natural sciences. Marx did not separate human society and its multiple forms from its material foundations. The necessary goods, their production, their elaboration, and their consumption—that vast process obeyed, according to him, inescapable laws. That which the living organism is to the physical world, society, he said, is to the concrete bases of human existence. Fundamentally pessimist, Marx thought that natural laws do not favour the economic process. A sort of hiatus opened here, once more, between man and nature. It was the very play of material laws and forces that ruined society. If Nature was thus destructive, she must be *corrected* by *regulating* human existence. That was to be the rôle of Socialism. Capitalism, on the contrary, was the free and consequently disastrous play of energies. Socialism would reduce it to order. *It would do this for all peoples, on the plane of men's labour.*

Marx thus liquidated in his turn the rationalist optimism which, in the period of prosperity, had closed the gap between nature and society by rationalizing Nature herself. What Marx wanted was *complete social justice,* that is to say, *Revolution.* But his German successors once more submerged his doctrine in an evolutionary and therefore optimist conception. This Socialist opportunism, seconded by Bismarckism, was the germ of the Socialist nationalism which was to substitute *justice between nations* for *justice between classes* and to break all the Socialist

Internationals. Be it noted that "Deutscher Sozialismus" was no more a political idea than Bismarckism itself.

Little was left in the end of Bismarckian and Wilhelmian Germany. Humanities reserved for a small section of the upper middle class, victim of the scholastic pedantry against which Nietzsche protested with such vigour; Christianity weighed down by the cumbrous framework of the Catholic Centre, which regimented the churches, and by the twenty-eight territorial churches of Evangelical Protestantism; liberalism mixed with an authoritarian monarchism that carried the upper and lower middle classes into economic materialism; finally, enfeebled elements of international Socialism in the trade-union organizations of the proletariat and in Social Democracy—this picture has more shadow than light. Here, again, the Germans appear, especially from 1900 to 1914, the most vulnerable people of Europe.

2. *Nietzsche*

To these general causes should be added the conscious work of a few wholesale iconoclasts.

Schopenhauer was, of course, the earliest. His influence followed immediately upon romanticism. It may be observed toward the middle of the nineteenth century, a little after the collapse of liberalism. His philosophy expressed the profound and tragic disillusion that weighed on men's minds during the whole decade from 1850 to 1860. *Nature and man*, as they appeared in the light of recent scientific discoveries, *did not correspond*, said Schopenhauer, *to human hopes*. In Greek thought, in Christianity, and in the Enlightenment, man had expressed his belief in his own effort, in his own value. After relentlessly deducing its consequences from the Copernican act, modern science showed the dreams to be extinguished, the aspirations of the past destroyed. All the cruelty of the nineteenth century, the cruelty that Thomas Mann, himself a disciple of Schopenhauer, so strongly emphasized in his *Betrachtungen eines Unpolitischen* of 1917, was revealed in the work of the philosopher of pessimism. Human life assumed for him the aspect of a bankruptcy. In the very act of guiding it, nature seemed to pronounce its doom. How could we see in it a divine, universal Spirit that guaranteed to us outside birth and death, outside the limits of our ephemeral existence, access to a superior order? There was no hope of salvation such as Platonism and Christianity offered. There were no longer any transcendental, absolute values. The best thing was to *forget* existence, or to *make it disappear.*

This pessimism was, above all else, negative. *It suggests a disappointed optimism.* The fundamental question was man's value. Was he immortal thought or purely nature? Let us not forget the *Vitalismus,* hostile to all intellectualism, the " vitalism " latent in German thought since romanticism. It imagined that man removes himself from life in proportion as his thinking improves, that a clear consciousness is a cause of decay because logical thought separates man from creative nature. It was necessary, it was said, that man, to be worthy of life, should be directly moved by her, by spontaneous instinct, *that he should cease to oppose to her the abstract schemes of his intelligence.* A certain adoration of life was thus equivalent to contempt of the mind. This was the opposite attitude to that of Schopenhauer. He made of universal life an obscure will, and tended to absorb human existence in it, while vitalism adored life in its universal manifestations and regarded human existence as of value only in so far as it drew from that perennial source. Vitalism took as its point of departure the feeling of life, its instinctive, obscure impulse.

Freudism took from this its immense significance. It showed, on the contrary, that if man blindly obeys the vital impulse he destroys himself. It is just the desire for life and for intense joy that dooms him to final destruction. *Considered as a creative power, life is possible only if we resist our natural impulses. Resistance keeps instinct in order.* What is needed is not to oppose to life Greek reason or Christian salvation, but to understand that the same forces work, according to our capacity for resistance, for the exaltation or the decay of our being. No doubt nature gets the better of us in the end. Nevertheless, there is in man, for the duration of his life, an internal force that affirms a possibility of higher life.

Nietzsche seems to have sought a position midway between pessimism and vitalism. His importance in the process we are describing comes from the fact that he radically destroyed the old values, with truly heroic courage, to substitute for them a Super-humanity. He showed the existence of European nihilism with more frankness than anyone else. It was for that reason that he wanted a new table of values. He found it only in an *individual* solution. He was thus, with Kierkegaard, the *great bourgeois* who returned invincibly to individualism. Kierkegaard tried to save Christianity. Nietzsche claimed quite simply to save the *higher individual*, proceeding then to charge him with the supervision of the inferior classes.

Thus we must make a distinction in Nietzsche's final philosophy between the *critical* part, which condemns all humanism, and the *constructive* part, which concerns superhumanity. This philosophy was based on researches Nietzsche had made between 1884 and 1888 into modern biologism.

Nietzsche thus inferred that if there are no final causes in the universe, man should liberate himself from the past, from the spirit of apathy, *and mould the universe to his own desire.* A sort of necrosis forms in us and weighs constantly on our minds. The world, however, is pure energy. Thus we need a matter both *emotive* and *thinking.* This will be the body, inseparable from thought, the latter being known only through and with the body. The body and biology will be our best guides. Waste and compensation are in conflict in us. An internal discipline regulates the instincts, sharing the alimentation between them. A *morality* is infused into biology, the supreme end of Humanity being in *that sense of victorious corporal and spiritual plenitude, that accumulation of potential energy, which alone will enable a strong* élite *to master the masses.* If the sentient individual is only a part of the true personality, a small reasoning entity in a greater, a society is similarly made of the opposition between the elementary instincts and the logical reason. This is the famous opposition between the *preyed-on* and the *preying.*

Nietzsche saw in Machiavelli and Machiavellism the true rationale of governmental methods, which should be in agreement with modern biology and the laws of Life. Men being essentially evil and perfidious, they can be well governed only by *imposture.* That is the only means of assuring the existence of the State in the long run, since few individuals desire freedom with the responsibility implied in command. As for Gobineau and his racial consciousness, he strongly attracted Nietzsche by his violent anti-intellectualism. Gobineau envisaged the *energetic, superior Barbarian* who is the final outcome of the masses. Morality, for him, is only life in action. It simply presupposes the right of attack and the right of defence, the necessity of war and the insufficiency of pacifism, and the distinction between masters and slaves. *Men tyrannize over themselves in order to tyrannize over others.*

Such was the explanation of the Nietzschean conception of decadence. Decadence forms an integral part of life just as the lesser reason is part of the greater. It is in the *unconscious* and the *spontaneous* that strength and vitality reside. Luther and the *Sturm und Drang* movement had already said so. The clear consciousness paralyses the afflux of strength that comes to us from our communion with the universe. Its steps are justified when it remains in contact with life; but its schematism becomes fatal when it separates from life.

It is necessary, therefore, that man shall be and remain an ardent will. On the other hand, collectivities are lasting only if they have *a common will*, admitted by all, imposed on all by pain and punishment. This will will be the accomplishment of *leaders*, of a tradition which they incarnate and dictate to the multitudes. Men are confined within the community by an accepted constraint. They find what there is in them of freedom driven out. The conflict is thus latent between any of that freedom that is retained and the external norms consecrated in general by religion and by the civil government.

We can clearly see in the Nietzschean criticism the origins of Nazi anti-Semitism and of Nazi contempt for the Internationals.

The Semites, according to Nietzsche, engendered the Hebraic epidemic and constructed a pessimist theocracy that instituted the priesthood of the sacred lie. The Hebrews were told that in disobeying their God they had wrought their own misfortune. This was the doctrine of *national sin*, invented and maintained by the priesthood. The Jews also instituted asceticism. The sacerdotal wave coming from the Indies swept over them in Babylonia. Immersed in the study of Wellhausen, Nietzsche evoked the Jahveh who symbolized national strength, joy, and hope. When anarchy came, the old God would not do and was replaced by another, an angered and exacting God. Hence the absurd mechanism of salvation, which assured the priestly caste perpetual enjoyment of its privileges. The Jews had *defiled* the joy of living, vital energy, carnal well-being, force. That was the explanation of their decadence.

Nietzsche passed to the ancient Greeks. He noted that Plato had sought in the contemplation of Ideas a corrective for the latent Eros, for the fever of passion that devours human beings. The philosopher accomplished in Greece a task analogous to that of the priest. The Greeks before Socrates had represented a fortunate epoch. Men of action, true "beasts," they were complete examples of humanity. Their virtue emanated from the very power of their personality. As for the Sophists, they still found grace in Nietzsche's eyes. But he objected especially to the plebeian Socrates, the philosopher who had flattered the Delphic priesthood, a type of decadent hostile to the true genius of Greece. It was he, perhaps a man of Semitic origin, who invented analysis, making use of reason to kill Athenian aristocratism, neglecting the irrational realities, and bringing philosophy back to an ordinary, second-rate moral system.

These considerations on Socrates brought Nietzsche to Plato, the philosopher-priest who repudiated science and allied himself with the priesthood, basing himself on gregarious thinking and embellishing the Socratic dialectic, after establishing a fundamental opposition between *instinct* and *reason*. In the person of Plato, Nietzsche saw the most essential elements of Greek humanism. For Plato, the reason was that which was *stable* and *lasting*, it was the sum of the *eternal values*, of *Ideas* in relation to which the concrete is but a crude approximation. Plato instilled the belief into men's souls that they lived in an eternal region.

This, in Nietzsche's view, was the true origin of Christianity, which was the heir both of Judaism and of Hellenism. Christianity conquered the Roman Empire, which destroyed Jerusalem. It was in order to undermine the adversary that the story was imagined of the Crucified, *the God of Love conquering through weakness*, the God of the poor devils. This time the end had come of the Chosen People. Jesus knew Israel only in tears, not in its strength. *Jesus was the Saviour of the little man.* He hastened the universal revolt of the slaves. He gripped us by the love of the lowly emanating from his whole person. He was a decadent, he too, extirpating from his heart all noble pride. He also knew nothing of the State, of society, of civilization, work, war.

Saint Paul distorted that Christian gift. The Jewish proletarians, members of the first Christian cenacula, saw in Jesus the prophet who revolted against the priesthood and the Roman Empire. Nietzsche imagined himself to have discovered, opposed to the great Roman solitude, the close solidarity of the common people. Saint Paul was thus the Jewish people pursuing in the Roman Empire a labour of *termites*. He eliminated from the Jewish conception the idea of Race. He invented Christ sacrificed by the Father for the sins of the world. He returned to the redeemer gods of Asia and of Alexandrine philosophy.

For him there was complete equality between immortal souls.
Here was the great levelling, the collapse of all that was higher in
man.   This time the crowd set itself up as judge of the Mighty.

That was why the Lutheran Reformation itself found no favour
in Nietzsche's eyes.   He reproached it not only with returning to
Paulism but with substituting democracy for aristocracy.   Was
not Luther the *yokel* who brought the Word within the compre-
hension of all, who introduced into Christianity "a churlish,
unpolished faith"?   His liberty was the shout of the crowd set on
domination.   The universal priesthood was the recommencement of the great revolt that should substitute the priesthood of
the people for hierarchy and the selection of the strong.   *Luther's
Reformation was a Christianity for peasants!*

Nietzsche felt no less aversion from liberal democracy.
Rousseau was his explanation of the decay of the French
aristocracy.   Rousseau was the French Luther.   The French
Revolution, he said, was but a sinister farce.   It needed a
Napoleon to renew the art of government, the Napoleon whom
the Germans stupidly brought down, thus ruining the unity of
Europe.   Democracy refused to recognize great men and *élites*.
It was the heir of the universal priesthood and let loose the
nstincts of sheep.   What was more, it mixed the blood of
diverse races.   Nietzsche, following Gobineau, deplored the
physiological pressure of the oppressed, the decadence of the
French people, won over by second-rate English ideas that had
come from the plebs driven by the landlords from its holdings.

It was from that that the parliamentary régime had come, the
régime of which the decadent French people had been the best
soldier.   The rise of the middle class, the cheapening of communications, urbanization, and the mixing of classes in the great
cities were all factors that had facilitated the formation of the
proletariat and of the plebeian *conquistadores*.   The peoples had
given way to nomadism.   The nationalities had fallen from their
greatness.   A horrible social mixture had been effected, creating
a race of gregarious, docile, laborious animals, content with a
monotonous well-being.   Here was indeed the terrible crushing
machine of democracy, rendering impossible the selection of
the fittest.   What was liberalism but government of the herd
by the herd?   An absurd diatribe.   Nietzsche was full of the
spectacle offered to him by the Germany hyperindustrialized by
Bismarck.   He knew nothing of the Western democracies.   All
he took note of was calumnies of them.

Thus, in his eyes Socialism and anarchism were continuations of the Christian Reformation and the French Revolution, which were simply potential anarchical Socialism. Why attribute so much importance to individuals? Nietzsche thought he understood the Socialist demand as of Christian inspiration, since it defended *imprescriptible rights*. The Christians taught the social revolution through talking of the Kingdom for which they were waiting, in which the first should be last. To the Socialist the defects of the plebs were but the sign of age-long oppression. He laid upon the *élite* all responsibility for the collective degeneration. He thus excited base appetites. It was true that democracy was itself on the fatal downward path, spreading average comfort and enlarging the possessing class. Nietzsche was here the forerunner of Georges Sorel. He preached preventive resistance against the social revolution. His own aspiration was for the formation of a Republic *sui generis, in which authority would force the citizens to serve a great cause, to follow an Order, a Master.* He wanted a *new Cæsar* to organize a unified Mankind.

To this had the lack of political culture brought Nietzsche. It made of him on certain points, undoubtedly, a forerunner of high quality, but a forerunner of Nazism. He did not foresee what would become of his fine dream of aristocratic selection when, after a defeat, that dream became an obsession with the German middle classes. Nietzsche returned to his eternal diatribe against Socialism; against Spinoza, the philosopher who believed only in clear thought and imagined that through it man participated in the divine; against the Jew who wanted to conquer the world by *intellectualizing* it; and finally against Pascal, who completed that work of spiritual destruction. Only Descartes found grace in his eyes because his thought was that of seventeenth-century aristocratism. In Germany, Kant and Hegel were for Nietzsche only the heirs of a debilitated Lutheranism! Everything was just decadence, and contemporary art, too sensuous, announced the ruin of our culture. Here was the tragic negation of thousands of years of effort. Nietzsche prayed for the catastrophe which would plunge the weak into the abyss and would place the levers of command in the hands of the strong.

Nietzsche saw clearly the evil from which Europe was suffering. *It is no longer believed*, he said, *that the world has a meaning.* If the physical universe is without end, what becomes of the destiny of man? *Men no longer live with a sense of a moral order.* Men feel their impotence, not only in face of nature, but *against themselves.*

The appetite for domination reigns everywhere, even among the weak. This means the eclipse of the highest divine and human authorities. Here we see all the nobility of the Nietzschean appeal. The strongest, for him, were those who, comprehending life, would make others comprehend it. What he did not know was that one day a Hitler would say in his turn that the system he imposed on Germany was in conformity with the eternal laws of Life!

Why, exclaimed Nietzsche, despair of the earth? Are we to see nothing but the immense mechanism that is preparing to break us? Are we to proceed to nihilism and to think that in consequence of the eternal Return our wretched plight will always recommence? Nietzsche did not think so. We know his solution. Men *of high intelligence and strong will* would break the existing societies, which were decrepit. Great thinkers and artists would maintain the *cult of intellectual superiority*. New philosophers would legislate and would establish the true hierarchy of values. Thereafter there would always be two moral systems, that of the *Leaders* and that of the *Herd*, that of the *Masters* and that of the *Slaves*. Keen prevision, but prevision of the *Führertum* and of the *Gefolgschaft*, the leadership and the following, of the Nazis!

Thanks to that selection of the strong, thought Nietzsche, we could conceive a lasting universe, but without transcendental support. What we should then need to comprehend *would be that one and the same Force inspires in individuals the elementary instincts and lucid consciousness, and in collectivities obscure or violent tendencies and the reflective thought that ends in a disciplinary organization.* That is the eternal German problem. Nietzsche solved it by the Will to power. That Will chooses from the qualities offered to us those that we prefer. These qualities preferred by our will are the *values*. We thus heroically deliver our inner value to the forces without. The true values are *quality-forces* that build up a *person* with given materials. It is a judgment of value that makes the unity of our person, at the same time as that of the world. To will to realize *that which is of most value* is to will that which will certainly be realized. Value is immanent in life. An admirable doctrine in itself, but one of which it is possible to make terrible use in the name of force or of what is considered to be true power.

That, according to Nietzsche, would be the true Renaissance. It would be a matter of choice, and therefore of judgment. If a vital connexion is established between the thinking subject and its object, it may be conceived that the being chooses its direction within the real, amid the dangers which nature holds; and that knowledge through the senses and knowledge through the reason, both daughters of inquietude, must join together, though the resulting knowledge will never have more than a *relative* value. The hierarchy to be created is incessantly menaced. The divine is incarnated in the world only in the process of incessantly vanishing there. *The more intense is life, the more need it has of clear ideas.* Science is there to arm us for action. Nietzsche was not afraid to say that we adopt the most consistent system of sophisms *in spite of its fundamental inexactitude,* the system best adapted to get us on in life. Everywhere evolution is simply energy and impulse, will to power that makes its way by utilizing better and better organized qualities or thoughts. As life is born and dies, so the alternation between regeneration and decadence is inevitable.

Thus the corporal organism is an apparatus installed to extract from living matter the consciousness which it virtually conceals. The body teaches us how societies are born and reared. The co-ordination of our internal phenomena is only partial, though it attains the rigidity we call reason. The intelligent will works always on instincts. If man is lord of the earth, it is because he inventively co-ordinates his organic habits.

It was for that reason that Nietzsche attached the greatest importance to human selection. He thought as *a true racialist.* Peoples of genius emerge from an alloying of unequal races. But, in general, promiscuity must be hated. On this capital point Nietzsche did not share Gobineau's opinion. *We must discover,* he said, *the dosages of blood that prepare the sovereign Race.* A curious thought, which the Nazis were one day to adopt for their own purposes, after reading Houston Stewart Chamberlain. Nietzsche, severe in regard to Anglo-French decadence, spoke of German imperfections, but in order to deduce from them a prognosis of vitality—*The future belongs to Germany because she has a young soul.* In the past the Jews were the race of intact vigour and refined spirit; at that time mankind had need of them. Let Germany, *by making use of the Jews,* seize intellectual primacy and give Leaders to Europe. Russia was good only for the supplying of *muzhiks,* peasants. Let us have German force, then, and German leaders, for a decadent West and for the barbarism of peasant Russia.

Nietzsche thus sought a middle course. When the gregarious

instincts carry the day, they slowly kill mankind; when the aristocratic instincts reign tyrannically, they, too, kill it, but more quickly.   What was needed was thus (1) a *gregarious* selection, to conserve the health of societies; (2) an *aristocratic* selection, to raise them to a higher level.   Be it noted that Nietzsche advocated *an absolute planning.*   He would have had European labour transformed into a *giant automaton.*   Thanks to its immense yield, there would be a fair level of existence for all, with a surplus for the aristocracy.   That would be the economy of the future.

Hide, then, from the workers the fact that they are machines, by cultivating their solidarity.   Create the idealism that enables the most irksome tasks to be performed with cheerfulness.   Especially, abolish wages, giving the worker fees and work a soul.   Utilize the *social Machiavellism* that will create *the social Republic of to-morrow*, in which the workers will obey principles and not masters, which will satisfy their self-respect.   A sublime demo-cracy—a democracy of voluntary slaves who accept their slavery!

What was to be done for the future *élite*?   Strong men would be bound to make their appearance in that new social State.   They would assist civilization to absorb evil and to draw vigour from it.   The higher man is *inhuman*, but it is through that that he is *superhuman*.   He is the new Barbarian who will associate with his superabundant genius the most rigorous discipline.   He will live in creative enthusiasm, but retaining a sense of pro-portion.   The mankind of the future will need *philosophers*, not *Cæsars*.   A magnificent phrase, marking exactly the delimitation between Nietzsche and Nazism.

Once the human tragedy was determined, when man had accepted the struggle against the world, without any hope except of victory attained in and by defeat itself, it would be possible to mould societies in conformity with that tragic datum.   Nietz-sche then imagined the era of wars ended, the planet at last pacified, the fusion of races completed.   The new mankind would comprise a class of simple labourers, of the *Chinese* type, and a caste of *masters* which Nietzsche supposed would combine *Jewish intelligence* and *Slavo-Prussian* qualities!   Each of these categories would have its moral system and its beliefs.   The life of the Superman would then be possible.   The union between Christ and Dionysus, between mildness and force, between Christianity and paganism, between power and love, would then be achieved.   It would be the fulfilment of Hölderlin's dream, of Richard Wagner's.

Have we not here, though on a higher plane, the exact prefiguration of the Germany of the Third Reich? Nietzsche's philosophy was and remained the great novelty in the thought of that period, the symbol of the world to come. German philosophy tried, of course, after Nietzsche, to remount that terrible slope. Its adepts gathered round Dilthey. They showed the danger of the natural sciences when they run counter to the mental sciences; they revealed their incapacity to solve the problems of human existence and history. A new conception was evolved beyond the Rhine, that of existential philosophy. With Husserl it combated pseudoscientific positivism, and attempted to define true science. With Heidegger it took up again all the metaphysical problems, seeking to understand nature through man, and creating an entirely new anthropology, so as to break the formidable destructive power of biological realism, while returning almost to the pre-Copernican conceptions of the ancient Greeks.

Was that a solution? It meant leaving to the phenomena of the external world their true value and admitting that they include ourselves. It is impossible to hold to-day that nature is conditioned by man. Husserl, Heidegger, and Jaspers did nothing but destroy the ancient authorities in their own way. Their thought, like that of Schopenhauer, betrays disappointment and disillusion. They represent a period that had abandoned hope. For they plunged finite and limited Man into the ocean of Being, forbidding him the Beyond, depriving him of all normative absolute values, denying all morality that could serve as a principle of conduct, and cutting man off from all eternal reality. *Has German thought raised itself from the Nietzschean hoodoo?*

What we see beyond the "superhumanism" of Nietzsche, the true conquering hero of that half-century before the First World War, is *the apologia for German vitality*, and especially the idea of a future society to be built up by Germany on the principle of the Leader in command, the *élite* supporting him, and the masses following him. That idea went marching on. It was to be found again in the form of Wilhelmian pan-Germanism, and then, after war and defeat, was to be seen taking entire possession of the Germany of the Third Reich.

3. *Pan-Germanism*

When we make an exact analysis of the data of the phenomenon, we easily see that pan-Germanism before 1914–18 itself attempted a criticism of international values and the elaboration of a programme of war and conquest to which the Nietzschean will to power was no stranger.

It is easy to show that the pan-Germanism of 1815 to 1918 presents an aspect similar to that of Nietzscheanism. As regards its negative tendencies it was anti-Semitic, anti-Roman, and radically hostile to œcumenical Christianity (which it deliberately set out to Germanize), to democratic liberalism, and to all the Socialist Internationals.

Doctrinal anti-Semitism appears especially, in its present form, in Houston Stewart Chamberlain. It already existed potentially in earlier German thought. When, after the French Revolution, about 1792, Hölderlin and Hegel discussed at Tübingen the possibility of making Germany into a National Community that would also be a Religion of the German people, they already declared themselves anti-Semitic in principle, considering Judaism as an irreconcilable enemy of a religion of that type. A curious symptom, showing that at its outset romanticist thought held Judaism responsible for the rationalism that was declared to be deadly and of which it was so readily said that it was corrupting all nations, especially those of the West.

Fichte attacked the Jewish mind. He charged it with ranging facts only in a mechanical and abstract order. Was it not Spinoza, the Jewish philosopher, who had vitiated the whole of Western thought? And was it not necessary to replace Israelite prophetism by a German prophetism, of which Fichte himself would be the first coryphæus? This anti-Judaism was to develop later, between 1850 and 1860, suddenly and on an extraordinary scale. The ferocious anti-Judaism of Richard Wagner is well known. It is easy to explain it by the whole philosophy of the musician-poet. Driesmans, a notorious pan-German, was both anti-Latin and anti-Jew. According to him it was Semitism that corrupted the Greeks. It was precisely from Semitism that Socratic doubt had proceeded, and then the vain subtlety of Alexandrianism, in short, the whole of ancient decadence. As for Houston Stewart Chamberlain, the famous author of *The Foundations of the Twentieth Century*, he was the inventor of Jewish materialism. It was to him, among many others, that we owe the celebrated demonstration that the Jews could not have given birth to Jesus, who was obviously an Aryan. An argument of capital importance, since anti-Semite thought made use of it to detach Christianity from the Old Testament.

This anti-Semitism spread freely under William II. It was certainly not the Nazis who invented it. It was not difficult for the ruling caste to renew the tradition of it after 1917–18, as we shall see later. The arguments varied little. Rosenberg was not the first to demonstrate that Saint Paul " Judaized" Christianity by turning it away from its true path. The hatred of all that is international shows itself clearly in all these acid criticisms. And it might be said that the Germans of that period, already a tragic one, perceived the extraordinary resemblance between Israel's destiny and their own. Is it not for that reason that the conflict between the international Race and the Race that desired to be purely national, between two sorts of racial unrest, was so profound?

In the orbit of pan-Germanism ancient and Christian humanism suffered a similar fate to that of Judaism. When the first pan-Germans turned, like Hölderlin, to Greece, it was usually to see there the sacred Community, the sovereign Race, not Greek universalism. The distinction is of importance. Many German poets and artists dreamed in the nineteenth century of uniting Hellenism and Christianity. It was their favourite theme. But this always meant the Hellenism of the agora and the community, Dionysiac rather than Apolline. What they saw before all else in Greece was the *strong and triumphant nationality*, with Socratism and Platonism relegated to obscurity.

The decisive demonstration for Greece was attempted by the historian Curtius, between 1876 and 1882. Before the Median wars, he said, the Greeks had been split up as the Germans were in a later age under the Holy Roman Empire. Subsequently the Greeks were unified, and it was then that they enjoyed supremacy. Salamis and Fehrbellin, so many centuries apart, were one and the same thing! Greece here was the model of the great military State under whose hegemony the neighbouring States were reduced to vassals. Attica and Prussia had the same destiny. Both showed the same devotion to the State. Bismarck was compared to Pericles. For it was he who had destroyed democracy and its fatal conception of human rights. What mattered the mutilation of liberties so long as power was gained? For such men as Curtius the eternal value of Greece and of the ancient world was found not in the universalism and the influence of their thought but in the effective hegemony exercised under their domination.

This apologia for a violent Greece, as model for a future

Germany, was found again, though perhaps less blatantly, in the Wilhelmian ideology. H. S. Chamberlain took up once more the comparison between Germany and Greece. Driesmans set the corrupted and corrupting Semites against the strong and healthy Greeks. So there was constituted throughout the nineteenth and into the twentieth century, from the distant days of Hölderlin, a sort of tradition concerning the interpretation of Greek civilization. Nothing was more typical than this tendency to dwell, in contrast to the Hellenism of the eighteenth century, entirely on the value of Greek energetics. But was not the germ of this to be found in the *Sturm und Drang* period, and in certain odes of Goethe, especially the *Wanderers Sturmlied*?

So much for Greece. As for the Latin mind, implicit in the Roman Idea, for historical motives that are well known it was the object of the most constant and determined attacks. We know how Fichte treated it, when he traced it back in its entirety to the most arid and the most abstract intellectualism, and finally compared it to the Jewish mind. It dealt, he said, only with concepts that described dead realities. For him the Franks were impure Teutons who had installed themselves in a country under Roman domination and had there adopted an idiom that was equally impure, because it was not original. The Latin collectivities, the philosopher added, were composed of elements that were simply in juxtaposition, individuals and groups without an autonomous life of their own. Germany was thus contaminated when she underwent the slightest Latinization.

Hegel certainly showed more justice to the Romano-Latin world. He understood the immense historic importance of the part played by the Roman Idea. Similarly, the great effort of German Catholic theology in the nineteenth century aimed at restoring the dogma and the ecclesiastical system of Roman Catholicism, introducing into it the community ideas of the romantics. But Rome itself stopped the development, assuredly dangerous, of that thought.

On the other hand, when Fichte claimed that authentic Christianity had been able to develop freely only among the Teutons, he "nationalized" or "Germanized" Christianity. He attacked Roman or Italian scepticism, which made of religion simply a political and social instrument. The Reformation found grace in his eyes only in so far as it was German, obeying the deep aspirations of the German soul. On this plane, Hegel arrived at analogous conclusions.

The Catholic romantics, for their part, could not condemn the Roman Idea. They sought instead to turn toward the national side, to show that Germany alone was capable of renewing and regenerating it. They insisted on the alliance between the imperial German nation and the Papacy in the Middle Ages, on all that Italy owed to the Teutons, who, they thought, had played the part of a vivifying lymph for all Europe. The great Latin mistake, according to Görres, was *the Italian Renaissance*. He saw the same fundamental Latin corruption in humanism, in the Renaissance, and later in the age of Louis XIV and the free-thought of the eighteenth century. Here came the eternal protest against a certain "Christianization" of Germania by Rome. It joined the criticism of the German *Aufklärung* and the Anglo-French Enlightenment. Rome and France were the objects of the same attacks. It was the conscious revolt against all Western humanism. It was for the Teutons, to whom the future belonged, to revivify the whole Roman order.

Hegel believed that the introduction of Christianity into Germany had made the Teutons furious. The atrocities that had accompanied that Christianization were, for him, the sign of a *predestination*. If the Teutons had thus revolted against the Christianity introduced from Rome, it was because they alone were capable of creating *the true Christianity*. Certainly pagan imperial Rome had been great. Nevertheless, the Teuton world was bound to rise against that tyrannical greatness.

These considerations called for a demonstration to serve as pendant to that of Curtius. It was furnished by Mommsen. His Rome resembles Curtius's Greece. It is not the Rome of Catholic universalism or of the Renaissance. It is ancient Rome, a model for Germany and her coming hegemony.

Strange views, but in a steady and continuous tradition. They took definite shape under William II, at the time when the future National Socialist system was beginning to show through the flourishing pan-Germanism. Hasse was able to maintain, about 1905, that the German Catholics should be detached from Italo-Roman influence and that a national Catholic Church was necessary to Germany. In that crucible, in fact, it would be possible to melt together traditional Catholicism, Lutheranism, and the sects that were pullulating in certain German States. It would be the great religious fusion. The idea of *a warrior religion, a heroic religion*, the prelude to the "soldier nation" of the Nazis, a religion to take the place of the Christian religion of weakness, humility, and love, took possession of many minds that had been infatuated by the reading of Nietzsche. Luther became in their eyes the Reformer who had led the German people to the source of its true genius. All else was but alien intoxication. Driemans explained Roman orthodoxy by the Celtic, and thus inferior, element of the German people. The geographer Ratzel charged the Roman Church with having favoured territorial fragmentation and made of mediæval Germany "a Greece in fragments." Maximilian Harden, finally, reproached the German Catholics with lacking the national colonizing spirit.

The anti-liberal criticism dated back to romanticism and its vigorous campaign against the *Aufklärung*. When he spoke of the Jews or the Latins, Fichte had in mind intellectualism and intelligence in themselves, with their fixed, immobile vocabulary, which could convey only fixed or dead facts. This time it was the France of Louis XIV or of the eighteenth century that was under fire. That great century, according to Fichte, was but cankered thought. French philosophy, he said, was associated only with inert concepts. It believed only in things that were ready made. How could such a people know the secret of collective life? How could it assure living and organized collaboration between individuals? Incapable of raising itself to true unity, never conceiving more than a collection of disconnected individuals, it oscillated between revolution and stagnation, between anarchy and despotism. We know the use, the abuse, of that system for which the thought of that period was responsible!

Here again Hegel saw more clearly than Fichte: he realized that Western rationalism had given the world critical doubt, abstract and normative thought, the Cartesian method that submitted all things to the test of reason. Hegel did not fail, moreover, to grasp the importance of the French Revolution. He reproached the Revolution, however, for its individualism, though recognizing that it had to destroy and actually did destroy a collective injustice—the *ancien régime*. As for the Catholic Görres, he saw in that Revolution once more the spirit of the Italian Renaissance. Moreover, whatever one's judgment might be of that historic phenomenon, that political Revolution could not deprive Germany, in Görres' view, of the hegemony she must one day exercise *in virtue of the Lutheran Reformation—a religious Revolution.*

No doubt a section of German opinion was converted, between 1815 and 1898, to liberal ideas, which it defended with great courage. The failure of the March Revolution of 1848 and of the Frankfort Constitution, followed by Bismarck's victories, struck a mortal blow at liberalism. The pan-Germans of Bismarck's day showed themselves more and more harsh against France. The day must come for her destruction, said Paul de Lagarde long before Hitler. Germany would take from her all the territory she needed. Constantin Frantz expressed the same view. The economist Friedrich List attacked France because she represented the detested Latin thought. The Latin race, he added, had not the requisite qualities for raising a nation to the supreme degree of power and wealth. Bismarck himself said that the Latins were used up, and had entirely fulfilled their destiny. They had but to disappear.

This offensive against Western liberalism, against democracy and the parliamentary institution, assumed new dimensions between 1890 and 1918. This was the period of the great intellectual assault that was the prelude to the military offensive. H. S. Chamberlain said repeatedly that the French Revolution had not given France what the Lutheran Reformation gave Germany. About 1900 a writer of the calibre of Julius Hart proclaimed the decadence of the Latin world. If we were to believe him, Napoleon was the last of the Latins. The Mediterranean race, said Wilser, had to be replaced, for it was finished. Did not the higher elements of French culture derive from the Teutons who long ago fertilized the Gallic soil? *In the kings of France there was a greatness that could only be of Teutonic origin.* As for the Celt, he was well known. He was the incarnation of sensuality, superficiality, and boastfulness, of submission to Roman orthodoxy, and of backstairs politics. France, it was said after Nietzsche, had weakened her Germanic blood by the Revolution of 1789. Those French were a decrepit people! Why not drive them into the West, taking the best elements, those of the East, for Germany?

How low, before 1919, was the level of that criticism! There was Maximilian Harden threatening the "female" France with an offensive from the "male" Germany, who, if she did not submit, would "quench her flame in blood"! And a little later there was Thomas Mann himself, in his *Betrachtungen* of 1917, resuming *ad nauseam* all these anti-Western arguments. It might be supposed that he aimed at accumulating, not without talent, a complete arsenal of them.

To combat Britain and France in their thought, their morality, their colonial empires, to see in the European West, in contrast with Germany, nothing but decadence and factors of collapse—such was the end pursued by that literature, which between 1900 and 1918 burst all bounds. The most venomous of the Nazi attacks on France in our day are all to be found already elaborated in that immense work of undermining undertaken against her, with such methodical persistence, since the Revolution of 1789. It dates from long ago, the false image of the Western democracies that haunts the credulous brains of Germany! It was against the qualities that made the greatness of the democracies that the German launched out the most readily. He does not possess them. Hence his resentment, his destructive fury.

Nietzsche's criticism of international Socialism reappears in pan-German literature. What could be more opposed, in theory at all events, to the idea of the *Volksgemeinschaft*, the racial and national community, than Marxism, the creator of the labour International? It was as well, however, to show a certain caution in this matter. For German Socialism was in certain respects one of the essential and efficacious forms of pan-Germanism. This can be demonstrated for the First and the Second International. Divest international Socialism of its internationalism, and you have National Socialism. From revolutionary Socialism, the former hope of the proletarian classes of all countries, the transition was made to the Socialism that was no more than a *national solidarism*, an absolute mania for ordering everything for the benefit of the most intransigent and the most dictatorial nationalism that the world has known.

For, in the history of Socialism, Germany did not have the initiatory mission with which she is generally credited. What she did was to capture the Socialist movement in her own interest. Later, in creating National Socialism, she captured the energies of the Communists for herself. It is easy, moreover, to discover in the most widespread of the pan-German literature the criticism of Slavism, of Russia and her defects, a criticism that was transformed after 1917 into anti-Communist propaganda. But, while attacking Slavism, pan-Slavism, and Communism, German criticism soon turned its eyes to the wide *Russian spaces*. There was talk of fighting Russia in the Balkans, in Asia Minor, in China, in Poland, and in the Baltic States. From this was born the theory of the "Mitteleuropa" which, under the hegemony and control of Germany, should organize against both the East and the West.

When he resumed in his last philosophical works his formidable argumentation against all forms of humanism, Nietzsche began to express, with the intuition of genius, the ideas that were in the air. It might be said that after 1890 the pan-Germans were able to profit from the lesson his work instilled as though of its own accord. All in all, their criticism is nothing but a systematic popularization of that of Nietzsche himself. Nobody knew that better than the Nazis.

The positive programme of pan-Germanism has certain elements in common with the later Nietzscheanism, though on this plane the difference is more marked than in the criticism of the Internationals. On the other hand, this same programme announced with the utmost precision that of National Socialism. In the history of pan-Germanism there is nothing to indicate that it was a product of war and defeat. Hitlerism merely adapted pre-war ideas to the mentality of the masses.

Yet, if *pan-Germanism* is on no account to be confused with *Bismarckism*, these two factors, essential elements in the history of contemporary Germany, certainly influenced each other. Bismarck's work, the creation of the Second Reich and the place the new empire took in the centre of Europe, encouraged pan-Germanism, its hopes and its ambitions, especially after the fall of the Iron Chancellor. Conversely, pan-Germanism led Bismarckism into a path which it scarcely foresaw at the outset. It was natural that Prussian hegemony should have brought the programme in view to practical completion by supplying the means for doing so. It is thus not surprising that under William II the pan-Germans asked whether *Prussian force* could be united with *imperialist ambitions*, in order to establish *a culture worthy of the name*. The pan-Germans believed in that alliance, but there is no sign yet of the culture.

The collapse of traditional values and of humanism in Germany had alike as its cause and its result the triumph of biologism.

In view of that it is understandable why Nietzsche, immediately before elaborating his final philosophy, returned to the study of biology and turned to contemporary sociology. The phenomenon was connected with the economic crisis. Men feared for their future. They asked why they were alive. They were bewildered and seized with a sort of collective metaphysical distress. Nowhere was that distress deeper than in Germany. Nowhere had mechanization and technicalization proceeded at a more overwhelming pace. *Had the Germans reached the stage of life for life's sake? Were they to see nothing more than the Reich for its own sake?* Nietzsche's solution, middle-class, individualistic, and aristocratic, was not the solution for a people haunted by that apprehension.

In its fury of industrialization and spiritual destruction the German soul was as though emptied of its substance. It thirsted for primitive nature, for a purely biological or dynamic existence. It was clear' how the Aryan, that is to say the German who claimed to save the natural, elementary, spontaneous instincts, was constituted physiologically and psychologically, as against the Jew who was supposed to be pure intelligence and who was accused of defeatist nihilism. This biologism made its appearance between 1890 and 1900. Men's minds clung desperately to natural history rather than human history, which inspired in them nothing but scepticism. They fled from the great city and its artificial civilization. The youth movement (*Jugendbewegung*) was the most striking sign of this state of mind.

It was then that there began to be adopted beyond the Rhine the *eschatology of Race*, the *hope centred in the Community*, the *religion of membership of the nationality*. It was a providential *ersatz*. A crude objectivism took the place of the old values. There came a cult of prehistory or subhistory. Contempt was shown for clear perception and its logic in consideration of that primitive background. Men persuaded themselves that the spirit engenders nothing but ideologies. The suspicion of ideology was a spiritual evil that spread everywhere. A terrible Asianism seemed to spread over German thought, with somewhat rare exceptions, ignoring the satisfied scientism of the universities. Thus *even the need for eternity* was killed. Philosophy descended to the level of a servant of the sciences. The disciplinary organizations, so compact in that country, had emasculated the individuals. Schools and universities, official Churches, political parties, trade unions and professional associations, were suffocating the people in ready-made moulds that claimed to shape all existence. It was precisely with that vacuum, that deficiency, that the great pan-German aspiration tried to cope.

The form that that hope took on the eve of the First World War was a prefiguration of the principal National Socialist theses concerning action and the future of Germany in Europe and in the world.

To begin with, there was the theme of the Nordic Race and its absolute superiority over other races, a theme blared forth by

Hitler's *Mein Kampf*, Rosenberg's *Der Mythus des 20. Jahrhunderts* (*The Myth of the Twentieth Century*), and the works of H. F. K. Günther. This racialism appears in Germany in certain writings of the eighteenth century, notably in the work of Herder. The idea of the national genius and of popular songs belonged at that time to the sphere of the broadest and the most generous cosmopolitanism. But it was pregnant with unforeseen developments. The religious feeling of the epoch, lacking concrete bases, was already in search of *Volkstum*, racialism. Germany was ready on the eve of romanticism to consider herself as a future holy Community, a future Greece. In this regard the poetic work of Hölderlin was a symptom of the greatest importance. In 1809, in Jahn's *Deutsches Volkstum*, the idea of the sanctified Race, of Germany heir of Greece, was expressed with the utmost clearness. The Germans were to be the second Holy Race because they were *a résumé of all human nature*. In 1854 Arndt repeated in his *Pro.Populo Germanico* that the German race was superior by virtue of its courage and of the combative spirit that enables man to carve a place for himself in the world. The German race was, indeed, descended from the Germanic race from which the Anglo-Saxons came, and which has always developed all over the earth its will to power. Let the German realize his unity of race, and he would exercise world domination.

In the first half of the nineteenth century, and even in Bismarck's day, pan-Germanism preserved its religious and philosophic character. It claimed to be working for the true faith of the future, *for a national religion* that would be superior to all the creeds. This Evangel, revivified by the Germans, would regenerate all peoples, and after the crushing of France and Russia it would reconstitute Europe. This affirmation was to be found among Protestant and Catholic romantics, in Paul de Lagarde, Constantin Frantz, and Richard Wagner. It is precisely this conception of a National Community (*Volksgemeinschaft*) of a religious type that was at the root of the life-and-death struggle between the Third Reich and the Christian confessions.

A little later, under William II, there was added to it racialism properly so called. This only saw the light in Germany in the twenty-five years that preceded the First World War. From about 1890 the ideas of Gobineau spread in Germany, falling on a soil well prepared, as we have seen, by biology, anthropology, and sociology. The idea of racial unity and racial purity suddenly invaded the German field of thought, reinforcing the nationalism of which the earlier aspects had derived mainly from religion or from general theories of culture. Gobineau affirmed that the superiority of all the great human civilizations was due to Germanic blood. Is not that the essential argument of Rosenberg's *Der Mythus des 20. Jahrhunderts*?

One may recall here the theories of Wilser, who sought to show the intrinsic superiority of the Nordic, that is to say the blond dolichocephalic, man, and those of Woltmann, who devoted himself to the biological interpretation of intellectual and moral facts, affirming that Germans of pure blood must be forbidden to intermarry with other Germanic stocks. All in order that they might be a people of "masters," a *Herrenvolk*. But the true founder of racialism was Houston Stewart Chamberlain, with whom Hitler came into personal touch and to whom Rosenberg devoted a recent work. Son of a British admiral, with a profound knowledge of Germany and of Europe, Chamberlain studied natural science, and then Carlyle and his theory of hero-worship. He scarcely believed in an originally superior race. He well knew that no people is of perfectly pure race. But, in order that a race might be superior, it was not at all necessary for it to be pure. The greatest peoples are precisely those that are born of admixture. For races can *become* pure, can *be made* pure. Every people is superior that possesses knowledge, civilization, and culture of mind. That is the case with the Germanic peoples. They purify knowledge by treating it as a disinterested passion, civilization by creating the true social organization, and culture by liberating it from rationalism. They are made for enlightened despotism and the rule of the wise.

Without dwelling at greater length on doctrinal detail, we may see that this pre-war racialism took account of the social problem, that it embraced, so to say, a national and communal Socialism that became that of the Nazis. But it also had in view the military problem, though without going as far as Nazi *Soldatentum*, as far as the idea of a permanent and total mobilization of national energies and of the entire population for military purposes. The great question for most of the Wilhelmian pan-Germans was whether the German culture could wear the disciplinary and military carapace with which Prussia was providing it. Like the Greeks, and like their own ancestors, the primitive Teutons of the age before the migration of the peoples, the Germans wanted a *military* State and also a State of *culture*. Goethe perhaps had some vision of the problem in the second part of *Faust*, when he placed Arcadia, where Faust and Helena celebrated their mystical wedding, in a region strongly defended by Faust's armies. Nietzsche thought at one moment that the Bismarckian empire, militarily strong, would endow Europe with a great civilization. He consoled himself for his bitter disappointment by a doctrine of superhumanity which was for the benefit only of the rare elect.

The pan-Germans of the average level, who were legion in a Reich of apparent prosperity, demonstrated for their part *that militarism and art are in no way irreconcilable.* It is possible, they thought, to unite the sword and the myrtle, the slashing cut and the flowing cup. This alliance, if they were to be believed, would be the very thing to confer true superiority on German culture, which would gain refinement without losing strength. On the eve of the war a certain Friedrich Lang saw in Prussian militarism the purest emanation of German civilization. Thomas Mann maintained a similar thesis in his *Friedrich II. und die grosse Koalition.*

As for the Continental and colonial programme of pan-Germanism, elaborated in the time of William II, it, too, formed a prelude to the Nazi programme, *with this difference, that Nazism definitely placed its Continental preoccupation, " Mitteleuropa," in front of colonial or world preoccupations.* This programme conceived:

(1) a fight to the death with France, a decrepit people, the remains of which, about twenty million, must be regrouped around the central plateau; Picardy, Artois, and Normandy to be integrated in the Reich and the east and the south of France colonized, so that the German race would reach to the Mediterranean;

(2) a fight to the death between Prussia and Austria, so that central Europe might be organized; of this process the Reformation, Frederick II, and Bismarck represented the first three stages, and the fourth would be the *absolute hegemony of Germany in central and western Europe, thanks to the annexation of the German provinces of Austria;*

(3) the addition of the smaller States of Europe, Scandinavia, the Netherlands, Switzerland, and the Balkan States, to Germany, so as to constitute "the world-wide Empire of the Germanic Race and People," and to realize the *Civis germanicus sum* of William II, the great *Civitas Germanica,* which would draw useful lessons from the *Civitas Romana* and would substitute a *real Empire* for the Utopian cosmopolitanism of the Internationals.

This scheme, chosen out of a large number, is propounded in

Reimer's *Ein Alldeutsches Deutschland*, which appeared in 1905.
Its kinship with the foreign programme of Hitler and Rosenberg
is obvious.

The hatred of democracy and the longing for a Germanic
Leader, a "Führer" who would seize control of Germany's
destiny in order to guide it, are no less apparent in the literature
that was flooding all Germany on the eve of the offensive of 1914.
It was an appeal in the first place for territorial unity, Germany
being enabled to combine the advantages of unitarism with those
of federalism, so as to become *a model for all peoples*. On the
political plane, the formula of enlightened and providential
despotism, together with the idea that the German people need
to be *led* and *directed*, remained in the foreground. A sort of
democracy based on the direction and rule of a competent *Élite*
would thus be substituted for the disintegrated mass of individuals
that the Western democracies had created by their doctrine of
the sovereignty of the people—especially France, which was
declared to be condemned to oscillate eternally between anarchy
and dictatorship. Germany, for her part, would always reconcile
authority with liberty, monarchy with the republic, thus elaborating the perfect Constitution, inspired by a sort of educative
constraint.

It was thus the ideal of the "Führer" or of "Führertum,"
the idea of an authoritarian régime. Already Fichte and Hegel
had expressed the aspiration for a Master, a strong man able to
mould the German masses, a royal Will able to incarnate the
sovereignty of the State. The State would thus be at one and
the same time a *spiritual* and a *material* force. This Bonapartism *à l'allemande*, based on federalism and on the hegemony
of a conscious disciplinary principle, passed into Bismarckism.
Prussian hegemony was its best instrument. On the eve of the
war, in face of the weakness of rulers, the blunders of diplomacy,
and the impotence of Parliament, did not Maximilian Harden call
in his articles in *Zukunft* for the Strong Man who would settle
accounts dictatorially with a worm-eaten monarchy?

Whence the apologia for the army, for national militarization,
and for war. For Fichte and Hegel, already, war was a matter of
logical necessity. War alone "classed" peoples and established
among them the indispensable hierarchy. These two were
followed by all the pan-Germans in the glorification of war as the
generator of true justice, of that justice between peoples of which
one day Möller van den Bruck was to write. But this warlike

activity needs a definite aim. This is to be found precisely in the famous theory of " *Volk ohne Raum*," a people without room to live, which was no Nazi invention. At the outset of the nineteenth century pan-Germanism, regarding Germany as a concrete geographical and historical reality, had recourse to scientific arguments in order to justify German expansion and war.

Did not Arndt protest in 1803 against neighbour States that were robbing Germany of the air, light, and space she needed for development? Was not a similar justification offered for the partition of Poland, while acquisitive glances were being cast upon Holland, Switzerland, and the Baltic countries? Hegel had further said that neither thought nor culture nor religion could exist *without material bases*, that every people has *its day*, that the *Germanic day* had come, and with it the right of sovereignty that belonged to Germany. He added the historical to the geographical demonstration, saying that the evolution of the Teutons reproduced in brief that of other peoples and would prolong it to a period no other people had attained. The Germanic Empire would thus be *that of historic totality*.

Later came Pertz, Ranke, Max Duncker, Droysen, Curtius, Mommsen, and Treitschke, with the demonstration that all history ended in German hegemony, and that the surviving political forms would coincide with those organized by Prussia for Germany. Finally, under William II, Ratzel and Dix resumed and expanded the geographical demonstration. The existing partition of the globe, they said, was abnormal and subject to revision, and Germany had not her due place in it. War alone enabled a people placed at a disadvantage to penetrate into neighbouring territory. The fact that restricted spaces had a dense population and that wide spaces were sparsely populated created a demand for air and a special dynamism. What else was the conflict of nations but *the struggle between different spatial conceptions*? Germany owed it to herself to equalize her spatial dream with the spatial dream of the Anglo-Saxons. The historical demonstration was furnished by a certain Karl Lamprecht, who reduced concrete history to the methods employed by peoples for organizing greater and greater multitudes in enlarged spaces. The world belonged to the three great Germanic Powers, Britain, the United States, and Germany. There was no discussion as yet of the Russian or "Eurasian" space.

There need be no surprise at meeting with the first outline of

a programme of Continental and colonial expansion in Arndt and
Jahn. But before 1850 Friedrich List was more precise. He
saw Germany constituting "the heart of a durable Continental
alliance," and he advocated colonial activity directed toward the
Near East. Moltke, too, had bold views on France, Holland,
and certain territories of the East. Bismarck was more moderate,
but Treitschke had big ideas and exalted the Germanism which,
thanks to Austria, would become Danubian, then Balkan, and
finally Oriental. Paul de Lagarde and Constantin Frantz laid
down what Germany should one day have the right to take from
the West, the East, and the South. For they dreamed of a
federation of Central Europe of which Germany would be the
centre.

It will be seen that these theorists' "Mitteleuropa" implied
colonizing activities within relatively modest limits. But under
William II imagination and scheming were given free scope.
Numberless associations were founded to advocate programmes
emanating from them, to spread imperialist ideas, and to worry
the life out of people in high places. It was not enough to war
against the Triple Entente. German power must be installed
in the very heart of the Continent. After the fall of Bismarck,
colonial ambitions grew under the action of boundless jealousy.
Based on the colonies already acquired, and encouraged by the
Boer War, a tireless propaganda demonstrated *the necessity of the
German colonial Empire*. While Rohrbach wrote his *Deutsches
Denken in der Welt*, the Kaiser proceeded to Morocco and to
Palestine. German activities simultaneously threatened the
United States and South America, France in North Africa and
Morocco, Russia in the Balkans, in Asia Minor, and in China,
Belgium and Portugal in Central Africa, and finally Britain in
Egypt, in Central Africa, in China, and on the seven seas.

Thus, in the hundred years between 1815 and 1918, pan-
Germanism passed through three great stages—the opening of
the nineteenth century, the Bismarckian period, and the era of
William II. Originally religious and philosophical and limited
to a few isolated dreamers, and lacking a solid basis so long as
national unity had not been achieved, it was hesitant. Under
Bismarck the Prussian policy and the military successes left it
in the shade, while preparing strong positions for it. Bismarck
was too realist to give support to so many unhealthy ambitions.
Nevertheless, racialism, scientific theories, and the Continental
and colonial programme had already assumed considerable

dimensions and some precision.   Once Bismarck had disappeared
from the political scene, the flood passed on, submerging every
obstacle.   There was a sudden and unprecedented crop of
theories and programmes.   The means of action were at hand.
The administration and the army had Prussified the Second Reich.
The offensive of 1914 was the first manifestation of the sacred
union between the dream of greatness and its instruments of
realization.

Was not this a perfectly plain story?   Is not the whole of
the Nazi programme contained potentially in pre-war pan-
Germanism?   Add, in the hour of defeat, anti-Judaism and
anti-Communism, preach the doctrine not only to soldiers and
to intellectuals but above all to masses not far from destitution,
and it will be understood why, after a dozen years of a democracy
unable to master Germany and also ill-supported from abroad,
the sudden violent Hitlerite galvanization became possible.

BOOK III

THE HITLER REICH

CHAPTER VII

WEIMAR REPUBLIC AND NATIONAL SOCIALIST PARTY

THE genesis of National Socialist racialism is indissolubly bound up with the history of the Weimar Republic. Nazism gained exactly what parliamentary democracy lost. Nazism was the direct heir of the final philosophy of Nietzsche and of pre-war pan-Germanism, and proceeded to its own definitive criticism of the European Internationals and to a mysticism of community type; but the collapse of Weimar, the tragedy of the Internationals represented by the great political parties of that period, found its natural counterpart in the victory and the arrival in power of National Socialism (the "National Socialist German Labour Party" as it called itself). The two historic phenomena were rigorously complementary.

It was a strange contrast in virtue of which a sudden violent galvanization of the national energies, without precedent in the past, followed a social and political decomposition which was itself unexampled. The paradoxical and crushing force of this phenomenon dominated the whole career of Germany after the First World War. It is this phenomenon that needs to be understood. The new and, indeed, disconcerting aspect presented by the vanquished German collectivity between 1918 and 1933 consisted in reality neither in the Republican dissolution nor in the extraordinary *Gleichschaltung* that abruptly brought everything in the Germany of 1933 to a common denominator. It consisted in the *immediate passage* from one stage to the other.

Goebbels accurately defined the strangeness of the fact when he affirmed that, thanks to National Socialism and its desperate effort, Germany was compelled to concentrate on her own needs, applying the most relentlessly consistent collective energy in place of the earlier slackness and *laisser faire*, which he described so exactly by the German term *Schlaffheit*. But a people that

256

passed so quickly from one extreme to the other, and made use of such means in order to assure the internal cohesion of its various elements, was not a people in health. Nor could Europe have a healthy life with such a collectivity in her midst.

The Weimar pluralism, the multiplicity of States, parties, creeds, and professional organizations, was the very substance of the German people, a substance transmitted from the past territorial epoch, passing through the imperfect Bismarckian unification, to the post-war period. But the system that replaced it overnight, with its dictatorship based on the close union of mystical racialism with Prussian discipline and of mass instincts with technical achievement, was no longer the substance of the people. Imitating American methods of propaganda, the dictatorship of Italian Fascism, and that of Russian Communism, it was virtually superposed on the population of Germany. Like a monstrous cephalopod, it held the people in its contracted tentacles.

Do not speak, then, of the *authoritarian State*. Place no faith in the intimate union alleged by the National Socialist leaders to exist between them and the German people. The leaders of the party may be compared to a bizarre *deus ex machina*. They made out of nothing a formidable machinery of power that responded neither to the infinite diversity nor to the true aspirations of the German masses. Their creation was mainly artificial and arbitrary. In that respect it was a continuation of Bismarckian industrialization and its misdeeds. It simplified and rationalized Germany to excess, destroying the country's civilization and humanism. It made of that country, once so rich in European culture, a sort of monstrous executioner, charged with the destruction of the heritage of thousands of years, supremely the country of iconoclasts.

1. *The social origins of Nazism and the activities of the former ruling caste*

It is impossible to grasp the extent and the tragedy of the phenomenon without an accurate picture of the German collectivity around 1929-30, at the beginning of the last crisis before the arrival of the Hitler régime, the crisis that came about half-way through the inter-war period.

It has been maintained that National Socialism originated among the German middle classes. The assertion is not wrong

in itself.   But is that the whole explanation, the whole truth?   It
does not seem to be.   For the German people of that time was
nothing but an oligarchically ruled feudalism, aristocratic and
capitalist, landed and industrial, very greatly reduced in strength,
face to face with two immense camps each representing almost
half of the population—the middle classes on one side and the
proletariat on the other.   This classification, which, of course, is
valid for the whole inter-war period, permits only one true
interpretation of the Hitlerite phenomenon.

The oligarchy, including families, did not consist of more than
half a million persons.   There entered into its composition the
whole of the aristocracy made up of the great landowners or
"junkers," the great industrialists, business men, and bankers,
the high officials of the civil, diplomatic, and military services,
and finally a few privileged persons with large private incomes.
Under William II that oligarchy had been identical with the
ruling caste, holding in its hands the substance of power, a large
part of the public fortune, and the effective direction of the
administration, the military forces, and foreign policy.   This
aristocracy of the nobles and the moneyed class had associated
its destinies in the past with those of the imperial court.   Strongly
organized in syndicates, cartels, or trusts, and fiercely ambitious,
it had found itself saddled after the armistice with the direct
responsibility before the Reich and the German people for the
war and the defeat.   Was it not Prussia that in 1918, under
Ludendorff's baton, had carried out the supreme offensive against
the West, on the morrow of the Russian Revolution?

The oligarchy thus defined found facing it after the war three
elements or masses, which should be carefully distinguished from
each other.

The first of these comprised on one hand the workless ex-
soldiers of the great defeated army, and on the other the youths,
not old enough to be mobilized or even in barracks, and with
little hope of making their way in life.   It was from this troubled
quarter that there was one day to rise, fully armed, the Hitlerite
party.   We can see the opportunity that presented itself here of
gaining the leadership of the despairing unorganized masses, by
means of a soldiery of a new type, militarized and politically
fanaticized.   In due course various formations came into the
news, from the volunteer corps of the "Baltikum" to the
"Stahlhelm" and the "Reichsbanner," not forgetting the Reichswehr proper and the police.   A sort of diffused militarism thus

formed round the reduced army, but without any direct link with it.

Then came the middle classes proper. They were divided into two distinct categories, the *owning class* and the *salaried*. The former included the peasant proprietors, the small and medium factory owners, and the mass of commercial and handicraft workers. Among them were numbers of "proletaroids," small owners who lived no better than the workers. The salaried persons, belonging to the liberal professions, the official class, and that of employees, were entirely dependent on their salary. That fact exposed them to rapid proletarization, in a country menaced with a succession of tragic crises. These middle classes, representing about thirty million people, seventeen to eighteen millions of them in employment, were not organized. Their claims and their aspirations were of infinite variety. They were split up between various parties such as the Centre, the Social Democrats, the Democrats, and even the German Nationalists. They, too, created a certain number of small formations, without influence, such as the Economic Union.

Finally there was the proletariat, again of thirty millions, eighteen millions being workers, a body ravaged by unemployment. This proletariat, which comprised many elements of very varied character, but was very largely made up of industrial workers, was much better organized than the middle classes. The Catholic proletarians had the support of the Centre Party and the Christian trade unions. The Socialist proletarians ranged themselves under the banner of the Social Democracy and the Free trade unions. The Communist proletarians had their party, divided into two parliamentary groups.

The middle classes thus represented a body very much *split up* socially, politically, economically, and professionally. They were placed, or rather squeezed, between the organizations of the landowners and capitalists and the proletarian organizations. In a country so industrialized as Germany, the social struggle was thus carried on between the organized oligarchy and the organized proletariat, that is to say, above the heads of the middle classes.

It is generally supposed that Hitlerite National Socialism had started among the middle classes *proletarianized* by the inflation of 1923 and by the great crisis of 1929–32 that had followed four years of economic pseudo-recovery, and then extended progressively on one side among the oligarchy of the Right, which might have need of it for breaking Marxism and the organized resistance of the proletariat, and on the other side among the proletariat itself, cruelly hit by unemployment and partly reduced to the condition of a "fifth estate," and driven by despair towards a nationalism, making big promises, that called itself "German Socialist." There is a good deal of truth in this generalization, but it does not correspond exactly to reality.

It must be admitted, on the contrary, even though the genesis of Hitlerism is still incompletely revealed, that the initiative came from the directing caste. That caste seems to have come very early to the idea of promoting a *militarized party*, a sort of Prætorian Guard in the service of the reaction, and in addition to have organized, when it saw defeat approaching and measured its own responsibility, a simultaneous propaganda of anti-Judaism and anti-Communism.

It did not wait, in fact, for the armistice in order to regroup its constituent elements and its forces, whether of conservatism, nationalism, or, especially, pan-Germanism. It acted under the inspiration of Ludendorff, who was himself thoroughly imbued with the idea that the armistice could only be a simple interruption of hostilities, and that after a military defeat regarded as temporary the war should be continued by other means or under other forms. The famous Herrenklub (roughly "Lords' Club") of Berlin grouped round itself a pseudo-*élite* whose members shared between them the various tasks to be accomplished, acting, moreover, in accordance with the rules of the strictest of discipline.

Its first care was for the organization of *Freikorps* or bodies of armed volunteers, led by ex-officers who had remained faithful to the monarchical ideal and institutions. These volunteer corps, whose history is as yet little known and presents the most complex aspects, were recruited with ease among discharged soldiers unable to find work. Defeat and unemployment automatically built them up. All that was needed was accommodation and money. These improvised troops were thus installed in the regions of East Prussia and the Baltic, where they were maintained by the great landowners, for whom they thus formed a Prætorian Guard. Their equipment was seen to by the Reichswehr itself. Similar volunteer corps were formed in other parts of Germany, notably in South Germany, in Bavaria, and even in the occupied Rhineland. We thus see rising behind the official Reichswehr and police, at a very early date, thanks to the efforts of the ruling caste, formations of every sort, from which were one day to proceed the militarized party of National

Socialism and the new army. It may be inferred *that the militariza-tion of Germany began from the defeat of 1918.*

But why was there also begun so early, and also directed from above, the anti-Jewish and anti-Communist campaign?

Let us place ourselves within the minds of that ruling oligarchy, at a time when defeat had brought the downfall of the monarchy and of the territorial dynasties. That oligarchy was responsible for the ills that poured from all sides over the German people, and for the humiliations it suffered. But it did not abandon the struggle. With Ludendorff, and so many other generals or politicians, it was fully determined to continue to pursue the pan-German programme. It thus needed, first of all, scapegoats upon whom to divert the anger of the masses. This caste was intelligent enough to know that the appeal both to the anti-capitalism and to the anti-Socialism of the multitude, especially of the middle classes, never fails.

It would be a great mistake to suppose that Hitler and his followers were the first to organize in Germany the ferocious anti-Jewish propaganda that is so familiar. That propaganda dated from long before the war. Germany had always had elements of anti-Semitism, if only because of the easy successes of the Israelites within her gates and the high places they obtained in the principal professions. The racialism of Houston Stewart Chamberlain had already assembled the most persuasive elements of anti-Jewish argumentation. After the war and the defeat the ruling caste needed but to take them up again. Thus we see opinion being prepared from 1917 on, from the moment when disaster was seen to be inevitable. An anti-Semitic review, *Auf Vorposten* ("On Outpost Duty"), was started; then the notorious *Protocols of the Elders of Zion* was republished, and finally a volume on the origins of the war was published by the Wilhelm-strasse, the Foreign Office, itself.

The review was intended for the German people. It set out to rejuvenate the ideas of pre-war pan-Germanism on racialism and anti-Judaism. It laid down that in order to make any German regeneration possible it was necessary to destroy the financial International on one hand and the Marxist and Socialist Inter-national on the other—both Jewish in origin and inspiration. This double annihilation, it said, would carry the German nation into the front rank of the European nations, because, as the central European country, "*das Land der Mitte*," she was equally distant from Western plutocracy and from the Communism that

was then rising in Russia under Lenin.   With these two irreconcilable enemies laid low, Germany would enjoy incontestable
hegemony over the old Continent.

In this way the intrinsic greatness and superiority of the German
Race were affirmed.   It was insisted that that race dated back
before the Græco-Roman and Christian cultures.   What could
be more natural and more timely than these theses?   The subject
with which they dealt was that which was to be developed
between 1917 and 1933 by all the nationalist thought of Germany,
on the most diverse planes and with infinite variations.[1]   From
that moment, however, the German ruling caste directed its
relentless propaganda to racialism, anti-Semitism, and anti-
Communism of the crudest sort.   It descended to the lowest
demagogy, and did not recoil from any untruth.   Before Hitler,
it made of the Jew the antithesis of the typical German, and made
him responsible for Germanic decay, for war and defeat and all
the miseries they had brought.   There was no excuse, no
remission for the Jew.   *Like the Man of Sorrows, he was to bear the
suffering and the burden of all the sins of the Germans.*

The *Protocols of the Elders of Zion* first appeared in Germany
in 1917.   Its true origins are known.   A French lawyer, Maurice
Joly, had published in 1864 a violent pamphlet against Napoleon
III, which had brought him several months of imprisonment.
The pamphlet was entitled *Entretiens de Montesquieu et de Machiavel
aux Enfers*, and showed Machiavelli instructing the author of the
Esprit des Lois on the means and methods to which demagogic
dictatorship could have recourse in order to win favour with the
masses, capture public opinion, and come into power.   Montesquieu is represented as the innocent who is "taught a thing or
two."   At a time when Russian Tsarism was trying to further
its own interests by turning popular wrath against the Jews of
Russia, either by inventing "ritual murder" or Jewish ambitions
for the conquest of the world, or by organizing terrible pogroms,
a Russian named Sergius Nilus copied and reproduced a large
part of this pamphlet, which later was developed into *The Protocols
of the Elders of Zion.*

The *Protocols* affirmed that at the Zionist Congress of the
Universal Israelite Alliance at Basle in 1897 the Jews had decided
to provoke war in order to establish their domination over the
world.   The Elders of Zion, said this work, had formed a secret

---

[1] See *Doctrinaires de la Révolution allemande* (Paris, Sorlot, 1938; second edition,
1939), by E. Vermeil.

international association that pursued an ambitious dream of hegemony, and the book gave a series of pretended minutes of meetings in the course of which all the details of the plot were settled. In order to attain their end, the Elders of Zion dreamed of destroying the Christian States, the stages of their progress being marked by democracy, Socialism, Communism, and anarchy. The first thing, they said, was to undermine the confidence of peoples in their governments. It would be easy to circumvent the leaders, and the people were no more than a herd. War, by exhausting peoples, would assure the reign of money. The Jews would then, after having seized possession of the products of prime necessity and the means of transport, be the masters of the world.

We thus see the double source, French and Russian, of this anti-Judaism, which shrank from no lie. The ostensible author, Gottfried von Beck, had taken cover under a pseudonym, and was no other than the notorious anti-Semite Baron von Haussen, who had made every effort to separate Ballin from William II. Haussen, who was a member of the Herrenklub and was closely associated with Ludendorff, died in 1927. He had not hesitated to publish this fantastic story in order to show to the most credulous public in the world that the Jews were responsible for the war, and consequently for the evils it had brought with it. The author's idea had been that the work should lead in Germany itself to a whole course of practical activity, embracing the organization of pogroms, the confiscation of Jewish fortunes, and the launching outside Germany of a campaign for international anti-Judaism. Baron von Haussen actually envisaged a Jewish Ghetto for all Europe in a region of southern Russia, the confiscation of Jewish fortunes serving to liquidate the cost of the world war. This, he added, would give Germany the leadership of political affairs in Europe. She would then create *a sort of national and at the same time universal religion*, of truly *Germanic* essence, absorbing the two Christian confessions and excluding Judaism. A Germanic Emperor, supreme Head of this religion, would reign over a wiser Europe. This would be the *Pax Teutonica*. These were exactly the theses that Nazism took up later.

While the review *Auf Vorposten* organized propaganda within Germany, the *Protocols* were obviously for propaganda abroad. In Germany they gave rise to a vigorous polemic. A professor of Hebrew and Chaldean at Berlin, named Strack, proved them a forgery, assembling a mass of irrefutable arguments. But that did not induce the anti-Semites to disarm. They saw in the *Protocols* a means of action too precious to be so lightly abandoned. It is absolutely true that the argument of the *Protocols* was presented point by point in the speeches and writings of Hitler. For him, the Allies were only in appearance the victors in the war. The true victory was gained by international Jewry, which sought to complete the ruin of Germany by imposing democracy and parliamentarism upon her.

As to the Wilhelmstrasse volume on the origins of the war, it was intended primarily for the German diplomatic service. It sought to show that the Jewish International and British Free-masonry were alone responsible for the war.

The three publications were thus closely connected. Together they expressed the essential aspirations of anti-Judaic and pan-German racialism. They were completed by Ludendorff's review *Judentum und Freimaurerei*, edited by Major Henning, a former staff officer.

Alongside anti-Judaism came anti-Bolshevism. It is as well to give its true origin and its exact significance.

The Germans foresaw their defeat as early as 1916, and set out to weaken the Allies in advance of it. They had been working upon the Russian political and military world in the effort to produce the disintegration of the ruling caste and the army. Sovietism, as is well known, was partly their work. They set before themselves, in fact, these three aims: to destroy an enemy who had shown himself very formidable at times, and to put an end to the war on two fronts; to exhibit Germany in the sight of the Allies as the surest bulwark against Communism (the threat of which would hang over all bourgeoisies and plutocracies alike after the war), in order to obtain better conditions of peace and to prepare the future; and to strike a strong blow against international finance, which had invested so much money in the exploitation of Russia's mineral resources.

Not that there could be any question of perpetuating in Russia a régime of that sort. Judaism, Communism, and even the Weimar Republic were to be used as scapegoats, in order to destroy them for ever. But it was possible, while working for their destruction, to make use of them for definite momentary purposes. Was not the Soviet régime a nightmare that haunted the brain of the possessing classes of the whole world? Why not show the world, said Ludendorff, what internationalism is capable of being in practice, what a danger to Western civilization was represented by this Bolshevism, which could only be explained by Russia being at least a hundred years behind the times? The international crisis was moving, in fact, in the direction of Communism. The wave of sovietism was a menace to conquered Germany. In fighting sovietism, though she had aided its start and its triumph in Russia, Germany was sure to gain credit in the eyes of the world, and to assure herself of the sympathy of the middle classes even among her former enemies. She would herself sow the soil which sovietism had tilled for her.

It was a Machiavellian calculation, but a clever one, and it explains the plan of military intervention which Ludendorff prepared for Russia. The beaten German General was able to make use of the foreign holders of Russian securities, whose losses amounted in all to several thousand millions of gold roubles. Ludendorff seems to have anticipated that, once the Weimar Republic was thrown down, Germany and the Allies, this time united, would make a smashing attack on Russia. Ludendorff would gladly have led the operation against that régime, new as it was and scarcely installed. Russia's creditors would then have recovered their lost securities, and at the same time the Bolshevik monster would have been destroyed. Germany would have received as reward certain territories that would have assured to her the raw materials she needed. What Ludendorff wanted above all was French assistance. In his idea the two armies together would first restore order in Russia and then found a series of States under the Continental influence of the united France and Germany. Russia would thus be restored to the European economy, and, no doubt, rapid eastward expansion would follow, Germany ultimately occupying the so-called "Eurasian" space, which remained throughout the Hitler régime the object of her dreams. But it was necessary to act quickly, for the very reason that the forced demobilization and the unemployment were increasing the opportunities of sovietism in Germany itself.

Thus this double action, anti-Jewish and anti-Communist, was connected with support from abroad. The *Protocols of the Elders of Zion* was intended for foreign consumption. There were good, solid reasons for interesting Western plutocracy and capitalism in Russia. In the person of Ludendorff and through the agency of her ruling caste, which had been responsible for war and defeat, Germany invited the Western Powers who had just beaten her to join her in action against Russia.

2. *The Kapp putsch and Hitler's beginnings*

With these two campaigns in progress, all that remained to do was to proceed to a direct offensive against the Weimar Republic, and this offensive culminated in the Kapp-Lüttwitz putsch of March 14, 1920. The Republican parliamentary régime had been in existence in Germany, at all events nominally, since the end of 1918. In the first half of 1919 the National Assembly had laid the foundations of a new Constitution, which was promulgated on August 11, and the two great parties of the Weimar democracy, the Centre and the Social Democracy, had signed the Treaty of Versailles. The young Republic, built up on the old Bismarckian compromises, partly revised and adapted to the new circumstances, took upon itself at its start the whole odium of the signature and acceptance of the treaty. It met at once with the many difficulties of a constitutional and parliamentary machinery which, in view of its clumsiness and complexity, could not function normally and serve as a reliable framework for post-war Germany. This Republic was, moreover, doomed from the outset because, in its fierce struggle against revolutionary Socialism, it had appealed to the most formidable and the most irreconcilable forces of the Reaction and of the demobilized army.

It was natural that the former ruling caste, which in pure opportunism had accepted the democratic régime for the moment, regarding it as arising out of the punishment that had threatened it, should work against it through the volunteer armed bodies it had organized. It also made use of the anti-Jewish and anti-Communist campaign that was aimed against the whole of the German Left, from the Democrats to the neo-Communists.

Not, indeed, that the Weimar Republic was incapable of self-defence. On the contrary, it successfully parried the first blow aimed against it. But its resistance was not to be very prolonged.

For one thing, the Social Democracy, which had had such a fine array of seats in 1919, had lost considerably to the Independent Socialists, owing to the disappointments the working masses had suffered. Moreover, the middle class soon betrayed the Republic in process of organization. It could only regard with indifference a Republican Government incapable of effective action, and it was suffering from its desperate economic situation and from the growing inflation. It saw no signs of any policy of true national regeneration. Hence the growing success of Right-wing opposition; and hence, above all, the hatching of a plot aimed at nothing less than the destruction of the Republic. Led by Kapp, on March 13, 1920, the Ehrhardt Brigade, one of the volunteer corps of the Baltic region, entered Berlin. At the same moment, von Kahr secured in Bavaria the triumph of the middle-class reactionaries. But the union of the Left quickly put an end to Kapp's attempted *coup d'état*. At that moment it would have been possible to use the exceptional circumstances to establish a solid democracy in Germany. Once more the opportunity was missed. And on June 6, 1920, there took place the fatal elections that brought almost complete ruin to the Democratic Party, a weakening of the Social Democracy, and the victory of the reactionary parties, the German Nationals and the Populists. The fate of the Republic was sealed, less than a year after the promulgation of its Constitution.

The most important thing in these unhappy events was the lesson the ruling caste drew from them. It realized very well that the movement had lacked discipline, that it was essential to have support from abroad, and above all, *that nothing could be done without the German masses*, who were still tired after war and defeat and still refractory to any anti-Jewish or anti-Marxist propaganda. It seems that at this time Ludendorff and his accomplices had accurately foreseen and discounted *the proletariza-tion of the middle classes and its consequences*. This group preserved its inextinguishable confidence. It repeated, with entire con-viction, that one day the possessing classes of the whole world would be grateful to a Germany that had destroyed sovietism and assured the triumph of the white race over the coloured races. A familiar theme, which Oswald Spengler and Möller van den Bruck were to treat brilliantly in works that became famous and well served National Socialism.

But what was Hitler doing about 1920? Would it not be worth while to arrange a meeting between the oligarchical Right wing and the tribune of the people? The Hitler movement had just assumed the name of National Socialism. The movement had proceeded from the fanatical annexationism of 1917, and as a political instrument it had been forged complete by the Bavarian Reichswehr, and in particular by Ludendorff himself. It was with this aid that Hitler and Röhm had secured the first successes of the movement. The famous twenty-five point programme dates actually from 1920; it was a programme well devised to capture the middle classes, and contained the elements of all the later theses of Nazism.   The first National Socialists did not fall into the errors of the Marxism they were fighting.   They did not reduce their policy to scientific formulas.   Their grouping had already the aspect of a lodge or an Order.

The party's first "cell," about a couple of dozen men of the lower middle class in Munich, was headed by a certain Drexler, a locksmith by trade, a man full of candour and faith, who had come, like Hitler himself, into conflict with the Social Democratic trade unions.   Drexler and Hitler had solid reasons for hating Marxism.   They imagined a new German Socialism that should save Europe and the world by liberating them from international high finance and Communist Marxism.   Their programme claimed to be strictly "national."   The patriotic party of Munich, the Vaterlandspartei, did not satisfy them because it was composed entirely of professors, artists, and lawyers, and had no connexion with the common people.   This little group of workers and Socialists was the first germ of a sort of Socialist and popular pan-Germanism.   It dated from March 1918.   Its members bore witness to the utmost confidence in the army and the General Staff.   They proposed to work together for the creation of the "productive nation," for the purest nationalism and the most intransigent defence of the interests of the working class.   There was talk among them of uniting the middle class and the proletariat in common action for the future Germany.   It was a curious but perfectly natural fact that Drexler borrowed many of his slogans from Walter Rathenau.

In January 1919 Drexler founded the "German Labour Party" (Deutsche Arbeiterpartei).   After the collapse of Bavarian Communism the control at Munich, behind the Weimar façade, was held by the Reichswehr, whose officers were determined to begin all over again.   *The idea that the war was not ended and that the struggle was still going on for the greatness of Germany—such was the bond between the military and Drexler's party, which Hitler entered with him.*

This military element included, however, not only the Reichs-wehr but the Bavarian volunteer corps, the Einwohnerwehr, and especially the reactionary "Orgesch" or Escherich Organization; the latter extended at the time throughout Germany.   It was from these volunteer corps that there came Hitler's friend Röhm, *miles perpetuus*, the typical mercenary, the veritable incarnation of eternal war, one of the most authentic representatives of that "soldier" spirit that characterized Germany more and more after the war. Röhm had brought into the Drexler group a number of military and police officers and soldiers, together with Dietrich Eckart and Gottfried Feder. In this little group were to be found the shouters for the "Nordic" race, for German *Blut und Boden* (blood and soil), for "German Socialism," which was to efface all distinctions between middle class and proletariat; anti-Judaism, anti-capitalism, anti-Marxism—all the elements of the future Nazism.

It was into this company that Hitler made his entry. At the time he was an entirely typical Austrian pan-German. He was working for the union of Austria, Bohemia, and Bavaria. He admired Schönerer, the leader of the movement, but would have liked him to have *contact with the masses*, like Lueger, the leader of the Christian Social Party and mayor of Vienna. The spectacle that Vienna offered to Hitler led him into anti-Judaism and racialism. On the morrow of the war, in which he had served as a private, at barely thirty years of age he was already one of the most feverishly active of propagandists.

Furthered by the Völkischer Schutz- und Trutzbund, anti-Semitism was then the rage at Munich. The Jews were held responsible for the Communist Republic. The word "Marxism" was flung about as a synonym for international Socialism. The term served alike for the Social Democrats, the Independents, and the Communists. To these three aspects of Socialism was opposed *National Socialism*. The soul of the party, which at this moment took its definitive name of "National-Sozialistische Deutsche Arbeiterpartei" (N.S.D.A.P.), was hatred of the Jews and of the Socialist Internationals. Hence the curious distinction, owed by Hitler to Gottfried Feder, between Jewish capitalism, which was claimed to be destructive and acquisitive (*raffend*), and German industrial capitalism, considered as creative and fruitful (*schaffend*). For in Socialism *à l'allemande*, true national solidarism, employers and proletariat must each occupy their natural place.

On the very day of the Kapp-Lüttwitz putsch, the Reichswehr and the volunteer corps replaced the Hoffmann Government in Munich by a Right-wing coalition under von Kahr. From then on the new Prime Minister of Bavaria gave National Socialism his support. The National Socialists, with their mass following, had little trouble in overcoming the aristocratic nationalism of the "Völkische," the racialists. But the party was still purely Bavarian. At the Salzburg congress it admitted Austrian elements. It was at Salzburg that Rudolf Jung, leader of the Austrian Nazis, revealed to Hitler that the Jews sought always to Judaize nations, that the Lutheran Reformation was only half German because it did not dissociate Christianity from the Old Testament, and finally that Western high finance and Russian Bolshevism were complementary terms and phenomena, run by the Jews for the domination of the world.

Here we see the direct connexion between pre-war pan-Germanism and Nazism. Use was made of Paul de Lagarde, Houston Stewart Chamberlain, Spengler, and even certain Russian *émigrés*. It was possible at one and the same time to exalt the imperial régime of the Prussian army, as Hitler did later in *Mein Kampf*, and to preach a national Socialism, while combating democracy, the "system" established in Germany by the Jews. This barren ideology was not of the sort to displease the ruling caste.

In a case like this, hostility exists even before the enemy makes his appearance.[1] The pseudo-Revolution of 1918 had taken a terribly imprudent step. It had called for the collaboration of the very people against whom it appeared to have risen. No party in Germany had had the simple courage to rule in its own name. Not only that, but the new Government had signed the Treaty of Versailles in place of the régime that had fallen—a second grave offence to be answered for. The middle class was already beginning to dissociate itself from the Government and to oppose it. It was turning its eyes toward National Socialism, especially in Bavaria, where, since the Soviet Republic of Kurt Eisner, the middle classes had moved to the Right.

It was just this Bavarian mass that Hitler moulded, in these years in which he was passing through his apprenticeship as a tribune of the people. He excelled all his comrades in activity. The aristocratic nationalism of the "Völkische" began to weaken in the latter half of 1920. Hitler's aim was to conquer the masses. He was a masterly agitator. His placards were drawn up in the direct and primitive style that makes people "sit up." Theatrically organized meetings rapidly followed each other. He formed an "Ordnertruppe," the germ of the future Storm Troopers, hefty "militants" who shouted down any opposition, interrupted the meetings of the Weimar parties, and had no hesitation in using brute force against the enemy. These

---

[1] The pan-Germans had attacked the very idea of the Weimar Republic before ever that Republic was born.

new methods of political struggle, introduced by Hitler and his henchmen, were a great success. In December 1920 the first Nazi newspaper, the *Völkischer Beobachter*, was bought. Hitler's sudden rise was already approaching the miraculous. He was the "Wundermann" for whom everybody had been waiting. And Röhm continually brought officers and soldiers into this Nazi Party, which already had not less than 3000 members.

It is reasonable to suppose that it was about this time, between 1920 and 1921, that a working agreement was effected between the Berlin movement and that of Bavaria, between the pan-Germanism of the North and that of the South. In the North, propaganda had had success among many middle-class people who had lost everything and sighed for the monarchy and for better times. But the Prussian proletariat remained for a time entirely impervious to this capitalist or aristocratic nationalism. It was just in Bavaria, among the first Nazis, that the Prussian ruling caste found what it was seeking—contact with the masses of the lower middle class and proletariat.

What the ruling caste feared above all was the danger of a social revolution spreading and growing in Germany. Nothing, it seemed, could any longer stop the vertiginous fall of the mark. The number of unemployed, moreover, was ceaselessly growing, owing to the demobilization and the economic depression. The ruling class realized that as the crisis grew it would have two main results, the proletarization of the middle class and the partial bolshevization of the proletariat. It was necessary to parry this danger while profiting by the advantages it offered. The desperate masses could be captured by means of anti-Semitism, anti-Bolshevism, and even a measure of anti-capitalism. It was clearly in the course of 1920–21 that the Herrenklub discovered Hitler and his party, Hitler and Gottfried Feder. They were supplied with the publications of the Berlin organization. Above all, they were promised subsidies. And Hitler proved the most amenable of converts.

The historian may even ask himself whether Hitler was not "formed" by the leaders in Berlin, with a view to the ends they were pursuing. It was arranged for him to have lessons in public speaking. It was apparently at that moment that Hitler visited Siegfried Wagner at Bayreuth, where he also came into contact with Houston Stewart Chamberlain, long notorious as a racialist and pan-German. It is known that letters were exchanged between Hitler and that strange Germanized Englishman.

Thus the Herrenklub took into its hands the destinies of Hitler and Hitlerism. It maintained him, gave him instructions, and brought its supporters to his side. It induced him to make the venture of an anti-Semitic campaign on the receptive soil of Bavaria, and then an anti-Bolshevist campaign in that country, which had had experience of a Soviet Republic. Hitler, as a proletarianized man of the lower middle class, covered by his quasi-symbolical "little man's" personality the intrigues of the ruling caste. It was for that caste that he was to gain the confidence of the masses. For the employers were well aware that inflation and unemployment were bound to increase, and they therefore had every interest in seeing to it that before the crisis attained its culmination the responsibility for it should be placed on the shoulders of the *Jews*, of *Marxism*, and of the *Weimar Republic*.

The industrialists now decided to take on no workers who were not National Socialists. Once the party had reached a certain size, the cards would be savagely thrown on the table. The party would destroy parliamentary democracy, would subject the German States to relentless centralization, and would let loose anti-Judaism everywhere, confiscating Jewish fortunes. As for anti-Communism, it was just what foreign nations would approve. Why not proceed then to reorganize the German economic system and to rearm on an immense scale? The Reich would then have its factories working at full pressure and would possess the most modern of armies.

After well and truly flooding them with its anti-Jewish and anti-Communist propaganda, Germany would bring Austria and Czechoslovakia, Hungary and Poland, the Balkans, Roumania, and Turkey within her sphere of economic action. She would then actively spread racialism in the colonies, especially by blaming the Jews for the evils that afflicted them. She would tell the natives that the peoples that were enslaving them were but the servants of international capitalism. The Reich would tell them that Germany has no colonies and does not want any. It would thus find in the neighbour nations many sympathizers who had a horror of Jews and of Russia and would be delighted to see at the head of Europe, furnished with a very legitimate hegemony, *creative pan-Germanism*.

Such were the secret thoughts of those who prepared the great tragedy. But did the ruling caste, foreseeing inflation, unemployment, and the consequences, intend to *make use of the crisis?* It is probable. By deliberate short deliveries the heavy industries provoked, to begin with, the occupation of the Ruhr. They pushed the crisis to the point at which the majority of the nation would joyfully welcome the rulers' intervention. In 1921 they began to speculate on the probability that Hitler, covering this dangerous game with his popularity, would become *a sort of national idol,* while strictly conforming to the mass of instructions sent him.

In this way, thought these circles, *the territorial and political union of Germany would be secured, bringing success where Bismarck had failed.* By playing on the horror of the mass of the middle class for Western capitalism (Ruhr occupation) and for Communism (Bavarian and Saxon attempts), Prussians and Bavarians, Württembergers and Badeners, Saxons and Hessians, would be made into *Germans* without distinction. This national and racial awakening would sweep away the Internationals of every sort— social, economic and financial, religious or philosophical. This time, Germany would teach Europe her national religion. She would constitute a confederated European Empire, under the orders of a Germanic "Führer." And she would reduce the colonial populations to economic enslavement.

Thanks to Hitler, the true monarchical and oligarchical character of this precious system and of these insane ambitions would be concealed from the crowd. The leaders would proceed to their goal with patience and perseverance, firmness and discipline. The future religion, which would unite Greek Catholicism, Roman Catholicism, and Lutheran Protestantism, would be the supreme consecration of the reconstructed edifice. A new Church, a new mediævalism would rise in Europe, under the ægis of Germany. In Asia support would be given to Japan, so as to compromise British interests in India. This would be the work of a hundred years. Such was the precise purpose of the collaboration secretly established between the pan-Germanism of the former leaders, of the *Ludendorff* type, and the neo-pan-Germanism of the middle classes, of the *Hitler* type. The Hitlerite propaganda was obviously inspired by this programme. It seemed new to the ignorant and politically untutored masses, but their credulity, their distress, and their despair spread it throughout the nation with frightful rapidity.

That is why the Press and publication services of the National Socialists took over the old anti-Judaic publications of the Herrenklub. The essence of these publications passed into

Mein Kampf, into Rosenberg's *The Myth of the Twentieth Century,* and even into Ferdinand Fried's *Ende des Kapitalismus.*

3. *The Munich putsch* (1921–23)

Thus, between 1921 and 1923 Hitler was simply the manager for the ruling caste, which had definitely decided to lead the masses through his intermediary. Before the war William II had listened to the advice of the pan-Germans. After the war their orders were carried out by Hitler. On February 3, 1921, in the Zirkus Krone at Munich, he ventured on his first great demonstration. From that moment his ideas on home and foreign policy were outlined with some clearness. For the rest, he was already the comrade and friend of Ludendorff.

On the plane of home policy, the struggle began against "blue-white" Bavarian particularism. The London ultimatum was about to be issued. It was a good opportunity for action against the rival nationalists, the Völkische and the Vaterlands-partei. On February 3 Hitler addressed an audience of four thousand; soon the figure had grown to eight thousand. Every sort of dubious element crowded round him. Rosenberg, Eckart, and Rudolf Hess, his principal collaborators, were present. No other speaker was his equal in fire and hysterical fury. He was believed in. Already he was called "Führer." He himself began to believe in his mission. He was the Cæsar of propaganda, the orator who had the ear of the crowd, menacing the men of Weimar with the gallows or the block, and, on the other hand, ridiculing the Right-wing nationalists.

Hitler seems to have gone to Berlin at the beginning of the summer of 1921, to get into touch with North Prussian circles. He spoke at the Herrenklub. He negotiated with the heads of the Conservative party of the former Prussian Herrenhaus (Upper Chamber), Graf von Behr and Graf von Wartenburg. Then he returned quickly to Bavaria to put an end to trouble that had broken out within his own party. On July 14 he was master of the situation. In the Nazi movement the "toffs" had won the day against the "little men." There was no longer any question of a sort of semi-Socialism. The idea was scouted. At the back of the party in process of formation stood the money powers. Those who were paying the piper had called the tune.

The elements of a new foreign policy also became clear.

Toward the West, to begin with. The movement revealed

itself as both *anti-Jewish* and *anti-British*. But it was also *anti-French*, for France, it was said, had surrendered to the Jews. Anti-Semites of all countries, unite! The appeal of Marx and Engels was twisted round. Hitler, in his speeches, mouthed incessantly against Albion, against her record in Ireland, against her tyranny in India. Disarm, he shouted, if that will make an end of the payment of Reparations! Such was his reply to the 132 milliards demanded in the London ultimatum in May 1921. After all, why not consider a *rapprochement* with France against Britain?

Ludendorff and General Hofmann supported this thesis against Russia also. All Russia, declared Rosenberg, was in revolt against the Jewish terror. Hitler went one better, saying that Bolshevism had begun to totter and that the Russian workers were turning against "those bloodthirsty dogs of Jews." For expounding these pretty politics in the newspapers there was Rosenberg; for the silly crowd Hitler would do. This was the moment when Arnold Rechberg, the potassium magnate, proposed to the Entente an armed intervention against Russia, published fiery articles against the Soviets in the *Völkischer Beobachter*, and collaborated with Ludendorff. Russia had, of course, just lost the war against Poland. In spite of that it was declared that she intended to swallow her neighbour. Rosenberg preached a crusade against her. This was playing the game of the White Russians. Munich became the Coblenz of the Russian *émigrés*.

In these quarters there was avid study of the *Protocols of the Elders of Zion*. Jews and Bolsheviks were denounced in the same breath. After the eternal Wandering Jew went the eternal anti-Semite! At the end of May 1921 the Russian monarchists held their congress in Upper Bavaria, at Bad Reichenhall. As for Hitler and Rosenberg, in their diatribes they cheerfully declared that every Jew is a born Bolshevist.

From 1921 on Hitler was master of the party. Its political programme had been completed and laid down. The main lines of the programme were of extraordinary simplicity. But how could it be carried out behind the federal and democratic façade of Weimar? The man who was to risk the attempt for the benefit of the pan-German rulers who maintained him was a political child of the First World War. He incarnated the ideal of the ex-soldier, a great admirer of Frederick II and of Bismarck, capable of criticizing the Wilhelmian régime while exalting all that that régime might have had in the way of solid qualities. Did he dream from the first of being the Leader, the "Führer," of Germany? It is not certain. Probably Mussolini's example was held up before him. On the other hand, Hitler was not an innocent. He knew a good deal, especially of the technical order. He grasped the situation that had been created for him, and set out to profit by it.

He was certainly not a man of character. He could scarcely manage any half-measure between hesitation and screaming. There was nothing of the higher qualities of the soldier in his nature. He was a civilian, and a shifty one, well aware of the use that could be made of an army as a simple instrument of policy. Hitler was also without any steady purpose or fixed directive. Beware of regarding him as a creature of instincts, a sort of prophet guided by inner voices. It would be more to the point to compare him to a sleep-walker. For he had assurance; he also had a certain capacity for logic. He drew the right conclusion and extracted the desired result from each situation, each moment. *Mein Kampf* has the appearance of a confused and chaotic book; that Hitlerite Bible is none the less full of clear and tolerably well-expressed ideas.

He succeeded, in fact, in giving in *Mein Kampf* and in his speeches a popular version of the thesis of the *Protocols of the Elders of Zion*. He knew how to throw on the Jews the whole responsibility for the war and for the troubles from which Germany was suffering, to rail against Bolshevism, and to ridicule the Weimar parties and parliamentary machinery, and with all these devices he made marvellous play. His was a simple brain, but it was perfectly well aware of the tactics to be employed in the service of the Machiavellism of the great and the doltish credulity of the German masses. In spite of his incontestable qualities, his appearance was certainly the most commonplace imaginable, the most typical of a certain class. But when he spoke he really hit out. He demolished his adversary in a few sentences of invective. Unquestionably Germany's rulers had found in him the man they wanted.

With him they also found their party, the single party on the Italian model. Out of this party Hitler made a true civilian army, drawn from every quarter, from the volunteer corps and from the unemployed of the middle classes and proletariat. The S.A. (Storm Troopers) and the S.S. (Hitler's bodyguard) made their appearance. The S.A. was organized by August 3, 1921.

Its call to arms read: "This organization will represent the idea of the defence of a free people. . . . What it will have to do first of all is to form in the souls of our young adepts an indomitable will for action. It will have to drive into their heads by hammer-blows in lines of fire that it is not history that makes men but men that make history." The new formation was to be a "training school for the struggle soon to be sustained for internal liberty." Thanks to it, the Nazi movement would be in a position "to proceed itself to the offensive." In fact, the Hitlerite Storm Troops (S.A.) were the Ehrhardt Brigade in fresh hands.

At that time there was a veritable breeding-ground of regular and irregular militarism in Bavaria. But the military leaders had neither programme nor agreed lines of action. Their differences enabled the Munich Government to rule in relative tranquillity. It was Röhm who regrouped all these scattered forces round Hitler. The Einwohnerwehr was dissolved and the other volunteer corps, in particular the famous "Organisation Consul," the new name adopted by the Ehrhardt Brigade after its defeat in Berlin, were merged in the S.A. In short, Röhm made of the party a military force. It is from this period that the conflict dated between Hitler's political tendencies and Röhm's paramilitary effort, a conflict that ended in the tragic "execution" of June 30, 1934.

At the same time the meaning of Hitlerite "Socialism" grew clear. What Hitler now envisaged was a sort of selection of leaders, men of decision, within a national economic system *that would respect private property*. There was talk of an "aristocracy of production," or of a "directing power." Under the cover of a new type of enlightened despotism the traditional inequality of classes and the old social hierarchy were to be maintained. Hitler claimed to be rebuilding Germany on three pillars: (1) the army and the corps of officers; (2) the administration and the bureaucracy; (3) the whole of the really pure "Aryan" Germans.

A fighting minority—that was the future. In Hitler's hands the party became an aristocracy. The *Élite* stood out against the Masses. The tribune was doing excellent work for the Herrenklub, with his aristocracy of biological origin and his conception of "militant natures" (*Kampfnaturen*). In the hands of this party the masses would no longer be anything but a docile instrument. The party would forge them into shape, and make them yield up all the organized energy of which they were capable. National Socialism was to become a *machine*, a power machine. Rosenberg provided it with its doctrine, but Eckart gave the party its style, its bearing, its true character. In Hitler's phrase, it was to be "the numerical minority that must become the majority of sacrifice and of will."

The party held its first congress at the end of January 1922. (It was still at Munich because it could not do without the Bavarian Reichswehr.) For the moment Hitler stood out against invitations from Berlin. He had to spend, however, three months in prison for interrupting a meeting held by his adversaries. There was talk of expelling him from Bavaria, and he even disappeared for a moment from the political scene. We find him next in Berlin, once more addressing the Herrenklub. He now came into touch with von Gräfe and with von Borsig, the biggest German employer. After the assassination of Rathenau, Hitler returned to Bavaria, where the laws for the protection of the Republic were being applied with some energy, but in such a way that though the Left wing was in power with a coalition between the Centre and the Social Democrats, the Right wing continued to do whatever it pleased. The Bavarians were fighting only for their particularism, and Hitler raised up before them the spectre of Prussia. In September 1922 came the utter failure of the putsch prepared by the Bavarian Reichswehr.

Things were moving. In Italy came the Fascist March on Rome. After November 1922 it began to be declared that Hitler would one day be the German Mussolini. The wind was blowing in the direction of Cæsarism. The thing that created the strongest impression in Germany was the coolness and imperturbability with which the Italian *coup d'état* was carried out. Here was the true Revolution, the "cool Revolution" the German lower middle class wanted, the Revolution without blows or bloodshed, though not without secret tortures. Thenceforth Hitler never ceased to imitate Mussolini.

Inflation was on Germany's threshold. It had begun in 1919 as a simple fall in the value of money. In 1922 it was transformed into a collapse of moral values. It was the sign of nihilism in practice. Terrible were the months between the murder of Rathenau and the occupation of the Ruhr! It was a period of agonized anticipation. Had the Nazi leaders any suspicion of the frightful policy on which the great industrialists were recklessly embarking? Did they fully realize the baseness of these accomplices and backers of theirs? They preferred to spread the idea that the Weimar Republic was the main culprit and that it was itself destroying all private fortunes. They deluded the crowd into the belief that that democratic State was in the hands of the Jews.

So all those of little sense ran wildly after Hitler. He was more than ever the idol of the day. The tribune went from meeting to meeting. He addressed himself to the middle class, the middle class that Rosenberg defined at the beginning of 1923 as "the heroine of National Socialism." This Nazi doctrinaire was able to coin that phrase with a solemn face. The middle classes were told that they were being ground between capitalism, with its *Zinsknechtschaft* or "bondage to interest," and Marxism. This pretty little argument gained more and more credence amid the strange mixture of anti-capitalism and anti-Communism that was peculiar to Germany. It was now declared that nationalism was eminently what Germany needed, and that all internationalism was Jewish in spirit.

Unless, indeed, Nazism itself was to be called the anti-Semitic International! Many Nazis began to accuse the Jews of having embroiled Russians and Germans, who ought to have made common cause, and also of having embroiled French and Germans, and British and Germans. Was Hitler sacrificing the legitimate patriotism of his audiences to international anti-Semitism and anti-Bolshevism? It may be. *Or rather, he was substituting for the nationalism of the past a sort of neo-nationalism with its poisoned sting directed against a part of the German people itself.* Deviations were, however, inevitable, and Nazi nationalism had no lack either of opportunities or of resources. When the Ruhr was occupied, Nazism turned against Western capitalism, leaving anti-Communism alone for the time. No one who has any knowledge of German thought would be surprised at these twists and turns. In any case, Hitler did not lose sight of the Social Democracy.

In January 1923, at the moment when the occupation of the Ruhr was beginning, the Bavarian Government forbade the party congress. Could Hitler allow his prestige to be ruined? To prevent that he turned once more to the Reichswehr. Röhm and General von Epp were ready to save him. They helped Hitler to triumph over the Weimar rulers. *The civilian republic recoiled in face of the army.* Thanks to the army, Hitler became the strong man against whom nothing could prevail. The number of adherents of the party grew. In April 1923 National Socialism was making giant strides. It had its first triumph.

The masses were never tired of listening to Hitler. From then on, French opinion should have kept a sharp watch on him.

Money flowed into the party exchequer. Hitler bought from Eckart the *Völkischer Beobachter*, and triumphed in Northern Bavaria, at Nuremberg, over his rival Julius Streicher, who had implanted Nazism there. On the other hand, he concluded a sort of convention with the "Völkische," the Right-wing nationalists led by such men as von Gräfe, Wulle, and Henning. At the same moment a grave danger began to menace him. Could he remain the master of his party and of its policy? He was a prisoner of the Reichswehr. He had against him Chancellor Cuno and Ludendorff. As for the irregular forces, they were stealing his Storm Troopers from him. Without meaning to, Röhm was compelling Hitler to transform his party into a band of mercenaries with whom the officers of the Reichswehr could do what they liked. *In other words, Hitler no longer had the S.A. in his hands, because Röhm was trying to turn them into an army, a Nazi Reichswehr.* So great was the danger that in order to parry it and maintain his position Hitler organized the S.S. as his own personal force.

How to get rid of the growing pressure of the military? In May 1923 Hitler made a first attempt but failed. This defeat was so serious that a good part of his followers left him. Nothing could be done in Germany without the Reichswehr. A little later Class, the leader of the Berlin pan-Germans and of the Alldeutscher Verband, tried to constitute with the Reichswehr, alongside Parliament, a national Government, a sort of Directory, at the head of which he would place himself in company with von Seeckt. He wanted Hitler to come in as representing Bavaria. Hitler thus found himself caught between the Bavarian blue-and-white and Ludendorff's black-white-red. On September 2, Ludendorff organized at Nuremberg a military festival, an immense demonstration of the volunteer corps or "Wehrverbände." It was "Der Deutsche Tag." In his speech General Ludendorff recalled that Germany's unity and strength had been the achievement of the Hohenzollerns. Why had the German people destroyed it? Ludendorff, who did not speak the language of the Nazis, enjoyed immense prestige. He was absolute master of the Right. Hitler found himself compelled to march at the General's side in the great parade. That symbolized dualism! The credulous public saw in it only the union between the

Führer and his people. But it was Ludendorff who had organized this demonstration. Was Hitler to find himself imprisoned in a golden cage?

Röhm had understood. He undertook the task of liberating the Führer by giving him the leadership of the Deutscher Kampfbund, which embraced all the paramilitary formations, including the S.A. He proposed to get rid of Bavarian competition and to give the power to Hitler. They would seize the police and the government by legal means with the aid of illegal pressure. This was the Nazi interpretation of legality. Röhm's stroke succeeded. Hitler was now installed as head of the Kampfbund. He had the support of all the illegal military formations.

Simultaneously, on September 26, von Kahr was appointed Commissary-General, and a state of siege was declared in Bavaria. The Bavarian Government rose against the Weimar Government of the Reich. Munich declared war on Berlin. What would happen to the Reich? North and South eyed each other. The Right wing at Berlin, ferociously hostile to the Republic, placed all its hopes in von Kahr. At Munich the Right depended on the generals and on the great industrialists of the North. Ludendorff and Hitler were in agreement on one point—to make an end of the Republican generals and with the Republic itself. Would the coup that had failed in Berlin in 1920 succeed in Munich in 1923? On October 25 Director-General Minoux, a former collaborator of Stinnes, came to offer to von Kahr *the collaboration of the great industrialists and of von Seeckt, representing the Prussian Reichswehr.* Ludendorff hesitated. Collusion between the industrialists and von Seeckt seemed to disturb him. Was it intended, he asked himself, to rule with Jews like Warburg and Melchior?

Meanwhile von Lossow, commander of the Bavarian Reichswehr, collected all the Bavarian military forces. He had the prestige of the army, and arms and money, and he carried the day against Hitler, who was obliged to follow his lead. The Reichswehr had Hitler in its grip. It was paying the S.A. and their partisans. This time was it to be a march on Berlin, the Berlin of the Weimar régime? What was it proposed to do with the Hitlerite party and its 15,000 members? The party was short of funds. But the money came. Wealthy individuals, Hanfstängl, Frau Helene Bechstein, Frau Gertrud von Seidlitz, made up the shortage. The *Völkischer Beobachter* became a daily paper. All sorts of people, enthusiastic because Hitler had promised to defend private property, lavished their fortunes on him. Money came from north and south and from abroad.

With all this support, why did not Hitler this time take seriously his rôle of "Führer"? With such resources, why did he not instil a new faith into the masses? This Redeemer spent his days lobbying generals and industrialists. *He had everything in his favour, mass support and the support of the oligarchy.* At bottom that "frigid power" the ruling *élite* despised him: he was good enough for the crowd and would be easily got rid of. Hitler, nevertheless, went on his course. He declared that "heads will roll" and that if the German people had to be saved by dint of inhumanity he would go to any length. He knew that he would save Germany only *by the most pitiless dictatorship.* Between him and the Reichswehr, which was indispensable to him, still stood Ludendorff. No matter! Göring announced that the advent of the Führer would mean the most formidable terrorism. All who resisted would feel it. That was what Göring and Hitler called the "revolutionary" mentality.

The time thus seemed ripe for a putsch. Bavaria was threatening to secede from the Reich. Germany must at all costs be saved from that threatened dismemberment, from a Danubian monarchy and the Jesuit peril. There was not a moment to lose! On November 8, von Kahr announced a great programme speech in the Bürgerbräukeller. Hitler determined to interrupt him and to proclaim *the national Revolution.* This time he would have his revenge for Ludendorff's Nuremberg "Deutscher Tag." Storm Troopers surrounded the hall, took possession of it, and set up their machine-guns. Hitler jumped on to the platform with his revolver and fired it into the air. Göring and he declared the national Revolution begun! This time Hitler threw his cards on the table. He would be the head of the new Government. As for Ludendorff, he would command the national Reichswehr. Control of the police would be seized. Hitler would carry through the national Revolution or would disappear. So, at least, he himself said. Ludendorff was compelled to follow him, *though he did not want to admit that this time he was obeying Hitler.* The generals were furious. What of that! The Nazis went on with the job. They arrested the Social Democratic city councillors and the chief burgomaster, Schmid.

Was it to be the end of the Weimar régime at Munich? Would the Republic next be submerged throughout the Reich? Not yet. For the Bavarian Government suddenly took courage.

Bit by bit it destroyed the self-styled "national Revolution." Then came the famous drama of the Feldherrnhalle.[1] Fourteen dead on the pavement! Capitulation was unavoidable. The putsch had failed. The police had remained loyal to Weimar.

In reality the plot had been badly prepared. The military organization had proved insufficient, and General von Lossow had made serious mistakes. And the leaders had lacked courage. It would all have to be begun over again. But the population of Munich remained still fanatically pro-Hitler and pro-Ludendorff. For the rest, Hitler drew some profit from his failure. For one fact had been established—*the contemptible quality of the Bavarian military*, who had abandoned Ludendorff at the supreme moment. And one result had been achieved, *the complete rupture between the Hitlerite party and the Reichswehr*. This was definitive liberation. The Nazi Party came into real existence on November 9, 1923.

4. *The triumph of the Party*

Von Kahr and von Lossow had abandoned Hitler and his supporters at the critical moment. Neither of them had the revolutionary temperament. Not that they had deliberately betrayed Hitler. Their courage had failed them, and they fell into the void of contempt and oblivion. Their attitude and the very failure of the putsch rendered Hitler most valuable service. In face of them Hitler took shape as a young patriot deceived by those who had sworn to give him their support. Thereafter public opinion held him to be the one who, like the German army of 1918, had been "stabbed in the back." That was enough for his personality to be given a symbolic aspect in the eyes of the crowd.

Hitler was condemned by the popular tribunal, a Weimar institution, to five years' detention in a fortress. He was set free after a few months, but was formally prohibited from speaking in public. He continued his propaganda none the less, gathering round him all those who were one day to constitute the directing body of the party. The prohibition of public speaking helped him forward: thanks to it Hitler's figure was enveloped in a sort of romantic aura. It was magnified in the mysterious penumbra that formed round him.

The true significance of his trial lay, however, in Ludendorff's

---

[1] The Munich putsch, the first attempt made by Hitler and Ludendorff to seize power. The procession they organized was fired on by the police.

declarations against the Roman Catholic Church and the wealthy
and cultivated classes.   Before the Munich judges Ludendorff
made no secret of his detestation of Bavarian ultramontanism
and federalism.   He openly charged those movements with playing France's game, and with betraying the Prussian cause and
therefore the greatness and the very unity of Germany.   He
declared himself ready to build up a strong Germany on Bismarck's foundation.   His claim was to be bringing back to the
German people not, indeed, the monarchy itself, *but the will to exist
of a free people*—free in the collective sense in which Germany
understands freedom.

It is a curious thing that, while Ludendorff turned away from
the dynasties and the ruling caste and addressed himself to the
people, Hitler, who had come from the people, turned toward
the social and economic oligarchy.   Ludendorff's and Hitler's
paths   crossed,   being   essentially   complementary.   Hitler
announced that he was going to break Marxism.   He shouted
his admiration for Richard Wagner, for the Bayreuth circle, and
for the pan-Germanism that Houston Stewart Chamberlain
supported there.   He represented himself as the "Trommler,"
the "drummer" of the morrow, the man who would continue
to shake the German masses, now that they had become soft and
amorphous, until the terrible awakening that would make
Germany once more strong.

After the trial, and even before the law had been invoked
against Hitler to expel him from Bavaria, the German Republic
seemed to consolidate itself.   It entered the period of euphoria
that was introduced by the restoration of the currency.   For
four years it was to live under the illusion of recovery, though
it owed its momentary prosperity entirely to foreign capital.
During those years the Hitlerite party grew, and the old nationalism was partly submerged beneath the movement that had
captured the masses; the grave crisis of 1929 came, and National
Socialism had its first decisive triumph, in the elections of
September 14, 1930.

Hitler's prison had quickly been turned into the party offices.
The party had had to choose between Hitler and Ludendorff.
The popular tribune wanted a vast popular movement in favour
of Greater Germany.   He scorned the old-style nationalism of
the *Deutschvölkische*, the "German racialists."   Ludendorff,
however, held to the alliance with von Gräfe, Wulle, and their
associates: their party had thirty-two seats in the Reichstag, a

figure by no means to be despised.   Hitler seemed for a moment to accept union between *Völkische* and National Socialists, though on the condition that the latter should lead the dance. He was well aware that Ludendorff had not the support of the masses—the old General was much too aristocratic and haughty for that.   In other words, Hitler *felt that time was working for him and that the future was his.*

At the elections of December 7, 1924, the *Völkische* suddenly collapsed.   Their Reichstag membership dropped from thirty-two to fourteen.   Hitler very shrewdly profited from their discomfiture, which was due to the stabilization of the currency, to the Dawes Plan, to a very tranquil foreign policy, to at least apparent agreement with France, and to the restart of economic activity.   It was the moment of the commencement of the ruthless industrial rationalization that produced the great unemployment crisis of 1931–32.   Germany was temporarily consolidating her position, and the National Socialist tide ebbed.

On December 17, 1924, Hitler emerged from the fortress of Landsberg.   Whom did he visit at once?   Pöhner, the Munich chief of police.   Why?   *To prepare the final breach with Ludendorff.* For Ludendorff had become impossible in South Germany, owing to his desperate struggle against Rome and Catholicism. Hitler realized the old General's political incapacity.   What he himself offered Held, the Bavarian Prime Minister, was peace with Rome.   Ludendorff should be ignored, and the struggle should be against Marxism, not against Catholicism.   This was the true road to popularity in Bavaria.   Leave the Bavarian Centre Party and the German Nationals in peace.   The ex-prisoner went to the support of the Bavarian reactionaries.   It was to this end that he entered into relations with Pöhner.   Why not try to unite *pan-Germanism* with *monarchism?*   The Führer-to-be might be a wild revolutionary at public meetings, but he was still at bottom the server of those in power and place.   Until November 1923 he had supported the Reichswehr.   But after the occupation of the Ruhr, the acceptance of the Dawes Plan, and the entry of the German Nationals into the Government, civilians took over the direction of political affairs.   The Reichswehr held aloof.   Where, in any case, now that the period of inflation was ended, was the money to be found for the paramilitary formations?

The day of the bourgeoisie had dawned.   Accordingly, it was for the benefit of the bourgeoisie that Hitler began the fight against parliamentarism and democracy.   He no longer troubled about the conquest of North Germany for his party. It would suffice to make Bavaria a solid centre of National Socialism. For that purpose he needed *the favour of the masters of the moment*. That was what Hitler called "keeping within the bounds of legality."

In vain did the Nationalists of the north, von Gräfe, Wulle, von Henning, and the rest, accuse him of wanting to be Pope in Bavaria. In vain did they censure his clericalism. Hitler broke ostentatiously with them in a big programme speech in the Bürgerbräukeller on February 27, 1925. He was careful to make no attack on Catholicism. He kept scrupulously within the lines traced for him by the Herrenklub. His attack was directed against Judaism and Marxism. This time, as in *Mein Kampf*, he set the "*Aryan*" against the *Jew*. His success was immense. He knew the slogans to which the crowd would respond. At the same moment he published in the *Völkischer Beobachter* a dogmatic definition of the normal Führer, *the man who managed the masses, who moulded that human material (Menschenmaterial)*. Men are, of course, different, but in the name of racialism they would be made into a coherent mass. For Hitler the character of his subordinates scarcely counted. What did he care for morality or for political principles! Were rules and regulations to be laid down for the impulses of men's hearts and for their instinctive feelings? This entire unscrupulousness was the path the Nazi deliberately trod, the path of the prudence and calculation of the brute let loose.

Hitler was completing his training and perfecting himself as the loud-mouthed tribune; but that did not mean that his Bavarian policy had the least chance of success. Up to then he had made use of the Bavarian Government as a weapon against Weimar and the North. But why not win the North for National Socialism? Why not follow the advice of Gregor Strasser, *who had realized that the centre of gravity of the Nazi movement was shifting northward*? Not, indeed, that Strasser was in revolt against Hitler; on the contrary, he placed himself under his ægis. But he entirely changed the balance of Nazism. He, too, showed extraordinary talent as an agitator. In a very short time he established a Nazi movement that covered the whole of the north of Germany. Seven regions or *Gaue* were formed—Schleswig, Hamburg, Mecklenburg, Pomerania, Göttingen, Lüneburg, and Hanover. Later came Berlin and, in the south-west, Baden. At this time there was considerable confusion in the party, for Hitler, too, was trying to conquer the South. He failed in Württemberg, but had some success in Saxony.

Gregor Strasser continued, however, the most vigorous propaganda in the north. He took Goebbels as an assistant. What Gregor Strasser and Goebbels wanted was to direct Nazism *toward the east, toward true Socialism.* Nazism was to be *the dictatorship of the Socialist Idea in the State.* Strasser could do without anti-Semitism and anti-Marxism. He could give praise to the Social Democrats themselves. He was not, like Hitler, playing the game of industrial Cæsarism. With his brother Otto he represented the Hitlerite *Left wing*, with a more sincere doctrine, that of struggle against Western plutocracy and capitalism. What he wanted *was that Nazism should follow Russia and the East in general in their struggle against Western capitalism.* Germany was hesitating between capitalism and Communism. Hitler was content with a false compromise, which the employers wanted in order to deceive the masses in Germany and opinion abroad. He was acting as a demagogue in the exact sense of the word. The Strassers had conceived *a more honest and more Socialist Nazism, looking frankly to the East.* On November 22, 1925, Gregor Strasser convened the first congress of the northern *Gaue.* His conception of National Socialism was launched in opposition to Hitler's. That is enough to explain why he was mercilessly slaughtered on June 30, 1934. Strasser did not recoil from the social revolution. He was for the method of the putsch, for bombs and violent measures. It was just this violent but straightforward method that Hitler rejected. He knew perfectly well whose game he was playing. He never forgave the Strassers for that year 1925, which very nearly destroyed his career.

About the beginning of 1926, indeed, Hitler was no longer sure that he could form a unified party for the whole of Germany. That year was filled with passionate discussions of the *orientation* of the future party, of its intellectual and doctrinal tendencies. Some wanted the true " *Volksgemeinschaft*" or " national community," others a pseudo-corporativism that should respect the old social hierarchy and leave the employers in the saddle, under Gottfried Feder's system. The Strassers said again and again that they wanted to lead the offensive *against the Anglo-Saxon spirit.* The German people should defend all those who were oppressed by Western capitalism. Hitler, on the contrary, spoke always of making peace with Britain in order to secure her benevolent neutrality, of combating Judaism, and of founding the great Empire of the pure "Aryans." The same struggle went on in student circles. It might be said that in Germany itself, in face

of the demagogic pan-Germanism forged by the employers and
Hitler, there had risen a sort of Slavized pan-Germanism that
did not recoil from collusion with Russia.

All these discussions, so vital for the future, turned upon the
same problem—whether to have the *nationalism* of the Hitler
type, with its racial doctrine and its lust for domination, or the
Socialism of the Strasser type. Goebbels tried to find a compromise under which National Socialism should combine the
two tendencies. But Hitler was on the look-out for any
dangerous policy of that sort. He knew better than anyone
what help he could count on from the ruling caste. He profited,
in fact, by the famous quarrel over the settlement concerning the
private fortunes of the fallen dynasties, the *Fürstenabfindung*, to
carry his point of view. Naturally the Nazis of the North were
up in arms, in the name of their Socialism, against the measure
put forward, which left the princes their fortunes. Hitler
shrewdly *took the part* of the princes. He destroyed the growing
opposition in the North. At the same time *he pronounced himself
against alliance with Russia and in favour of alliance with Italy*, in
conformity with the programme of *Mein Kampf*. Goebbels then
played false with Strasser and turned to Hitler.

Thus was imposed, little by little, upon the Nazis of the North
and their Socialist tendencies the dictatorship of the Munich
party, founded on more or less secret connivance with the German
Right wing. Strasser was beaten and superseded. Hitler was
freed on his right from the Wulle or von Gräfe type of aristocratic
nationalism, aloof from the masses, and on his left from the
troublesome Socialism of the Strasser tendency. He had emerged
as victor in all these battles. He was able to convene the Weimar
Congress at the beginning of July 1926. He was able to proceed
to the Ruhr and address the great industrialists. In the following
year he was able to renew his oratorical prowess and to gain
favour with the employers. He was asking nothing impossible
from the great industrialists or the junkers. He contented
himself, faithful to the twenty-five points of 1920 as amended by
him, *with defending private property*. He even pronounced himself
in favour of economic liberalism. He demanded of it, however,
that it should take sides without qualification *with the people and
the State*. He considered that since 1895 the employers had
changed their outlook and gained a better understanding of the
people's needs. That being so, he could associate them with his
dictatorial enterprise. What he demanded was simply *a less*

despotic capitalism. His system, entirely empirical, would provide a wise hierarchy of capitalists and high servants of the State. It would be a Jacob's ladder, a hybrid solution of the conflict between capital and labour, which would this time be united in common service rendered to the totalitarian State.

On this basis it would be possible to invent every imaginable formula—the entire devotion of the individual to the Community, the Community being the providential guardian of the individual: or, if you will, Nationalism and Socialism. The essential thing was to preserve the grain of salt—capitalism—in this solidarist Socialism. Hitler therefore exerted himself to wrest the S.A. from all those who were trying to bring them over to Strasser, to a more consistent Socialism. Now Goebbels could go to Berlin to make the conquest of the capital. He could borrow from Möller van den Bruck the phrase "Third Reich" and invent the word "system" for the future State. If he went too readily beyond the bounds of "legality," he would have force at his back. Hitler was on good terms with the Bavarian Government, and also on good terms with the ruling caste in the north. Already the Hitlerite party had gained the day against the "Stahlhelm," the "Jungdeutscher Orden," and nationalists such as Seldte and Mahraun; it celebrated its orgies at its first congress at Nuremberg in September 1927. At the Reichstag elections of May 1928 the Party already obtained twelve seats.

In October 1928 Hitler began a vigorous reorganization of the Party. He created twenty-five regions or *Gaue*, cleverly breaking up the Ruhr region, which was Strasser's. The "Hitler-Jugend" (Hitler Youth) made its appearance. The Party had 60,000 members. In vain did Gregor and Otto Strasser try to save their positions, to achieve the triumph of the Socialism that offered a very much fairer prospect for the future than Hitler's speeches. Men like Gottfried Feder and Darré gathered round Hitler, provided material for his theses, and so arranged the cards that everyone stood to gain. The middle class was going under, victim of the inflation. National Socialism could thus announce the death of the middle class and hold out a hand to the Socialists and even to the Communists. The game was very cleverly played. Their supporters would rest content with the Hitlerite formula of a national economic system controlled by the power of the State but not carried on by the resources of the State. Behind this formula the whole employing class could take refuge. That was the class that must not be

upset! You want to know what Socialism is? That's easy!
The true Socialism is a mixture of *forced labour* and of *military
service*. The idea of the *soldier* State made its appearance. The
immemorial State-by-Divine-Right would still be with them,
but its head would be a General Staff. What was the use of the
quarrel between Hitler and the Strassers over anti-Semitism?
The useful Jews would be retained. The others would do for
the Nazis to graze on.

The Strassers had a political system and convictions. *Hitler
had neither*. It was precisely in this that his strength lay. The
Strassers nursed a chimerical dream, but intelligently and honestly.
Hitler had not the slightest respect for the fourteen theses of the
German Revolution which they promulgated in 1929. These
theses were certainly of much more importance than the Nazi
twenty-five points of 1920, amended by Hitler in 1928 in accordance with the principle of respect for property, and they brought
the Strassers popularity among the leaders of the young intellectuals. The Nazis of the North had *learnt to think*. Hitler
had no use for a rational and well-constructed doctrine. What
he wanted was brute force, heavy-handed barbarism, the brain-
less bruisers (*Kampfnaturen*) whom he gathered round him for the
final sweeping away of the old social order, for his nihilist revolution of destruction. All he needed was a hammer with which
to smash the old idols.

It was at this moment that there appeared in Germany a new
proletariat, with a new national feeling, ready to receive National
Socialism as a providential gift, as the drowning man's straw.
Only those who know the extent of the distress of the German
masses between 1929 and 1932, rendered desperate by unemployment, proletarization, and destitution, can appreciate what
Germany passed through in those years. There was little to
choose between the fate of the middle classes and that of the
proletariat properly so called. Men's minds were seized by a
relentless solidarity, a furious resentment, an indescribable
horror of the social downfall that wounded German pride to the
quick. It is impossible for any foreigner who did not study
that crisis on the spot to picture it. That crisis suffices in itself to
explain the final triumph of Hitlerism in 1930 and the rapidity
with which the Party, with its 107 seats in the Reichstag, demolished the parliamentary machinery, the Weimar democracy,
and all the past, finishing with the symbolic Reichstag fire of
March 1933.

Hitler knew that nothing could be achieved without the Reichswehr and the industrial oligarchy, and in the course of the last years before his arrival in power he had broken finally with the Strasser tendency and had been discreetly courting the great ones of this world, the higher race of industrialists and manufacturers. On the other hand, he shouted to the masses, who had grown very anti-capitalist since the inflation, that he meant to destroy the omnipotence of money. For the sacredness of property he substituted the sacredness of the Nation. He preached racialism, the Nordic man, the exaltation of the "Aryan" German and of the white race; he appealed to the corporative spirit in industry, and with all this propaganda, fiery but crafty, full of fury but carefully considered with a view to its effect on the masses, he was able to undermine the popularity of the Weimar parties, especially the Centre and the Social Democracy. And between 1930 and 1933 there was a series of dramatic successes. The Nazi flood was on the move, and nothing more could stop it. Millions followed Hitler. It was a fine flood of irrational passion, but directed by men who were coolly exploiting it and who knew what they were about.

The *coup d'état* of 1933 had become possible. It is perfectly easy to explain. It proceeded from an agreement between the old ruling caste and the Nazi Party. It was the triumph not of a doctrine but of the monstrous coupling of two forces, that of *money* and that of *popular fury*, Hitler serving as intermediary between the two. At bottom, the situation in Germany at that time was not revolutionary in the normal sense of the word. The people were not ready to rise against their oppressors. They had been deceived by talk of a régime over which they would be masters. The pretended Hitlerite revolution was the outcome not of any deep will of the masses but of a sort of violent mass dynamism from which the ruling Right wing expected to profit by canalizing it. It seems very probable that it was von Papen who, thanks to his ascendency over Hindenburg, organized the *coup d'état*. This *coup d'état* was simply a "*Kombination*," a scheme prepared through fifteen years of diabolical intrigues and spectacular mass demonstrations. It owed its success to terrorism, the terrorism which, in a country that has an army and a police system but no longer any justice, paralyses the whole population. Certainly there was no lack of actively creative elements of good will; those elements exist everywhere. But they had no means of uniting to save the nation. The establishment of the Third Reich, like the whole of the preparation for it, had been the result of a purely artificial process. The German Nationals and the Nazis, Hugenberg and Hitler and their supporters, when they formed the Government of January 30, 1933, were all equally "nihilist." *Each partner was out to oust the other.* The Nazis' aim was to make a clean sweep of the past by means of ruthless *Gleichschaltung*, and to create an order of things under which the Party would be able to impose its domination on the entire nation, setting up a machinery of power to which any resistance would be impossible. *To mix discipline with destruction, to give cool direction to irrational passions, to make use of order to produce disorder, to rule Germany by means of a sort of masculine Order, an imitation of the Teutonic Order— such was the self-appointed mission of Nazism.*

CHAPTER VIII

THE SOLDIER NATION

FROM the day of Hitler's arrival in power, the German nation became a "soldier" nation. This characteristic implied a style and rhythm of life entirely different from those of the West. It was a total and permanent mobilization of all individual and collective energies. If we could not carry it out ourselves, was there not a danger precisely in the shifting of level thus produced and accentuated between the so-called "totalitarian" régimes and the Western democracies?

This complete militarization presupposes *Gleichschaltung*—the imposition of absolute conformity in thought and action. Centred on the myth of the *Volksgemeinschaft*, or national community, and on Prussian disciplinary simplism, the Third Reich rose up in face of German diversities, reducing, so to speak, all ideas, all wills, and all activities to a common denominator. One single current was to pass through the nation and its still heterogeneous elements to galvanize them, destroying, if necessary, every obstacle in its path.[1]

Germany, we said above, was revolutionary in the measure in which her territories or States approached unity, approached a cohesion which, after centuries of dualism, should imply final

[1] *Gleich haltung* is a term borrowed from electrical engineering, its technical meaning being "synchronization" (of alternating current machines).

harmony between *statecraft* and *culture*, the latter being required, however, to bear all the expenses and all the sacrifices of the operation, modelling itself on the most brutal type of statecraft. After the magnificent harvest of classicism and romanticism, Prussia seemed incapable of integrating the energies proceeding from a century-long effort. But, thanks to her hegemony and to industrialization, the victory was hers. Her power was now more sovereign than ever. The South now brought to Prussia nothing but a simple myth of biological origin. A crude mythology and Prussian training were driving Germany into limitless continental expansion, destroying the original forms of the Germanism of the periphery, and integrating everything in the nation conceived *as the secret of absolute collective efficiency, as a pure instrument of domination.*

The Nazi régime made of the German people an army, of each German worker a soldier. It tended to efface the distinction between the *civil* and the *military*. The machinery of power that crushed the German people with its weight was intended to form an army of *minds* by means of propaganda, an army of *executants* of every sort by means of the Labour Front, and finally the *army proper*, furnished with the most modern armament.

1. *The governmental machinery*

The *coup d'état* of 1933 succeeded owing to a strange mixture of romanticism and realism. Incredible forces of upheaval were associated with social and political conservatism of the most reactionary sort. *Dynamism* and *retardation*, push and pull, were paradoxically united. On the Right were people who simply wanted the restoration of any sort of governmental authority, a renewal of patriotism, economic reorganization, and a more active foreign policy. On the other hand, in the Nazi Party there were moderate forces that desired only the welfare of the masses and a social policy worthy of the country. But these two currents of opinion *scarcely counted.* Union had been effected between *the Right wing that was resuming the old method of power or of conquest* and *a sort of popular* élite, *without any true doctrine, that claimed to be rebuilding the military Germany on the ruins of the past.* The old pan-Germanism had been born again in the ashes of 1918, and brought up to date as a popular, vulgar pan-Germanism, the fruit of fifteen years of persistent activity on the part of Hitler and his party.

The Nazi régime must thus be conceived not as *an authoritarian State*, but as a *machinery of power*, existing for its own sake, and superposed on a people whom the decomposition of Weimar had reduced to the most complete amorphousness and who had been deprived of all capacity of resistance by an unemployment crisis that had produced unprecedented destitution. This machinery of power imposed on the people its new cadres, its brutal will, and its imperious demands. The idea that comes into our minds is that of a General Staff both civil and military in competence, endeavouring to bring the civil population on to a totally military plane. The Nazis had the feeling, quite rightly, that the mass of the Germans, after all their sufferings, could be moulded exactly as desired. That is why the most relentless dictatorship followed the decay of the Republic, and, in Goebbels' phrase, absolute *Gleichschaltung* followed the most complete laxity.

But this sudden change would not have been possible if the *coup d'état* had not had the support of the Reichswehr and the police, who betrayed the Republic, for which they had never had anything but contempt. The old ruling caste assisted the creation in Germany of a mass solidarism, a *national Communism* which it counted on subjecting and directing as it desired. The question then was what would be the relations between the Hitlerite Party, with its leaders and its centralized bureaucracy, on one side and the Reichswehr and the great industrialists on the other. The question is difficult to answer; the essential thing is to bear in mind that these different kinds of force were in action together and must never be entirely dissociated.

This is the explanation of the curious fusion of fervent nationalism with the cold calculation, the "realist romanticism," that characterized the Nazi Revolution. The mystery of Germany was still the *Reich* and *Prussia*. The union between limitless ambitions and a rigorously disciplinarian order, between vast schemes and concern for the greatest technical rigour, necessarily assumes the aspect of an unleashed dynamism, the dynamism that the Germans like to call "revolutionary," using the term in a special sense. We have here, in fact, a sort of *organized iconoclasm*.

The National Socialists were well aware that the German masses in their desperation would be full of enthusiasm for the coming Reich, for a grandiose vision of power, for a fierce and furious myth. To understand this one needs to re-read the analyses of Dr Le Bon, or those of Georges Sorel in his *Réflexions sur la Violence*, and finally to return to Machiavellism, as described, for example, by Maurice Joly in his *Entretiens entre Montesquieu et Machiavel aux Enfers*. The art of leading the masses and of directing public opinion is terrible when it is brought to bear on distress and when it is sure of its resources.

As the Germany of that time was a democratic parliamentary Republic, the preaching of this national mythology could only destroy the whole established order, make a clean sweep of the past, and spread in the nation, this time on the popular plane, the "nihilism" of thought and belief that was to be observed among the intellectuals before the First World War. That nihilism was the more evident and the more effective because it bore, both in theory and in practice, on the values of the international order that were represented precisely by the Weimar régime and the Weimar parties.

In this way there was produced in the mentality of the German public, through tragic circumstances which were very ably capitalized by the ruling caste and the Hitlerite agitators, a sort of vacuum, a great intellectual gap or "no man's land," which they set out to fill by means of ardent nationalist propaganda. Workless youths with no prospects played their special part. These youths overturned the heavy and solid historical obstacles that had at all times blocked the way to the nation's unity and internal cohesion. They consigned them to limbo. These obstacles melted like wax under the sun in the frightful crucible in which the beliefs of the past disappeared. It was in that traditionless vacuum that Hitlerite neo-pan-Germanism was created. It was that incredible phenomenon that made it possible for the machinery of power to be constructed in all its rigour, and to take possession of the amorphous masses and confine them within a framework of ruthless discipline.

The Nazi *Weltanschauung* (general outlook) was thus framed for the masses and for them alone. Men's minds had to be *occupied*, the frightful gap that had been produced in them had to be filled, they had to be inspired and given a sort of blind faith, vague and ardent, before concrete exploits, effective conquests, what the Führer later called *Aktionen*, were proposed to them. *To act for the sake of action, in order not to despair; to believe for the sake of belief, in order not to fall into the void.* There was no question of any programme, only of hatred of the Jew and adoration of the *Volksgemeinschaft*, the racial Community, for the sake of cultivating on the political plane a dull solidarism habitual to the Germans.

That was what the Nazis called *die Massen politisieren*, making the masses politically minded. In reality they were entirely divorced from politics, by separating them for all time from the Weimar order, which, whatever faults may be alleged against it, did imply the participation of all, Catholics and Socialists included, in public affairs.

The masses then, owing to a state of distress that discredited the Republic, and to a propaganda that gave them fictitious consolation, fell into the required state of passivity, and of completely uncritical receptivity, that provided a case for *Gleichschaltung*. They accepted the machinery of power; they allowed it to regiment them, like all those Germans of the older generation who were to be seen in Berlin marching four abreast on the day after the Reichstag fire, copying the hordes of young Nazis in uniform. To attain these ends, use was made of an "ideology," in the exact sense of the term, which, after rendering suspect all the values of the past, caught the masses in its net—a formidable *ersatz* lavished on them in order to produce the desired intoxication.

There was thus nothing whatever in this of any true national regeneration or any real popular collaboration. Nothing whatever to recall the French Revolution, in spite of the similarity which Hitler seems to admit, in *Mein Kampf*, between that and the movement he led to triumph. This was not a people carving out its destiny. Far from it: the failure of Weimar proved that the people were unable to do that by themselves, caught as they were in their historic pluralism, a pluralism that could only be overcome by *repudiating* it and substituting for it the *tabula rasa* of nihilism. Men's minds were brought to unity among ruins. The new "system" descended upon them, as it descended upon men's bodies and wills. That is the essence of Cæsarism. To cover this shame, the Nazis tried to give currency to the legend of a secret harmony between the subconscious instinct of the German crowd and the conscious will of the leaders. That was simply a lie, and the greatest lie of all. It was not difficult to unify the social classes, even composite classes like the bourgeoisie, when defeat, inflation, and the rest had reduced them all to one level. By that method the militant Hitlerite Party supplanted the older parties, the over-organized, worn-out Centre, the lethargic, convictionless Social Democracy, and the Democrats who had been played out since 1920. The Socialist trade unions offered no better resistance than the Christian ones.

Thus the masses had the illusion of political activity at the very moment when they had in fact been entirely divorced from it and had become the victims of *Gleichschaltung* and dictatorship. The rational machinery of parliamentary democracy worked no longer; irrationalism took its place. It was a suppression, not a renewal of the State. The masses had become simply a *Gefolgschaft*, a mass of "followers." The more contradictory and heady the propaganda became, the better it succeeded with people whom the methods of free parliamentary discussion had wearied because it bore on more and more vast and technical problems. The new doctrine served above all for demolishing the old order. But the Nazis ridiculed the idea of gaining convinced adherents and true believers. They made the masses not *conscious* but *drunk*. It is in this sense that the Nazi Revolution was made, as was said, *without doctrine*. Let the old obligations disappear, since it was dictatorship that was wanted.

Over against the masses stood the State and the "Führertum," the hierarchy of "leaders." What did they amount to? The "*élite*" represented cold cynicism, thoughtful calculation, a sort of highly technical rationalism that carried out "operations" with a sure hand, making use of an ailing people. Did this *élite* believe in the party's "*Weltanschauung*"? Was it genuinely racialist? How can we tell? It only believed in the ideas it propagated in so far as they served its general propaganda and captured and dominated men's minds. The essential thing in its eyes was the *Machtinstrument*, its instrument of power, that is to say, the propaganda organization, the ".working community" (*Arbeitsgemeinschaft*), and the army. Discipline, of course, but a discipline of destruction so far as concerned the past, *and of purely military reconstruction* in regard to the future.

Thus was the necessary mould made for the masses in process of fusion. It was necessary that the instrument should be irresistible, and that its momentum should gather up all the coagulated German energies. A truly diabolical conception, since its one and only concern was to throw down every obstacle and to bring to bear everywhere the whole power of Germany. It was from this purpose that there proceeded the spirit of forced camaraderie, and the revival of the idea of the Teutonic Order, once famous, which had earned such glory in the conquest of Eastern Europe. It was a purely masculine Order, confined to initiates, to those with "knowledge"—knowledge of nothing but the cynical nihilism that was the definition of their existence.

In the presence of the masses they seemed to be performing pseudo-religious rites, rites that bound the masses to their evil purposes. It might be said that Germany had abandoned her age-long culture and fallen back into the primitive state.

This pretended *élite* was *pure activism*. So long as it met with no resistance, it went straight along its course. "*Ich mache Aktionen*," said Hitler. He offered peace only in order to establish a conquest achieved or an act of domination accomplished. And he continued with a sort of sleepwalker's sureness, until the day should come of the final catastrophe that would awaken him. A demoniac Machiavellism, to which no bounds were set, acted through that machinery of power. It was not, perhaps, the most convinced Nazis that were the most efficient. At bottom this play of pure brutality and cold cruelty excluded all conviction. In face of it individual liberties and collective autonomies disappeared. The Party was the State. The State was but the Party's instrument. In other words, the State was part of the machinery of power. The *élite* played the part of the motor, of a radical force always in action and at work.

The ruling caste had proposed to canalize to its profit the energies released by the decomposition of Weimar. It was mistaken, deluded. In taking the risk of the *coup d'état* it had precipitated its whole membership into the tragic affray. It had hoped to moderate the rebels; instead of that, it had delivered up the State to them and to their schemes of direct action. The rebels had made violence their element and rupture with the established order their method. Their *élite* was not of the sort that would proceed of its own initiative to great works of national regeneration. The *élite* was but a body of mercenaries in the pay of the Führer. It was his creation, his creature. It included satisfied and not yet satisfied careerists, third- and fourth-rate persons whom a stroke of luck had suddenly placed in positions of power, an anonymous power made ten times stronger by its collective character.

Here was the new "master class" (*Herrenschicht*), the new ruling caste, less socially exclusive than the old one, bolder because rawer, a body of which each member was working desperately to supplant his colleague. A very practical process of selection, brutal from start to finish. These were the "militants," the born bravoes (*Kampfnaturen*) whom Hitler loved, men who loved the game for its own sake, torture for its own sake, the Reich for its own sake. A master-minority pursuing nothing

but pure power and pure success, masters in the primitive biological sense of the word. This minority that feared no risk had
risen against the parties that had never risked anything. So it won
against them, as pure activity is bound to win against pure passivity.

The Leader became a mythical figure, an adored divinity, the
Man of Providence. This is just the magic that proceeds from
devil-may-care extremism. The masses, completely dazed,
submit. At the back of the cult of *Blut und Boden*, blood and soil,
was the dream of total domination. The much-used word
"*Gemeinschaft*" (community) meant little: it was the Party, the
Order, that had the sole decision of all things, despite its ferocious
internal dissensions. It suggested a new sort of Salvation Army,
with the same vigour, the same gestures, the same audacity. The
Party was required to keep up this mad pace. This time
centrifugal forces were finally annihilated. The "Gauleiter" or
regional bosses were petty kings, bound to the Führer by the
most rigorous subordination. There was certainly a grandeur,
an atrocious grandeur, in this formidable system. The Party
and the bureaucracy were intermingled, and that is why the
bureaucracy did not stifle the revolution. All things were
forcibly integrated in the instrument of domination. That
instrument demanded of every person incessant activity. Based
on the people, it aimed at *exhausting* them. No pause, no rest.
"We are destined," wrote Möller van den Bruck, "never to let
the others rest."

That pyramid of Nazi power could at all events blunt its point
easily enough. Any critical situation that discredited it might
reduce the pyramid to rubble. Always at high tension, the
framework might suddenly give way. For the weakness of the
Hitlerite Party lay *in its very totality and its extreme centralization*.
One blow at its head and, like an enormous insect on the body of
the people, the whole system would collapse, its tentacles being
suddenly paralysed. It was not a true Order. Either the nation
would come to its end beneath it, or it would die a natural death
and the nation would at last be freed from its grip.

It would be possible to reign for a few years with the aid of the
Gestapo, of political terrorism, of concentration camps, and of
intimidation. But how could these refinements of atrocity be
rendered permanent? That ferocious energy, applied to a sort
of wild amoralism, that brutal policy of decision, that carefully
calculated display of robustness, suggesting the existence of
forces that in fact were of doubtful reality, that use of morality

and legality where convenient, coupled with incessant violations of both in other directions, that appeal to sentimentality, that sadist domination through the exploitation of human baseness—could all this last long?

The appeal to envy and jealousy, the use of informers, the indulgence in the most cowardly of cruelties—all this is not government. That mode of rule is the counterpart of utter weakness. The liberal bourgeoisie and moderate Socialism were suddenly struck down by that irresistible blow, plainly launched from the depths of the collective soul. The ruling caste had itself prepared this pseudo-revolution, this reaction, coolly directing it and allowing it to gather impetus from the dark passions of the blind masses. Was it, would it be, the victim of it? Would the great landowners and industrialists and bankers find themselves faced with a State Socialism of a military nature, little removed from Communism, and able one day to expropriate them entirely, after it had been shaped by their own hands and financed by their own subsidies? Was the army in the service of the régime, and would it allow itself to be dragged by it into the immoral adventures that were common gossip? That was the secret of the morrow. But the mere fact that such questions could be asked proved that men were faced with an instrument of domination unique in all the world, an instrument in face of which the latent opposition remained the victim of long-standing disunity and the old pluralism.

What, in such conditions, could Hitlerite legality be like?

Two terms exactly described the régime—"Volksstaat" and "Führerstaat," people's State and leader's State. In essence they meant the same thing. "People" and "Leader" were complementary terms, "people," in the ordinary sense of the word, losing all concreteness and becoming an abstraction. To reduce the people to a purely instinctive and unconscious will, to cast it into pure irrationalism, to claim that the "Führer" incarnates its past and its future, the whole rhythm of its history, in his own person, was to destroy the people on the pretext of "nationalizing" it, to make of it the docile instrument of an ambitious and brutal clique. To imagine that the "Führer" grasped by direct intuition and carried out by immediate action the will of the masses was to establish a purely fictitious relation between the German people and the dictatorship at its head. Nothing but brutal success, facile demonstrations of strength applied to weak States, could justify such a conception and such a practice of public law. This pseudo-mysticism amounted to complete contempt of the mass of the people.

The Hitlerite leaders used to say that only the doctrine, the *Weltanschauung*, was totalitarian, and that the State was its instrument, the form taken by the substance of the people under the pestle of the Party. The "Führer" and his Party created the mould into which the amorphous masses must be run. The masses had to be "shaped" for the future struggles. But it was assumed that that mould corresponded exactly to the collective will. From this point of view it was absurd to establish a sort of artificial distinction between Hitler and the German people. The State was here simply the result of the interaction, mysterious and yet real, between "Führer," "Volk," and "Partei." The State was the people turned athlete. It was totalitarian only in the proportion, still hypothetical, in which the people lent itself to that pressure. The State created nothing by itself: it was "created" by the action of the "Führer" and the Party on the people. That is why Hitler said in *Mein Kampf* that the State is created *by the Race*, and that the Race is the primordial element. The agreement between the unconscious will of the multitude and the conscious activity of the "Führer" and his Party is precisely the Race :

" We Aryans can only figure a State under the aspect of a *living organism* that serves as clothing for a given people and, not content with assuring the existence of that people, works also to develop its intellectual and spiritual capacities, in order to lead it to the highest liberty."

Spurious romanticism. It made of the State the permanent creation of the "Führer" and assimilated the "Führer" to a sort of eternally creative Divinity. The conscious Race, incarnate in the "Führer," worked on the unconscious Race incarnate in the "Volk." The State was totalitarian only if the mutual penetration and the harmony of the two elements were complete. If the State was thus reborn every moment, a written Constitution was useless. It would be but a Nessus' shirt for the impatient and impetuous Nazi ! This was what was called, in the Nazi jargon, "constitutional realism." An old German idea, in virtue of which every juridical Charter paralyses life. Why this network of prescriptions? Why be bound to anything *a priori*? The State was in one or another "constitution" (*Verfassung*) from moment to moment. Here were the old romanticist theses popularized, if not rejuvenated.

There was conformity with "legality," but not with any external or juridical legality. The true law was *the inner law*, which was bound up with the *historic destiny* of a people. Under the action of "Führer" and Party, the people "became." Racialism was a cloak for the dictatorship of formulæ borrowed from the crudest vitalism. It invented a law that was both common law and statute law. The Weimar Constitution still subsisted in so far as Nazism had not modified it, but it had lost all binding character. The law of the Third Reich "broke up" the Weimar law. Creative and dynamic law destroyed established law. In the past it had been impossible to modify the Constitution except by a two-thirds majority. Now the "Führer" did what he chose and the jurists discussed the question whether this or that remark of his formed a constitutional precedent.

When the "Führer" had received the power from the palsied hands of the old rulers he was able immediately (1) to align (*gleichschalten*) the territorial States by imposing on them "Statthalter" or Governors devoted to him; (2) to destroy the great political parties, replacing them by the single party making up the whole composition of the Reichstag; and (3) to destroy the great professional organizations and trade unions on Right and Left. The Plenary Powers law of March 24, 1933, renewed at a stroke the whole body of legislation. A show was made of consulting the people by a plebiscite. In reality the nation was compelled to abdicate, placing its sovereignty in the hands of the "Führer."

Through this act an end was made of the many delegations of power. Under the Republic the people had delegated its sovereignty to many authorities, none of which had full sovereignty. Now it had remitted its entire sovereignty to the "Führer" and the Party. The people became nothing more than a mystical affirmation. There remained the governmental machinery. The Party was considered to be forming itself *spontaneously* within the governmental machinery, or, what amounted to the same thing, by the *free choice* of the "Führer." Let there be no talk of Republic and Monarchy—these were empty words. The Reich was virtually totalitarian and of indefinite extent. Such was the meaning of the relationship between "Führer" and "Gefolgschaft," Leader and Following. It was a curious mixture of responsible liberty and absolute obedience. The masses were worked and pounded into shape. They lost their liberty in order that, through the good offices of the "Führer" and the Party, the Race should be free. All federalism had disappeared.

The "Führer" and his Party thus acted *from aloft*, though they had come *from below*. They forcibly co-ordinated the elements that in the past had been pluralist and disunited. In the authoritarian State of the Bismarckian model, the *Obrigkeitsstaat*, the imperial monarchy had ruled without direct contact with the masses. In the Weimar democracy (*Volksstaat*) the people had ruled without real effect, owing to the plurality of organs representing it. National Socialism quite simply replaced the authoritarian State and the pluralist democracy by the *machinery of power*.

The Third Reich was thus a popular State, a People installed in its territory, but aiming at acquiring its "*Lebensraum*," or room to live, in order to develop all its potential energy there, a Race disposing of blood and soil for the incessant renewal of its activity, a Socialist State in which the common interest prevails in theory over the individual interest, in which the public service is the sole criterion of law and justice, a governmental machinery implying at every step in the hierarchy the fundamental relation between leaders and executants. The Nazi Greater Germany was a very different thing from the Bismarckian Empire plus Austria. *Its territory participated in the revolutionary dynamism that characterized the régime.* The quarrel over the republican and imperial flags was ended—the one and only permitted symbol was the red flag with the swastika.

The "Führer" was thus the head of the Party and the head of the State. The Party, as a "militant" militia, set itself up against the State considered as a formless mass. Liaison was established by personal union between *Party* and *bureaucracy*. This was assured by the nazification of the official. The Party prevented the State from becoming bogged in a ponderous bureaucracy. It continually urged it on. Legislation and execution were one and the same thing, at least in principle. The three powers were no more than the three aspects of one sole activity exerted upon the masses to be trained as fighters.

Hitler united in his person all the prerogatives of a party leader. He renewed the "militant" *élite* responsible for militarizing the masses. This militarization was an undefined task. For this very reason the Party was to be in a condition of permanent liability to respond to any call. The masses were deprived of their former structure and were given their new shape. This operation implied an immense and terrible simplification. There must not be too many intermediaries. There was a solid central headquarters, the Brown House, and from this the will of the Party was communicated to the masses. The Party must act with the fanaticism and intolerance that were indispensable. It would employ "Terror," the intimidation produced by propaganda and especially by repression behind the scenes.

The single party then became a corporation at public law. A deputy leader, Rudolf Hess, a treasurer, and a central office (*Kanzlei*), and the work of direction could go on, orders being communicated to the "Gauleiter" (regional bosses) and by them to district and local groups. The party had its organized services and its troops—S.A., S.S., and motorized units. How should it not have these last, since it was the "motor" of the State? Its members were submitted to special jurisdiction. They enjoyed certain privileges and immunities. The Party thus had relative autonomy, and it was alone in this respect. It was an Order in so far as it created a pseudo-religious myth. It had its capital at Munich, its congresses at Nuremberg, and its Leader at Berchtesgaden.

After 1933 it became necessary both to consolidate and to renew the Party. At the outset it was far from having attained unity. In February 1934 its members took an oath of loyalty to Hitler. Then, in co-operation with the Stahlhelm, it liquidated the conflict between the old and the new generation. On June 30 of the same year an action of extreme violence, and of unheard-of brutality, put an end not only to attempts of the Right wing to organize reaction with the aid of the great religious bodies, and of the Left to achieve a more radical social revolution, but to every move in the direction of absorbing the Reichswehr in the Party and making an army of Nazi inspiration and tendency. The Führer, who in this action espoused the cause of the Reichswehr, purged the S.A. and S.S., demanded of them loyalty and austerity, and imposed on them a new twelve-point catechism. The congress of 1934 completed this internal reorganization. With the introduction of 1935 of obligatory military service the Nuremberg congress of that year was able to celebrate the grand trilogy of Führer, Party, and Army.

But how to renew the Party? Whence was the pseudo-*élite* to be recruited? This *élite* comprised those whom Hitler so well called "Söhne des Chaos" in his speech of July 13, 1934. In the course of time a distinction developed automatically between the old and the new *élite*. It was not forgotten that the Teutonic Order had died a natural death when it became incapable of renewal. It was all very well to gather into the famous "Ordens-burgen" several thousands of future leaders. This puerile scheme could not rejuvenate the Party, for there were appearing in its ranks a more radical youth and elements of proletarian origin. While those Nazis who had come from the old ruling classes to which, in spite of their connivance and their aid to it, the Nazi movement was a menace, acquired growing influence in the Party and were trying to pave the way for a monarchical restoration, young elements from other classes were dreaming of an absolutely new type of man and of society, were talking of entirely destroying the West and its bourgeoisie, and were trying to create a true Order, a sincere German Socialism, aiming at *consistent planning*, for the total and universal Revolution. In a country like Germany the *Jugendbewegung* (youth movement) never ends. Germany always contains a young generation potentially in revolt.

Before the last war the German youth demanded freedom and railed against a civilization that was suffocating it; before this war it had arrived at a sort of generalized despotism that aimed at destroying freedom everywhere. It was looking beyond the Nazism of the day. It entirely rejected the middle-class civilian existence of the past. It had embraced militarism for its own sake. It had conceived the collective existence for its own sake. Not that it did not protest against certain things in its own ranks, which were full of contradictions and conflicting tendencies. That young *élite* wanted to be pure, free from demagogic lies, free from corruption. It was thinking of a higher asceticism that would put an end to the original, ponderously solidarist National Socialism. The Nazi Party was far from being a homogeneous entity. It was in full ferment, torn between Restoration and Revolution, between West and East.

For the moment the personalities of the Führer and his immediate acolytes remained predominant. Hitler was: (1) Direct leader *of the whole people*, heir to all the powers of the former President, which he combined with those of the former Chancellor, both source and executive organ of the nation's laws, the plebiscite being there in order to maintain the illusion that the people was delegating its sovereignty to its "Führer"; (2) Head of a *unitary State*, since the law of March 31, 1933, had aligned the territorial States with the Reich and replaced their governments by

"Statthalter," Governors devoted to the Führer; (3) Head of the *Government*, and of its *Ministers*; since every bureaucratic or collegial system had disappeared and the Führer's orders were immediately carried out by the whole of the ministerial and administrative machinery, by the complete system of great Ministries that Germany now had; and (4) Head of the *Army*, with all its constituent elements. His power was absolute, but strictly bound to that of the apparatus of domination just described.

2. *Doctrine and propaganda*

There is a National Socialist doctrine. It is precisely this that is "totalitarian," that is to say, accepted in principle by all Germans. It makes of Germany a complete whole, self-sufficing. It is less a matter of deep conviction than of intellectual schematism. In other words, doctrine is here simply a sort of projection of the system on the plane of thought. This doctrine is negative in the sense that it prohibits in Germany every sort of international belief that might be a rival to National Socialism. It is positive in the sense that it determines the values that are to be recognized by the German people as its own. This doctrine is dispensed in Germany by appropriate propaganda.

The alpha and omega of Nazi racialism are the combination of anti-Judaism and anti-Bolshevism. The Jew and the Bolshevik are, of course, simply *pretexts* or *symbols*. The Enemy to be fought is the antithesis of national German racialism—Internationalism in any form, and Humanism in so far as it tends to embrace nations in a system of common and eternal standards and to subordinate them to a spiritual power comparable to that of the mediæval Church. It is said that we are returning to the Middle Ages. But the victory of Nazism would bring the return to a *German* mediævalism, the spiritual power being in this case the Nazi *Weltanschauung* itself.

Alfred Rosenberg considers that for fifteen centuries the European nations have submitted more or less to a universalist conception of the world. He adds that each of the great universalist conceptions of Europe was represented in Germany by a particular political and social section. National Socialism, he says, recognizes only one principle, that of the national honour. From now on the nations of Europe are entering the nationalist era, that is to say, the German era.

To begin with, there must be condemnation, by holding it up to public obloquy, of the international Race that has elements in all nations, namely the Jew. Why is the Jew to be the principal scapegoat? In a country like Germany there are a thousand practical or theoretical reasons. The chief one is *a similitude of destiny*, which generally escapes common observation. Germany has never possessed or defended in the world a political Idea that was her direct property. According to circumstances, the national feeling is depressed or exalted in Germany without ever coinciding exactly with the actual substance of the people, its institutions, and its activities. The German makes desperate efforts to equate Prussia with the Reich and the Reich with "Volkstum," with the whole body of the German race, including the indeterminate mass of Germans living in small groups everywhere in the world. He does not succeed. Feeble and receptive in face of foreign influences when he is concentrated in his territorial cells, he rejects those influences when he regards himself as a member of a pseudo-mystical Community and a Race.

In his own house he finds the elements of a Race that suffers a fate analogous to his own. It will be pointed out that the Jews represent only a hundredth part of the German population. That makes little difference. They, too, have no specific political Idea. They, too, are defined only by their membership of a racial entity, a human unit of a supranational order. This does not prevent them from adopting the political principles of the democratic nations when they are able to assimilate them. The *Germanic nation* of the future is rising against the *Jewish supranation*, also of the future. The Germans, like the Jews, are *a people that is more than a people*. They know no peace, and they can give no peace to others.

In associating her pretended regeneration with the fight against Judaism, Nazi Germany tendered extraordinary homage to Israel. The German masses were on the move at the very time when the Jews aspired to settlement. In the great opposition between the settled and the nomad, it was the Germans who, returning to primitivity, went over to nomadism. We see here the profound reason for the hostility nurtured by Germany in general against the West. For Rome represents the principle of settlement toward which the Jews are working to-day, the principle of property, of law, of the interest that integrates the nation in the territory and erects the State upon an effective sovereignty. Thus understood, as we have seen, the Roman Idea engendered Papal Catholicism, the Italian Renaissance, the French genius, and Anglo-Saxon Calvinism.

But the German soul is badly situated between the settled nations of the West and the nomads of the East. It is full of doubts and hesitations. It oscillates between the Catholicism of the South and the dour Protestantism of the North. Industrialization, by producing a great exodus from country to town, *delivered Germany over to dynamism*, to the idea of nomadism or *Lebensraum* ("room to live"), to indefinite expansion. Born of immense distress, the principle of the "Führer" coagulated the mass of the Germans and made of it a foreign body in Europe, a fire-ball with an unforeseeable path. On this plane the German destiny joins the Jewish, while still in opposition to it, for the Jews are moving towards a sovereign State attached to a particular territory. In its terror of encirclement the "soldier" (*soldatische*) German nation, collected round its leaders, is tending to take the place in this world of the Israel of the past.

It is precisely because Germany wishes to expand as a national Race that she fights desperately against every system that would impose limiting standards on her, and therefore against all internationalism. Her fight against the Jews is symbolic of her fight against every external obstacle, against what she calls *slavery*. She wants to accomplish among the nations the very work of dissociation with which she charges the Jews. She adopts the Jewish method, and in order that she may follow it in freedom *it is necessary that she shall expel the Jew himself.* Thus the terms, "Jew" and "Aryan" are rigorously complementary. The "Aryan" is a sort of *Jew in reverse*. The German persecutes himself in persecuting the Jew. And the Nazi can only be defined *in relation to the Jew.*

Alongside this essential element, the rest is but secondary, whether it be the crushing superiority of Jew over German in certain recognized fields, or the power of the Jewish critical spirit in comparison with the false and credulous idealism of the Germans, or a matter of still lower considerations and of pure material interest. Anti-Jewish propaganda in Germany scarcely mentions these secondary causes. It confines itself to wholesale charges. It charges the Jew with aiming, as Germany does, at domination over the world, with having brought about the First World War and Germany's defeat, and with poisoning the whole of the German people. That is why in *Mein Kampf* Hitler openly advises the Germans *to imitate the Jews*, consecrating themselves to their Race as the Jews do to theirs. Rosenberg insists more than Hitler on Jewish intellectualism, on Asiatic Semitism as a hotbed of corruption, and on the wealth piled up by Jews in Germany; but he thinks, none the less, exactly as his Leader does.

Thus, in order to demolish the other internationalisms, it will suffice to show that they are "*Judaized*," that they are emanations of eternal Judaism. That is the line taken by Nazi doctrine.

Beginning with the Black International (of the Roman Catholic Church), Hitler writes about it in *Mein Kampf* with a certain moderation, not wanting to give a shock at the very outset to the religious feelings of the Austrians or the Bavarians. He contents himself with reproaching German Catholicism with not being national enough, by which he means not anti-Semitic enough. Rosenberg, the Balt, is not so considerate. Popularizing Nietzsche's demonstration, he shows that Catholicism is simply primitive Christianity diverted from its true path and Judaized by Saint Paul. Roman universalism exasperates Rosenberg because it is irreconcilably hostile to races and nations that abuse their sovereignty, and because it establishes common standards, the common morality which Germany calls "slavery." This Nazi doctrinaire goes so far as to praise French free-thought as an opponent of the Church, although elsewhere he condemns its uncompromising intellectualism and the Revolution of 1789 that was its outcome. But he accuses Catholicism of being an immobile monism, a fixed dogmatism, and of exerting everywhere its passion for enforcing uniformity, as though Nazism in its triumph did not fall into errors of that sort!

The lesson from Nietzsche has been learnt. It is in preaching original sin and Christian humility that Rome has destroyed human energy and diverted that great current of vitality, the German will to power. Rosenberg protests, after so many others, against the Christianization of the Teutons. The Church, he says, is at the root of all the German weaknesses. Luther did, indeed, endeavour to Germanize Christianity, but he did not carry his endeavour far enough. And if there are few German Catholics ready to Germanize Catholicism, there are many Protestants, in particular the "German Christians," and the adherents of the "German Faith Movement," ready to lead Lutheranism away from the œcumenical path, to lure it into anti-Semitism, and to separate it from the Old Testament. Thus the transcendental Christianity of sin and redemption would give place to a so-called "heroic" Christianity that would exalt force and would be derived from an "Aryan" Christ.

The attack on Western political and economic liberalism is aimed directly against democracy itself. Here the Nazis include France, Britain, and the United States in the same reprobation. Naturally, Nazism sees Western democracy in the light of the failings of German parliamentarism and of the troubles it met with, for the simple reason that liberalism never conquered German politics. Fundamentally egalitarian, allowing individual values spontaneous expression and automatic emergence from the people, democracy is the antithesis of Hitlerite pseudo-aristocratism. It is attacked because it cannot conceive political life without opposition to the Government, and because it believes in the virtues of free discussion between different opinions or interests and in the general will of the politically educated people.

There would be no harm if the Nazis contented themselves with pointing out the antithesis, inevitable in democracy, between liberty and equality. They attack Western plutocracy bitterly. But it is especially the Jew, once more, whom they imagine that they find at the back of the Western Liberal. For them the Liberal, like the Jew, is a man out of his proper place, a man divorced from "blood and soil," inferior both to the peasant and to the artisan. Not a word about the grandeur of Calvinism or the achievements of the middle class, which Jaurès lyrically praised in *L'Armée Nouvelle*. Nothing but insulting sarcasms for 1789. Rosenberg discovers in that Revolution the Roman and republican Idea, to which he reproaches it with devoting "the dictatorship of the intelligentsia." Always the same clichés about the State as existing for its own sake, about individualism, paper constitutions, the "crust of ready-made ideas," the methods that make of the Western woman "an intellectual depraved by eroticism." All the rancours of the average German find expression in these pages.

Worse still are the tirades against Marxism and Communism. It is still the eternal Jew, as Socialist or Communist leader. Closely related to the West that exploits the urban proletariat, trying to replace the Celestial City of the Christian International, or the democratic ideal of the bourgeois International, by the purely terrestrial objective of the working-class International, Communism, says this Nazi, is the most terrible ferment of corruption to which the Jew can have recourse for the destruction

of nations. The charge Hitler brings in *Mein Kampf* against
the Social Democracy is that *of separating the proletariat from the
nation*. The Jew talks to the worker of his wretchedness in
order to kill his sense of racial and national allegiance. For
Rosenberg, Jewish Marxism devitalizes the workers by uprooting
them and setting them on the international plane; maintains
the class struggle by promising to employers and employed the
same panacea for social evils; denies the true property that
corresponds to each man's creative capacity; and finally preaches
pacifism in order to deliver up the German nation to the hostile
world that surrounds it. Judæo-Socialism attacks colonial
empires, the culture and the divinity of nations, and all that is of
racial substance.

This Nazi criticism passes all German history through a sieve
from this point of view. Its purpose is simply to extirpate every
element of the past that recalls humanism. The first German
Empire is therefore reproached with having tried to impose on
Europe and on Germany the standards of the ancient world
and of Christianity; the seventeenth and eighteenth centuries
are blamed for the philosophy of the Enlightenment and
liberal influences; the Bismarckian empire for its opportunist
parliamentarism and Socialism and its toleration of the Jews;
and the Weimar Republic for having opened wide the floodgates
and totally corrupted Germany on the morrow of her defeat.

So were the arguments of Nietzsche combined with those of
pre-war pan-Germanism. The subject of Europe's "maladies"
was resumed by the Nazis. They proceed, they said, from clarity
of thought and from intellectualism. Fundamentally there was no
change in the argument. This criticism carried its attack to every
point in the European periphery, to the Catholicism of the South,
the liberalism of the West, and the Communism of the East. It
was helped by the fact of the mutual hatred and the active mutual
hostility of the old Internationals.

Racialism is the positive aspect of the Nazi doctrine. Hitler
gives an adequate definition of it (*Mein Kampf*, 1936 edition,
p. 439):

"As a State, the German Reich must include all Germans, with
the task not only of collecting and maintaining the most valuable
stocks of original racial elements in this people, but of slowly and
surely raising them to the dominant position."

It is the gist of H. S. Chamberlain's doctrine.

The Christians used to talk of the Kingdom of God and the

dominion of Satan. The Hitlerites talk of the Reich and the
Gegenreich or counter-Reich. The German by race is the Aryan,
and it is he who is set against the Jew. The relations between
Germany and the world are thus reduced to those existing
between the Nordic element, free from all Jewish alloy, and the
peoples corrupted by the Jewish strain, in which the inferior racial
elements predominate. The German Race, composed of Aryans,
is a "natural" and "primitive" datum. German individuals
exist only in so far as they belong to the Race.

This Race is "Volkstum." A biological link, strong and
fundamental in a different way from the linguistic link. To
Germanize populations by resting content with imposing the
German language on them is to risk mixing Nordic purity with
inferior elements. Hitler well knows that Germany is a mixture
of various races, a mixture furthered by a wide periphery of ill-
established frontiers, by the Thirty Years War, and by immigration on a vast scale. But these elements can be fused by galvaniz-
ing them in relation to the common Enemy, the Jew, and by
subordinating them to the Nordics. Let this operation succeed,
and the Germans will be the masters of the world. Nordism will
play the part of catalyst.

Rosenberg compares this discovery with that of Copernicus.
The State no longer revolves round the individual; on the
contrary, the individual is centred on the State and gravitates
round the "Volk," the people. Since it is inevitably composite,
the *Volkstum* must be crystallized round a dominant racial
element. Hitlerite racialism thus applies to the Reich the
corporate Idea which the Christians apply to the Church when
they talk of the mystical Body of Christ, an idea the European
monarchies of the past also utilized for their dynastic conceptions.
But National Socialism is before all else the heir of the dream of
the eighteenth and nineteenth centuries, the dream of an organic
religious German Community, a sort of new Greece or revivified
Church which, in contrast with the individualist and absolutist
Western State, would be a body existing before its members and
claiming total sacrifice from them. This racial Idea claims to live
in men's brains as an image or Myth and in reality as Reich.
Here imagination and militarization keep pace together.

The aim is, in fact, to establish a harmony between the body,
taken as point of departure, and the spirit, considered as point of
arrival. Spiritual activity will henceforth be exhausted in the
accomplishment of functions regulated on the model of the body.

The Race is the matrix of the German people, which, proceeding from it, lives and develops as an organized body. Thereafter, apparently, the German considers himself simply as a healthy body whose purpose is a determined technical function, each person's activity being the measure of his freedom—his freedom within the national body that has to be "shaped."

This crude and vulgar biologism breaks with the sciences, with the notion of the spirit, with humanism. If man is a microcosm and a living organism, he belongs to all the kingdoms. He can therefore be studied under every aspect, in accordance with the most diverse sciences. The thing that is frightful is to see him only from the biological angle. But the bodily ideas and symbols of racialism are an integral part of its political system. This is a complete bankruptcy of the values represented precisely by the mental sciences. In a country like Germany, men's souls are delivered up to the most terrible confusion, to a sort of anarchy in the void. No form of humanism has been able to hold them and impose on them a lasting rule. Then has come this authoritarian biologism, a poor "*ersatz*" for so many fugitive gods!

Rosenberg defines with some precision the term "blood," which makes its appearance so often in National Socialist ideology. Applied to the social body, the term signifies "the current of red blood, of real life, that goes surging through the circulatory system of every authentic race and culture." To be an Aryan thus means to feel passing through one the current that traverses the whole national body. As for individual life, blood signifies the unconscious and spontaneous region of life that brings to man the determinations of the Race. Rational activity separates us from that obscure existential depth. When it regards itself as an end in itself, it removes us from the national Community. There must no longer be any opposition between the individual ego and the people.

In the past, romanticism conferred on collectivities and nations the attribute of personality. To-day Nazism confers on the German Community the attributes of the body, of the biological organism. If, says this base philosophy, the individual plunges into the depths of his being, he grasps there by direct revelation the "commandments of the blood." Dreams, religious rites, and ancestral myths may serve this revelation. It is from these appeals and these mysterious orders that the *Gesittung*, the normal attitude of the individual belonging to a community, emanates.

This degenerate romanticism Rosenberg calls revolutionary science. He opposes the *continuity* of action to the *discontinuity* of the clear consciousness. The liaison between the two, he thinks, is assured by *intuition*, which thinks solely in *symbols*, not in *concepts*. This is still the old anti-intellectual cliché.

The national Myth thus decomposes into symbols which are revealed to the intuition by signs, colours, or sounds. In Nazism the uniform and badges, the quasi-ritual gestures, and the swastika on a red field have a special virtue. The framing of this national symbolism in representative figures of remarkable men or women is claimed as a return to the Greeks. We have here all the elements of a pseudo-religion. Not that that religion repudiates the promptings of reason and of technical activity; but it aims at subordinating them to the racial Myth. "*Deutschtum*," Germanism, is manifested by a determined policy, by a relentless war, as well as by an appropriate common end, philosophy, and literature.

This is what this primitive romanticism calls uniting obscure forces with clear intelligence. The new thing in this linking is its application to racial ends. It is an emptier and more artificial chimera than the Western rationalism which the Germans revile because they confuse it with their own errors. This absurd racialism kills in Germans, as if in exasperation, every diversity and every autonomy, however legitimate and natural. Territorial States, political parties, religious confessions, professional and trade union organizations, all are ended in Germany. "We have not," writes Rosenberg, "to conserve the forms of yesterday, *but to concentrate the force of blood and that of will*, for the individual personality as for all the ethnic elements of Germany, *on a Germany one, strong, and great.*"

The notion of "soil" follows that of "blood" and conforms to it. *Lebensraum*, "room to live," is simply indefinitely expansible space, because proportionate to the strength the blood gives, through well-established circulation, to the whole body of Germany. This space grows with the very cohesion of the Race. The Race is more than its members, more than the State, more than the instruments of which it makes use. It *pre-exists* all these.

This biologism calls for precisions. It is not enough to tell the Germans that they must breed pure. It must be proved to them that the *Nordic* element preponderates among them and that racial crystallization must proceed round it. A racialist like

H. F. K. Günther takes up H. S. Chamberlain's problem in apparently more scientific terms. Each man is part of an "hereditary mass" (*Erbmasse*) of which our body and soul are but a particular expression. All that matters is selection, that is to say, the prevalence of Nordism over the other racial elements of Germany. Industrialization has menaced this prevalence by mixing all races in the towns. Nordic superiority is expressed in physiological and psychological qualities which Günther analyses at great length. The Nordic is the master, the dominator, the Leader *par excellence*. He possesses both drive and technical dependability. He is to be found in every higher civilization. And the way for Germany to cultivate the Nordic qualities is to Prussify herself. The Nordic spirit, it is added, is the very feeling for life in its full expansion, *for the life that renounces itself rather than accept too narrow limitations*. The Nordic spirit is totalitarian by definition. *It was born in the vast spaces of the north German and Russian plain*. It loves limitless horizons. It was the Nordic race, not the Mediterranean race, that originated the ancient culture. Günther brings a mass of erudition to the support of the theses of Rosenberg's *Mythus des 20. Jahrhunderts* ("Myth of the Twentieth Century").

Günther admits however, that Nordism is degenerating. This is "de-Germanization." He explains it, of course, by Christianity. Every time Germanism tried to lift its head, in the mediæval cities or in the Lutheran Reformation, Christianity overthrew it. Later Liberalism, Socialism, and Judaism treated it with the same brutality. The Nordics have often betrayed their own cause. And Germany, menaced on the West by capitalism and on the East by Communism, must "re-Nordicize" herself to achieve her destiny. That means that she must *create a new nobility*, as Walther Darré counsels her. This new nobility must no longer separate itself from the German peasantry. The new *élite* will be composed not only of individuals but of *families* in which the gift of the Leader will be hereditary. Germany will thus do better than the modern democracies, which exhaust peoples by their mode of selection. This new nobility will be a true *Order*, worthy of its great ancestor, the Teutonic Order. Was not that Order the first national State to dare to struggle against the universal Church?

What is wanted is thus an *organized élite*, responsible for guiding the people. It will nationalize the masses, which feed in their wretchedness on international Socialism. The masses are intolerant and brutal by nature. This fact must be utilized, and Nordism made into a popular reality, violent and irresistible. For Hitler recognizes certain natural virtues in the masses—the spirit of comradeship, solidarity in distress, modesty of needs, and especially the capacity for sacrifice. These masses must no longer be offered an abstract programme. Inspiring images must be set before them. Rational policy and organization must come after prophecy and mysticism. Luther, Frederick II, and Wagner worked through suggestion as much as through direct argument. Hitler followed the same line as those great figures.

The complementary term to "mass" is "person." What place does it occupy in the racialist system? By a strange paradox, the word *Persönlichkeit*, personality, is constantly in Nazi mouths. The personality is the responsible leader, furnished with special power. It is equivalent simply to militancy, combativeness. It implies the most rigorous obedience on the part of the "following" (*Gefolgschaft*). Amorphousness for the masses, dictatorship for the leaders—that is the Hitlerite system. An active minority is alone capable of guiding the multitude. For the weak are legion, while aggressive natures are not very numerous. This crude militarism implies a sort of democracy of pure force. We are asked to believe that it has found the secret of the old Germanic democracy. In every healthy organization, we are told, it is the strongest who maintain the circulation of life and the balance of the parts.

In this absurd sociology—absurd because primitive and retrogressive—man is distinguished from the animals only by the fact that he can invent a thousand tricks for maintaining his ascendancy. The law of the jungle is the favourite theme of the speeches at Nuremberg. When Hitler appeals at Nuremberg to the example of Prussian discipline, he misuses the term. His imitation of Prussian discipline is of the crudest. He adds that in the racialist system the collective institution alone has any lasting value, and, like the Catholic priesthood, it cannot be compromised by individual failings. The régime will have in its service none but born fighters, *Kampfnaturen*.

The Leader is not only the strong man; he is also the *dreamer*, the *visionary*, the inventor of *myths* offering an image to the popular will. Just as contemporary aviation has materialized the myth of Icarus, and the well-being acquired by men may be set alongside the myth of Paradise, so, it is claimed, the Germans will materialize the myth of the Vikings. This, it is added, is not Cæsarism.

The Cæsar is a demigod who rules through the bureaucracy and the army. The Hitlerite Leader unites *authority* with *popularity*. He is a faithful reflection of the *Volkstum*. He incarnates the collective "style of life." He has in the highest degree the Germanic virtues—faithfulness, the sense of honour, and heroism.

Nazism claims to be a discipline. In this regard it looks toward the strongest German State, Prussia. Its cleverness consists simply in its intimate mixture of Prussia and the Reich, disciplinary methods and the mysticism of the national Community. This latter is no longer the rich tradition of culture that in the past could be contrasted with the impoverishing action of Prussia, and thus nothing now prevents Prussian force from placing itself completely in the service of the régime. Nor does anything prevent the régime from utilizing the Prussian State and taking over its hegemony.

In fact, the Hitlerite leaders went farther than Bismarck, farther even than Spengler and the theses he published in *Preussentum und Sozialismus*. Hitler, in *Mein Kampf*, is unceasing in his praises of Prussia, of her ideally heroic virtues, and of her formation, the great triumph of German statecraft, an "artificial" and deliberate formation, he says, in contrast with the "natural" development of Britain and France. The existing militarism emanates from the Prussian method and spirit. Rosenberg calls the Nazis "the Prussians of the twentieth century." Prussia, according to him, brought to the Third Reich the union between the *worker* and the *soldier*.

This primacy of Prussia implies that of Germany among the nations of the Continent. We have here once more Spengler's pet idea that Prussia was called upon to defend all Europe from the menace of the lower classes (Bolshevism) and from alien races (Jews and the yellow and black races). Germany is to be the national State affirming its creative will, *the State supremely fitted to exercise hegemony*. It was a short stage from the *Volk ohne Raum* (people without space) to *Lebensraum* (living space, or room to live). Everything is eloquent here of a revolutionary, that is to say *destructive*, dynamism. For there are peoples on the up grade and peoples on the down grade. Germany thus has, in principle, unrestricted rights over the small States and the decadent nations. Why? *Because she knows the eternal laws of Life.* Her mission is essentially providential. The right of the strongest is based both on *nature* and on *reason*. The complaint about the place the victorious Allies had reserved for Germany in

Europe is succeeded by the brutal and violent affirmation of the will to domination. Germany is the Mother of Peoples, the *vagina nationum*.

Hitlerite propaganda worked to impress this doctrine on all men's minds. *Mein Kampf* was its first manual.

The aim was to engender in the nation and abroad what Hitler calls "spiritual terror" (*der geistige Terror*), to effect the intimidation of minds deprived by fear and distress of all spontaneous thought and ready to adopt unresistingly the affirmations required of everybody. It was a masterful utilization of doubt and resulting lassitude in face of a situation that was too complex and problems that were too difficult. A sort of general "nihilism" took possession of the masses. There came a void in public opinion. It was filled by the "*ersatz*" of slogans repeated a hundred times.

Just a few points of view, said Hitler, of vast scope. It was on this nihilism that the militarization of thought was grafted. The citizen was treated as a soldier who must not know the secrets of strategy, but who nevertheless must risk his whole person and his whole existence in the battle. A generalized militarization of the intelligence, kept alive by the leaders and accepted by the mass. Indecision and general lack of determination, says Hitler, are worse than imperfect or even lying slogans. Once more, *cohesion for the sake of cohesion, and with a view to total military reconstruction.*

It is natural that this propaganda should be directed especially to youth. Indecision and uncertainty are the mark of a bourgeoisie and a proletariat that are behind the times. Thus the young must be extricated from these decrepit surroundings and placed in an intellectual and moral atmosphere in which the Nazi affirmations appear obviously right. A "lightning" propaganda thus produces "the common will." That will is at first the will of a minority; propaganda makes it an affair of the majority. That is the way totalitarianism is reached. Simple images, ardent myths suggested to elementary brains, huge spectacular demonstrations and vehement speeches, symbols, badges, uniforms, resort to lying and false doctrine, to hatred and rancour, all this calculated primitiveness, so deliberately brought to bear, assembles all the methods already invented in America and, later, in Russia. Hitler knows what he owes to the Soviets.

It was in the name of this propaganda that Hitler, in his famous speech of May 21, 1935, presented himself to the Western democracies as the Leader of a people who, he said, followed him "spontaneously" and had invested him with "total responsibility." Goebbels found the phrase for this propaganda —"*romantic realism.*" The German had passed abruptly from the sad grey everyday life, the depressing "*Alltag,*" to the great collective intoxications lavished on him in festivals and celebrations. Parliamentarism and free discussion, it was claimed, were not meant to be interposed between the leaders and the people. This violent fixation of men's minds on a few points, this affirmation of a mysterious parity between the will of the multitude and that of the rulers, were the antithesis of middle-class or Socialist intellectualism. And it was pretended that there was a liberation of the "intact will" and the "perfectly conserved energies" which Goebbels declared that the Germans still possessed in 1918.

Thus propaganda both *nationalized* and *socialized* the masses. It was more than simple propaganda by persuasion. Bound up with military training, it was a system of education, a complete pedagogy, a sort of culture, simple in its formulæ but clever in the employment of its methods, the aim of which was to mould all men's souls alike. It is what is called "moral armament" of the people, or, if you will, *bringing the individual into the state of the people.* Such means are simply the exact counterpart of the intellectual anarchy engendered by total nihilism. They pursue a single aim—*pure action, activism for its own sake,* a sort of unrestrained and unlimited revolutionary dynamism. The only test of the propaganda is its success. It is a spiritual dictatorship installed upon total material and intellectual distress.

That is why Goebbels declares that in a totalitarian régime there is no further need for popularity. The Leader does not seek popularity. Since there is fundamental agreement between his will and that of the mass, he can *impose* his will *by force* on the crowd. Like Frederick II, the Leader is servant of the State. And it is in the name of that providential service that he demands absolute obedience. Nazism can speak, in a sense, of *legal* and *plebiscitary* means. Propaganda is a *plebiscite starting from the top.* The crowd is put through a plebiscite. This, it is claimed, makes the Third Reich a "moral" Reich, because it is brought to the acceptance of a totalitarian truth. The Nazis charge William II, the Austrian pan-German Schoenerer, and Primo de Rivera with having aimed at military dictatorship *without contact with the people.* The soldier nation is dictatorship accepted by all, a sort *of dictatorship integrated in principle in the substance of the people.*

For the people is an end in itself. It grows and flourishes *naturally*, like a tree. The individual is there only to participate in that growth, which alone forms the basis of law. He is there to make of his people a "world" people, ready to make itself felt everywhere. It is a sort of *national, not class, Communism.* This Communism distributes burdens between the members of the community, but *without committing itself to absolute social justice.* Propaganda persuades each person that that is the *true* Socialism. This Socialism is simply a crude and brutal solidarism. But it charges itself, in regard to other nations, precisely with effecting their internal decomposition, acting as a virus or, in Goebbels' image, as a *poison gas* that penetrates the most solid objects. Nazism claims to have what Bismarckism had not—*a political Idea.* The old nationalism was inspired only by a vague romantic ideal. The Idea, however, loses its shadowiness and gains concrete substance when it descends to the crowd and invades practical existence. It is by the Idea that Nazism unites the militants and creates the Order of to-morrow. Propaganda provides the link between Party and people. It passes the militarism achieved in the Party on to a popular mass that has to be won little by little for total militarism. All German teaching and culture is subordinated to that end, whether through physical regeneration and sportor through an intellectual training that assures to each one the indispensable technical knowledge.

That is why Nazism claims to make an end of the internationality of science and art. For the Nazis, research and creation are differentiated according to peoples and races. There is a "German" physics and a "German" mathematics. The theses of Spengler, in his *Decline of the West*, are pushed to absurdity. All the rest is but false internationalism—that is to say, Jewish, Catholic, Liberal, or Socialist. The *savant*, the *artist*, and the *soldier* are one. This is, indeed, the vulgar and atrocious form of ideas which were long familiar to the German *élite*. To realize this, read Thomas Mann's *Friedrich II. und die grosse Koalition* published at the outset of the First World War.

3. *The army of workers and soldiers*

It is within that framework that there took place, quite naturally, the organization of German labour, the social and economic ordering that made possible total military reconstruction.

A certain mysticism floats over this Community of Labour (*Arbeitsgemeinschaft*). That is why it may lead, by its own logic, to consequences transcending the existing régime. Hitler celebrates it in *Mein Kampf.* He starts from his own lower middle-class experience, from the gradual proletarization of that particular world, which lived apart from the workers' world and did not want on any terms, in its social decline, to rejoin that world. *A world without pity,* remarks Hitler, referring to the lower middle class, a world full of rancour and resentment, *because it has had a long struggle to climb the social ladder and has a horror of those whom it leaves behind.*

It would be impossible to supply a better description of the social origin of Nazism. Hitler was well aware both of the excesses of industrialization and of the responsibilities of the employers. But he was never a Socialist in the true sense of the word. His idea was to retain the capitalist and employer class in order to incorporate it in the régime of the Third Reich, to give it a new lease of life after having been carried into power by it, delivering over to it a mass *part proletarian and part proletarized,* a submissive mass of manual and intellectual workers, a mass in which the middle classes had been entirely absorbed. These desiderata of Hitler's paved the way for the desires of a ruling caste that believed it could escape from the chastisement it deserved *by profiting from a double decline to which it had largely contributed.*

This fundamental disequilibrium of the social classes was cloaked, so to speak, by Nazism beneath a mysticism that affirmed once more that Germany's social régime would be *in conformity with fundamental verities,* with the *Ursinn der Dinge,* as Hitler wrote in *Mein Kampf.* In 1933, at Nuremberg, he spoke of those eternal verities that respond to the sure instinct of the masses, an instinct that "forewarns and saves." The tribune did not hesitate to speak of the "social musicality" of the Germans! It implied the "genius" of the Leaders and the absolute submission of the Executants.

To utilize for the achievement of absolute domination Lutheran religious devotion and old-time patriarchalism; to declare that Nordism alone can conciliate the classes which Jewish Marxism sets at each other's throat, was the game for Hitler and his followers to play. They wanted to make men believe in a "brazen justice" that would constrain everyone to act in the interest of the community, so as to unite "individual capacity" and "racial value." Nowhere are the Hitlerite sophisms more appalling than on the social plane.

The leader of the Labour Front, Robert Ley, elaborates this definition of social *Soldatentum*. He gives it both a *religious* and a *disciplinary* tinge. Racialism, in his puerile phrase, expresses the Divine Will. The Führer is the new Christ, the heroic Christ who has suffered in order to destroy Liberal individualism, whence have come capitalism and Marxism. This leads Ley to a passionate defence of the *Arbeitsgemeinschaft*, the community of labour, as both *biological* and *religious*. It is the sacred Hive, the Church of organized labour, the Army of the discipline that is to cover the amorphous Weimar Germany with its close-meshed network. The occupational order to be built up will thus emanate from an internal harmony conditioned by Race. And this will be the union between the *creative instinct* and the *disciplined intelligence*.

Organized by the Order that is the Party, the army of labour will be the clamp that will hold the still inchoate and impotent mass. It will be a sort of *providential despotism*, based on *soldierly comradeship*. The German working masses will emerge from the debilitating Marxism, cured of their malady. They will rejoin the employers and the middle class in the National Community (*Volksgemeinschaft*). For it is the soul of the worker that is in question. Labour is the activity through which we introduce order into the chaos of universal matter. Chaos within us is *instinct*, and without is *soil*. Into it must be introduced *directing intelligence* and *organized space*. Here each will work according to his vocation, which is his destiny. Everyone will be *a soldier of the Reich*. Everyone has the right to work. The Labour Front, that Corporation of Corporations, thus absorbs into itself all classes and all categories of workers. It allays the class struggle from within. The *worker* and the *soldier* become indistinguishable. Their freedom is the degree of mastery they acquire, a mastery that is merged in the collective mastery.

This mysticism thus throws a veil of deceit over every real difficulty and every possible injustice. We are told that there is absolute equality between the German workers, from the greatest employer to the least labourer. But inequality is born again elsewhere. For that giant organization the Third Reich is governed by three principles—the responsibility of the Leader, the normal relations between leaders and executants, and so-called "honourable" agreements. On this principle, it is claimed, the employer will be unable to evade his mission. As for employees and workers, they will be consoled for the hard times by the feeling of the beauty of labour and the solidarity that unites them with their comrades. Each group of workers, each enterprise, is a "nucleus of force," and the union of these nuclei will restore Germany's lost prestige.

Between workers there will no longer be any contractual bond, governed by the "Roman" spirit, but a bond of religious member-ship, with a racial tinge. The cosmic laws will preside over the destinies of German labour. To work is to observe the discipline indispensable for all creation. A thoroughly "soldierly" moral system, claiming to restore the dignity of the worker, his elasticity, his energy, his joy in living. Nazism used this slogan, this constant apologia for the occupation, the "*Stand*," as a powerful lever with which to oust the Social Democracy and the Catholic Centre, with their feeble and antiquated ideologies, and to con-quer the middle classes by offering them a common programme.

From this emerged the so-called "corporative" organization, "*der ständische Aufbau.*" This labour corporation, embracing all the separate corporations, is nominally autonomous. It is supposed to settle its affairs itself, co-ordinating the divergent interests for the greatest good of the community. All this is pure show. In reality the corporations and the Labour Front have no autonomy. Here again the machinery of power dominates everything. The famous "*Führerprinzip,*" the "leader principle," is fundamental in it. The corporations are entirely dependent on the Party and its leaders. They are subjected to an unparalleled fury of regimentation. Rules, budget, meetings, agenda—all are decided in advance. The essential thing is that all the corporations shall docilely carry out, on the plane of the nation's labour, the will of the Government.

Everyone, except Jews, must belong to the Labour Front. All other trade unions or professional associations were suppressed. Membership is ostensibly permissive but in fact obligatory. Workers and employees have obeyed without a murmur, able only to offer tacit resistance by the indirect means of sabotage or inertia. The employers hesitated, waited to be asked, and entered the Front only one by one. The structure of the Front is horizontal regionally and vertical occupationally.   The leader, Robert Ley, is entirely devoted to Hitler.

Within the Labour Front, from which every idea of contract is excluded, the employer becomes the "Führer" in the enterprise. The rest of the personnel plays the part of "Gefolgschaft."   The Nazis have consequently held that the spirit of true Germanic democracy penetrates the whole social and economic organization. The employer fixes the conditions of work, prices, and wages in accordance with governmental directions.   It is an autocratic economy in an autarkic framework.   The right to strike disappears.   A worker's card is required for every engagement and every transfer.   The control is absolute and the freedom to transfer virtually non-existent.   The *Vertrauensräte* or "trust councils" do not represent the interests of the workers.   They have nothing in common with the Weimar *Betriebsräte* or factory councils.   They are purely consultative.   The Labour Trustee (*Treuhänder der Arbeit*) imposes Nazi law on each economic region.

In this Labour Front the employers are clearly not on the same footing as the other social categories.   Hitler has pointed out that "the great industrialists have reached a dominant position through their capacity and their own efforts."   *They are of superior race.*   They will therefore be respected.   That is how "industrial peace" is assured.   You have, as Ley says, "the truly Socialist drill-ground and barracks," and, in Goebbels' words, "a *Socialism of soldiers*, hard and fierce, a Socialism of *action*, not of pale theory, *a Socialism that concerns not a class but a whole people, the Socialism that inspired the Kings of Prussia when they created our army and our body of officials, the Socialism of which the enthusiasm vibrated in the march of the Prussian grenadiers.*"   Hitlerism is a "master" class dominating the obedient working masses.   It is *an economic system under command.*

This organization of labour, which proceeds in its camps to a preparatory mixing of social classes, spreads the net of its Chambers of Labour over the whole country.   This ensures that the orders from the Government are strictly carried out.   A certain autonomy is allowed to the employers and managers, but there is none at all for employees and workers.   The agricultural corporation has been organized in the same spirit.   Its *Arbeitsgemeinschaft* or labour "community," closely bound to the Party, absolutely dominates all economic and intellectual activity.   The principles of the Labour Front are those of "autarky" (self-sufficiency) and of the utmost possible militarization—autarky for foodstuffs and raw materials, militarization in the work of the farms, shops, and factories.

At the base of the institutions which thus regulate the whole of German labour are almost always the ideas of Gottfried Feder, whom Hitler discovered in the early days at Munich. Feder talked of "reagrarianizing" Germany by directing back to the countryside part of the unsettled population of the great towns. Hitlerism realized that it was necessary to restore to the countryside a prosperous peasantry, and that the subsidies to agriculture had been entirely absorbed by the great landowners. The law of hereditary domains, which sought to tie the peasant families to the soil, and the peasant corporation, are the institutions by means of which the régime proposed to endow Germany with a considerable category of *solid and stable peasant proprietors*, each permitted to own up to 125 hectares (310 acres), enough to maintain a family without engaging in capitalist enterprise. Nearly half the arable land, with about 850,000 peasant owners, comes within this category.

The effort was made to remove the peasant from the influence of supply and demand by fixing minimum prices for cereals and produce. In this rigid system the peasant has become a sort of social official, compelled to adapt his production to the requirements of national consumption. He is the peasant-soldier, heir of the great Nordic tradition dear to Walther Darré, the Minister of Agriculture, who is hostile to the Roman idea of individual ownership, and an enthusiastic disciple of the Germanic idea, which conceived freedom as *service* rendered to the community. This is the peasant *Soldatentum* (soldierliness) which, according to Darré, was the basis of the great Prussian tradition of the officer and official devoted to the *Staatsräson*, the principle of the service of the State. It is owing to this mysticism and to the adoption of the appropriate measures that it has been possible to organize in Germany a sort of *alimentary autarky*. But that autarky has not been able to escape from a grave deficit, imposing privations on the people and producing a discontent that has long been visibly welling up from under this disciplinary crust.

Feder also traced the broad lines of the solution to be found for industry. He attacked the very idea of *profit-making* and of *individual profit*. The opposition between Jew and "Aryan" served as a symbol for the contrast to be established between the *profit* system and the system of *social service*. Hitlerism claimed to be creating the basis of true property, that which aims simply at *meeting the needs of the people.* That is why Nazism tolerated the great industrial enterprises. The sacred names of Krupp, Thyssen, and Mannesmann were officially recognized. These "creative employers" were, however, retained only in so far as they were bent to the service of the dictatorial State in the matter of rearmament. The idea of the profit-sharing system demanded by Feder was, naturally, dismissed. The Nazi socializers were no more than the accomplices of the astute magnates who subsidized them. Rearmament permitted the wheels of the vast German industrial machine to turn, and the workers to work, under a system of fixed wages that enabled the enterprises to continue to reap fine dividends.

As for finance, Feder had dreamed, as is well known, of liberating Germany from capitalism, from what he called "bondage to interest" (*Zinsknechtschaft*). Feder was in revolt against the unhealthy accumulation of capital that engendered the tyranny of interest and dividend. He charged the public finances with turning into private finance. He conceived money as a draft on work done, and moved in a circle of ideas that recalled those of J. G. Fichte and his closed commercial State. Feder wanted the State *to remain entirely master of money* and to demand disinterested labour of its citizens. The State, he said, would itself create money, *in proportion to the work done.* He thought that in that way inflation could be avoided, and that the stability of money should be effected by measuring it in terms of a precise number of hours of work. The Reichsbank should assure the circulation of the medium of payment. Thanks to this pretty system, Feder added, *Germany would conquer.* Feder forgot only one thing, that imports have to be paid for in gold currency.

Clearly German industry was prospering between 1933 and 1938. But this prosperity was due entirely to *State contracts.* These contracts had to do mainly with rearmament, and the prosperity of industry was thus based entirely on unproductive expenditure. The consumable goods industries were deliberately neglected. Thus unproductive expenditure steadily gained upon productive. *Armaments grew and permitted territorial conquests, but the conditions of living deteriorated.* The average of salaries and wages diminished. The total of earnings grew from 26 to 32 milliards of marks, but the number of employed persons had increased by several millions. The condition of the workers had been maintained at a *constant* but *very low* level.

Since the economic recovery was a function of rearmament, industry was booming, but there was a grave shortage of skilled labour and technicians. The problem of exports and foreign trade was not satisfactorily solved. The total value of imports and exports continually fell. Resort had to be made to the barter system. Foreign commercial debts remained unsettled. And the tragic question began to be asked, *What will happen if the State becomes saturated with armaments and is compelled to reduce or terminate its orders?*

In fact, during the first Four-Year Plan, Germany followed classical procedure, thanks to Dr Schacht. It was not the control of exchange alone (dating from 1931) that neutralized the inflation of credit. The old debt had been wiped out, and there was a considerable margin for fresh indebtedness. Moreover, Germany possessed an enormous industrial equipment. And thanks to important undertakings, and especially to excessive armament, she had been able to keep wages at a very low level, to begin an expansion of short-term credit, and to take the most elementary precautions, making a considerable fiscal effort, appealing for voluntary contributions, and assuring considerable profits to industry. All this was a long way from Gottfried Feder's doctrine. As there was drastic control of consumption, *the expansion of credit was prevented from reaching the consumer*, money was brought back *into the banks*, and, at whatever cost, prices were stabilized.

But this bold financial policy, while it assured stability, met with grave difficulties under the second Four-Year Plan. This time unproductive expenditure so greatly exceeded productive that Dr Schacht himself raised the alarm. A return had to be made to an old invention of Brüning's, taxation bonds (*Steuerscheine*). How could inflation be avoided while suspending the restrictions imposed on consumption? The Germany of 1938–39 bore witness to a *failing control over events* that recalls that of the pre-war months of 1914. Too many political amateurs were taking the place of the technicians in this domain. Had not the time come to choose between frantic militarism and the equipment of Central Europe? Hitler made himself the defender of capitalism and the adversary of Communism. He did not want to proceed like the Russians to violent expropriation. But with his taxation bonds he was arriving at the same result.

The Party and the economic system were thus carried away by a sort of revolutionary dynamism. Behind the first phase of the

Hitlerite revolution the second phase was beginning to show itself. Just as the Party was divided between conservative reaction and a very daring Left-wing extremism, so the Labour Front was being carried away by the pressure of the young generation, which agreed neither with the psychology of the Prussian officer nor with the demagogy of the Third Reich. The majority, dismissing reasonable solutions, were thinking of a State Socialism more comprehensive than had already been introduced, *a sort of integrally planned "totales Wehrreich"* (totally militarized Reich). The demand was for a consistent dynamism, denuded of hypocrisy.

To get an idea of this state of feeling it is necessary to read *Der Arbeiter*, by E. Jünger. This new-style Nazi dreams of a labour democracy that would be a true synthesis of the most authentic nationalism and the sincerest Socialism. *This time the opposition between the remainder of the aristocracy or of the capitalist class and the proletarized or proletarian masses would disappear.* A relentless technical planning would take its place, embracing *all* the members of the Community without distinction. This would be the most radical anti-bourgeoisism, the end of the old social and economic organization. The old system enjoyed the comforts of *technical progress*. It turned technical achievement to the consecration of social injustice and the flabbiness of a prosperous few. The new system would be inspired by *Russian planning* and would make of Germany a *classless State*. Labour and its rational needs would take the place of demagogic leaders and profiteers. There would be no more peasants, employers, and workers. The labourer, whatever his work, would be the *soldier* of the future. The *Soldatentum* of the Third Reich would attain its true level. There would no longer be any difference between the *combatant* and the *non-combatant*.

And then this total mobilization would be extended to the whole *world*. Pure domination (*Herrschaft*) would take the place of progress in the optimistic eighteenth-century sense of the word. The waters of Fascism and Communism would mix. These two would be integral labour and pure preparation for war. Prussia would realize herself through Russia and Russia through Prussia. For the proletarians were represented in the Hitlerite Party. They were penetrating it with their substance. They were developing their ideas under the very eyes of the present leaders, who sensed the coming of their twilight. In short, the machinery of power seemed to be swamping the Party itself. It was sufficient for itself, and becoming an end in itself. The mass was becoming radicalized. It was entering into the very fabric of Nazism, and abandoning its passivity. Like the Girondins of the past, the existing Nazis could no longer arrest the formidable dynamism of the movement. If it was not prevented from doing so, the vast machine would make a clean sweep everywhere.

The new army would be the crown of the edifice.

The old Prusso-German army had been a force supporting tradition, one of the most solid supports of the decaying Wilhelmian régime. On the eve of 1914 Harden had declared that the army was the only intact power in Germany, the only one not dangerously "gangrened" by Socialism. It clearly had its system of morals, its rule of life, its sterling patriotism, and a collective conception that was inspired on certain points by Western Christianity and in particular by the Lutheran ideas on defensive war. War and violence were for it the *ultima ratio*; a sort of inevitable offshoot of politics. In any case, even if, faced with the deliberate barbarism of the present day, one is tempted to idealize the picture, this army held aloof from politics. The German officer was proud of what he called his "correctness." It is true that, though the German army did its duty in 1914, it may have had no clear knowledge of the ends for which it was being sacrificed. For the offensive of 1914 was no *ultima ratio*. Pan-Germanism was the moral condemnation of the German army.

War, total mobilization, and defeat had profoundly modified the German military organism. The Nazis were now ready to declare with Göring that the officer and the soldier have a duty to be crafty, crooked, Machiavellian. The army must serve the Party and its diabolical doctrine. And this, unquestionably, was a fundamental change.

It is certain that the Reichswehr, as built up by the Allies with their own hands, did not support the Weimar Republic. In 1932–33 it did nothing to save it. When Hitler came into power, and especially when he began to reconstruct the military machine, the Reichswehr played his game, which was plainly also its own. But it inevitably became more and more the instrument of the National Socialist Party. It ran the risk of thus losing, as every other constituted body had done, its autonomy and its moral dignity.

The German army thus vacillated between a parliamentary

democracy that it never wanted and a dynamic Revolution which, little by little, dragged it into the worst adventures of pan-Germanism. Monarchical in origin, its only means of recovering the balance and the traditionalism for which certain conservatives longed was through its own return to monarchy. But could it return? Did not any return seem more and more improbable? In other words, it was no longer possible to see how it could become what it should be, the instrument of an order to be restored within the framework of reasonable solutions. And as youth became more and more nazified, the very substance of the army changed profoundly, though it was never able to identify itself entirely with the régime.

The consequence of this false situation was that the direction of the new "Wehrmacht" lacked firmness and clearness. Its attitude remained mysterious. It was divided in objective. The German corps of officers was in a sort of intermediate state, in a regrettable confusion that deprived the army of the unity of will that it should have had.

The fundamental issue was whether the army personnel accepted or not the "soldier" ideal of the Third Reich which we have just been analysing. That ideal tended to abolish the old frontiers between the *civil* and the *military*. It carried the "Wehrmacht" beyond the traditional mission of the army. Was the army to be confused with the "Wehrreich," the purely military Empire of which some dreamed in Germany? Was it to become the *absolute power* that would end by devouring everything in Germany, economic life, culture, private life, society itself with its liberties, its diversities, its autonomies? *Would the army make itself the docile instrument of the greatest revolution of all times, a nameless, unprecedented revolution*, before which the Western world would recoil, a sort of *military Communism à la prussienne*, under which peace would be reduced to submitting to the exigencies of war, not war to the exigencies of peace? Thus understood, the German Revolution would be total German mobilization, with a permanent war economy, with integrally military education and culture, the end of civilian existence. *The army would absorb the nation*, and planning would be merged in the economic aspects of military organization.

In order to understand how such ideas gained currency in present-day Germany it is as well to retrace the broad lines of the history of the military institution since the First World War.

The mobilization between 1914 and 1918, on an ever-increasing scale, made of the German army, for the first time, a sort of absolutely independent power. The very part played by the personality of Ludendorff through those four years well shows how the military power had rapidly absorbed the civil and political power, which had already shown itself almost non-existent under the imperial monarchy. Neither the Emperor nor his chancellors nor the Reichstag had been able to stand against the army. The collapse of Weimar was foreshadowed in that of the imperial régime.

That, no doubt, is why for such a man as Ludendorff the armistice counted always as *merely an interruption*: the game was to go on. Instead of being a consolidating element, the army, even in the form of the simple "Reichswehr" of 100,000 men, and the police that completed it, maintained themselves on the plane of absolute militarism. The army considered war as a normal and permanent state. This enables us to realize the immense mistake made by the Allies. They did not see that, in order to maintain the Weimar democracy, it should have been given, as it could have been, a Republican army, and not a nucleus of Prussian militarist resistance.

It is probable that the failure of the 1923 putsch showed Hitler that it was neither possible nor even desirable to substitute for the regular army, restricted as it was, the S.A. and the Brown-shirt militia, working through an insurrectional movement and in concert with Ludendorff. The Reichswehr, aided by the police, defended itself well at that moment. It was the resolute attitude of the Reichswehr that made the putsch abortive. But Hitler learned the lesson of his failure. He was a great admirer of the Prussian army, and later wrote an apologia for it in *Mein Kampf*; and *he resolved to leave it to continue its tradition, and to act in regard to it as he acted in regard to the employers*. It was better to respect it while drawing it little by little toward the revolution he was preparing. The Brownshirts must not, he thought, become a sort of second army, a clandestine army capable of rivalry with the regular army.

From then on there developed a gulf within the Nazi Party between two radically different views, one favourable to collaboration with the Reichswehr and the other favouring the constitution of a separate army, integrally National Socialist. The Hitler-Röhm duel had begun.

Röhm wanted to reinforce the S.A. and S.S. little by little, and to draw from them a truly revolutionary army. *The Reichswehr would then have sunk to a militia, a national guard without intrinsic value or any great future.* Violence would then have suddenly won the day against the constitutional order. There would quickly have been an end of the old Germany and of its rulers. Wild and undisciplined irregulars would have held in their hands the fate of the nation. This solution was wanted also by the Strassers, who would have been glad to send the generals of the old régime, such men as Groener and Schleicher, to the gallows. But Hitler was not so extremist as this. *Just as he needed the employers, so he needed the Reichswehr as the nucleus of the future military reconstruction.* He would undoubtedly have been in grave danger if one day a military dictatorship had supplanted his own. He took that risk, himself persuading the military that it was in their interest to put an'end to the revolutionary Socialism of the Nazi Left wing. This situation was an exact parallel to the political situation. Between the Reichswehr and the employers on one side, and the Party and the Brown militia on the other, Hitler established a balance. *He was the man of compromise, perhaps in that respect the successor of Bismarck.*

This explains why from 1923 to 1933 the attitude of the Reichswehr to Hitlerism remained undecided. The Reichswehr had no love for the Weimar Republic. Its hatred and contempt condemned to death the Weimar democracy, which could only have lived and developed if it had had at its disposal a truly Republican army. On the other hand, the Reichswehr distrusted the S.A. and S.S. It leaned on nothing but itself and its intrinsic strength. Toward 1932, when the situation was becoming tragic, Groener considered that it would be necessary to disband the Brownshirts. But Schleicher, who took his place a little later, prepared a sort of military *pronunciamento* with the army against Hindenburg and von Papen. The Reichswehr would thus, in the person of Schleicher, have taken the initiative of a military dictatorship in order to re-establish order. The question is whether the whole army would have followed Schleicher, who was seeking, in his own way, a compromise with the Weimar democracy. It is certainly doubtful. For the Reichswehr, in accordance with its old tradition, watched jealously over its autonomy.

When the *coup d'état* came on January 30, 1933, the Reichswehr simply followed the example of the ruling caste. It accepted that solution, thinking, like the employers, that it would be able to use the Hitler movement, a pseudo-revolutionary mass movement which might restore to the country the dynamism it needed. But National Socialism made only a show of placing itself in the service of this reactionary dictatorship. It might have been imagined that Hindenburg and the Reichswehr were going to win the upper hand and, so to speak, canalize the unloosed Nazi energies. This was pure illusion. Nazism quickly called the tune. Thereafter Hitler's choice was made. He would respect the army, thinking of the " Wehrmacht" that would later take the place of the Reichswehr.

This was exactly the course taken in the massacre of June 30, 1934. On that day Hitler, under the advice of the employers and of the Reichswehr itself, brutally cut short Röhm's attempt, not hesitating to sacrifice his best fellow-fighter. *He did not want a revolutionary Brown army*. Now, from 1935 on, there would be the new army, the great military reconstruction, uniting all the forces of the nation. This is clear proof of the persistent collusion between Hitler and the conservative elements, which were determined to resume power politics in their own interest. But was Hitler going to tow this restored army in his wake? Had he been content on June 30, 1934, to *retard* the movement which Röhm wanted to *precipitate*?

For the moment there was a visible *rapprochement* between Nazism and the regular army. Hitler had worked well for the Reichswehr. Now that he was President and Chancellor of the Reich he could administer the oath to the army. Not, indeed, that the army was ready to be a simple instrument in the hands of the Nazis. But this army, which had lived from 1918 to 1932 *outside the Weimar system*, and thus in complete autonomy, was thenceforth reformed and developed *within the Hitlerite system*. The *Party* and the *army* collaborated to a certain extent, varying according to circumstances. Through the Hitler Youth the army was enriched by elements formed and educated by the Party. The army imagined, with General von Blomberg, that it would preserve its independence. The re-establishment of compulsory military service on March 16, 1935, was clearly what the army wanted. But would the army be any longer, as in the past, the "great school of the nation"?

The ultimate result was a sort of permanent duality. There was the Party and there was the army. Hitler might ask himself whether he was going to be at the mercy of an army and a General Staff both of which would be growing beyond all bounds. On the other hand, would the young elements of that army, which would soon be in the majority, continue to range themselves behind Hitler? In the Hitler Jugend and the labour service these youths were impregnated with Hitlerite ideas before entering the barracks. *In fact, both propositions or possibilities remained true.* The army tried to preserve its autonomy, but irresistibly moved toward Nazism. In it the forces of *conservation* were in conflict with *revolutionary dynamism.*

The Allies had tolerated the introduction of conscription, the remilitarization of the Rhineland, and the intervention in Spain, in 1935 and 1936, and through this the Wehrmacht was greatly indebted to Hitler and his Party. The staggering blows that followed, the work of the Wehrmacht itself, in 1938 and 1939, added further to this debt. The Wehrmacht had thus evolved in such a way as to return stage by stage to Ludendorff's conception, that of *total war*, at the very moment when the hundred-per-cent-Hitlerite jurists had arrived at the idea of *total enmity between the Western bourgeoisie and the "soldier" nations.* The Wehrmacht had entered the path of absolute militarism. It had substituted Ludendorff for Clausewitz, Banse and Haushofer for the past healthy traditions and relative moderation. In short, the army had become *the prisoner of Nazism.* It was to be an instrument of destruction and upheaval, not of conservation or ordered reconstruction. It could not be otherwise, since Hitler attached his whole propaganda, conceived as "fourth arm" and "broadened strategy," to that course.

In penetrating the army with its spirit, the Party itself penetrated more and more into the life of the nation. Thus the Restoration to which the ruling caste aspired in 1933 had turned into *a sort of German Communism.* The proletarian elements had multiplied both in the Party and in the army. The partisans of more and more absolute *planning*, of more and more declared and total military *mobilization*, of a true *mystico-military Communism*, similar, *mutatis mutandis*, to the old pre-Christian Germanic society, grew formidable. Was Germany then anything but a country in a masked state of siege, of terrorism made legal? Was not the idea of *military adventure* the guiding idea of the régime?

Whether of juridical or military origin, whether devised by Carl Schmitt or by Ludendorff, defended by the Nazis or by the Wehrmacht, the deliberate confusion of *civil* with *military* that was *Soldatentum* was installed in Germany. That is just what was meant by the notion of the "soldier" Race. War became for it *prima ratio.* We were far now from Lutheran hesitations and purely defensive war. It was considered that the nation must be kept in a state of *perpetual aggressiveness on principle*. There were no longer two organizations, one for peace and the other for war. There was but one "state," one situation, of neither absolute peace nor absolute war. Between two overt wars there existed a zone that was no longer peace and was already dominated by the exigencies of war. The law of preparation for war governed everything. A crushing military instrument descended with all its weight, like a giant carapace, upon a nation sapped from within and ready to obey in all things. *The civil order had abdicated. The military order was automatically taking its place.*

But there was a risk of exhaustion, a risk of the total absorption of the people in the army, with no more reserves, psychological or economic, to be maintained by peace. This conception and practice would turn against the army itself. The army would no longer be the *refuge of order* that it is in other countries. The Reichswehr had placed itself *above* the Weimar State. That had been its mistake, the irremediable error that had prevented it from being an element of renewal. Now it was falling *beneath* Nazism and the Third Reich. It was becoming demagogic. The officer was descending to the level of the wily politician and the unscrupulous adventurer.

The army had thus given way to the temptation to misuse the formless masses led by intoxication combined with terrorism. With National Socialism it returned to the methods it had followed in 1917 and 1918 for reviving public opinion. It recommenced the monstrous masterpiece of Prussian discipline which tragic circumstances had then engendered. Once more the multitude had to be *technicized* and *rationalized*. Everything that menaced that ruthless subjection to technique must disappear. Any humanity was here clearly weakness. A frightful realism took possession of men's minds and wills. Military domination of the people—such was the aim. But this realism was romantic because it made use of the racial myth. The people's energies were swallowed up in the abyss of absolute militarization. The machinery of power seemed to be digging its claws into the palpitating body of the subjugated nation.

The war economy proved it. Unemployment had been brought down by rearmament. The Germany of 1934 could still fear either forced disarmament or preventive war. The Allies called for neither. Thus in less than four years, between 1935 and 1939, the German will to *simple security* became a *will to*

victory, encouraged as it was by the Western passivity. Thereafter Germany could overthrow the whole European order,
destroying prosperous civilian life and the age-long traditions of
normal existence. She could go *beyond Communism*. There
were military men who understood nothing of this. They did
not know what it was that they were aiding and abetting. Others
were satisfied with Ludendorff's doctrine. Autarky, super-
armament, and the manufacture of "*ersatz*" materials were but
various aspects of this German *Soldatentum*. It was a socialization
like any other. It implied the nationalization or collectivization
of enterprises.

While the Revolution engendered rearmament, rearmament
in turn animated and promoted the Revolution. The two four-
year plans had revolutionary effects. War economy, however, in
time of relative peace, without the requisite accumulated reserves,
presented the gravest dangers. Moreover, war material ages
very rapidly. The pace could only be increased. It was a
vicious circle. It is well enough to cut out profits in time of
war; it is more serious in peace-time. This war economy was
one of the elements of the *Bolshevoid planning* that threatened to
take possession of all Germany. The machinery of power was
exhausting the people. Nazi radicalism was turning against itself
and threatened to end by making it impossible to go to war.

Accordingly Nazism had recourse, in Hitler's phrase, to the
broadened strategy. *It made use of the army to produce anguish, fear,
and cowardice*. The idea of *Blitzkrieg*, of a single deathly night,
haunted men's minds. War and Revolution allied themselves
together. The Trotskyist idea of the *coup d'état* rose, fully
armed, out of Nazism itself. The weight of armaments became,
even more than before 1914, an end in itself. State Socialism
gripped the country's internal energies in order the better to
release its forces abroad. This fatal Napoleonism was blind to
the fact that it is impossible to solve problems of foreign policy
in this way. Abandoned to the Nazi madness, Germany was
rushing toward catastrophe. For she despised the spiritual
forces, being herself in a state of complete moral collapse. While
the military mistakes were yet to come, diplomatic blunders
accumulated as before 1914. The difference could no longer be
seen between the *desirable* and the *attainable*. Men turned their
backs on Bismarckian realism, underestimating the adversary.
An epidemic of Byzantinism spread among the generals round
Hitler, a much worse Byzantinism even than that of the Wilhelmian

court. Shut off from the world, Germany took her illusions and her dreams for the concrete world of the morrow. *She thought herself a creative Race—with her end approaching.*

Parades and demonstrations intoxicated the public, but killed the true military spirit. They substituted bluff for effectual preparation. Relatively easy successes against small States furthered this illusionism. Read the works of Jünger and Banse, to realize the abyss down which Germany was plunging. A group of mediocrities, totally sceptical in their hearts, were dragging the country to ruin. Hitler's "Aktionen" dominated and determined everything.

An absurd pugnacity took possession of the young. They were enthusiasts for the *miles perpetuus*, for the eternal soldier of fortune, for the *trade of soldiering*. The soldier of the morrow was to be both a *volunteer* and a *mercenary*. Complete Cæsarism substituted for the national army, the people's army, an instrument handled by specialists in war. These professional troops destroyed the last vestiges of democratism. The nation thus mobilized by this nucleus of fanatics knew the intoxication of exaltation, but its state was the work of cool, resolute, persevering technicians. It was *amoral* soldiering by definition. It was the *ersatz* for all the lost values. This doctrine, Banse's "*Wehrphilosophie*," destroyed among the young officers all that remained of sound morality, honour, and humanity. Banse proposed to start from the nucleus of mercenaries and to militarize the whole nation, to manufacture "heroism" in those who were not spontaneously heroic.

That is what pure biological materialism had led to. *Gleichschaltung* had ruined true comradeship in the corps of officers. Over against the traditionalists, the monarchists, and the Christians stood the new-style *condottieri*, the brutes bred by the régime, the pretended Nazi nobility. Above generals without courage, passive because they had been terrorized like everyone else, floated the absurd mirage of the "Führer *of genius*." The "Wehrmacht," which alone could have restored order, swallowed everything—the Nazi doctrine, the "Heil, Hitler," and the rest. A few officers saw things clearly and told the truth. But what chance had they?

On February 4, 1938,[1] this sinister process was plain to all

---

[1] On February 4, 1938, General Blomberg was dismissed (on the pretext of his marriage), von Keitel succeeding him, and von Neurath was replaced as Foreign Secretary by Ribbentrop.

eyes. It was realized that, beneath the enforced surface unity, a clique of madmen were leading to perdition a helpless people of whom so many yearned for the return to order. If the generals blindly followed Hitler, Germany was finished. The promises of June 30, 1934, had not been kept. Potsdam Day buried Potsdam. The outer world had given *carte blanche* to the pretended Nazi *élite*. Hitler was able to act with a sleepwalker's immunity before the eyes of a doomed civilian society. The Western democracies had capitulated at the same time as the German generals. The German people was being suffocated by its army.

That is why the structure of the Machinery of Power that is Nazism, with its doctrine and its propaganda, its social or economic planning and its whole-hogging militarization, constituted for Germany and Europe the clearest and most extreme danger. *This unleashed force could be mastered only by a greater force.* The proof of this was the series of upheavals in Europe caused by the régime on the international plane between 1933 and 1939.

CHAPTER IX

THE POLICY OF THE ACCOMPLISHED FACT AND THE DESTRUCTION OF INTERNATIONAL LAW

FROM its very structure, the régime of the Third Reich is directed entirely toward paramountcy in foreign policy. While the machinery of government imposed itself on every element of the nation, racialism affirmed the providential hegemony of Germany in Europe. War economy and superarmament "shaped" the soldier-people. In the tow of the Party, the army now saw nothing but the effects of a brutal policy of decision—the accomplished fact, the "actions" to be embarked on, and war as their consequence. Galvanized internally, Germany had acquired in a few years the terrible freedom that led her to overthrow the whole European order. She might be compared to a meteor whose slightest deviation alarms a whole continent.

1. *Racialism and international law*

At the end of 1933 the Third Reich hastened to break with the League of Nations. Thereafter it proceeded to demolish bit by bit the whole international constitution of the old Europe. How much of that constitution remains, and by what will the lost institutions and charters be replaced?

The Nazis like to call themselves the creators and representatives of a new conception and practice of relations between peoples. As for the internal order established in Germany, they claim to be returning to the eternal verities, the divine laws of nature. They believe themselves to have discovered in racialism the means of grasping the essential elements of each human community, what they call, in their own jargon, the *Artgemeinschaften*. Their doctrine clearly inspires their activities in foreign policy. The question is whether the doctrine is there to *explain* or to *disguise* the brutal method of the accomplished fact.

Beyond any question this doctrine proceeds directly from German romanticism, from its reaction against rationalism and the Enlightenment, against internationalism and universalism as abstractions. It derives in equal measure from a crude biologism, at once Darwinian and utilitarian. The Nazis talk of races that are entities or quantities determined by a sort of *mass heredity*, manifesting human culture under the most various forms. Nazism coarsens and vulgarizes, in fact, the meditation on organic life that made its appearance in Germany at the end of the eighteenth century. The nations of the past, each with its "national genius," have become, after a series of transformations, races condemned to fight eternally between themselves for pre-eminence.

For Nazism, the diversity of races is an inescapable fact, and so is the hierarchy that sets superior against inferior races. There seems to be no room here for any generalized idea, any standard imposed on the nations of the world, other than that of permanent war. Nazi thought goes even farther. If we are to believe the Nazis, the Nordic race possesses absolute superiority. It is the origin and the condition of all the higher cultures the world has known. It has therefore a universal character. The German "Aryan" asserts himself simply by repudiating the Internationals, which amounts to saying that *he monopolizes universalism for his own advantage*. He declares that law (*Recht*) has its sole source in the Race, in *Volkstum*. Each people has "its right," proportionate to its might, to its potential. There is no formal and abstract right or legality, valid for all peoples. *Legality is that which "serves" the people. Usefulness to the community is the measure of legality.*

This amounts to declaring that legality resides only in the feeling

that this or that people is in the right.   The "Führer" claims to
incarnate the conscience of the people, and, at all events in theory,
never to be in conflict with it.   Legality and morality together
proceed from this conscience of the people.   There can never,
the Nazis say, be any opposition between legality and morality.
They re-edit the fundamental theses of the German historical
school.   The "Volksgeist," the spirit of the people, is the sole
criterion.   Thus enlarged, the doctrine incurs grave objections.
Can a people be the possessor of a juridical conscience that is truly
consistent and faithful to itself?   How does that collective
juridical conviction manifest itself, and how can it be recognized?
May there not be a contradiction between it and positive legality?
Finally, is it possible to establish a fundamental identity between
that juridical conviction and usefulness to the community?

On such a plane it is rather difficult to figure international
law.   According to Hitler and Rosenberg, all foreign politics is
simply a struggle between peoples or races, an intellectual and
moral struggle or a struggle with material arms.   It is a cruel
conception, with neither illusions nor scruples, based entirely, as
never was doctrine before, on the principle that might is right.
Nature, we are to suppose, throws creatures into the world and
thereafter impassively watches the free play of their unchained
forces.   She gives preference to the one who possesses most
courage, daring, and capacity for work.   On him she confers
the right to dominate.   Humanism and humanitarianism are
henceforth meaningless.   They imply nothing but stupidity and
cowardice!   For mankind grows and progresses only *through war*.
To enlarge his potential of energy and his *Lebensraum* is the duty
of every man; and every collectivity has the same duty.

Foreign politics is thus the common effort that unites people of
the same blood and the same race in a realm, *a realm always
extensible*, since every increase of power means more air, more
light, and a larger surface, for perfect freedom of movement.
The true frontiers, those of *eternal law*, are necessarily movable.
They are permanently changing according to the fluctuations of
the universal struggle.   No doubt there is a certain contradiction
between the idea of a *natural balance* between nations and this
conception of law.   Hitlerite nationalism is rapacious.   It
fights for the German people, unceasingly, since one day, according to *Mein Kampf*, the Continent should contain 250 *millions* of
Germans.   How could it honestly talk of "collaboration" with
the European nations?

We know Hitler's and Rosenberg's programme. Nordism, according to them, must one day lead the white race to final triumph over the inferior social classes and the coloured races. This is Oswald Spengler's thesis, modified to suit the taste of an intoxicated multitude. These are the dreams of normal pan-Germanism. It is true that between 1933 and the present day they have undergone a certain evolution. Listening to the speeches or to the simple talk of the Nazi leaders, it would have been easy to believe that intransigent racialism was but a memory, that Germany had not the slightest desire for war, and that new hostilities would simply plunge the German people into new difficulties. In short, Hitler seemed to have no further wish to attain his ends by violence. In the past he had often talked of the "family" of European nations, making an exception only of Russia. To the dark and sinister pessimism of absolute racialism presented to the German youth at the Nuremberg congresses there was added the vision of an harmonious Europe, offered to the foreign nations. Was this oscillation of ideas or simple artifice?

That is the whole question. Thus we need to consult the Hitlerite jurists. Were they caught in a contradiction? Was there any real contradiction?

It is certainly difficult to conceive international law otherwise than on a universal plane. It would be difficult to imagine an international law that was purely German. It is true that Nazism, true to itself, condemns universalist and liberal science, substituting for it a science essentially German. That does not prevent Nazi doctrine from simultaneously affirming that the racial factor is a governing condition of the science of international law, and that racialism is of universal value.

Before 1933 there was a great variety in Germany of doctrines concerning international law. National Socialism put an end to it by proclaiming what it called "controlled freedom of opinion" (*geordnete Meinungsfreiheit*). *Gleichschaltung* played its part here as everywhere else. Hitler's speech of May 17, 1933, already demanded it. The jurists had to give way before National Socialism. Resistance was impossible. International law itself, although its seat of authority was outside Germany, must get down or get out.

During the nineteenth century a certain positivism had ruled in this domain. The essential source of national law was seen *in the will of the sovereign States*. This will found precise expression in contracts, treaties, and pacts of every sort. The Germans had accepted it just as their neighbours had done. But since 1850 the Italians had already inclined to the ideas of the historic school and of nationalism. Only since the First World War has German international law parted with positivism.

If true law can proceed only from the racial substance of a people, from what the Hitlerite jurists call racial conviction concerning law (*völkische Rechtsüberzeugung*), then international law can no longer *dominate* peoples, rule them, be "*übervölkisch.*" There will be as many systems of international law as nations. So it was that the jurist Schecher denied in 1933 the existence of any true international law. For him, every statute bearing upon the relations between nations was *part of a particular State.* The German jurists gave no answer to the question that arose, whether racialism could form the basis of international law. They simply declared, persistently, that National Socialism must recognize international law in the traditional sense of the term. It was a simple matter of opportunism. One jurist, Nicolai, added that this international law was reduced to very little under racialism. It really did not matter. *That is to say, Nazism desired the contradiction and deliberately maintained it.* It set itself to recognize international law and at the same time to minimize it.

In spite of everything, the difficulty continued. And the Hitlerite jurists wriggled out of it in all sorts of ways. The older generation set the accent on the necessary recognition of an international law, leaving aside Race and "*Volkstum*" as far as possible. A later generation, a hundred per cent. Nazi, did exactly the opposite. It was simply a question of proportion.

Naturally all the jurists of the régime agreed, without a single exception, in condemning the Treaty of Versailles and the Articles concerning disarmament. They maintained the tradition started in 1919. The new feature was the growing passion and violence with which the argument was resumed. On the other hand, the struggle for the famous "equality of rights" (*Gleichberechtigung*) took a new turn. The standards for treaties were measured by different criteria. The system they created was called "dictation." It was claimed that an unjust, dictated treaty, a "*Diktat,*" had no share in the sanctity of treaties. It was repeated that the struggle for equality of rights provided the opportunity to found a new theoretical basis for international law. In other words, *the German case was made to fit the world.* Germany no longer talked of treaty revision. *Natural* law was invoked against the existing juridical situation.

International law was thus to be based on natural law, on the life in common of all peoples *under a just order*. This was the idea of *justice between nations*, defended in particular by Möller van den Bruck. The great authority (*Instanz*) was Life. It was not will, the human "*Satzung*" (ordering), that made the world, any more than precepts make morality. What was wanted was the creation of *a natural order*, in revolt against the abuse of abstract standards. An old German cliché, brought in again and again in Nazi thought, in which it assumed its brutal vulgar form. Justice, morality, law, all count for nothing in face of nature, life, organic realities. One jurist, Victor Bruns, talked continually of the Community (*Gemeinschaft*) as the object of law, adding that the Community excluded all preponderance. In the Community each nation was the equal of every other one. This equality was the very principle of justice. Each State was independent, *but solely in the measure of its capacity for self-defence*. *The possession of arms* was the fundamental right of the Community.

Each people has the same right as the rest to its *Lebensraum*. The only clear thing is the possession of arms. All the rest, says Bruns, is vague and indeterminate. Has he any conception of a pre-established harmony between States? He does not even ask himself whether it is possible or not. One State is as sovereign as another. Similarly each State is as free, in the dynamic sense of the term, as any other to bring to bear its potential of force. Each State therefore submits itself to international law if it chooses, its "*Wehrhoheit*" or "military supremacy" being the essential consideration. It would be impossible to achieve a more subtle association of the traditional notion of law and the racialist claim. But it will deceive nobody.

For the rest, there is nothing specifically Nazi in a theory thus presented. There is no talk, apparently, of Race or "*Volkstum*." These terms are left in the background. The jurists Wolz and Wolgast, for instance, content themselves with suggesting the picture of a state of absolute tranquillity and pacific collaboration such as the world has never yet seen. In thus mingling the racialist principle with that of equality, an order of "juxtaposition" (*Nebenordnung*) is supposed to be reached, a pacific harmony of peoples.

The paradox is evident. The perspectives of National Socialism are very different. All these jurists skirt the true problem without ever frankly dealing with it. For them the basis of international law is the Treaty of Versailles. That is enough. As, from the German point of view, it is necessary to destroy the Versailles order, once that has been done what remains of international law? Apart from this, no difficulty is felt in treating all international statute law as abstract, theoretical, and sterile. Or it is declared that it conflicts with German sovereignty. "*Weltrecht*," it is declared—a system of law valid for the whole world—is not wanted. The cloven hoof shows itself here. National Socialism, we are told, admits the equality of nations, "in the sense of equality of material rights" (*im Sinne materieller Gleichberechtigung*). That means that there is no longer formal and absolute equality. There is only a doubtful precarious equality, fundamentally restless and expansionist, because *dynamic*.

The return is constantly made to the deployment of living energies, together with all desired political and military resources. The national honour is invoked. The theoreticians declare that the "individual" interests of the participating States are absolutely essential. It is a return to the "*jus volontarium*" of Grotius, opposed to the "*jus naturale*" as "*jus necessarium*." The community is but a façade. So-called "vital interests" will always be at call to permit the barriers of law to be blown up if they seem too rigid. The treaty is in no way sovereign in the juridical order. Treaties are and always will be just scraps of paper. *Life comes before law.*

Obviously a certain hypocrisy is at play in all these solutions. The sections of the edifice fit together badly. But other Nazi jurists make a franker attempt to build upon Race. They talk no longer, like their former colleagues, of States. They make play instead with "*Volkstum*."

Heinrich Rogge seems to constitute the transition between the older and the younger group. He plainly minimizes international law. A disciple of Möller van den Bruck and of neo-conservatism, he considers war as the central phenomenon of relations between peoples. Fundamentally pessimist, he sees nothing anywhere but eternal struggle, and progress is for him a meaningless word. Thus the law of nations (*Völkerrecht*) is the law of war (*Kriegsrecht*). But, he asks, is it not possible to discipline this eternal struggle? The concept of national honour will serve that purpose. Each people has its "right to honour" (*Recht auf Ehre*). The Community of peoples will be founded, therefore, on the sentiment common to them, that of honour. This is the old rule of the Middle Ages, the "*Ritterfehde*" ("knightly feud"), applied to all international life. Hence Rogge's hostility to pacts and his preference for direct agreements between man and man and between country and country. Since 1933 Rogge has modelled himself closely on the sayings of the Hitlerite leaders. No more pacts of assistance, no more collective agreements, no more sanctions or arbitrations. The nations are divided simply into great, medium, and small Powers.

From these dismal premises, however, Rogge claims to deduce an harmonious world. According to him the law of nations should comprise simply the law of neutrality, the law of war, and the rules relating to these two categories. Rogge has the same idea of peace as Hitler. Carl Schmitt goes further. He raises the question of the *homogeneity of peoples in the international Community*. In order to constitute a League of Nations, must all of them have the same structure? Here our jurist comes to Race, to "*Artgemeinschaft*" or community of type, to the determination of the strictly original elements that may exist in a grouping. Carl Schmitt is careful to make no attempt to define that homogeneity. He avoids pure racialism, which is not to the taste of this recruit to Nazism. He insists on the fact that if the League of Nations is renewed, very different systems will have to be admitted into it, whether liberal or totalitarian. When there is a treaty between nations, the admission of a partner of different structure involves a modification of the treaty. Nazi thought remains attached to some sort of compromise on this subject.

Other theoreticians take the racial idea entirely seriously, and proceed to apply it to international law. Nicolai writes that international law is simply the law concerning foreign peoples (*Aussenvolksrecht*). Every consistent racialist minimizes juridical organization. Is not his essential aim to *liberate the racial State as far as possible from every juridical obligation*? If there is peace and collaboration between peoples, it will be due solely to the confidence which the States called "free" of all obligations will nevertheless have in their partners. It is a minimum of security.

Another racialist theoretician, Kraaz, simply denies the existence of international law. Another admits the possibility of an association between peoples of the same racial origin. Gürke defends the following thesis: it is not international law that founds collaboration between peoples; it is their racial

agreement that in the first place engenders international law.
Gürke seeks for a link in the political and juridical ideas of peoples.
He considers that international law comprises various individual
juridical systems.   Naturally the Jews and the Russians are excluded from this picture.   But how can Gürke then hold that certain juridical principles of an international order may be common
to different races?   Who does not see the contradiction?

It may be asked, what is the exact relation between people
(*Volk*) and State (*Staat*)?   Is it the Race or the State that engenders
law?   For Gürke the only State that exists is the racial State.
This alone is a "subject" of international Law.   Why should
not the problem of minorities be solved by means of the State that
includes several nationalities (*Nationalitätenstaat*)?   Here we see
the appearance of Germany's *hegemonic* tendency, for we are told
of the elementary and primitive instinct (*Urinstinkt*) that dictates
its promptings to each people.   The most absolute Machiavellism
then becomes the rule of all thought.   And *total enmity* between
races or cultures is its direct consequence.

All these argumentations make for the total ruin of international law.   As regards private international law, it is laid
down that the German tribunals should apply rules of foreign
origin as little as possible.   Public international law is assimilated
to the law of contract (*Vertragsrecht*).   All universal standards
are rejected.   Yet, how is it possible to do without them?   And,
especially, who does not see that in order to have a treaty it is
necessary for the contracting wills to be strictly bound by it?
When one reminds a Nazi that *pacta sunt servanda*, he just smiles.

It follows obviously that all international law that is not
contractual in form is a contradiction.   Law is thus reduced to
a bargain struck between two parties.   What becomes, then, of
the juridical organization of peace?   The League of Nations
disappears entirely in face of Nazi criticism, since the Nazi
deliberately rejects every liberal and democratic principle,
abandons the equality of nations, and refuses to admit any sort
of collective sanction or the arbitration or even the existence
of The Hague Court.   He protests in advance against every
administration that is independent of any State, the International
Labour Organization included.

Thus there is an antagonism in principle between the idea of a
racial law and that of a law imposing precise obligations on all.
Everywhere in Nazi doctrine reign doubt, uncertainty, and
hypocrisy.   *To recognize the existence of international law is to deny*

racial law. To affirm racial law is to destroy international law. Hence the fact that Nazism is compelled to admit either a Community of absolutely homogeneous peoples, each Race being saturated, or the full sovereignty of each and the absence of any external obligation. In any case, there is an end of international law, and the way is made smooth for Hitler's formulæ.

These doctrines seem to correspond to two different stages through which the foreign policy of the Third Reich has passed. The older generation was preoccupied above all with equality of rights, which was secured in 1936. Then it was that the younger generation, the racialists, entered the lists. The game had been played. Fundamentally, the solution envisaged after all the confusion was inconsistent with National Socialism. *For a system of independent States, equal and with the same right to life and struggle, is still a liberal conception.* In the external order, National Socialism takes its stand on the principles of the old individualism. *The Reich is granted that which is refused to the individual.*

The difference from Fascism is obvious. The racial theory is built upon the right of peoples to dispose (entirely) of themselves. Within the State, however, it does not permit citizens to dispose freely of themselves. That is to say, once more, *it contains liberal elements.* It recalls the Italian nationalist theory of the nineteenth century. That theory was based on the historic school rather than on racialism. It admitted the existence of collective individualities of a spiritual and not a racial order. The Italians thought it was possible to establish on this basis not only Italian unity, with its democratic structure, but also the League of Nations. At the same time, they pursued an irredentist foreign policy, aiming at a certain racial saturation. It was at that moment that Germany gave currency to the modernized Hegelian theory of the "*Machtstaat*," the "Power-State," from which proceeded through initiative from above the Bismarckian Reich, excluding Austria.

What happened after the First World War? Racially saturated, Italy brought in Fascism with the aid of Hegel, while providing herself with an entirely modern political system. Germany, on the contrary, brought in National Socialism under the influence of the old Italian school, that is to say, virtually, of irredentism. All Germans must be united in Greater Germany. On the German side there was no visible imperialism, but an appearance of federalism, a doctrine envisaging equality *between racial States*, but implying a grave contradiction. On the Italian side there was *Imperium Romanum*, a State envisaging absolute unity and built up on several racial cultures. It is true that the Italians defend themselves from the charge of imperialism and, like the Germans, claim to envisage a harmony *between States that have become Fascist*. That is why Italy declared unceasingly that she desired peace.

Italian practice in foreign politics, like German, *ran counter to this ideal of peace*. The ideal was *nevertheless* maintained. It must be said, however, that the Germans were less democratic than the Italians, who in the past dreamed, under the influence of the French Revolution, of a harmony between democratic States. The Germans merely wanted collaboration between totalitarian States, under their direction. They imagined that they would attain peace equally with the French Revolution and the old Italian school. This was pure utopianism. In practice the Italo-German activities made with growing clearness for the "*Machtstaat*," which, pursuing its own ends and working solely in its own interest, evaded every international obligation. Here every liberal and democratic *Utopia* was abandoned in favour of *realism, that is to say, imperialism, through competition, the struggle for existence, and perpetual war*.

We are thus faced with a sort of juxtaposition or co-existence between the search for absolute power for the State and the vision of a balanced Community of Totalitarian States. National Socialism deliberately dismisses every idea of an *objective* science of international law. Science is subordinated to the Race, its dynamism, and its success. In that attitude, on the other hand, there is nothing of science left, and if the German jurists talk of a science of international law they thereupon admit principles contrary to racialism. The Hitlerite jurists evade the difficulty by leaving aside the actual content of international law. They build in the air a system *for the future* and call that chimera international law. Under the cover of that convenient Utopia, the Reich can manage to get along. Conflict in the field of positive law is thus avoided.

Do the Germans believe in this future of collaboration between peoples? They do not. They entertain the idea in order *to mask* the aims of their foreign policy, to serve their people and what they call its "expediency." The opposition remains absolute between racialist doctrine and the Hitlerite appeals to balance or harmony. Racialism explodes in principle *every* community of peoples. It destroys *every* obligation of an international nature. It is impossible to believe in the sincerity either of the Nazi jurists or of their future League of peoples. Behind that façade rises a hidden law of nations that explains and supports the foreign policy of the Third Reich. *This law may serve several foreign policies at the same time.* It is based in reality on the concrete and brutal data of geography and history. It is a pure affair of "geopolitics." The myth of Nazi peace is the same thing as the total hegemony of Germany.

The Nazis are past masters of the art of masking their true aims by making demands which they know to be impossible. Their pretended science of international law is purely pragmatical. They are inspired at one and the same time by the egalitarianism of free competition and by racialist nationalism. Their conception of law is rigorously *sociological.* Actual juridical settlement oscillates between a wholly arbitrary settlement and the absolute settlement arrived at in accordance with standards imposed on all. But international law does not exist without mutual concessions and an effort to accommodate the interests at stake. As the constraint resulting from war and victory may be substituted for these compromises, there is true international law only where there is organization of a durable peace. On this point Nazi doctrine and practice are a perpetual scouting of law.

Clearly it is open to question whether a treaty based on victory and constraint constitutes a basis for the international order. The idea of a revision is perfectly acceptable. *But Nazism leaps to the opposite extreme, the total absence of juridical constraint.* Accusing the Treaty of Versailles of having been inspired by violence, it repudiates every juridical system. Hitler set out not to suppress but to *reverse,* to Germany's advantage, the relation between victor and vanquished.

On this point a comparison may be made between the Bolshevist and the Nazi doctrine. Korovin, a well-known Russian jurist, establishes an opposition between the systems of capitalist origin and those of the Soviet Union. But he admits that an international law may in case of need unite the two systems. Sovietism minimizes but *recognizes* international law. In fact, there is no agreement between it and Nazism. The Russian system admits that the oppositions between States are *transient.* National Socialism, on the contrary, sees in them a *normal* reality. Bolshevism desires homogeneity of States on the *social* basis; for it the existing situation is but transitory. Nazism minimizes *law in itself,* a very different thing. The Soviet Union is already a concrete Community of various peoples with *the same social structure*. That is worth more than the Hitlerite façade. In other words, Nazism signifies a *total eclipse* of international law. Its triumph would be the end of all civilization and of any sort of social order.

2. *The first programme of foreign policy*

The confrontation of Hitlerite leaders with Hitlerite jurists brings into view the curious oscillation, so characteristic of German thought in general, between the *agonistic* conception of international life and the *utopian* conception of a Community of homogeneous peoples. Involuntarily one is led to think here of the opposition between the sovereign territorial States of Germany and the Reich, between a fragmented or combative reality and a common ideal, between *anarchy of fact* and a *dreamed communion*. This paradox has passed from Germany to Europe and to the world. The Western democracies are nations very firmly delimited, within which individuals and groups enjoy a relative liberty. Russia is trying to realize a vast social Community on a proletarian basis. Germany is destroying liberty within her territory, only to install in Europe, while apparently dreaming of an ideal Community, the anarchy of struggle between nations. She talks of peace but makes war. She makes war and talks of peace. The deliberate oscillations of doctrine become, through propaganda and action, a practice that can only sow confusion everywhere.

In the twenty-five points of 1920 there was little enough on foreign policy and the ends it should pursue. The first Article proclaimed Greater Germany and the right of the German people to self-determination. Articles 2 and 3 demanded the abolition of the Treaty of Versailles and the Treaty of Saint-Germain, absolute parity between Germany and other nations, and the restitution of the German colonies. Taken together, these demands had, nevertheless, some importance.

The programme for Germany's foreign policy contained in the principal writings of Hitler and Rosenberg comprises, like Nazi doctrine in general, a negative part and a positive part.

The Third Reich must take action against France and Russia to bring them down after isolating them from each other, because these two nations are the seat of the most detested universalisms —Judaism, Catholicism, democratic Liberalism, and Socialism. On the other hand, thanks to the benevolent neutrality of Britain and the northern countries, Germany constitutes "Mitteleuropa" in concert with Italy. It is thus desired before all else to prevent France and Russia from jointly opposing the movement that drives the Germanic mass to expand north-eastwards in the direction of Poland and the Baltic, and especially to surmount the mountain barrier in the south and work in the direction of the two thousand-kilometre European isthmuses, that of the south-west, where, thanks to the alliance with Italy and eventual action in Spain, it is possible to reach the western Mediterranean, and that of the south-east, which may lead Germany through the Balkans to the Black Sea via Roumania and Turkey.

The Hitlerite leaders point out, to begin with, that racialist Germany is embarking on a new foreign policy, that that Germany has unsatisfactory frontiers and must conquer a *Lebensraum*, a "vital space" proportionate to her population potential and her military strength, and that the Reich must prepare itself for this vast territorial increase.

As regards the first point, the programme for foreign policy is bound up with the general racialist doctrine. Nowhere do the Hitlerite leaders say more clearly that the Race must prevail over the State, which is but its instrument and would be nothing without it. "We Aryans," says Hitler, "can represent ourselves expressly as a State only *under the aspect of a living organism* that serves as shelter for a particular people and which, not content with assuring the people's existence, strives also to develop the people's intellectual and spiritual capacities in order to lead it to the highest liberty."

Rosenberg makes clear what it is that is "totalitarian." It is not the State, which is but an instrument, but the Race as the fundamental reality, and the doctrine that expresses its soul. Thus conceived, the German Race must have its full potential of strength. Above all, it must be free to bring that potential to bear *as it thinks best, in accordance with its profound instinct*, unconscious in the mass, conscious in the leader, and in doing so it must provide itself with a social organization of military type, known as *Soldatentum*.

This Germany is confined within too narrow frontiers. Hitler rejects not only the limits of 1919, but also those of 1914. According to him the German frontiers have never corresponded to the geographical, economic, and military necessities of the Reich. They are purely fortuitous. This German people, so full of vitality, as is proved by its birth-rate and its conception of life, moves in a space too restricted for its needs and aspirations. It has therefore, *by nature*, the *right* to carve out its legitimate place in the world of to-day, to make good its opportunities. God and posterity will approve the most sanguinary wars, on condition that they are carried on in this spirit. That is Germany's sacred cause.

"The foreign policy of the racial State," Hitler writes further, "must assure the existence in this world of the Race organized by the State. To do this it must create a normal, durable, and natural relation between the number and growth of the people on one hand, and the extent and excellence of the soil or the territory on the other." For "political frontiers are created by men and modified by men." The notion of *frontier* is here related to that of *race*. Like the race, the frontier can be expanded without limit, since racialism requires that all Germans shall belong to the Community and that the so-called "lower" races shall be subjected to the Aryan or Nordic Race.

If, then, there is an antinomy between race and frontier, it is necessary to prepare to break down the artificial, transitory frontiers, and to increase the national domain. The Reich thus maintains itself, *temporarily*, within the narrow space assigned to it by the course of history. But there it disposes of two points of departure, the national *myth*, the image of the people as it regards itself in its perfect unity and totality, and the *military* instrument that will complete the Reich. The existing Germany is but a nucleus, a starting-point. It is true that Hitler and Rosenberg disagree on the subject of Germany's possible expansion. Hitler speaks of 250 millions of Germans in Europe in a century's time, which assumes the total Germanization of Europe and the absolute hegemony of Germany. Rosenberg is more modest: he contents himself with 100 millions.

Such is the basis, in terms of the natural antinomy between Reich, Race, and frontiers, of German dynamism. The thing to be done is to throw down the obstacles. These obstacles are France in the west and in the east Russia.

Keeping to the text of *Mein Kampf*, the famous pages on France, written on the morrow of Locarno (1925) and never disavowed by the "Führer," bear witness to unremitting hatred. Hatred to order and for purposes of propaganda, no doubt, based on grotesque assertions, a strange medley of true and false. France is well protected along all her frontiers and may count, on the east, on Weimar benevolence; she is dominated by Jews, who cleverly associate stock exchange policy with chauvinism; she is an empire that, again with the aid of the Jews, is "negrifying" Europe, drawing upon the coloured troops of her vast colonies and installing on European soil an African State filled with inferior beings; she detests Germany and wants at all costs to prevent her from constituting a homogeneous Power, maintaining her fragmentation, occupying the left bank of the Rhine for all time, and assuring her own Continental hegemony; she has "stolen" Alsace-Lorraine from her neighbour. Conclusion: accounts must be settled with France, isolating her not only from Russia but from Italy and above all from Britain, and thoroughly beating her, so as to give the greatest possible extension to the Reich in the east.

France, in the eyes of the tribune, is above all the country that represents and defends the treaties of 1919, the League of Nations, and the pacts of collective security. Concerned to give no offence to Britain, the tribune affects to ignore her participation in this system. Hitler repeats the German jurists' contention that Germany was not responsible for the war of 1914, though he admits with Rosenberg that the offensive of 1914 was the first act of the German Revolution. Naturally Hitler draws a distinction between the German statesmen, who made mistakes, and the German people, which regarded itself as unjustly attacked. But criticism of the Treaty of Versailles furnishes him with splendid matter for agitation. He dares to compare that treaty with those which Germany concluded in the east with Russia and Roumania. Is not the advantage with these latter, since Versailles condemned Germany to perpetual *slavery* and *disarmament*?

Hitler and Rosenberg, like so many other German publicists of 1914, were always ready for any upheaval that might assure the victory of Germanism on the Continent, amid their continual protests against the injustice of Versailles. Little did they care for any inconsistency. Fundamentally, in Hitler's view, Versailles kept alive an inescapable relationship of *vanquished* and *victors*. That was the essential point. He spoke of the reciprocal confidence that would one day unite vanquished and victors. But, since the law of life is the primacy of the strongest, his real thought was that it *was necessary to reverse to Germany's profit the relationship which defeat threatened to perpetuate.* There was the same fury against the League of Nations, its Covenant, and the whole system of collective security. Germany was the sufferer from them all. Hence revision was necessary. But it was not

revision that the tribune wanted.   What he wanted was *freedom*,
that is to say, *the destruction of every international obligation*.   The
agreement between this programme and the juridical theories
just described was complete.

Hitler thus wanted to liquidate France, with her whole historic
tradition, every principle of her policy, and therewith the whole
tradition of the West, of Versailles or Geneva.   France represented in his eyes an order that extended beyond her bounds, but
which she supported, a detestable and detested order.   She was
the scapegoat of the West.   *To strike at France would be to strike at
the heart of humanism*, to bring down at a single blow Catholicism,
Liberalism, the best Socialist tradition, and a remarkable Israelite
élite.

The arguments against Russia were mixed up with those Hitler
produced against Communism.   They admirably served the
campaign intended to show the West that Germany was its
rampart against Bolshevism.   Hitler spoke of conquering Russia
and covering the cost out of her territory.   He regretted that
Wilhelmian Germany had not followed that policy before 1914.
In his view, as in Rosenberg's, Russia would be beaten because,
like her former ally France, she had been *de-Germanized*, Jews
having taken the place of those Baltic barons who had brought
her such success.

The precise point of these diatribes is clear.   Hitler did not
content himself with saying that Germany could not tolerate two
great military States to right and left of her.   His double
campaign, anti-French and anti-Russian, enabled him to satisfy
the German middle classes by combating both Western *plutocracy*
and the *Communism* of the East.   For the lower middle class had
two simultaneous hates, that of the great capitalists who condemn
it to decay and proletarization, and that of Socialism, which aims
at making the middle class and the proletariat indistinguishable.
Hitler calculated well.   Did he not show in *Mein Kampf* that
the lower middle-class man will put up with anything except the
renunciation of the social rank he has so slowly and so laboriously
achieved?   At the same time, Hitler could turn to the old ruling
caste in Germany and tell it that he was saving it from the
proletarian revolution.

Such was his argument.   It called for construction, for a
programme.   To achieve its aims, German diplomacy must
make an end of the methods of the past, and especially of the
planless policy for which Hitler so bitterly reproached it, and play

a very cautious game. Instead of beginning by spreading over the world in the effort to occupy foreign markets which steadily eluded their grasp, instead of squandering their energies all over the world, the Germans would do well to concentrate on Europe, creating "Mitteleuropa" by occupying the space indispensable for the deployment of their energies. They should dig themselves in there as a formidable wedge between West and East. It was a view exactly in accord with Wilhelmian imperialism, but it took for granted a supposition which the Germans were too ready to accept as a dogma—that the Western Powers were decadent and the Soviet Union entirely impotent. Quite apart from its assumption of Britain's benevolent neutrality, which was the most enormous of all the blunders that Hitlerism made.

The two Hitlerite leaders thus claimed to do better than their predecessors. It was impossible, they said, to preserve the strength and energy of the German people if they were to be required to keep down their birth-rate or to content themselves with internal colonization. It was equally out of the question to rely on pushing exports without limit in order to procure imports without limit, for the Germans would then be confined entirely to industry and commerce. *The Wilhelmian Reich*, said Hitler, *should have followed a policy of territorial conquest in Europe, returning in the East to the tradition of the Teutonic Order, which had been interrupted since the fifteenth century.* It should have associated itself deliberately with the British, who in 1900 had offered Germany an alliance against Russia. There is nothing to be gained by dwelling on the two Nazi leaders' criticisms of Weimar diplomacy, which they accused of spinelessness in face of the Allied demands, and of which they had no desire to admit that in many respects it had smoothed the path for Nazism.

What, then, was to be done?

Since the thrust was to be made toward the south and east, the first thing needed was to safeguard the rear. The Reich, they considered, had nothing to fear from the Scandinavian or the Baltic States. The essential thing was to secure in advance an assurance of neutrality. As for British neutrality, that was a more delicate question. Hitler put forth a mass of specious arguments, recalling the racial kinship between the two countries and making use, as Ludendorff had done in 1918, of the "Balance of Power" theory. Britain, he supposed, wanted to put an end to France's Continental hegemony. She would not have won the war until that hegemony was destroyed. Very well! Germany would help her. Hitler was not afraid, indeed, to remind the British that Prussian militarism had just as much perseverance as they had. As always, more or less veiled menace was mixed with flatteries and promises.

Turning southward, and first of all to the south-west, the tribune perceived there the natural ally all ready—Italy. For he had his own idea of alliances. A weak and humiliated country like Weimar Germany was no attraction to anyone. A strong Germany would have friends. She would even find Europe rallying round her. Italy had been converted to Fascism. That meant that she had recovered the sense of her Germanic origins. She ignored the appeals of the Habsburg legitimists. The Italo-German alliance was thus a natural thing. "Italy's reason for coming into the war," says *Mein Kampf,* "was certainly not to aggrandize France; her reason was much more probably to make an end of her detested Adriatic rival. Every reinforcement of French power on the Continent clearly means a future obstacle in Italy's path." The destruction of France would suit Italy just as well as it would Britain. Hitler's crude mentality saw nothing beyond that.

Then there was the South-east, and the East in general: access to the Black Sea and the eastern Mediterranean. "We National Socialists," wrote Hitler, "are deliberately breaking with the foreign policy Germany pursued before the war. . . . We are making an end of the eternal thrust of the Germans to the South and West of Europe, and are looking toward the countries of the East." The passage is not clear, but no doubt means that Germany wants to beat France without conquering her and will leave Italy to her own destiny. The term "the countries of the East" is vague. Elsewhere, however, we read that German Austria "must return one day to the great German mother-country," and that "common blood presupposes common empire." The tribune goes no further. He simply leaves it to be understood that there must be a sort of general thrust to the South-east, toward Russia, and toward the Baltic North.

It is precisely because he means to take up again the colonizing work of the Teutonic Order in the East that Hitler passes rapidly over the colonies. After a strong criticism of the pre-war colonial policy he declares that he sees little to approve in colonial enterprises. Germany's destiny lies in Europe, in her *natural* space.

Such are the broad lines of the foreign policy of *Mein Kampf.*

Hitler is content to indicate the general direction. It is a very different thing from simple equality of rights or treatment. The German people must conquer by arms the place to which it is predestined. The pre-1914 phrase was "the place in the sun." The reference in Hitlerism is to a place determined by fate, by Providence, or by " geopolitics." It is to a virtual right, a draft on the future, demanding that a given force should be employed to secure it.

While Hitler thus limits his designs to Europe, Rosenberg looks out to vaster horizons. Like Spengler, he considers the problem of the lower classes in revolt and that of the coloured races. The Far East disturbs him, with the nationalist and Communist China of Sun Yat-sen and the Kuomintang, the China that Japan menaces, and also with India, of which Rosenberg foresees that it will soon be giving trouble to the British. Rosenberg goes farther, however, than Spengler. He does not entrust to Prussia alone the task of preserving Europe from Bolshevism, from invasion, and from the decline of the white race. He hopes that America will quickly be converted to racialism and will support in Europe the struggle Germany has begun, for the saving of the white race from Bolshevism and the coloured peoples. When Germany has her hundred million inhabitants, the association of the United States, Germany, Italy, and Japan will be invincible. It will rule the world. Such were the first hopes of National Socialism in world affairs. They will not be reproached for lack of scope.

These views clearly implied that Germany, once her European programme had been carried out, would tolerate the British Empire and British domination of the seas, and that, on the other hand, she would assure to Italy the primacy in the Mediterranean. Perhaps she would reserve to herself what she calls "the Eurasian space," that is to say, the space occupied by Russia, of which Germany would take possession in the event of the dismemberment of Russia. Here is the germ of the theory of the extremists.

Between this programme and that which the pan-Germans had elaborated on the eve of the First World War, the difference is not absolute. The Nazi leaders are clearly the heirs of a tradition and a plan. To prove it there is no need at all to recall the views of Paul de Lagarde or the various systems concerning Central Europe that were published under William II, down to the famous "Mitteleuropa" of Friedrich Naumann.

The Wilhelmian pan-Germans thought that Germany had

been mistaken after 1871 in resting on her laurels. Like the
French under Louis Philippe, the Germans had had but one idea,
to enrich themselves. The German people had fallen into
materialism. It had installed itself in the Bismarckian Reich as if
that was to be its final home. Never had the pan-Germans
accepted the Bismarckian idea of German *saturation*. Or rather,
they had admitted it only for the period 1871–90, during which
it was necessary to consolidate the young Reich. They had
accepted with enthusiasm the world policy of William II. At
the same time, breaking with the Bismarck tradition, they sought
to reveal to the people the secrets of foreign policy. They set
out to persuade it that the victory of 1871 had opened out to
German ambitions an unlimited field.

Hitler inherited this overmastering preoccupation. But he
was not after colonies. For the time, as we have seen, he wanted
only an *intra-European* policy. Certainly the dream of "Mitteleuropa" had been entertained under William II. There was a
return to Friedrich List, to the idea of a Zollverein for Central
Europe, and the Berlin-Bagdad schemes were to prolong this
Customs Union to Asia Minor. After the First World War this
idea was taken up again by the "Tat" group. There was thus
a certain continuity down to Hitler. The Hitlerite leaders,
however, could not forgive Wilhelmianism *for having mixed up the
Continental and the colonial programme*. That did not prevent them,
on attaining power, from quickly reviving colonial claims. But
it remains true that these still occupied a secondary place in their
policy.

3. *Accomplished facts*

The foreign policy pursued since 1933 by the Third Reich
presents certain aspects and reveals certain characteristics that
were scarcely suggested by the earlier programme.

There reappeared very clearly the curious alternation that was
revealed by the juridical theories. On the one hand there was
the affirmation of the full racialist system, with the notion of *total
war*, founded on that of *total enmity*. On the other hand there
was kept in the background, in the guise of an ultimate Utopia,
to serve as a bait for the credulous publics of the West, the idea
of Peace, German Peace, thinly disguising that of a harmony
conceivable and possible only among *homogeneous*, and therefore
totalitarian, peoples. There existed alongside each other a peace
propaganda in favour of the abolition of recourse to war, and

successive acts of violent breach with the post-war international status. Such was the paradox that needs explaining.

In order to grasp it better, we need a careful definition of the Hitlerite concept of "broadened strategy."

When Hitler said that he wanted peace, that declaration did not in the least mean that he was not continuing his Revolution in the direction of German hegemony. Quite the contrary, for the successive ruptures were intended precisely to lead to the "Pax Teutonica." If these successive ruptures—the reintroduction of obligatory military service, the remilitarization of the Rhineland, the intervention in Spain, and the annexation of Austria, the Sudeten territory, and Bohemia and Moravia—could succeed *without a general war*, so much the better. It is true that the general war broke out in 1939 owing to a new rupture, a "last straw" of some size. Consequently Hitler, when he addressed the nations, made no attempt at any apologia for that war in itself, though its principle was the very essence of racialism.

Instead, he created a sort of *intermediate* state, a sinister penumbra between peace and war, a state of things that was neither peace nor war—conforming in this perfectly well to his jurists' ideas on international law, on war and peace.

Perhaps he was returning to a pet idea of Clausewitz, the idea that in face of relatively weak States the simple existence of a strong army may suffice. The essential thing then was, beneath the cover of the vague and boundless fear, the "spiritual terror" inspired by Germany in the neighbour nations, to achieve the ultimate aim by successive stages, especially by attacking small States incapable of resistance, which were easily frightened by a crushing military machine, and which could thus be penetrated without striking a blow. To acquire in this way, bit by bit, hegemony in Central Europe, was to constitute an excellent basis from which to proceed.

Propaganda was to be connected up, as a *fourth arm*, with the land, sea, and air forces, and so to produce such fear that, with the Great Powers remaining immobile and, as it were, mesmerized, it would be possible to incorporate in the Reich the territories considered as belonging to it by natural law. Hitler was able to show to the Germans that they had no need of war to accomplish their mission, that their leader was making no call on them while lavishing upon them resounding successes. Would the Western democracies, won over by the passiveness of Right and Left, accept the situation and bow before the accomplished fact? As

for Russia, she remained immobile and silent, suggesting the view
that she did not want war on any account, and had not the
slightest desire to interfere in the affairs of the rest of Europe.
When he spoke of peace, Hitler speculated on the German
people's desire for peace, which it shared with the other peoples,
and on the subsequent German peace which would be total
hegemony. Between these two modalities, the victims would be
the weak States, whatever their size. This time the relation
between victors and vanquished would be fixed. A hegemonic
Germany would not be seen imitating Bismarck's moderation.
Here the world was faced, beyond possibility of any illusion,
with *unlimited revolutionism*, making play both with subtle
prudence and with brutal audacity, with peace and war. War
became permanent without being true war; peace became
permanent without being true peace. Hitler's "Aktionen,"
marching from success to success, would have destroyed the
established order, broken the small States and weakened the
strongest Powers, if the conquest of Poland had not put an end
to the succession of tragic adventures and incredible exhibitions
of weakness.

Hitler and his acolytes were moving in pure dynamism.[1]
Among them there was a strange mixture of condottierism and
cool calculation. Their perfidy was without bounds; meanwhile
they were convinced that the German era was beginning for
Europe. Nobody can deny that Hitler, while very cleverly
making use of the passivism in his own and other countries,
wanted peace. Why the "Aktionen"? Simply because, without
being of sufficient dimensions, at least in the "Führer's" opinion,
to break the peace and bring real and general war, they prepared
the way for future hegemony. It was a miscalculation, for this
method could not but show the menaced nations that to want
peace meant to want *total servitude* to Germany.

The critical period in the history of Europe during these last
years was the period 1935–38, during which *Germany imagined
herself to be able to pass from the simple preoccupation with security to
the certainty of crushing triumph.* She had been allowed the opportunity to arm to the teeth and in three years to get the preponderance of force on her side. And she had not wasted a moment
in profiting from this almost undreamt-of opportunity. The
neighbour nations, stupefied, had seen how she was proceeding

---

[1] The word is Nazi by whole-hearted adoption though not in origin. It might
be regarded as a euphemism for "aggressiveness."

to future order through existing disorder.   Finally they realized that, keeping within a sort of chiaroscuro between consistent racialism and the idea of collaboration between peoples, the Hitlerite leaders and their rabble of jurists were preparing, stage by stage, the enslavement of Europe.

Obviously a peace offensive had followed the first rearmament after the campaign for equality of rights.   None the less, they took up once more the subject of the "*Lebensraum,*" the "room to live," to be conquered.   From 1935 onwards, Hitler's speeches dwelt incessantly, and with growing insistence, on the lack of room to live from which the German people was suffering.   On March 7, 1936, he said: "Here, on a very restricted territory, not all of which is fertile, live 67,000,000 people."   The tribune added that the German people had only one-eighteenth of the space per head that the Russian people had!   On September 9 of the same year Hitler declared at Nuremberg that this fact condemned Germany "to internal disarmament and to destitution." The allusions to the vast territories of the Soviet Union multiplied. "We are not in the happy situation of those Bolshevist Jews who have too much land.   If the Urals with their immense resources of raw material, and Siberia with its rich forests, and the Ukraine with its immense areas under grain, were situated in Germany, then, under the National Socialist Government, she would be *swimming in wealth.*"

Even when Germany was proceeding to one annexation after another, this declaration was repeated.   The speech of April 28, 1939, which set out to justify the conquest of Bohemia and Moravia, returned once more to the theme of *Lebensraum.*   "I have always kept within the limits of the claims that were closely bound up with Germany's need of room to live, *and therefore with the eternal property of the German nation.*"   And he added later in the speech, turning to Roosevelt: "I have re-established the historic and millenary unity of the German *Lebensraum.*"   Had not the United States fifteen times as much space as Germany? Was not Hitler attaining his ends *without shedding blood?*

The argument concerning peace in Europe appears again and again from 1933 onwards.   On May 17, 1933, Hitler declared that no European war "would be able to establish a better situation in place of the existing one."   Even decisive successes obtained by violence, he said, would only increase the European disequilibrium and sow the seed of future conflicts.   Such cynicism would indeed be hard to beat.   But in the course of the years that followed this theme was taken up a hundred times over. On May 21, 1935, Hitler exclaimed: "Germany has realized the simple, elementary fact that no war could put an end to the universal poverty of Europe." He added that he had no desire at all for the glory of the victorious general. He desired the glory, more difficult to obtain, of the *peaceful builder*. Or again, drawing upon his recollections as an ex-soldier, he claimed to have a horror of war. But he insisted none the less on *peace with honour*, and we know what that meant. At the end of his speech on April 28, 1939, Hitler dared to claim that he was serving the cause of justice, prosperity, progress, and peace, for all mankind. And he resumed this theme later, after the tragic campaign in Poland.

In agreement with his jurists, Hitler quibbled over the respect shown by Germany for other peoples. He called for harmony between nations. He turned to the youth of Germany, who had suffered so much from the consequences of defeat. He declared that Nazism, as a general conception of life, imposed on its followers "universal obligations of principle." "We," he exclaimed, "attached to our own people by boundless love and faithfulness, also respect the national rights of other people *in virtue of that same state of mind*, and we want from the bottom of our hearts to live with them in peace and friendship." In his speech of May 17, 1933, he went so far as to disclaim the very idea of "Germanization," mainly because that process made use only of the language. Hitler wanted to reach men's souls. And from the moment when foreigners are regarded as inferiors there is nothing to be done but reduce them to slavery. Hitler repeated these sayings on May 21, 1935. He noted that each nation, Poland included, *remained true to itself*. If Germany was in favour of peace, it was "for the very reason of this special conception held by National Socialism of the people and the State." Hitler added that there were no longer any unoccupied lands in Europe, and that in consequence there was nothing to be gained by increasing any population by the addition of new units. And on March 7, 1936, he maintained once more that peoples are "historic realities."

How were such declarations to be reconciled with the notion of the absolute sovereignty claimed for Germany? Why send Germans to Spain to reinforce the Moors fighting the Spaniards themselves? The same inconsistency weighs upon the declarations of the "Führer" and on the theories of his jurists.

If Germany meant to respect her neighbours it was because she desired equality of rights for herself. This was Hitler's great *leit-motiv* between 1933 and 1936. He was prudent. He began by leaving pure racialism on one side. All he wanted was to put an end to the unequal treatment of Germany and to abolish the relationship of victors and vanquished, since that relationship was not in Germany's interest. This did not prevent him from refusing the same equality of rights to Russia. Moreover, that equality was inconsistent with pure Nazism. We can see how cleverly Hitler juggled with contradictory conceptions.

There was the same Machiavellism in the declarations concerning France and Russia.

The opposition was flagrant between the argumentation of *Mein Kampf* and the assurances Hitler lavished upon France from 1933 onwards. "It would be a tremendous event," he said on October 14, 1933, "for all humanity if the two peoples could banish violence once for all from their common life. The German people is ready to do this." After the return of the Saar to the Reich, the tribune declared that there remained no territorial conflict between France and Germany. How many times he returned to this theme in the years that followed! Yet Hitler continued his propaganda in Alsace-Lorraine. He made use of that glacis for introducing anti-Judaism into France. In addition to this, he swooped upon French democracy, especially after 1936, and upon the Popular Front in particular, declaring that these contained the germs and were the mouthpieces of Bolshevism.

No longer desiring to attack France *manu militari*, Hitler meditated upon a political and moral offensive. He repeated incessantly that democracy is the channel for Bolshevism. "I consider it possible that in such a case, to avoid a worse solution, *coalition governments may be formed, masked as a Popular Front or something of the sort*, and that they may try, perhaps with success, to eliminate the last vestiges of resistance to Bolshevism that are still to be found in these peoples." The allusion is clear.

These arguments led Hitler to the theory of the *necessity for intervention*. On May 21, 1935, he said that Nazism was not an export article, but on March 7, 1936, he sketched a new move, intervening in French affairs and using France's *internal politics* as a pretext for the remilitarization of the Rhine. Here French democracy was expressly confused with Bolshevism, though Nazism has close kinship with Russian Communism and its absolute planning system. This was the depth of perfidy. On November 6, 1938, Hitler returned to the same theme at Weimar.

Specious arguments, but well calculated for attracting to the Hitlerite cause the French bourgeoisie, which he was merely out to betray.

We see the same duplicity in regard to Russia. There were some assurances of friendship, particularly in a speech of March 23, 1933, and also close relationships of various sorts. The Rapallo and Berlin agreements had been extended by a protocol that was ratified at Moscow in May 1933. This juridical bond was precarious. Any trifle might destroy it. But it had been in existence a long time, and there had been busy economic relations between the two countries down to 1936. From then on the volume of business diminished. It was recovering before the present war.

First place was given to the very vigorous anti-Communist campaign, directed less against Russia than *against universal revolution*, with the main object of filling the Western middle class with panic and of breaking every bond between France and Russia. When he spoke of Europe, Hitler spoke *as if Russia was not part of Europe*. On May 21, 1935, he insisted on the elements that separated Germany from Russia. He wanted peace, but no military support from Bolshevism. In 1936, when he denounced Locarno, he invoked as pretext the Franco-Russian pact that had just been ratified by the French Chamber. *While refusing all co-operation with Russia, he drew, nevertheless, a subtle distinction between Russia herself and Bolshevism, which was out for world domination.* Europe existed in two halves: (1) Russia; (2) the peoples to whom Germany was bound. At the Nuremberg Congress of 1936 the attack was delivered with yet more energy. The struggle against Bolshevism took the place of the struggle against the Versailles Treaty, with the three familiar theses: the Jews were the makers of Communism; Germany could make splendid use of Russian territories and resources; a crusade was necessary against the Soviets and the democracies ought to take part in it. In 1937 Hitler declared that intervention in Russia was inevitable and that Germany would then be *a model for the other half of the old Continent*.

Thus the programme of *Mein Kampf* was pursued point by point. Without war, by the most insidious of propaganda, aimed at associating Democracy and Bolshevism in order the better to keep them apart, the Third Reich tried to break the bond between West and East.

If we consider Hitler's naval pact in 1935 with Britain, on the subject of which he later made menacing reservations; the assurances lavished upon France, mixed with diatribes against democracy; and the cautious attitude to Russia as Russia, the impression remains that Nazism had no desire to create any great concern among the Powers that had formed the Triple Entente before 1914, and that it desired to maintain the anti-Communist propaganda that gained Hitler so much sympathy among the Western middle classes. It was just this that enabled him to go determinedly to work against the small States on the German periphery, beginning with those with German minorities.

Few references were made to the Scandinavian countries, which scarcely felt German pressure before 1938. The Schleswig problem might be taken up at any moment. By way of precaution agreements were made with Poland and with Belgium, in whose territory the conflict between Walloons and Flemings favoured Hitlerite propaganda. This propaganda was carried on busily in Holland and Switzerland, but those two countries were not really involved until after certain disturbing annexations and the appearance of the menace of general war.

The principal effort was directed to the south-west by the alliance with Italy and the constitution of the Berlin-Rome axis, without forgetting intervention in Spain, and to the south-east through the annexation of Austria and of Czechoslovakia, actions which were completed a little later by the Italian ally's occupation of Albania.

The way had been prepared for these destructive activities by three main moves: (1) the rupture with the League of Nations; (2) rearmament; (3) the remilitarization of the Rhine. By the first, for which Hitler, acting against the advice of his diplomats, assumed all responsibility, Germany recovered liberty of movement. Through the second she rapidly regained her former strength—a Samson recovering his locks; by the third, finally, she had reconquered her full sovereignty. On each occasion she had broken the most solemn engagements. In particular, the remilitarization of the Rhineland was the end of Locarno.

So came one after another, in truly lightning fashion, from 1936 to 1938 the intervention in Spain; in March 1938 the annexation of Austria; in September 1938, in agreement with the Western Powers, the annexation of the Sudeten territory; in February and March 1939 the annexation of Bohemia and Moravia; and in September 1939 the attack on Poland that started the Second World War.

All these States had been given the most formal guarantees. On May 21, 1935, Hitler had declared that he would respect in its entirety every treaty signed by Germany, even before 1933, and would conform in particular to the obligations of Locarno. "The German Government," he said, "by respecting the demilitarized zone (of the Rhineland), is contributing to the pacification of Europe. *But this respect weighs on our sovereignty as a crushing burden.*" Less than a month later Hitler tore up the Locarno pact. In the same speech Hitler promised to respect the Versailles clauses concerning territorial frontiers. In order to escape from the discrimination against it, the Government of the Third Reich "will respect absolutely the other points that concern the community of nations, *including the territorial stipulations*, and will not carry out the revisions inevitable in the course of time *except by the path of a peaceful agreement.*"

Hence the assurances lavished on Austria and Czechoslovakia. "Germany has neither the intention nor the desire to interfere in Austrian affairs, to annex Austria, for example, or attach her to herself" (May 21, 1935). On March 7, 1936, Hitler said, in regard to Czechoslovakia and Poland, that *Germany had no desire to attack those States.*

A very simple procedure emerges clearly from the practice thus followed during six years. To maintain Europe, by means of "broadened strategy," in a state intermediate between peace and war; to obtain the connivance and indulgence of the Western Powers; to hit at the small States that were incapable of defending themselves alone; to declare Germany's absolute need of "room to live" and at the same time to praise the collaboration of peoples, the purpose being to recover the lost sovereignty; to attack France and Russia only from within; to prepare action against the south-west by alliance with Italy and against the south-east by forcible annexations; finally, to start the cry of encirclement if the periphery defended itself—such was the line followed. The moment came when the European world decided that it would be duped no longer.

This foreign policy was the sign of a dynamic revolution with unlimited ambitions. It set aside Alfred Rosenberg because it found him too moderate. And it gave expression to its supreme designs, not by any means in the best-known works of the Nazi leaders, but in certain writings of the Nazi extremists—Jünger, Haushofer, Banse, Niekisch, and others.

Fundamentally, in order to avoid war while attaining the ends in view, it was proposed to employ new tactics. From this point of view, the eastern policy or the destruction of France were but *secondary* objectives. The former assured Germany of the indispensable raw materials; the latter freed her on the west. What was at work here was *an imperialism with world-wide aims*. Under cover of a false appeal to peace a mysticism of population, territory, and expansion developed here to its extreme conclusions. In face of the nations that possessed space through their empires rose those that had fewer possessions, *though their birth-rate entitled them to more*. A specious and a dangerous claim, since the *Slav* increase is greater than the *German*.

Thus the ruin of the existing empires must be accelerated, and the peoples not be allowed to come to their end in a Europe in which they were being stifled. A question of population and of the birth-rate. The victory was due in advance to those who had most of both. German confidence and audacity were due to the belief in the inevitable decay of the Western Powers, the British and French empires. It was believed in Germany that the shadow was moving over the colonial aggregations of the past. They were regarded as incapable of self-defence or of defending the primacy of the white race. *The Russian Empire was considered to have no more solidity. It was proposed to dismember it with the rest.* On all these ruins would then rise German hegemony, surrounded by the necessary *Lebensraum*!

Thus, facing the "revolutionary" Powers such as Germany, Italy, and Japan, stood the Powers of "conservation" such as Britain and France, and also, evidently, Stalinist Russia. The brutal simplicity of the picture is disconcerting. Victorious Germany, it was said, would substitute for the class struggle, the object of Socialism, Communism, and Judaism, *the struggle between nations*. Imperialism here became a providential mission, a tactic to be followed with a view to universal domination; Hitler carrying out for his own benefit, at the instance of the most audacious elements of the Party, the very plan that the *Protocols of the Elders of Zion* attributed to the Jews of the whole world. "Mächte des *Beharrens* und Mächte der *Erneuerung*!" Powers *holding tight* to what they had and Powers out to *change all that*! The future belonged to the young nations that had achieved unity between 1850 and 1870.

And what was to become of the small States? They no longer counted, and were doomed to disappear. They were created by the treaties of 1919, and how should they subsist when those treaties had gone? They had been but an episode in the fast-moving course of history. The notion of neutrality was rapidly changing. The smaller States of Europe could no longer pursue a policy worthy of the name. They must be absorbed. The fate of Austria, Czechoslovakia, and Poland, the fate threatening Denmark, the Baltic States, Holland, Switzerland, and the Balkans, all this depended on one and the same principle. There was talk of "protecting" these States. That meant that the notion of "*Gefolgschaft*," of the "following," was being applied to them. Their task was to conform to the "protectorate."

Germany played assiduously with the two pictures. She affirmed at one and the same time the theory of absolute domination and the principle of the free determination of peoples. She made use of the latter to shake the existing colonial edifices. But she employed methods that were the negation of this principle, since they involved proceeding to transfers of populations. It was a vast work of dissolution that had begun, led by iconoclasts devoid of scruples, and permitting Germany, if it was not interrupted, to deploy all her domination-seeking imperialism. This imperialism was of a different type to that of the nineteenth century, consisting in the sharing out of the world to the advantage of Germany alone. From European hegemony Germany would pass to world empire.

Hence the "true" interpretation of alliances. They are there to bring Germany *active partners*, working in the same direction as she, and including, if it must be so, *even France*, though a nazified France. Greater Germany would then be the nucleus and the principal director of a vast defensive association, based on her hegemony. There would be applied to the entire Continent the great Nazi system of *Führung* and *Gefolgschaft*, leaders and following. Europe would be replaced, in this system of leadership gone mad, by a universal Empire in which Germany would occupy the whole of the so-called "Eurasian" space. The wide territories thus brought under her dominion would reach vertically to the Danubian region, Turkey, the Middle East, and India, and horizontally from Flushing in the west to Vladivostok in the east.

Then would come Britain's turn. Germany, with France reduced to her western vassal, would have all Eurasia, including, that is to say, the Russian territories. Italy would hold the Mediterranean, Africa, and Asia Minor. Britain would retain her mastery of the seas and her Dominions. America and Japan would represent two distinct continental entities that would count. *This would mean the almost total liquidation of France and Russia.* The same result might alternatively be reached *by a German-Russian alliance* that would compel the Western Powers to capitulate.

Such were the designs put forward in their fanaticism by the hundred-per-cent. Nazis, those who wanted absolute planning, an army of mercenaries, and a world empire; those who regarded the first National Socialist programme as rather skimped, provincial, merely-European! Such was the element of *dream* and *Utopia* in the later policy.

That policy scarcely concealed its methods. And those methods may be compared to those of a terrible engine of destruction. They emanated, like the whole of Nazism, from a frantic romanticism that made use of the most rigorous discipline and the most perfected technique. The partial success obtained might have made reality of that Utopia. In face of such perspectives, middle-class nationalism cut a poor figure. It did not realize what was bound to result from the German rupture with the League of Nations, in an international void, where right no longer counted, and where there was room for the play of a sort of prophetic and visionary somnambulism free of all restraints and limitations.

In face of this flood of pushing and acquisitive pan-Germanism the threatened nations made no move: they were positively spell-bound by the phenomenon, and they still thought in their simplicity that National Socialism might grow reasonable. They did not see at first that every concession brought fresh encouragement to that forced dynamism. Thus, by their apathy, resulting from lack of foresight and lack of energy, they helped on a policy of *gambling upon opportunities*, which could only count on the weakness of the rest but which bore within itself the germ of death, because under the influence of its vision of greatness it hit out blindly right and left, automatically producing the coalition that was bound to bring it to ruin.

To sow disorder everywhere, to have nothing to do with bourgeois "statism," to destroy the established order root and branch, to rule over the ruins—was that the aim, or not? To destroy the position of the "saturated" nations, to create universal anarchy, to profit by the humbling of the *élites* in the existing democracies, to overthrow everything without having any plan of renewal, was that a policy for Germany and Europe?

In the first half of 1939 all sorts of opportunities offered themselves to Hitler. He could turn to the south-east, to the Ukraine and Roumania, and thence to the Black Sea. He could also turn to the north-east and attack Poland, in alliance with Russia. Finally, he could encircle France and occupy the Netherlands, in order to isolate Britain from the Continent. To-day we know the choice he made, without counting on the crushing onset of Russia. The Führer began by flattering Britain and ended by turning her against him. He first abused France and then made her the most alluring offers. Finally, after brutally denying that Russia had anything to do with Europe, he concluded an alliance with her. He reproached William II for having no programme. Was his own policy any more consistent? Now, with the maximum of power deployed, Germany had the maximum of difficulties and doubts. It would be dangerous to allow that dynamism free play at any time, in the idea that it might turn against Germany herself. For Germany was capable of placing the world under her heel and yet making no attempt at any sort of reorganization.

In their anti-British fury the Nazis did not see that the British Empire is essentially the model of a spiritual and material empire *that knows how to leave mankind its freedom.* National Socialism talked of the injustice of Versailles but then allowed itself to commit far worse injustice. To Germany's misfortune it destroyed the federalism of Central Europe. *It made of it a coalition which no one could endure.* The biological Race brings death to nationalities without organizing anything in their place. Germany has been led in the opposite direction to that of her true mission. Hitler squandered the unprecedented opportunities he had in 1933 for reconstructing Germany, unifying her, consolidating her structure, and remaking Europe with the Western Powers after their liberation from the imperfect League of Nations they had created. Nothing would then have prevented Europe from solving the colonial problem, the problem of economic exchanges, and that of the distribution of raw materials.

Now the nations reduced to servitude must regain their independence and recover their vitality, for the final defeat of Germany's dictatorial violence. Germany contented herself with local aggressions, with partial successes gained against small neighbours, successes devoid of true merit or true greatness. She disorganized the old Continent without showing herself capable of offering it anything better than brutal domination.

Her power was not equal to her insane ambition. After her slow emergence from territorial fragmentation, her political intelligence was inadequate for assuring unaided the equilibrium of the Continent.

4. *The Second World War*

The historic evolution and the first developments of National Socialism from 1933 to 1939, as here described, make perfectly clear the true character and the true significance of the phenomenon—that of a more and more conscious and organized preparation for the Second World War.

But the part played by the German ruling classes, and in particular by the great industrialists, in the genesis of the Hitlerite Party and of the Third Reich, the new and original aspects of the governmental machinery, the development and propaganda of racialist mysticism, and finally the construction of two armies working in unison, that of the workers and that of the conscript soldiers—all these various traits, so striking in themselves, bring into full light the factor that determined the whole situation at the beginning of the present war, the industrial factor: a vast war production, greatly ahead of that of the other nations, whether of Europe, Russia, or America. Never before had German industry, with all its potential, all its highly perfected installations, all its technically trained personnel, played to such an extent the part of an instrument of war. This explains the fact that the Second World War began, even more than the first, under the conditions of massed industrial production. *It is this immense production that constituted from the first the German advantage.*

It has been rightly said that the failure of the Anglo-French Alliance between 1939 and 1940 was in no way due to any economic shortcoming, to inadequate resources in the possession of the two nations united in the defence of their common positions. If there was any failure, it was before all else *political* and *strategic*. Germany, and the totalitarian Powers in general, took full account of the geographical and economic realities. The famous "geopolitics" had helped them. They thought only in terms of these material realities. The potential of the Anglo-French Alliance was not only formidable in itself but greatly superior to that of Germany and Italy. The propaganda of the two Western nations had even been energetically saying so again and again, with the result of veiling the weaknesses of the combination and of giving to too many ill-informed people a false sense of security. If the position of the Alliance had corresponded to its resources, it would have been capable unaided of effectively countering the military power of the Third Reich and of maintaining peace on the Continent. But the Alliance had not had time to mobilize its real resources. For it had given no thought either to its political consolidation or to its strategic plan until the moment when it was overtaken by emergency and, what made matters worse, after the elimination of Russia, which had been put out of action in 1938 and subsequently bound to Germany by the well-known treaty.

In reality, German industry had been preparing for the Second World War ever since 1918.

At the very outset it had avoided the danger of the socialization of the great trusts, which had appeared possible if not probable toward the end of 1918. On November 15, Stinnes and Legien, the heavy industries and the Socialist trade unions, had concluded an agreement. The new Government and the Social Democracy had also come to terms. And in the Weimar Constitution the Government had lost no time in ratifying its compromises. As always, the industrialists had astutely concealed their political game. The big subsidies the Republic had granted them enabled them to proceed with technical organization on a huge scale. The Reichsverband der deutschen Industrie, the German federation of industries, may be regarded retrospectively as the initial form of the economic organization later taken up by the Nazis. It quickly restored the financial situation and considerably enriched itself, until the day came when Germany's former competitors, and particularly the Anglo-Saxon world, began to shower upon it great capital loans. Between 1924 and 1928 these grew to an enormous total. Consequently, with the ground thus prepared by the modernization of plant, the restoration of the financial situation, and the reopening of relations with the victor countries, German industry was soon able to go over to the offensive, organizing great trusts, securing assistance from the economic G.H.Q. organized by the army, producing synthetic petrol and rubber, and assuring itself in all essential domains of war production a considerable advance, which the system of autarky was to extend and consolidate.

In all Germany's plans of conquest, central and south-eastern Europe played a leading part in consequence of their great raw material resources. The Reich was then able, partly through its financial legislation and partly through the inactivity of the

Western Powers, to subjugate the Danubian countries, which from 1939 on found themselves transformed into economic colonies of Germany. Under the National Socialist régime, once the masses had been won over to the policy of nationalist and pan-German "push," the great trusts were able to gain possession openly of the principal parts of the political and social machine by organizing the Labour Front. Not, indeed, that they were hampered by a State so impotent and docile as the Weimar Republic. They had become in some degree the victims of the great corporative State which they had done so much to build. But, since this system was but the political façade of a totalitarian industry, they were able to find their place in it in the very interest of the German Community whose military victories were to serve their ends. In fact, they were almost part of the State. And the State could delegate part of its power to the great industrialists, turning them, in the mystical system of National Socialism, into "Leaders," "Führer" consecrated by it.

It is easier, in the light of these elementary but in themselves convincing facts, to measure the immense mistake made by the Western Powers in accepting not only the National Socialist régime itself, and the destruction of the League of Nations at the end of 1933, but above all the reintroduction of compulsory military service in Germany in 1935, the remilitarization of the Rhineland in 1936, and the conquests and annexations that followed. In any case, apart from that great and significant political tragedy, unprecedented in European history, Germany's industrial advance constituted about 1939 her true superiority, all the more since it was to be utilized in accordance with the military conceptions and practices made possible by the latest developments of the most perfected modern technique.

Such is the sinister reality of which the progress was marked by the succession of *faits accomplis* referred to earlier.

Germany made full use of her industrial advantages in the first year of the war, from September 1939 to September 1940, from the attack on Poland to the end of the "Battle of Britain."

On August 15, 1939, Germany had begun her total mobilization. Poland had mobilized only on August 31, a delay that cost her dearly. But what could she have done, even if she had mobilized earlier, against a country with such intensive industrial production? Three weeks sufficed for the total liquidation of the Polish State created after 1919. By the middle of September all western Poland had been conquered, and the Russian army lost no time in invading the eastern territory. A new partition, even more tragic than the earlier ones, was the immediate consequence of that double campaign, German and Russian.

That, it must be said, contained an important lesson. For it was known from the first, since 1918, that the Germans would plan to move eastward before attacking in the west. And later it was clear that an ill-prepared adversary would be unable to resist a powerful combination of tanks, aircraft, and well-trained troops of all arms.

The story of the long stagnation of the winter of 1939–40 is well known—the stagnation that followed the Anglo-French declaration of war and the installation of the Allied armies along the eastern frontier of France and in the Alps. Only the naval struggle between Britain and Germany, resumed in the forms of the last war by the blockade and the submarine warfare, announced that a second world war was in preparation. On the other hand, Russia had extended at the same time her offensive against most of the Baltic States. Estonia, Latvia, and Lithuania had quickly had to submit. Finland's turn came in March 1940.

The winter was scarcely over when Germany, after having seized, since 1938, Austria, Czechoslovakia, and most of Poland, struck at Denmark and Norway. Her technique and her method had not varied in the slightest since the aggression against Austria. It was still a powerful invasion of the territory of an infinitely weaker opponent, the frightful war machine pouncing upon it with all means of action closely and pitilessly combined. Not that the Norwegian campaign was an easy one for the Germans. It cost them grave losses. But there, too, their superiority in the air assured them a relatively rapid and a total triumph. By the end of April the fate of these two Scandinavian countries was sealed. And though there had been no war between Germany and Sweden, the latter country could not but be a docile instrument in Hitler's hands, a pawn easily moved in his terrible game.

There remained Britain and France. On May 10, 1940, the most fateful day of all, Mr Winston Churchill succeeded Mr Chamberlain in England, and the German offensive against Holland began. French armistices were concluded with Germany and Italy on June 21 and 24. In six weeks the strongest coalition in Europe had collapsed. In face of that adversary, much the most considerable of all, the German method had not changed in the least. It was still, as, indeed, it had been in 1914, the mass attack, led with a clear superiority of energy and of technical resources. Hitler committed his aggression against Holland, Belgium, and Luxemburg at the very moment when he had just concluded treaties of friendship with these small States. The offensive proper followed the "peace offensive." As in Norway, Germany had recourse, though on a much larger scale, to parachutists who had flown from her own territory and to the traitors of the Fifth Column she had formed throughout Western Europe. And above all, in forcing the passage of the Meuse between Sedan and Mézières with five armoured divisions, she had brought into full light not only the essential trait of her strategy but the central idea of her doctrine and practice, the idea of an instrument of war irresistible in itself. This was the great blow of the bulldozer against the Western world, the moment of the application of an age-long thought and effort. On May 18 and 20 the Germans reached Amiens and Abbeville. On the 27th the Belgian army capitulated, and soon after this came the Dunkirk evacuation, which saved about 225,000 British and 112,000 Allied soldiers, mostly French. France's defeat was inevitable.

What would Britain do? The part she played in 1940 deviated not by a hairbreadth from the line she had always followed. It was in conformity with the clearest historic traditions of Great Britain, who has never ceased to oppose to the ambitions of conquerors an insurmountable barrier. But it is not enough to say that the German army came up against the inflexible resistance of a country separated from the Continent by a broad arm of the sea. It must be borne in mind that if Britain, then defenceless, had been eliminated from the game by a German invasion, the enemy would have had every chance of winning against Russia. Moreover, the British resistance permitted the formation and consolidation of the alliance of Russia, the United States, and the British Empire. *In other words, it is thanks to British heroism that there was built up, in face of the Hitlerite ambitions whose unlimited scope we know, the new Triple Entente, the association of Powers that needed only time to crush Germany beneath its blows.* The supreme hour of destiny had struck. The British people and its Prime Minister realized it. They gained incomparable greatness by that Battle of Britain, which saved the world and made possible the liberation of France.

Many of the Germans, and not the least among them, considered that the only way to strike at the heart of the British Empire was by the invasion of England. It is well known how in September the British aviators struck in time at the invasion

ports.   The Germans had to abandon their main idea, their effort
having been frustrated in the air and on the sea before ever it
began.   Thanks to the British navy and air force the German tanks
were unable to cross the twenty miles of sea.   That was why, from
November 1940 on, air attacks on Britain were substituted for
invasion.   But they could not have either the same scope or the
same consequences.   The three objects in view were the ports,
the industrial centres, and the population itself, which had to be
terrorized.   It was not simply *"der geistige Terror,"* the moral
terrorism, of *Mein Kampf,* but physical terrorism.   The Londoner
faced it with the familiar calm courage, thus restoring the hopes of
all free peoples.

As for the maritime war, the battles of the Atlantic and the
Mediterranean, it may be said that Britain had won that, too, by
the spring of 1941.   At that time she had a tonnage exceeding
that which she had had at the beginning of the struggle.   She had
maintained (1) the mastery of the seas against the German and
Italian fleets; (2) the freedom of the imperial lanes of traffic against
the German and Italian submarines.   In June 1941, at the end
of a combat which Britain had fought almost alone, the Axis had
not attained its strategic ends in the Mediterranean.   The Battle
of Africa was not yet decided.   But the Allied armies of the Near
East had 750,000 men.   And the armies of the Axis met with
inflexible resistance.   *"Blitzkrieg"* had beaten France, but it
failed against Great Britain.

From then on the war became world-wide, thanks entirely to
the British resistance.

First came Hitler's offensive against Russia.   It had been in
preparation since 1940.   When it broke out, on the morning of
June 22, 1941, Britain was Russia's ally.   The Prime Minister's
decision, taken without hesitation, was at the same time an appeal
to America.   War had begun in the space between Russia and the
Atlantic, the latter largely dominated by the United States.   On
the two wings of the struggle two continents were to enter the
fray, one attacked and invaded by the German troops, the other
entirely unprepared militarily, no doubt, but drawn into the
fighting some months later by the Japanese offensive.   And
when, a year later, on November 8, 1942, the American troops
landed in North Africa, the African continent being directly
affected by a struggle that shook it to its darkest depths, the war
became indeed total.

We are now, at the moment of the publication of this book, a couple of years away from those memorable events. Since then Germany's allies have suffered terrible and debilitating ordeals. As for the Hitlerite Third Reich, it has lost the game in North Africa, and subsequently in Russia, while the Anglo-Saxon Allies are systematically destroying its western industries and positions from Norway to France, by means of the immense Allied bombings. Germany's military power is declining. Her defeat on this plane is certain. And the whole question is whether the peace that is coming will make it definitive.

In spite of its intrinsic power, in spite of its central position in Europe, in spite of the terrible destruction it has wrought among the nations of the periphery of the Continent, the Hitlerite empire will have lasted no more than half as long as Napoleon's enterprise. But the first German assault dates from 1914, and to-day we may almost talk of a Thirty Years War. Will the great victorious Allies be able to maintain their union and assure to the world the peace for which all mankind is most naturally, and so ardently, sighing? That is to-morrow's secret. But the light of an immense hope is passing across the world. For the course of events, as we have just traced it, shows us that, under the desperate effort of the peoples at war, the line is being restored and the world is being righted, not, certainly, of its own accord, but thanks to the collaboration of all men of good will. May that collaboration survive the war, the cruel necessities of which engendered it.

CONCLUSION

WHO would have the temerity to draft a Psychology of the German People? The science of the large human collectivities of our time is still in its infancy. The sociology of to-day is learned about primitive societies and ignorant of its contemporaries.

No matter. No one can forbid our venturing on a provisional reconstruction. It will naturally be based on the synthesis here attempted. Further, it will lead us to a final judgment which from the midst of to-day's tragedy will throw some light on the problems that we have to face.

I. There is no such thing as a Germanic race, any more than there is a Celtic race or a Slav race. Ethnologists distinguish six different races in the German population. Far from being of one pure race, the German people is even more heterogeneous than its neighbours. "The voice of the German Blood," as Hellpach writes, "would be a medley of voices." [1]

Germany contains 50 per cent. of Nordics, distributed between North and South in the proportion of 60 to 40 per cent. The Dinaric element is in a majority in the South. The Mediterranean race is but very scantily represented. The Faelic element in Hesse, Thuringia, and the South, the East-Baltic element centring in East Prussia, and lastly the so-called Eastern Race, are all of negligible importance.

This rapid analysis reveals the antithesis between North and South. It is easy to see why the racialists of to-day use this somewhat complacently to demonstrate the superiority of the Nordics, and next to them of the Dinarics. They pretend to forget the true nature of the exchanges which have taken place along the North-South axis, and especially the linguistic aspect of these exchanges. It was High German, the language of South and Central Germany, that carried the day against Low German, the speech of the North. The Reformation completed this

---

[1] W. Hellpach, *Politische Prognose für Deutschland* (1928), pp. 9–11.

victory with Luther's translation of the Bible, and the classicism of Weimar set the seal on it in the eighteenth century.

In the nineteenth and twentieth centuries, however, the pendulum swung in the opposite direction. With the ever-increasing Prussification of the united Germany the language of the North, now become classic in its turn, conquered the South, especially the official and middle classes. When Germany transformed herself into an industrial and military State, when the countryside of the South-west became depopulated for the benefit of the Ruhr, of Brandenburg, or of Saxony, then the Nordic genius, frigid, laconic, unsentimental, and of ruthless tenacity, won the day for ever. It took charge of the political destinies of the nation. There is nothing more suggestive than these exchanges between North and South.

The antithesis between East and West is still richer in diversity of direction. It corresponds to the historic formation of the German population. It implies, moreover, the problem not of races but of ethnic components (tribes, *Stämme*).

The Elbe, as an internal frontier, here comes into its own. The ethnic groups to the west of this river have admirably persisted, attaching themselves to the soil and absorbing any elements coming from without. They tend in general to be mobile in mind, liberal in politics, with a leaning towards international conciliation, for they have been strongly under the cultural influence of antiquity, of Christianity, and of the West. In the region east of the Elbe, on the contrary, the levelling effect of its colonization has begotten—especially in the half-Slavified Prussian North—political conservatism, a sense of social discipline, and a peculiar dynamism, relic of the colonizing tradition, which drives men toward territorial and warlike adventure.

From the end of the fifth century A.D. we see the tribes between the Rhine and the Elbe holding their own: Frisians and Low Saxons in the North, Franks and Thuringians in the Centre, Alemans and Bavarians in the South. The Middle Ages, the Reformation, the Thirty Years War, the wars of the French Revolution and Empire, and Bismarck's creation of the Reich, have here changed nothing. The regional environment un-failingly wins the day over temperaments and individualities which, taken as a whole, offer little resistance to its influence.

The Frisians, people of the North Sea, form a hardy population characterized by a curious blend of prudence and daring, by the laconic speech typical of lonely and monotonous landscapes, by the silent activity and the love of independence which have given birth to so many small republics in their country. The Low Saxons, who inhabit the birthplace of the primitive Germanic peoples, that is to say the genuinely Prussian and Nordic country between the Rhine, the Elbe, and the Harz, are energetic, dedicated to the toil of sea and land, faithful to their vernacular, to their traditions and customs, even to certain survivals of ancient Germanic religion and mythology. They have little love for Roman Law. They have an instinct for organization, for positive science, for decision and for action. They form a very vigorous ethnic group who have swarmed westwards as far as England, southwards as far as the Rhine, and westward to colonize Slav countries. This country was the home of Scharnhorst, of Hardenberg, and of Bismarck.

The region of the Rhine and the Main is the most varied in Germany. It is there that Rome has left its strongest imprint. The Frank is essentially mobile, quick of thought and speech, affable and generous, markedly individualistic too, because he lives in a country where land is minutely parcelled out. This is the country of big fairs, of vast factories, the country of Goethe, of scholars and inventors, where political qualities used to be the most outstanding and where the conception of the Reich flourished the most vigorously. No other ethnic group was more capable of breaking free from the dour stolidity and massive dullness of the usual German community. Western Catholicism and the ideas of the French Revolution here penetrated deeply. As for the Thuringians, they escaped Roman influence. More sentimental and religious, they created the "garden" of Germany, the paradise of flowers, of luxuriant verdure, of poetry, of music, of pietist or mystic Lutheran fervour. Theirs is also the country of the great commercial routes, of the book trade and intellectual exchanges, the country of the Reformation, of Bach, of Handel, of Schumann, of Wagner, and of Nietzsche.

The Alemannic group occupies the rich region that stretches along the upper courses of the Rhine, the Danube, and the Neckar. It has played no inconsiderable part in history, for it gave birth to several imperial houses: those of Hohenstaufen, Habsburg, and Hohenzollern. The Aleman's mind takes kindly to decentralization; his is a country of free cities and of vigorous democracy, where the aristocracy mixes freely with the people; where Schiller and Schubert in their day revolted against monarchic absolutism; a country where mediæval epic and lyric poetry flourished, and science and philosophy with Kepler and later Hegel and Schelling; and mysticism and pietism with Tauler, Suso, and Spener. Somewhat thick-blooded folk they are, the Alemans, reserved and introvert, often unable to find words for what they feel, souls in whom repression finds natural vent in explosion. People, in short, whose very fullness makes choice and decision difficult. As for the Bavarian, he loathes industry and commerce, loves music and dancing, is loyal to the established order, and clings fervently to his Catholicism. Though normally happy-go-lucky and light-hearted, calm and inclined to silence, he is by nature a fighter at his own times. Above all he is a peasant, inhabiting wild and lonely uplands where landed properties are of vast extent. It was in Bavaria that the great Christian dream was born of the conquest of Italy and of the East.

Such, in its elements and its most essential aspects, is Western Germany, rich in contrasts and in possibilities. Alongside it, the country east of the Elbe lived for centuries under Slav domination before it was colonized from Western Germany. Its towns are more geometrically laid out than the ancient tortuous cities of the West and South. The large landed estate, the "*Rittergut*," is there the normal thing. It has been fatal to the free development of the peasantry. The blending and levelling of the two populations contrasts with the relative fixity of western groupings. The German colonizing effort lasted an entire millennium, from A.D. 800 to about 1800. Having once crossed the Elbe, the western elements fused. This marked provincialization begot Prussianism, in this region of flat plains where ease of communication promoted Slav integration and the vigorous centralization of the Prussian State.

These vast movements from west to east, however, were succeeded (as in the relations between North and South) by an inverse movement from east to west. The active influence of Prussia followed, in fact, the east to west direction. *The ethnic, juridical, and political concentration of the region east of the Elbe was more effective in creating the modern unitarism than the ancient dreams of universal greatness, which, indeed, ran counter to the particularism of the West.* The Lutheran Reformation of the sixteenth century, which started out from the East spread to the North-east and to the North-west. Later, Silesian culture, which was very potent in the seventeenth and eighteenth centuries, was equally successful in capturing the West.   Finally the Industrial Revolution of the nineteenth century had the effect of draining the countryside of the East for the benefit of the Ruhr and of Brandenburg.

Thus constant exchanges in reverse directions took place along the two vertical and horizontal axes.   The striking differences that exist on the one hand between the plain of the North, the greatly subdivided Central Germany, and the plateaux of the South, and on the other hand between the West with its numerous ethnic varieties and the East with its racial and political uniformity, throw into full relief the opposition between the *North-east*, where all modern Prussian policy since 1750 has originated, and the *South-west*, home of the ancient imperial houses.   This is the radical antithesis between Prussia and Reich.

In so far as these ethnic differences have persisted through the centuries, it is justifiable to speak of a real *psychological pluralism* which, far from having disappeared under the Third Reich, certainly still exists beneath the dictatorial façade of the Hitlerite régime, and has increased and become even more complex with the territorial annexations of 1938–39.   On the other hand, though this pluralism persists, though the German people remains a complex people of many facets, perhaps even in danger of relapse into its ethnic, psychological, and political particularisms, there have nevertheless been at work in the course of history powerful factors making for *psychological uniformity*. We can recognize three of them: first the great work of linguistic, literary, and philosophic unification that was accomplished between 1500 and 1800—at the very time when territorial fragmentation condemned Germany to political impotence—and found its consecration in Romanticism; secondly, the enormous and, indeed, excessive industrialization of the Bismarck period between 1850 and 1914; thirdly and finally, the Hitlerite process of *Gleichschaltung*, after the last war, which aimed, even before Hitler's advent to power, at creating the one-type German, the German who would *Volk werden*, would become just a national unit, to use the terrible Nazi formula.

II. These factors of unification were not unrelated to the earlier pluralism.   They were, in fact, its effect and its corrective. Herein we are again face to face with the fundamental duality of Germany in the true meaning of the words.   Having analysed the various elements that go to the make-up of the real Germany, W. Hellpach, in his *Politische Prognose für Deutschland*, wonders whether there is any trait common to all the Germans of the twentieth century. He finds it in precisely this singular opposition, which we must now accurately define.

Taking account of the racial elements, the ethnic groups, the territories or States, the religious confessions, the political parties, the trade associations, and the innumerable other societies which have always continued to multiply beyond the Rhine, we find that the German as an individual seems to be the victim of this incredible psychological, political, and institutional pluralism, finding a series of screens interposed between himself and the nation. An inhabitant of the South, for instance, will be a Dinaric, a Bavarian, a Catholic, a member of the Centre Party, a proletarian trade unionist, before he is a citizen of the Reich. His vision is thus inevitably myopic, he is imprisoned by a narrow horizon within some limited and strictly disciplined trade or occupation.

But this same German never forgets the Reich, whether of the past or of the future. *Nothing but the Reich really kindles his enthusiasm*, be it the fallen Holy Roman Empire or Germany's future hegemony. Since the days of Bismarck the vision of this Reich has worked more and more potently on his mind in proportion as pan-Germanism—originally begotten in the brains of a few or limited to intellectuals—became popularized and took possession of the masses. This typical German found consolation for his narrow and dreary existence in dreaming of the Empire of the morrow. He thrilled with patriotism when he was reminded of the disastrous subdivisions of the Germany of old, the humiliations endured, the defeats due, like that of 1918, to so many internal dissensions. Formerly he would console himself by plunging into abstruse philosophy, into poetic dreams or universal constructive schemes. It is common knowledge that pan-Germanism exploited this great intellectual tradition.

The appreciation of this vital fact solves the problem of the Two Germanys. These two Germanys do not exist side by side. *They co-exist in principle in every German brain.* When living his everyday life like everyone else, and doing his honest day's work, the German is able to feel justly and to think justly. But he suffers from too much discipline in an over-organized world, and from too many conflicts between the groupings of every kind that infest his country. He then pictures to himself by way of contrast the Imperial Germany toward whose greatness all will collaborate in virtue of a peculiar mystic membership of all in their community. *This is why the real German problem has been and still is, whether we like it or not, the problem of unity in moderation and moderation in unity.* What must be avoided is allowing Germany to continue to conceive the indispensable internal cohesion of her national energies as an irresistible instrument of absolute domination and hegemony.

The Industrial Revolution of the nineteenth century was carried to such lengths that it produced, as we know, serious social maladjustments and an over-speedy urbanization. It was thus the cause of a rapid and brutal psychological simplification. Just as within some five decades the majority of large towns adopted a generalized type of dwelling, a certain uniform type of street and standardized way of life, so, superseding regional diversities, a new human type was to be seen evolving and spreading everywhere. It is not too rash to conceive the typical German coming into being with the Bismarck era. Count H. Keyserling, Walter Rathenau, Thomas Mann, Willy Hellpach in Germany, and Jacques Rivière, Louis Reynaud, and Maurice Betz in France, have tried to define the type. These considerations and my own personal experience tempt me to point out some of its fundamental characteristics.

The first I should phrase thus: *The German in general possesses no exact sense of reality.* All too often he lacks common sense, clear perception, and sure judgment. Why? Simply because he sees reality either in bits or *specialized* by the requirements of his daily work, or else *magnified out of all proportion* by the appeals of his imagination and his dreams. In either case he *narrows* or *idealizes* the world and thus distorts it. In this modern and contemporary world of ours he dreams incurably either of a social technique for ever being further perfected but for ever demanding violent dynamic action, or else of an ardent mysticism sustaining a faultless rational organization.

Hence comes the intellectual and moral indifference, the lack of personal principle, that so often strikes the foreigner. J. Rivière attributes *"Bonasserie"* to the German, easy-going softness. W. Hellpach describes him as *"Triebhaft Gut"* (impulsively good), a person of an elementary, vegetative kindliness that can ill co-exist with firm and clear-cut personal moral principle. The German would seem to accept his moral principles *from without*, by external persuasion or deliberate education. If this irks him, if so much "legality" galls him, he is brutal in his method of freeing himself from his enslavement to it. He is able to be very loyal to conventions and at the same time very hostile to them. Disgusted by the monastic rule which he has over-conscientiously applied, a Luther will abruptly fling it off to pursue that pure spiritual liberty which he finds in the Gospel and in Saint Paul. As long as the rule prevails, it is observed with the most meticulous rigour. When the rule vanishes, it disappears in a sudden explosion of feeling, of passion or fury.

When the German displays his individuality he does so in the form of icy rigidity, tear-drenched emotion, or vulgar coarseness. Perhaps this is why he is intolerant of happiness, his own or another's. If he is unhappy he casts the blame on other people. If he is happy he either declares himself unsatisfied or is carried away by dangerous exaltation. His military successes of 1864 to 1871, with the incredible material prosperity that followed them, and his successful offensive of 1914, went to his head. Then came the armistice of 1918 and total collapse. To-day we are witnessing an unprecedented outburst of savagery, of the instinct of domination that chooses defenceless individuals and weak States as its prey.

At heart the German rarely possesses the sense of true greatness that is based on strength and moderation. He is untrue to his own classic tradition, which extolled that mastery. He either persecutes his own great men in their lifetime or exalts and deifies them after their death. Goethe and Bismarck suffered that fate. The Weimar democracy was as much the victim of the mediocrity of those who represented it as of the bestial fury of its irreconcilable opponents. While so many colourless nonentities crowded the front of the political and parliamentary stage, strong unscrupulous personalities behind the scenes commanded the levers and pulled the strings that were to compass the irretrievable downfall of the Republic.

The German "*manque de crête*," writes J. Rivière: he has no psychological backbone. Not that he is lacking in vitality, especially when he is one of a group. But this vitality is rarely directed, rarely guided by a confident moral principle. A certain emptiness, a certain internal vacuum, yawns in the soul of many a German. In order to convince himself that he is somebody, the German invents for himself and attributes to himself heroic virtues, culled from history or tradition, which are in reality wholly foreign to him. He exists less in himself, in his own right, than by his deeds, by his achievement. Having no goal of his own, he is happy when someone sets him a task to perform, proclaiming that he is always ready to obey. Thus by force of toil, or of extravagant dreams, he creates lofty situations for himself, to which he proves unequal. He is the typical Sorcerer's Apprentice. A minority in Germany extol war; the majority hate it but accept and wage it. Military successes are not always the product of force of character. Often terrible in his deeds, often personally unconvinced, the German sees battle as a potent, mechanical operation. Similarly with racialism, which corresponds less to any profound faith than to a weapon of power destined to achieve domination and hegemony.

Values which to us seem fundamental have foundered in Germany more rapidly and more completely than anywhere else. Why? *Because the German mind does not clearly distinguish the true from the false, likes to believe itself superior alike to good and to evil, or confuses the real and the ideal.* It knows no mean between doctrinal pedantry and unbridled, lawless exuberance. The German finds it difficult to formulate a firm, exact moral judgment. He "learns" rather what is good or bad, by this or that utilitarian reckoning. He is credulous because he has few natural criteria. He can conceive truth only in relation to the mind that enunciates it, and often confuses it with ideology. Or, rather, he suspects it of ideology. The good is what you are able to do; the true is what you are able to make others believe. German thoroughness (*Gründlichkeit*), the conscientious exactitude which the German puts into his work, has nothing to do with respect for truth. It is merely a matter of technique, obstinately and ruthlessly pushed to the extreme. The German does not invent "*ersatz*" materials only. He loves intellectual substitutes no less. So he installs himself in a false world, seeing only a distorted vision of the universe. He contemplates the universal in false categories.

In his heart he believes that *everything is possible*. It amuses him to obliterate frontiers, territorial as well as conventional moral frontiers. His unstable mind seeking adventure looks for weak spots which permit escape or give opportunity for brutality. A sort of metaphysical Will or impersonal dynamism drives him irresistibly into the immense no man's land which he creates between true and false, good and evil, peace and war. Demanding a monopoly of everything, his will loves to paralyse other wills by terror. This will of his is governed at once by cold calculation and by a sort of *raptus* as furious as it is irrational. Though he is an admirable organizer, the German loses his head if his plan is foiled. With excessive patience and inexhaustible energy he can bring order into chaos, discipline amorphous masses, dominate and mould unresisting matter. He loses himself in his task and identifies his own personality with the object he is pursuing. A certain lack of genius tempts him, as Paul Valéry has shown, to aim at massive results disconcerting to other people. He thinks of everything, foresees everything, does everything necessary with that appalling concentration that so often accompanies absence of psychological insight.

That is why the German is a prey to education and even derives a monstrous self-assurance from this malleability. Feeling confident that he can do anything if he wants to, he acts with the Germanic innocence and guilelessness that Richard Wagner has glorified in the persons of Siegfried and Parsifal. His objectivity has become legendary, for he pursues an object *for its own sake*. He converts man into a tool, a means of dominating the world. *The task to be performed is in his eyes of more importance than the man who performs it.* This objectivity leads him into a collective megalomania that dreams of might unbounded and a future without limits. Hence that secret but sinister harmony between the small specialized job and the great work of expansion. His theoretic vision of the reality to be attained occupies and obsesses his brain. He *sacrifices himself* to his goal because he counts the goal of more importance than himself. He prefers a discussion about Paradise to Paradise itself.

That is to say he confuses the ideal and the real, the ideal being for him but the ideological sketch of the expected reality. His "*Tüchtigkeit*" is the sum of the mediocre qualities that ensure his certain arrival at the goal. As an organized nation the Germans become intolerable. They take vengeance for their impotence in the days of their territorial fragmentation. Their idealism has become progressively reduced to a programme which must be punctually carried out to satisfy their overweening ambitions. Here the vision serves to stimulate a violence they are ever ready to unleash. Hapless individuals bound by disciplinary obedience to ruthless leaders perform cruelly exhausting exploits. Thus the German people surrenders itself as the blind instrument of what it conceives to be its true greatness, its true power. Its sense of aristocracy is based solely on the efficiency or the brutal violence of the leaders and the subservience of the led.

It always believes firmly in the decadence of the democratic peoples who fail to follow its example. Himself lacking the qualities that give internal stability of soul, the German is taken in by superficial appearances in forming his critical judgments. He has never understood the profound reason for the stability the Western nations enjoy. He is perpetually predicting their end. Too much technique, too many all-powerful superiors, too many docile subordinates mean the dangerous reign of figures and numbers. The German people makes itself hated by its imperialism, at once restless and brutal, mystical and calculated. There is something inhuman in its methods that profoundly wounds the human soul. Its organized romanticism drives it to project into the Absolute, into its *Volkstum*, into its Race, the National Community to which—for ·so it claims—it belongs *by religion.* What it conceives to be "rational" it must make "real." And the very vastness of this conception militates against self-confidence and decision of character.

The famous German introvert profundity (*Innerlichkeit*) is most often only the complement of the extravert shallowness (*Aeusserlichkeit*) of a too rigorous organization. When German culture protests so violently against mechanization it does so because mechanization is for the German a perpetual menace. Nietzsche was very right when he said that this profundity was only a retreat and a refuge preceding a violent explosion of fury. The German flies to it from the pedantry he imposes on himself. He finds therein a spiritual vastness from which he afterwards escapes to plunge into technical achievement. If he revels in associations and military life, it is because he dreads beyond everything the infinite loneliness of his ego. The *Gemeinschaft,* the "community," is essential to him if he is to raise his head and stand erect.

We see why the German boasts that he is more primitive, more elemental, more *original* than Western nations. This has been an old contention ever since Fichte's *Reden an die deutsche Nation* (Addresses to the German Nation). A contention not yet stilled! Taine wrote: "The animal yonder dreams and feels and seeks to penetrate the Absolute, instead of chatting, observing, judging, analysing as we do." The most intensive factor in the German's make-up is the dull, instinctive, sentimental, and passion-ridden life, ill-equipped to explain itself in words or readily to obey principles. Nothing but external discipline is able to canalize and moderate this dynamism, and discipline suffices only up to the point at which it itself surrenders to the promptings of the subconscious. As the German confuses true and false, good and evil, real and ideal, so he fails to distinguish between the unconscious and the conscious. He defines originality as *Ursprünglichkeit*, which might more justly be termed primitiveness. Individuals in Germany feel themselves bound to each other by a social allegiance that is, or fain would be, a communion of souls. In general the German prefers private life to public, juridical, or political life. But he has pushed this preference so far, and has multiplied his "Invisible Churches" to such an extent, that the national edifice no longer holds together and the people has had to submit to a dictatorship that destroys that cherished family and private life, all true friendship and all true comradeship.

The famous German Wrath, the *furor teutonicus*, proceeds from simple souls who are distinguished only by their attachment to the social body. This collective allegiance has its sinister side. From group to group, from region to region, hatreds gain an intensity that makes them lethal. It is the same with international relationships. The German who speaks for a people of 80 millions is a thousandfold more bellicose than the German of the old territorial States. Unless restraint is exercised upon him, he will make the air of Europe less fit to breathe than it has ever been. The Germans become what Mauriac calls "the ever-furious people," furious by definition and by force of habit. Germany becomes a country whose youth is seized with loathing for humane civilization, and in breaking the spell thereof flings itself wholly into permanent and total militarism. The German is not a revolutionary who revolts individually against an established order which he deems evil or tyrannical. He is *collectively* revolutionary in virtue of a greater national cohesion, of a regrouping of energies that provides the social body with the much-vaunted liberty of movement thanks to which the most violent deeds of aggression are possible. "We are destined," wrote Möller van den Bruck, "never to leave the others in peace." The German loves a war of upheaval, movement for the sake of movement, destruction for the sake of destruction, the Reich for the Reich. Ernst Jünger has revived for contemporaries this type of Germanic warrior.

Thomas Mann in his *Betrachtungen* of 1917 maintained that German *Kultur*, supported by a synthetic and all-inclusive language which is better qualified to express the values of emotion than of reason, and is equally at home in working out great ideals, is above all a *musical* culture, in the sense that its primary aim is to reproduce the very rhythm of Universal Life, the profound and elemental movements of the soul or of social bodies rather than the nuances of individual psychology. The German, following Thomas Mann, likes to stress the opposition between *Kultur* and Civilization. He considers no culture worthy of the name which is not at all times ready to break away from convention and verbal formalism to preserve communion with Universal Life and its perpetual metamorphoses. We find the same tendency in German politics. Particularism persisted for a long time in Germany, and still persists behind the Hitlerite façade *because the German has in fact no clear and precise idea of the State*. We have seen that Bismarck's Empire was a State without a guiding political principle. The German mind has no conception of form. It will never accommodate itself in advance to a given framework. The Teutons who wrecked the Roman Empire acted not on a concrete plan but on an instinctive impulse. In exactly the same way the Germans wrecked the League of Nations and then the entire European order. National feeling in Germany has never been more than a feeling of linguistic or racial allegiance, confined at first to an *élite* and then gradually extending to the whole people. This national idea came *from above*. It was first conceived in a few minds before it penetrated to the masses, before it allied itself with Prussianism to carry out a programme.

III. These fundamental characteristics explain Nazism and Nazism in its turn reinforces these characteristics. By means of the calculated *Gleichschaltung* and the imposition of uniformity, which are an essential part of its governmental system, Nazism consciously creates, for a fixed purpose, what it believes to be a new type of German; but this type is in fact but the culmination of the psychological processes we have just been analysing. The Nazi doctrine is nothing more than the progressive degeneration of Germany's intellectual tradition. In the same way the psychology of the normal Nazi merely emphasizes and enormously exaggerates the characteristics of the German of the time of Bismarck and William II.

Nazism developed in the most highly subdivided social stratum, among the middle classes of modest independent means or salaries, in the country districts, and amid the agglomerations of the large towns. It devised for them promises, visions of the future, political, economic, and social slogans, which, at a time of appalling collective downfall and of acute distress, would appeal to those diverse and hitherto ill-organized elements,

The success gained by Nazi propaganda between 1920 and 1932 would have been inconceivable if the process of levelling-down had not been reinforced by other factors acting both on the middle classes threatened with proletarization and on the proletariat demoralized by unemployment.

War and defeat had already hit the ex-Servicemen hard. In the midst of their own misery they saw the old oligarchy still firmly entrenched in its feudal estates and its industrial power, and on the other hand the Social Democrats and the Catholics carried for the first time into political power by the Republic. The wrath of these defeated and precipitately demobilized troops vented itself first on the Spartacists and the Jews, whom the ruling caste, to avoid a just vengeance falling on itself, denounced to the soldiers as their enemies. Later came the turn of those who had chiefly benefited from parliamentary democracy.

The curtain had scarcely fallen on the first tragedy, that of the days immediately following the armistice, when it rose again on the drama of Inflation, a collective tragedy if ever there was one! The effect of the inflation of 1921 to 1923 was to reduce to one level not only the material conditions of everyone's existence, but all intellectual, moral, and political convictions. It prepared the masses for the *Gleichschaltung*, the levelling, of minds. It is not impossible that in allowing inflation to run its full course to its ultimate consequences, the ruling caste complacently foresaw the effect it would produce: the complete proletarization of the middle classes and a new direction of their thought. The complete collapse of the mark robbed those classes of their best traditions: foresight, thrift, family and moral allegiances. It begot an unbridled craving for immediate enjoyment, the spirit that sacrifices everything to the passing moment, the sense of a complete breach with the established order, especially from the moment when the normal relation between debtor and creditor was abolished. It would be impossible to overstate the comprehensiveness and the far-reaching effects of this terrifying phenomenon. If Britain and France sometimes show so little understanding of what is going on in Germany, it is because they were spared that tragic experience.

Then, after the inflation, with the bogus recovery of 1924 to 1928, due to the influx of foreign money, came a new wave of Americanization. It was the visible accompaniment of the sudden flood of Anglo-Saxon capital and the pitiless rationalization of industry that flung so many workers out of employment.

American intervention gave a powerful impetus to certain preferences and habits, to the giddy whirl of modernism. Large towns were covered with huge blocks of flats and commercial buildings; enormous workers' tenements everywhere sprang up, monstrous factories and gigantic stores; powerful trusts handled an incredible accumulation of capital out of all proportion to a national income that was parcelled out in innumerable minute sums for millions of impoverished recipients. The crisis preyed on mind and soul. And Germany became a sort of European America moulded and ruled by the machine.

New forms of life made their appearance. An immoderate taste for sport reinforced the purely biological and physical aspects of life. Cinema and wireless augmented the already excessive dynamism inculcated in men's minds. These external influences were the more successful since the acquired psychology of the average German was highly susceptible to them. This Americanization was further induced by the Russian example. And it attacked a people of completely passive moral receptivity.

The crisis of 1929 to 1932 set the seal on the process. This time foreign influences were rudely ejected. Germany found herself alone, completely alone in face of herself, in face of her destiny, in face of the ghastly drama that threatened her with complete internal disintegration. Nihilism swept away her last defences. The *furor teutonicus* was let loose in the void created by so much ruin. *The German mind broke with Western psychology, with rational, bourgeois order.* There was no question of conscious intellectual criticism. *One form of life was in arms against another form of life.* It was a question of two different rhythms. Germany chose the militarized, warlike life because she was psychologically conditioned for it. All her faults were intensified in this atmosphere of abnormal collective tension. Nazism was to stabilize this spiritual unanimity, based on the conditions of existence that plunged almost *all* Germans into the same misery.

Nazi propaganda played upon this very feeling of *uncertainty*, an uncertainty not confined to the middle classes, but common to the whole of Germany, a country tortured by proletarization and unemployment. You would have to have seen with your own eyes the Germany of 1933 if you were to understand why these masses—a full third of whom were suffering actual hunger, and the rest escaping it only by real feats of organization and sacrifice —lived in expectation of some means of salvation, some miracle, some providential Messiah. Accumulated trials had swept from German minds every lingering vestige of faith in the old values. Men weighed down by trouble were ripe for the racial myth, a convenient conception of the harmony between the unconscious desire of the masses and the conscious decision of their leaders. The Weimar democracy had not solved the problem of the national will. The whole of the evil was laid at the door of the old bourgeois politics, as too intellectual and too discursive. An abrupt reversion to primitive brutality called aloud for a Chief, a Leader, a man who would command, a propaganda able to reduce all minds to a common denominator, a dictatorship capable of imposing on all the same gestures and the same ideas.

Most assuredly Germany might have found another solution than this lapse into second-rate Cæsarism. She did not find it. On every hand the ideal and the real were once more blended in unprecedented confusion. The old idealism took the form of the Hitlerite "*Weltanschauung*," of a social programme that posed as "ideal," as being in conformity with the "original meaning of things" (*Ursinn der Dinge*). But this was followed by a ruthless realism enforced by every conceivable active means: propaganda, corporate organization, and the army. A new connexion was established between Germany's *dream* and Germany's *might*. To become *Nordic* meant nothing else than to subject the amorphous mass to a "Führer" and to one sole party. The internal dream was once again transmuted into an external discipline. From the moment when the race idea took root in their minds the Germans were bound to submit to the appropriate technique, to a thousand obligations, to all the severities of total mobilization, in order to achieve the national solidarity, the "*Volksgemeinschaft*," the Reich of the morrow.

This intensified collective psychology explains the success of the Hitlerite propaganda. The confusion between true and false, good and evil, the Conscious and the Unconscious, was the very life and soul of this propaganda so efficiently designed by Hitler and Goebbels. There was no question of mere credulity, but of *faith*, of active adherence, ready to proceed to the destruction of bourgeois order. Each person had to accept the same truth in relation to the German Community and its future. The German's legendary thoroughness, his *Gründlichkeit*, was applied laboriously to new ends. A formidable necessity weighed upon all this pedantry, the necessity of engaging in high-pressure preparation for war. It demanded the lie. By definition lying became a duty. Never before had the German mind invented so many intellectual substitutes, never before had it lived in so imaginary a world, never before in order to make its dreams come true had it risked so many tragic, because purely destructive, adventures.

Never before had the German indulged so cynically in that cult of immorality, innocent in its spontaneity and at the same time very cruel, to which he is addicted. To act, always to act, in obedience to the racial formula, in virtue of the absolute liberty now regained after so many broken bonds, the liberty that overleaps all obstacles. The Nazi questions nothing. He forges ahead through thick and thin. He obeys his leaders. Obedience has become a system. Loyalty to the Leader throws its mantle over him and justifies his crimes. This explains the atrocities, insufficiently grasped by the public, which the British White Book reveals. The Nazi is responsible only for carrying out the order he receives, not for the nature of that order. He does not discuss it. His will, offspring of Hitler's miracle, yearns after other miracles, seeing nothing ahead but infinite opportunities, more especially world-wide imperial "*loot*." He seeks out the adversary's weak point and swoops down on it. The field is free, since International Law has been destroyed.

This temptation is well calculated to overwhelm a mind in distress, to provoke an eruption of coldly furious collective wrath, of ingenious tortures devised for the Jews and for the Concentration Camp! These evil doings are explained by defeat, demobilization, the free-lance armies (*Freikorps*), destitution, the destruction of all faith, and total militarization; in their service the German displayed an unheard-of expansion of industrial mechanization, of ponderous corporative organization, of joyless force, of massive solidarity to order, and of appalling intellectual conformity. *For the Third Reich had to be fitted to undertake anything whatever.*

This result could not possibly have been achieved without that docile acceptance of instruction, without that intellectual and moral malleability which we have just noted. This radical indifference, this "*plasma germinatif*" of which Rivière speaks, when collectively successful engenders the worst manifestations of arrogance and brutality. The appalling German ingenuousness commits these crimes without mentioning them, without appearing to perform them, in the awe-inspiring silence of Hell where every cry is stifled. The German tortures the German to compensate himself for so many misfortunes, so much accumulated resentment, so many vast enterprises that have failed. The German has never thought himself so original as now, or so successful in achieving organized and compulsory comradeship: the very antithesis of the subtle personal choice on which friendship depends. The Germans now gather together in close-packed masses on any and every pretext. National festivals and the Nuremberg rallies amply satisfy their natural appetite for immense ritual ceremonies.

It is self-evident that only a masculine Order could govern on such lines. This generation of pedantic bandits has come from the middle classes, this body of men ready for anything, capable of every sort of fanaticism, a wild collection of petty Cæsars who have chosen Hitler as their symbolic Chieftain, a monstrous psychological abscess bursting over the entire nation. These men, the product of the battlefields of 1914–18 and the social ruin of 1918–33, hostile to all the refinements of intellect and culture, to all shades of religion, these men believe in nothing but the superiority of what they call "combative" characters. So they banish their womenfolk once more to housewifery and child-bearing and substitute for the citizen the *miles perpetuus*, the trooper ready for any adventure. They thus create a power-apparatus which but ill conceals the hatreds raging between one chief and another, one coterie and another, one tendency and another. They cultivate the warrior-spirit for its own sake, abolishing the frontiers between the civil and the military. This crack-brained militarism drove Germany to an absurd glorification of all her most inveterate vices.

In the course of these four years of war we have seen what the Nazis—let loose to rage unfettered over the continent of Europe which they conquered between 1938 and 1940—have achieved in the way of crimes, murders and executions, robbery and destruction. This is not the place to enter into detail. Let us confine ourselves to noting simply that all this looting, violence, and bloodshed was callously carried out, stage by stage, in accordance with a plan conceived and drawn up in advance. This plan was based on a theory of destruction for which the German General Staff and the National Socialist Party bear equal responsibility. Germany is already admitting in the speeches of her leaders that she will be defeated in this Second World War. She maintains, nevertheless, that the world cannot be conquered in one war, nor even in two, and that in the course

of this second act she will have made appreciable progress
toward her final aim if at its close she retains an adequate
economic and numerical superiority over other peoples, a
superiority of which she can make sure,

 (1) by subjecting the other nations to a pitiless ordeal of
   undernourishment from which the young generation
   will suffer most;
 (2) by beginning already to lay up the war resources for the
   struggle to come.

Such is the cause to which the traditional German soldier-
bandit is expected to devote his efforts and his sacrifices.

IV. A people of this type, having reached the point to which a
decade of National Socialism has brought it, inevitably tends to
a conception of life and to an actual practice to which we shall
give the name of "planism." This constitutes a problem of the
greatest gravity, for it involves the future and the significance of
German-Russian relations.

Western opinion is mistaken about Russia, because we look
at that continent solely from the point of view of class warfare
as we know it amongst ourselves. Dreading a social revolution,
the big capitalists present us with a picture of Russia as Hell.
Conversely the workers, won over by Russian ideas, picture the
Soviet Union as an earthly Paradise. The truth lies between
these two extremes. Like the Third Reich, the Soviet régime is
characterized *by an ever-growing planning system* that presupposes
a fixed *mode of life.*

In Russia a militant minority—the Communist Party—has
established a socialist order. It is true that the movement,
begotten of the proletariat, destroyed the middle classes. But
had Russia ever had experience of middle-class capitalism? This
had scarcely begun to make its appearance when it came into
conflict with Marxism. The drastic operation of 1917 was
possible only in Russia. National Socialism took good care not
to attempt it.

The solid foundation of Russian Socialism rests on the peasant
masses and the industrial working masses. These are distributed
over an area representing one-sixth of the globe, and the population increases by three million souls per annum. How were
these masses to be reorganized amidst the distress of 1917? A
new relation sprang up between town and country, between the
urban and the rural proletariat. In the past, thanks to serfdom

and in accordance with Western tradition, the town had dominated the country. The abolition of serfdom later transformed the Russian peasantry into an immense mass violently fermenting but lacking any organizing leadership. On the morrow of the defeat inflicted on Russia by Japan in 1904–5 the peasant crisis reached its height. Twelve years later there was total tragedy, tragedy for the worker, the peasant, the army, the entire nation.

Over this inconceivable chaos there arose a new conception of Life and of Man. This was the soul of Bolshevism. Russian literature had no doubt long been preparing it. This conception took up the Marxist theory, according to which the proletariat was the corner-stone of all future building. It started from the *working man*, the human *unit of toil*, the man who *has only his hands to work with*. This man, it contended, is exploited by the middle classes, who by the wage system convert him into a marketable commodity. This exploitation had to cease. The worker must be the constituent cell of the new social order. The militant party aimed at transforming industry and agriculture. It became the General Staff of the working army, the fighting army, and the army of all pledged to this one doctrine. This triple army would teach Russia the great economic laws of town and country. Lenin was to be the social chemist who would thus regroup the elements of the disintegrated community.

State Capitalism would then replace private capitalism and profit-making, while the worker, of whatever grade, would become an *official* worker, a *soldier* of the régime. The party recruited and supervised the executive officers of the national reorganization. In this gigantic system of collective labour, scientific, industrial, and agricultural, the individual was reduced to a mere atom. The entire nation lived on the everlasting dialogue between the *belly* and the *head*, between economic requirements and organized toil. The *Plan* was held up to the multitude, who gazed vacantly at the dance of the figures, at the Plan at once theoretic and in process of taking concrete shape. This was Shibboleth, the new god. This explains the realism and the absolutism of the Russian phraseology, which took heed only of the earthly life of man, his instincts, his desires, his needs. Here was a rational system for satisfying them, a despotic conception born of an unprecedented crisis and a nameless despair. It behoves us to grasp this fact, if we would understand the magnitude of this historic phenomenon.

This situation was the direct parent of Dictatorship, the only form of government conceivable in face of such difficulties. The very immensity of the Plan presupposed a classless society. This planning claimed that it offered salvation not only to Russia but to the entire world. Every worker, a mere scale on the dragon's body, would have his proper place and his prescribed part in the system. He must adapt himself. There must be total, disciplined organization. The Revolution must be permanent, exacting the unremitting mobilization of the national energies. This meant that Russia, an industrial, agricultural, and colonial country, would be exploited *by its united inhabitants*, skilfully commanded, ready to *sacrifice the present* for the vision of a better future.

The striking quality of Bolshevism is its *deliberate* and *preconceived* character. Here the revolutionaries preceded the Revolution, whereas in 1789 the Revolution begot the revolutionaries. This was a logical Revolution, not, like its predecessors, an irrational one. The Proletarian Revolution was "bound" to follow the bourgeois revolution. This new Revolution was to be final and universal. The past was abolished. True history only began with the new society. The Russian calendar was sufficient to wreck European unity. For this Revolution followed the World War and deduced from it its ultimate moral.

It thus transformed Western Socialism into a sort of orthodox planning. Marx, who was the continuation of the Left opposition of 1789, wanted people to change the world by rethinking it. The Russian intelligentsia adopted his doctrine as absolute in that vast continent, where reading was frequently a substitute for experience. They did violence to Russia in order to organize her. They made her the experimental field of Marxism, following the recipes of international science in order to achieve the final Planned State. A double Russian tradition presided over their operations: that of the Orthodox or Messianic Kingdom and that of the strong Police—and Military—State of the Tsars. A single group of intellectuals reduced everything to dogma, approaching all problems in the spirit of absolute religion and of soldierly simplification.

Now, Russian thought had been strongly subjected during the nineteenth century to the influence of German idealism, and in particular to that of Fichte and Hegel. It showed the same tendency to enclose the masses of the people in an organization calculated to abolish the injustices of Roman Law and of private property; the same escape into the past and into the future. If to this Romantic influence we add the influence of Western Socialism it is clear that the Russians took up again all the social ideas of nineteenth-century Western Europe. Their Socialism, which interpreted Hegel in a revolutionary sense, remained at first individualist. But in the desire to preserve the individual it ended by completely absorbing him into the social whole.

This Socialism was primarily *nihilist*. Setting aside God, the spirit, the soul, and the eternal values, it claimed that happiness lies simply in the possession of the things man needs, in the organization of a just society, in the liberation of *natural* man, stripped of his historic fripperies. It was on thoughts like these that Marxism seems to have acted, the Marxism that already looked upon civilization and its values as epiphenomena of economic reality, and believed that only the proletariat could set men free from the slavery imposed on them by the tyranny of social laws. The early Russian Marxists wanted the industrial development of Russia, because they thought it impossible that the Marxist experiment could succeed in a peasant country. They believed that only the factory could create the new man.

Little by little, however, *totalism* won the day. Lenin seems to have realized that the socialist experiment might be attempted in Russia *without capitalist development and without the preliminary creation of an industrial working class*. Accordingly he made of the Revolution a religion, a philosophy, and a militarized State, instead of a simple doctrine of economic determinism. He was inspired by the ideal of absolute integrity and integration. Thus there developed a Russianized Marxism with its Messianism, its myths, its exaltation of the revolutionary will, above all with the idea that the battle must be led by *an active minority*—a strange blend of idealism and materialism. The unique characteristic of Bolshevism is that *it believes in the power of an Idea which tallies with the instinct of the masses*. Let us anticipate and point out that it is precisely in this respect that the link with National Socialism is manifest. "Let us unite," said Lenin, "the peasant and the worker. It is fortunate that we are not confronted by a strong, well-organized middle class."

For, like Nazism, Bolshevism made a cult of force. In 1917 it was organized force that laid hold of the wholly disorganized Russian masses. Hence the *national* and at the same time the *universal* character of that Revolution. Lenin was a revolutionary in the Hebrew and Russian Messianic sense, but he was still and primarily, a statesman. He united in his own person two Russian traditions, that of the orthodox prophet and that of the despotic military State. For he had a horror alike of unbridled romanticism and of anarchy. His aim was to discipline Russia and prevent her from slipping down the slope to chaos. Assuredly he was not by nature cruel. Nevertheless, to achieve the result he aimed at, he preached a cruel policy. For him whatever served the Revolution was good, and whatever hampered it was evil. His was the dictatorship of one conception of the world: the analogy with Hitlerism is obvious.

The new State was therefore to continue both the Muscovite Kingdom and the Empire of Peter the Great. And this State was to be a Police State, authoritarian and military. When workers and peasants had grown accustomed to it and fully learned their lesson, then dictatorship could end. Only one thing Lenin forgot: the dictatorial omnipotence of the bureaucracy, of the privileged official who is better paid than the worker and earns much more than the peasant. Such was the Revolution imposed on Russia *from above*, a revolution both dynamic and uncompromising, asserting the primacy of politics over economic realities and economic problems, aiming at the Americanization of Russia and at making her a totalitarian State, a sort of inverted theocracy. The Russian Monarchy was upheld by an orthodoxy that exacted an adherence without reservations; similarly Communism is based on an integral conception of the world that is no less exacting for its initiates. A whole people was here subjected— as the German people were later—to a State catechism. The Messianic vocation of Russia was merged with the Messianic vocation of the proletariat. This national vocation brusquely ejected Trotskyism as merely international.

The Bolshevism of to-day, a veritable social Titan, possessed by its vision of the great Organized Collectivity, grips Russia in an iron vice that keeps her free of anarchy but imposes on her a pitiless dictatorship, being no doubt the only power capable of preserving her from the encompassing dangers. Like Hitler, Stalin is the sole judge of ultimate Truth in everything relating to the State and the direction of its policy. Considering, like his people, that there is no true liberty in the West, because nothing can there be changed, Stalin identifies liberty with the possibility of collective construction, even if living men are to be the means and the instrument of the world that is to be built.

The Second World War, the great offensive against Russia

which Germany ventured to launch on June 22, 1941, the German occupation, the Wehrmacht's subsequent forced retreat, and the military victories of the Red Army, inevitably modified this fundamental position. Stalin and the Communist Party remain, no doubt, scrupulously faithful to the letter of Lenin's dogma. But their policy leaves room for plenty of subtle and ingenious adaptations. The new and vital fact is that the new Red Army, product of the total mobilization of the Russian people, is predominantly composed (80 per cent.) of peasants. From the firing of the first shot, this war has been a national war. It has thrown together all social categories and all tendencies. It has played no small part in the reawakening of the Orthodox Church, a revival encouraged and ratified by the régime. Compelled to take heed of all regional and popular aspirations, the régime tempers its centralization by a certain degree of federalism, and is beginning to admit more or less democratic or ostensibly democratic forms and institutions. Stalin nurses his generals, his army, and his people, and the spirited vigour of his troops, stimulated and fostered by ever more brilliant triumphs, fully justifies this gradual widening and deepening of policy, with which the future lies.

If this is the essence of Russian Communism from Lenin to Stalin, it bears many striking resemblances to National Socialism. There is no identity, but an unquestionable analogy, and an analogy more profound than might at first sight be recognized.

In this, as in everything, Germany was poised between two worlds to both of which she was linked by firm and far-reaching influences, the Western democracies on the one hand and Communist Russia on the other. Nazism was a hybrid product containing a dash of Western democracy, preserved by a few negligible survivals from the Weimar Constitution, a dash of Italian Fascism due to a fairly obvious imitation of Mussolini-ism, and much more than a dash of Sovietism. For demonstration purposes we may ignore the Western and even the Fascist ingredients. For the Nazis insisted not only on their criticism of the West, but still more on the difference, the fundamental difference as they saw it, that distinguished their system from Fascism, contrasting their totalitarian doctrine with the purely political creation of Mussolini's State. In order to come into line with Hitlerism and satisfy the demands of the Axis, Italy plagiarized the German racial theory, but this temporary acquiescence only served to throw into relief the gulf that separated her from Germany. In Germany, as in Russia, there co-exists the tradition of a strong and despotic military State, whether it be Hohenzollern Prussia or Tsarist Russia, alongside the Messianic tradition, the providential mission of Germany or of Orthodox Russia. The co-existence of these two traditions is the only thing that matters.

On both sides, too, there exists an organized, militarized, active minority, a sort of Order that presides over the nation's destinies. Not that the Communist Party excludes women from politics as the Nazi Party does; but the general conception is the same. Only the method of recruitment differs.

Both régimes aimed at evolving the worker-type. Ernst Jünger did not write *Der Arbeiter* (The Worker) without being familiar with Russian ideology. But in the Hitlerite sense the word was necessarily more comprehensive because it applied to old social categories which the régime had allowed to persist. While the Russian Revolution was made by the elimination of a class— the proletariat of 1917 succeeding the bourgeoisie of 1789— the German Revolution sought only a formula for national coherence and in the main retained the old social order. Moreover, while Bolshevism perhaps addressed rather the peasant masses than the industrial workers, Nazism did the opposite, for the Third Reich was industrially over-equipped even after incorporating the entire peasantry of Germany into its ponderous corporative system. This German corporative system was the antithesis of Russian collectivization, for Germany, in her own way of course, made use of a middle-class capitalist order for a considerable experiment very different from Russia's. As we know, Nazism professed to respect private property and maintained a class distinction between the employer and the proletarian on the *Führer-Gefolgschaft* principle of Leader and Led. It limited rather than eliminated capitalist profit-making. Hitler confined himself to advocating a sense of social responsibility in the employer class, but firmly insisted on low wages and low profits for the proletariat of industrial workers and peasants.

Here again we find the same realistic organization, the same tragic dialogue between belly and brain, between the needs of the nation and the directed economy. But in Germany the brain gravely bullied the belly, imposing cruel restrictions according to the now symbolic formula: guns before butter. In every respect there was in both cases the desire to apply to the whole of earthly life and to the whole people a totalitarian disciplinary

system.   Germany based her system on a *new Prussification*, while
Russia reverted to her tradition of *Tsarist political despotism*.   By
a curious paradox a certain mysticism underlay this realism, a
realism which alike in Germany and Russia displayed the same
deliberate, preconceived, logical quality.   For the German
revolutionaries preceded what· they call their Revolution, a
revolution which, as we know, was a blend of demagogy and
social reaction.   Bolshevism came to birth round about 1903 and
Nazism somewhere about 1920, which allows both systems
approximately a dozen years of preparation for the Totalitarian
State with the same pretension to universal domination.

So the two régimes have a common origin: nihilism, radical
denial of all ancient values of a civilization rejected as out of date.
Passing from *nothing* to *everything*, from *nihilism* to *totality*, from a
clean sweep to a *definitive system*, both régimes claimed to substitute
for the old civilization a special symbolism which should provide
anchorage for the mind and prevent the distressed masses,
uprooted from their entire past, from plunging into chaos.   It is
beyond question that both these "totalisms" were intimately
related to the idealism of German Romanticism.

Fundamentally both established the same relation between the
spirit and economic reality.   They desired a perfectly rational
and regulated national economy, but at the same time a dynamic
economy since it must satisfy a people in the full flush of vitality
and expansionist urge.   It is true that Russia did not seek the
autarky in which Germany voluntarily imprisoned herself,
breaking—in this as in so many other matters—her normal ties
with her European neighbours, denying herself for the sake of
super-armament all traditional exchanges, and subordinating her
whole import and export system to her military aims.   Germany
achieved her economic integration in a laboratory retort the
while she respected the old social castes.

It would be possible to dwell at length on the part played in
these two States by the bureaucracy and the police.   Both
displayed the same excesses and the same dangers of repression.
The essential point, however, is that we find in both the same
interplay of national mysticism and planned organization, the
same submission of every mind to a State catechism, the same
tendency to the collectivization of the individual, to a conception
of the great human societies of to-morrow as so many working
hives.   The Revolution of 1933 imitated the Revolution of 1917.
Adapting it to different circumstances and to a country already equipped,

Nazism pirated for its own benefit whatever effectiveness and efficiency there might be in the Communist system. Starting like Russia from grave collective distress, the Nazi Revolution adopted ways and means which only the Russian example can explain. This prevented neither social reaction—since the Right collaborated in the *coup d'état* of 1933—nor even the furious anti-Bolshevik campaign so shrewdly conducted for the edification of the West.

Nazism went even further. The demagogy of the Hitlerite leaders who had allied themselves with the old ruling class tended to overleap itself. From 1926 onwards, after the great discussion in the bosom of the Party, a more sincere youth strained toward complete Socialism, toward more consistent planning, towards a total militarism for which super-armament was only the preparation. The rejuvenation of the Party; the possibility of a truly proletarian revolution; the vision of a professional army bidden to militarize the whole nation; imperialist world-dreams for foreign policy; increasing infiltration of German influence into the so-called "Eurasian" Russian spaces; all these were tendencies that sufficiently indicated that Germany would gladly have stepped into Russia's shoes if only she had been able to conquer her. The shadow of Russia was visibly extending over Germany, especially after the beginning of the present war, and of the German-Russian pact, though this did not necessarily imply the identity of the two systems or a lasting alliance between them. The National Socialist régime had preserved enough ties with Western capitalist tradition to be able to harp on either string and promote class warfare in the West by representing itself now as the friend and now as the foe of Bolshevism. Its real aim was to bring about the internal disintegration of the Western democracies. At the present moment, and after four years of savage warfare, the Germany of the Third Reich, defeated by Russia, is turning toward the Anglo-Saxons to stampede them with the fear of Bolshevism. She is shouting that England has become a mere vassal of the United States, that the British Empire is decadent, that France is impotent, that Germany alone is able to organize the spaces between Russia and America and protect them against what she calls "the Bolshevist chaos."

This wild Machiavellism confronts us with new perspectives which it is impossible to define with absolute precision. The aim of German propaganda is to bemuse and confuse the mind, to neutralize the resistance, to paralyse the will of her enemies. Hitler poses as a liberator while he reduces peoples to slavery.

He is intensifying his propaganda as the strength and material resources of the Allies increase. He knows how to exploit humanitarian, Christian, or Marxist pacifism. But his appeal will not outbid the appeal of Bolshevism, which is addressed entirely to certain class instincts, while National Socialism allures only the conservative middle classes and the Socialists and those who hover midway between. Hitler bowls for the Left and bats for the Right; his principle is *Divide et impera*. This may still prove to be the most immediate danger of to-morrow.

A people that allowed itself to be taken in by this double-faced propaganda would be committing national suicide. The weakness and the acquiescences of the democracies between 1935 and 1939 no doubt not only played Hitler's game for him, but also encouraged Stalin to exploit the situation. Amid the immense confusion of to-day, with no possibility for any one of us to form a perfectly clear conception of the problems confronting us, caution is advisable in consulting German *émigrés*. No doubt every one of them wants to see the end of the Hitler régime. So do we. But while some of them want us to accept in advance a military dictatorship beyond the Rhine to forestall the bolshevization of Germany, others frankly admit that they would like to see Hitlerism succeeded by a dictatorship of bolshevizing tendencies. It is for the Western democracies to make up their own minds as to what they want. On the day when Germans and Russians see proof of the democracies' vitality and will-to-win they will cease to repeat that the democracies are decadent and belong to a dying world.

V. In the writings of his middle period, between 1875 and 1882, Nietzsche dealt at length with the future United States of Europe. He held that we Europeans could reverse the course of the blood-stained history of the Continent, widen the physiological foundation of the race, shatter the narrow framework of nationality, and thus arrive at a great new political structure, that of the New European State. Nietzsche by no means denied the services which the conception of nationality and the reality of nationality had rendered to civilization. But he thought it would be possible to create a "European Race" by crossing the various nationalities, and that this race would multiply more quickly were it not for the sinister interest of certain dynasties and certain classes in maintaining the violent hostility and passionate hatred fostered by the régime of existing nationalities. In this connexion Nietzsche extolled the history and the virtues of the Jewish race, emphasizing its eminently European turn of mind and its longing to cease to be for ever the "Wandering Jew," and demanding that the Jewish spirit should be an essential ingredient in the future European spirit.

He was certainly under no illusion about the resistance this Europeanism would have to overcome. But he thought that, just as the greatest among the Germans of the best period had always sought to benefit by the good that came to them from without, so the "good Germans," the "really good Germans," would endeavour to cultivate qualities excelling those which made them simply Germans. He besought his fellow-country-men to slough their Germanism, or what we nowadays should call their pan-Germanism. He showed that the nations would be in no wise diminished in stature by holding in the New Federative Europe a place such as the sovereign cantons of Switzerland hold in the Swiss Confederation (or, we might add, the ancient German States in the Bismarckian Empire). Nietzsche knew that it would be necessary to win the support of the masses and of the peoples for this change, and that it would be possible to direct to the service of peace the passions which had hitherto been concentrated on war. Clearly, he added, this conception of a United Europe had a greatness quite other than Bismarck's conception of a German Empire. For the European Republic, like all republics, would be a product of democracy, proceeding logically from democracy, to which the multitudes, with good reason, are passionately attached.

But the most curious and the most prophetic thing in these reflections of Nietzsche's, at a time when his mind was visibly under French influence, is that he foresaw the obstacle to any such hope, and foretold that the foundation of a European Confedera-tion would be laid by the preliminary triumph of absolutism, by militarism, and by war. There would come either peaceful agreement or a resort to Napoleonic methods, that is to say to compulsory Europeanism. The small States would be devoured by the large States and these in their turn would become the Monster-States of the morrow. For there would remain only one Monster-State on each continent. But the Monster-State of Europe would fall disastrously to pieces, for it would lack an encircling ring of enemies to compel it to remain united. It is odd that Nietzsche seems not to have suspected that, if this Monster-State proved to be a German hegemony in Europe, the European nations of the periphery would have been so completely sickened and nauseated that Germany would have for ever lost all moral prestige in Europe, even before the ultimate victory or defeat of the Germanic Monster-State in battle with the other continents. Who nowadays could doubt it?

In any case, Nietzsche contended that, after absolutism had collapsed, the time would have come for European confederation. Not having been able to achieve unity by her own efforts, Europe would arrive at it, after the new Napoleonism, by dissolution. There would have to be a return to diversity, to European multiplicity, and through that to the possibility, the simple possibility, not of a ghastly Hitlerite uniformity but of a Continental Federation, a reconstruction of Western Europe.

To-day that historic moment is upon us. The task of the Western democracies is to counter the effects of German National Socialism and to create a Europe at once diverse and united, between the Atlantic eventually dominated by the United States and a Russia at full tide. A regenerate Germany will have to find herself a niche, if she can, in this New Europe, instead of subjecting the continent to the *Gleichschaltung*, the slavery, the appalling tyranny which the Nazis have inflicted on it, loosing upon it all imaginable ills. Thus, after losing the battle of 1940, we have not only to win the war despite that temporary defeat, but to be victors also in the war of propaganda by reinstating humanism in its rights. We have to proclaim a crusade against the whole spiritual, moral, and political tradition of Prusso-German imperialism. We have to destroy this Nazi Germany which is seeking to absorb Communism into its own imperialism, the better to disintegrate and then to dominate Europe.

We must then give Europe the opportunity of organizing herself under some constitution conformable to the interests of our civilization, offspring of Western humanism. We must first renew and consolidate the fundamental principles of this civilization of ours, adapting them to the exigencies of the tragic epoch in which we live. We now know that to compromise with Hitler under his pretext of averting the Bolshevist menace is to court ruin and slavery. What we must build is a Europe regenerated by Germany's own regeneration and by the establishment of normal relations between Germany and the Continental countries surrounding her, between the Continent and Great Britain, and between the British Empire and the French. This should not be beyond the power of the Western democracies in union with Central and Eastern Europe.

Since her gigantic re-armament Hitler's Germany has been confronted by an implacable dilemma: *either the absolute domination of Europe or total collapse.* Germany's enemies face a no less inexorable dilemma: *either victory over totalitarian Germany or ultimate exhaustion followed by annihilation.* After succeeding only in her Western offensive and failing in her offensive against Russia in the East, Germany may try to defend what she calls the European Fortress. Equally she may continue the war by patient and insidious propaganda aimed at demoralizing her enemies. Now that we have every prospect of defeating Hitler and ridding Europe and the world of him, we shall not let him demoralize us.

The prospects of the near or not-too-distant future are by no means clear. But the problem of our war aims has long since found its place on the agenda, and many books and articles have appeared concerning the constitution of the future Germany.

There has been a lot of argumentation, particularly about the delicate problem of the two Germanys.

Here we are faced by two extreme lines of thought. Some people, the Anglo-Saxons more particularly, emphasize the distinction between the Hitler régime and the German people, as if the German people, especially during the period of great victories, had not been wholeheartedly behind Hitler almost to a man. Those who hold this view are ready to treat the German people with the utmost generosity when once the régime and its leaders have disappeared. Some, on the other hand, talk of parcelling out Germany anew, reintroducing the old territorialism and bringing "The Germany" to life again.

These two theses seem to me equally inacceptable. The first because, even admitting as we do that National Socialism was originally a power-machine artificially imposed on the German people, we cannot separate this people even in thought from the régime that restored its cohesion, captured its entire youth, and lavished upon it intoxicating victories, tearing up the treaties of 1919 and annexing the greater part of Europe's territory. Even if a crushing military defeat were of itself to effect the desired separation of régime and people, it is by no means certain that it would at once obliterate the education imposed and all the habits acquired. Moreover, nothing could be more dangerous than by imprudent anticipation to make the conditions of peace depend on the disappearance of the régime. If that were done the eviction of Hitler and of the Nazi Party would involve us in the same embarrassment as the alleged promises of President Wilson's Fourteen Points. The Germans would ever after swear that we had broken faith. As for the present Russian play with the "Free Germans" in Moscow and other capitals, it seems to have been devised for special ends and in consequence to be irrelevant to our problem.

The second thesis is in my view no less untenable, because this present study has reached the conclusion that the old territorialism led, not to say condemned, Germany to a morbid nationalism, to the dreams and ambitions of the pan-Germanism that was the accompaniment of territorial fragmentation and later of that fatal pluralism which the enemies of democracy, the industrial and military castes, so skilfully exploited to help to engineer the fall of the Weimar Republic. It is not easy to see whose interest it would be to parcel out whatever remains of Germany after this war.

It is therefore important neither to absolve the German people, in an impulse of generous but facile indulgence, nor to thrust them back into a past that has for ever vanished, however great that past may have been in virtue of its culture.

We must first solve in East and South and West the problem of the amputations that appear indispensable. The Moscow Conference has already decided the future of Austria. No one could reasonably oppose the cession to Poland of East Prussia. And the question of the left bank of the Rhine is more vital than ever.

But the essential task in the political constitution of post-war Germany is to "de-Prussianize" the country, transferring its political centre of gravity from the North-east to the South-west, to the neighbourhood of Frankfort, the city that attempted nearly a hundred years ago to bring about a German synthesis on democratic lines. This solution would have the advantage of placing the new centre of gravity in the neighbourhood of, if not under the direct control of or in close dependence on, the United Western Nations.

If we are to strike directly at the heart of the enemy, the real enemy, *if we want to deal the final blow at the dream of a planned, all-dominating German Reich destined to govern not only Europe but the whole expanse of Russia, we must aim it at the myth and practice of* Lebensraum (*vital living space*) *in any and every form.* At any cost we must teach Germany not to equate herself with Europe according to Hitler's formula: "Either Germany will be Europe or she will cease to exist." We must at any cost prevent her from Germanizing Europe by systematically destroying the surrounding nations in her utterly ruthless way. Her deadly work is already far advanced. Germany will not cease to pursue this end even on the morrow of a second defeat. *Europe will be lost if the vitality and cohesion of the nations around Germany does not finally and definitely hold in check the vitality and cohesion of the Germans—unless the Germans themselves merge their vitality and cohesion in that of a restored Europe.*

There is no other problem than this. The victorious Allies will have it in their power to destroy—*if they wish*—the industrial and military predominance of a conquered and shrunken Germany. Complex as is the question of Germany's future status and her political re-education, this is not our most difficult task. The real difficulty will be to unite to-morrow the nations lying between the United States and Russia. *For the history of the years since 1918 has abundantly proved that their union must be very firmly based and very durable if it is to incorporate into a reorganized Europe a Germany reduced in size and militarily powerless.*

Small need to stress the necessity of the Franco-British alliance. We may think what we like of the relations between England and France as they have been formed by the four and a half centuries that separate us from the beginnings of the Reformation. England fought monarchical France in the colonial field and Napoleonic France on the Continent. But the results of the German industrial revolution ranged Britain on the side of France from the opening years of the twentieth century, and when Russia was out of action it was the coalition of France, Britain, and the United States that defeated Germany in 1918. The absence of America and the tension between Britain and France destroyed in less than twenty years the fruits of that dearly bought victory. *And even if we assume a second German defeat, the danger of German hegemony in Europe remains so great that France and Britain dare not risk forgetting that the common interests which unite them are vastly more important than their differences and the misunderstandings that might estrange them.* The most casual glance at the history of the last four and a half centuries shows, with dazzling clearness, that the two Western democracies have to defend a common heritage of thought and political institutions, of hard-won liberties and of successful civilization, against a Germany which has always remained a stranger to democracy and which possesses no democratic tradition. In face of this fact their divergencies are of wholly secondary importance.

It is, moreover, evident that Britain has never felt herself more closely bound to Europe, more dependent on Continental developments, than now, nor more firmly resolved to play a foremost part in shaping European destinies. But the British conception of Europe and its problems is by no means identical with the French. Great Britain's vision is at once less narrow than that of France—which is limited by immediate and imperative needs—and more inclined to be inspired by the moral principles governing the relations between peoples. On the other hand we well know that face to face with the United States, with Russia, and with Germany herself, Britain and France share a common anxiety about their falling birth-rate.[1] Better still, Britain understands the present German danger better than might sometimes be supposed from the diverse expressions of public opinion that appear about Germany and the future of the Third Reich, and from the curious weakness or ignorance displayed in some of these statements. Britain knows, and France too knows, that eventual alliances to east and west will not solve the European problem, and that, since Britain cannot maintain herself in insular isolation, a close alliance between Great Britain and France is one of the vital necessities of to-morrow.

Now, if this alliance is to have the solidity and breadth of view for which we hope, it must bring not only a reasonable settlement of the German problem but a general reorganization of Europe. It is here that Nietzsche's prophecy, made during his middle— his "French"—period, comes fully into its own. Having destroyed the Monster-State which the German philosopher foretold, having survived the appalling trials which that State has inflicted on the entire continent, the Europeans of Europe must unite.

It is not here our business to say how. These final pages aim at indicating general directives rather than at drawing up a detailed schedule, a task beyond the competence of any one individual, and impossible while the war is still unfinished. One thing is certain:

The Germans succeeded for a time in imposing their supranational system on Europe because the Peace Treaties of 1919 envisaged only national solutions, within the framework of a would-be universal League of Nations which failed to act effectively or even to maintain itself.

Obviously there can be no question of a centralized European State. We can see only one or several federative solutions.

[1] See P. Maillaud's article in *La France Libre*, February 2, 1944, p. 260.

There has already been talk of regional understandings in Europe, of a Union of the Scandinavian Countries including Finland, of an Iberian Block, of a Western Block embracing Great Britain, Holland, Belgium, Luxembourg, France, and even Switzerland. These groupings are perfectly conceivable, and they would in any case be merely the first stage on the road to the United States of Europe.

The question of the East and the South-east is more difficult.

Beginning with the East: the Allies appear to have been long since in agreement that the Polish State must be reconstituted, though details and methods have still to be thrashed out. Poland, lying between the New Germany and the New Russia, represents in fact an oasis of civilization and of Christianity well watered by the purest currents of Western thought, a State capable of forming a strong bulwark on the East, with of course no hostility toward Russia. Such a Poland, strong and relatively independent, would form one of the most important foundation stones of European peace, when once she has accomplished the almost crushing task of reconstruction which will fall on her after the incredible trials through which she is passing.

The same applies to Czechoslovakia. No one to-day disputes that she must resume her natural destiny and recover relative independence and legitimate sovereignty in reorganized Europe, the more so since, like Poland, she forms a predestined link between the Slav and Western worlds. What should be the fate of Slovakia, Ruthenia, and the Sudeten districts, are important questions outside the scope of this brief summary. We shall abstain also from attempting to draw up a plan for Czech-Polish federation.

The real problem is that of Austria and the European South-east.

The moment Austria is once again released from Germany, the moment a Greater Germany is no longer a possibility, the question of Austria will be as acute and as profoundly significant as ever.

The problem can only be solved if we realize the part that country can play, and ought to play, in a reborn Europe and in relation to a Germany relieved—as it is our duty to relieve her—from the preponderant influence of Prussia.

The well-known opposition between Potsdam and Weimar is now no more than an historic and a misleading memory. Starting from the elementary facts of history, from Bismarck's prussianized

Germany, we find that the only true antitheses to Prussia and Berlin are Austria and Vienna. The deed of March 11, 1938, was far more than the mere "*Finis Austriæ,*" far more than the mere absorption of Austria into Greater Germany. *The intention was to prussianize Austria and then Bohemia.* Any Western policy that tended to weaken Austria, or to allow her to be weakened, would be a disastrous mistake. It was to their own undoing that the Western Powers tolerated Prussia's victory over Austria at Sadowa. When Napoleon III abandoned Austria to Bismarck, in 1866, he was encouraging in advance (even though Bismarck himself in 1871 was still satisfied with Lesser Germany) the ominous outburst of the pan-Germanism that ultimately reached such an alarming pitch under William II, after the fall of the Iron Chancellor. Those who are hostile to Roman Catholic Austria, and who see in her nothing but social, political, and religious reaction, forget all that Socialism had accomplished in the municipal sphere, and often imagine, somewhat ingenuously, that Prusso-Lutheran Germany represented an advance on feudal, ultramontane Austria.

If, then, Austria must be separated from the Reich, she must not again be left isolated as she was after 1919. She, too, must be incorporated in a European Federation. Without her it would be impossible to organize the Danube basin. Five years of ruthless German domination, and the terrible losses suffered by the Austrian units which Germany systematically hounded to their death, have erected an impassable barrier between the Austrian proper and the German of the Reich. We can foresee a complete revulsion of the common people forcibly subjugated by the Nazi régime. It is not impossible that this revulsion may even bring about a reconciliation between the Socialists and the upholders of tradition, the Catholics, monarchists, and patriots. Austrian Socialists have acquired a sense of nationality, the other parties a wider social outlook. Once her incorporation in the Reich has been officially shaken off, there is no doubt that Austria will regain her self-confidence.

What would be the advantage of linking Austria with the fortunes of Bavaria, especially if we succeed in transferring the centre of gravity of the future Germany from the North-east to the South-west? Munich and Vienna never drew together in co-operation against Berlin. Bavaria has never belonged to any but the German world, and if she stepped to Austria's side it would only reinforce pan-Germanism in Austria. An Austria separated from Germany but not isolated would, on the other hand, be a factor of the first importance in federative union.

The problem of Transylvania undoubtedly presents formidable difficulties. If, however, it were made into a sort of autonomous province in which Roumanians, Hungarians, and Saxons—approximately equal in numbers—could enjoy a common administration modelled on that of the Swiss cantons, without aspiring to the prerogatives of a State, there would be nothing to prevent it from being directly attached to the suggested Federation. And we might hope that the Federation would be granted access to the sea—that is to say, a port on the Adriatic.

Without going into details, it would seem that in spite of the many difficulties—the study of which lies beyond the scope of this summary sketch—a Federation of South-east Europe would be possible, provided that none of the States involved were allowed to claim hegemony over the others and that the federal authority abstained from interference in their domestic affairs. The skeleton of such a Federation would be an economic and customs union, a common currency, and a federal army. If this Federation attained one day the stability we might hope for, what a number of local problems that now seem insoluble would become less acute!

From every point of view it is clear how important a European coalition would be that was based on France and Britain. Whether we like it or not, the United States and Russia are the two Great Powers, the two "Colossi," of the future. Marshal Smuts has said this repeatedly. German propaganda has said and repeated it *ad nauseam*, adding that Germany alone can powerfully organize the areas separating these two great continental Powers. The present war has modified the balance of world power by demonstrating the overwhelming superiority of the industrial potential of these two great countries. If on the cessation of hostilities Europe feels herself menaced, "encircled," divided, and uncertain of her future, this will not be because she has been impoverished by war but because she is reduced to material impotence. Since there can be no question of a German hegemony, it may well be wondered what will be Europe's eventual strength if a solid element of that strength is the new alliance between Britain and France.

On that point it can be shown that in respect of man-power, coal, iron, and raw materials generally, the combined colonial empires of Britain, France, Holland, and Belgium can confront the Continental Powers of West and East with an industrial potential at least equal to either of theirs. With Germany's military and industrial supremacy for ever obliterated, a Franco-British Alliance with all the resources of the European continent at call could stand up to any adversary. Its failure in 1940 was a political and strategic failure only—its potential strength against Germany was formidable. But it was not mobilized and ready to take immediate military action at the first moment of Germany's aggression.

Thus conceived and thus organized, the Europe of to-morrow, free from all aggressive intention towards either America or Russia, would be in a position to oppose any imperialism—whether arising from Germany in her midst or from America or Russia outside—which might threaten her security and her most sacred treasure, the diversity of her nationalities and of her culture. The component elements of Europe must unite precisely in order to preserve the riches of their civilization—incomparable riches, incalculably precious for mankind, riches which would infallibly be destroyed by any brutal imposition of uniformity from whatever direction this might come.

INDEX OF NAMES